HUMAN RIGHTS AND LABOR SOLIDARITY

PENNSYLVANIA STUDIES IN HUMAN RIGHTS

Series Editor: Bert B. Lockwood, Jr.

A complete list of books in the series
is available from the publisher.

HUMAN RIGHTS AND LABOR SOLIDARITY

TRADE UNIONS IN THE GLOBAL ECONOMY

SUSAN L. KANG

PENN

UNIVERSITY OF PENNSYLVANIA PRESS

PHILADELPHIA

Published by
University of Pennsylvania Press
Philadelphia, Pennsylvania 19104-4112
www.upenn.edu/pennpress

Printed in the United States of America
on acid-free paper

2 4 6 8 10 9 7 5 3 1

Library of Congress Cataloging-in-Publication Data

Kang, Susan L.
Human rights and labor solidarity : trade unions in the global economy / Susan L. Kang. — 1st ed.
p. cm. — (Pennsylvania studies in human rights)
Includes bibliographical references and index.
ISBN 978-0-8122-4410-6 (hardcover : alk. paper)
1. Labor unions. 2. Labor unions—Law and legislation. 3. Employee rights. 4. Human rights. I. Title. II. Series: Pennsylvania studies in human rights.
HD6476.K36 2012
331.88—dc23

2011049647

For my parents,

Young Chan Kang and Keesun Kang

CONTENTS

Preface ix

List of Abbreviations xi

Chapter 1. The Precarious Position of Trade Union Rights in the Global Political Economy 1

Chapter 2. Negotiations and Norms: The Development of Trade Union Rights in International Law and Institutions 18

Chapter 3. International Institutions and Their Protections of Trade Union Rights 41

Chapter 4. South Korea: International Ambitions and the Postdevelopmental State 66

Chapter 5. United Kingdom: New Labour and New Labor Rights? 113

Chapter 6. Canada: Federalism and Stalled Compliance 155

Conclusion. International Norms, Trade Union Rights, and Countering Neoliberalism 193

Appendix I. Kucera's Measure of Freedom of Association and Collective Bargaining 211

Appendix II. Number of Unions/Unionization Rate in Korea: 1987–2003 213

Appendix III. Case Disputes and U.S. Law 215

Notes 219

Bibliography 275

Index 303

Acknowledgments 321

PREFACE

This project was partly inspired by my brief personal participation in the United States labor movement. Through an internship with the Service Employees International Union in college and later activism and volunteer work with a local AFSCME and Hotel Employees and Restaurant Employees (HERE), I first encountered the everyday challenges that workers face as they attempt to exercise their basic rights to form, join, and act within their unions. During my participation in the AFL-CIO's Union Summer program in Seattle in 2001, fellow interns and I worked on a ballot initiative campaign that sought to guarantee legal collective bargaining rights for public home-care workers. Although this campaign to support a ballot initiative was eventually successful, I realized how precarious workers' positions truly were. While volunteering with a HERE local, I saw an International Labour Organization poster declaring that "Workers' Rights Are Human Rights." For the first time I recognized the connection between the difficulties of American trade union rights and larger struggles for human rights transnationally, which I had learned about through the 1990s anti-sweatshop movement. This connection with U.S. workers' situation led to my exploration of various international legal instruments to protect labor rights, especially the ILO Committee on Freedom of Association.

Although this book focuses on cases outside the United States, my research and interests have always kept the U.S. comparison close by. Problems with trade union rights in the United States are often marginalized; however, recent events have brought more attention to drastic shortcomings of U.S. law vis-à-vis our own trade union traditions. While the debate over the proposed Employee Free Choice Act, first introduced in Congress in 2007, became dominated by antiquated fears of authoritarian union struggles, I could not have predicted how relevant the legal questions of this book would become with the sudden explosion of public-sector trade union activity in early 2011, in places such as Wisconsin, Indiana, Ohio, and many other states. Like every legislature examined in this book, the legislatures in these states engaged in extralegal behavior to pass bills that decimated public workers' basic trade union rights. This suggests that even a country as detached from international norms as the United States still operates within the broader global normative frameworks. More information on the ways in which the case studies in this book relate to the United States can be found in Appendix III.

The primary focus in this book seeks to reconcile the competing logics of international relations in terms of state behavior. I investigate the competing influence of a well-established, but poorly enforced international norm of trade union rights against the more pressing concerns about economic competitiveness. Prior studies have demonstrated that normative arguments are not sufficient to change state behavior, but the cases in this book suggest that the transnational normative negotiation process that states participate in with international organizations can influence state behavior, under specific conditions. Because trade union rights protection is seen as a possible threat to a state's economic competitiveness, legal changes that better protect them require a significant overlap with a stronger state interest. Unlike the European Union, however, which provides clear material incentives for membership-seeking states to comply with certain democratic norms, institutions that protect trade union rights have little to offer. Thus, incentives for change are largely external to international institutions, and often relate to existing political goals and state institutions. Therefore, while the normative aspect of trade union rights, as part of the larger framework of universal human rights, does not always influence state behavior, this book demonstrates how it can serve as a possible strategic tool for activists in campaigns.

ABBREVIATIONS

AFL-CIO	American Federation of Labor-Congress of Industrial Organizations
BIAC	Business and Industry Advisory Council/Committee (associated with the OECD)
BCGEU	British Columbia Government and Service Employees' Union
BCTF	British Columbia Teachers' Federation
CESCR	Committee on Economic, Social and Cultural Rights (United Nations)
COIE	Committee of Independent Experts (Council of Europe)
CUPE-BC	Canadian Union of Public Employees-British Columbia
ECHR	European Court of Human Rights
ELSA	Employment, Labour and Social Affairs Committee (OECD)
FKTU	Federation of Korean Trade Unions
GCHQ	Government Communication Headquarters (U.K.)
HEU	Hospital Employments Union (British Columbia)
HSA	Health Science Association (British Columbia)
ICCPR	International Covenant on Civil and Political Rights
ICESCR	International Covenant on Economic, Social and Cultural Rights
ICFTU	International Confederation of Free Trade Unions
ILO	International Labour Organization
ILO Committee	International Labour Organization Committee on Freedom of Association
ILO	Committee of Experts on the Application of Conventions and Recommendations (CEACR)

ITUC	International Trade Union Confederation
KCTU	Korean Confederation of Trade Unions
KGEU	Korean Government Employees' Union
NLRB/NLRA	National Labor Relations Board/Act (United States)
NUPGE	National Union of Public and General Employees (Canada)
NUJ	National Union of Journalists (U.K.)
OECD	Organization for Economic Cooperation and Development
TULRRA	Trade Union and Labour Relations Adjustment Act (Korea 1996–1997 law)
TUAC	Trade Union Advisory Council/Committee (OECD)
TUC	Trades Union Congress (U.K.)

CHAPTER 1

The Precarious Position of Trade Union Rights in the Global Political Economy

> This year's ITUC survey shows that the majority of the world's workers still lack effective protection of their rights to organise trade unions and bargain collectively.
>
> —Guy Ryder, General Secretary of the International Trade Union Confederation, *ITUC 2010 Annual Survey of Trade Union Rights*

The Paradox of Trade Union Rights

The rights of workers to join and act within trade unions occupied an unclear place at the end of the twentieth century. These rights, also called trade union rights, include the rights for workers to join and form organizations, engage in collective bargaining, and engage in strikes and other actions to protect their interests.[1] Prominent state and nonstate actors expressed their support for trade union rights through the adoption and creation of various international instruments. States, nongovernmental organizations (NGOs), and UN bodies affirmed the importance of labor rights, including trade union rights, at the 1995 World Summit on Social Development in Copenhagen.[2] Clauses reaffirming the importance of trade union rights were incorporated into multilateral trade agreements such as the North American Free Trade Agreement (NAFTA). The United States even included trade union rights in its list of conditions necessary to lift its embargo on Cuba in the controversial Helms-Burton Act.[3] The European Union also included trade union rights in Articles

12 and 28 of its Charter of Fundamental Rights (2000).[4] Following debates about the role of labor standards and trade, the members of the International Labour Organization (ILO)[5] committed themselves to trade union rights, in creating and signing the Declaration on Fundamental Principles and Rights at Work (1998).[6]

Many key nonstate actors have also affirmed support for trade union rights. Widely publicized social movements, such as the Global North anti-sweatshop students' movement, highlighted the importance of these rights in the context of globalization. Multinational corporations expressed their support for these rights by including them in their corporate codes of conduct and by joining the 2000 UN Global Compact.[7] Even once reluctant multilateral financial institutions now publicly support trade union rights. The International Monetary Fund (IMF) endorsed trade union rights as part of its broader set of core labor standards in 1999, and the World Bank pledged in 2003 to condition its private-sector loans on core labor standards compliance, which included trade union rights.[8]

Yet information from trade unions suggests a discrepancy between these expressions of support and the actual persistence of trade union rights violations.[9] For example, in its 2000 annual report on global progress toward the 1998 Declaration, the ILO stated that globalization had eroded trade union rights such that "a significant representation gap has arisen in the world of work."[10] Similarly, the International Confederation of Free Trade Unions (ICFTU),[11] a global trade union federation, noted the increasing precariousness of trade union rights in a 2001 report. The general secretary of the IFCTU responded to the ILO's Declaration, stating: "There is something paradoxical in the contrast between the international community's increasing outspokenness on international labour standards and reality on the ground. Three years after the adoption of the ILO's Declaration on Fundamental Principles and Rights at Work, violations of trade union rights have reached a level never recorded before."[12]

This contrast between public statements of support for trade union rights and their widespread violation is this book's motivating puzzle. While trade union rights remain important on the international agenda, the international institutions that promote them do not enjoy strong enforcement mechanisms. Trade union rights, as part of the international regime on labor rights, are "universally adopted, but locally adapted."[13] These rights are enforced at the national level, and are thus at the mercy of state leaders who may consider them secondary to more pressing economic pressures. Therefore, the question remains: how can trade union rights as international norms influence domestic practice in the context of the new global economy?

Workers' Trade Union Rights as Human Rights

This book focuses on the subset of labor rights called "trade union rights."[14] They are included in the "core labor standards" determined by the ILO. Core labor standards are part of the larger global labor protection regime, protecting workers from the vulnerability of labor markets by promoting the decommodification of labor.[15] Core labor rights also include prohibitions on forced labor, limits on child labor, and protections against discrimination.[16] However, trade union rights, unlike many other labor rights, are "labor processes" because they neither provide a minimum floor of protections nor guarantee specific outcomes.[17] Rather, trade union rights protect the process by which workers participate in creating the conditions of their work and thereby provide a means for furthering workers' interests.[18] Trade union rights are distinct from *individual labor protections*, which include protections over job security, work hours, working conditions, and other substantive (rather than procedural) protections that states may provide workers.[19]

Trade union rights are included in a broad range of international legal sources, and most states have made multiple international legal commitments to these rights. These legal commitments exist on a continuum between hard law and soft law. Hard law, according to Abbott and Snidal, are those international legal arrangements that (1) create strong obligations that are legally binding on states, (2) consist of precise rules, and (3) include provisions for delegation to third parties for implementation and interpretation. Soft law describes the broad range of legal institutions that deviate in at least one of these dimensions.[20] Since trade union rights are included in many key human rights documents, they may be considered customary international law, creating obligations on states regardless of ratification status.[21] Therefore, trade union rights have become important international rules.

This book draws largely from the constructivist tradition in international relations, which argues that international norms, such as trade union rights, matter to states and shape their behavior. One of the key findings of constructivist scholarship is that states often follow international norms not only because of incentives, but also because of widely held standards of right and wrong. In other words, states will often follow norms because of a *logic of appropriateness* (legitimacy), rather than a *logic of consequences* (self-interest). Guided by the logic of appropriateness, states are more likely to follow norms that are well established and deeply ingrained within domestic and international contexts.[22] However, recent scholarship has pointed out that states' interpretation of international norms is an ongoing process. Actors' understandings of norms change over time and are especially impacted by political and economic conditions.[23]

New economic and political conditions have changed the way in which states approach trade union rights. While states rarely reject them, as trade union rights are long-standing and well-established norms, states may see strong protections of trade union rights as constraining their economic interests. Therefore, states will resist creating stronger protections of trade union rights unless they see doing so as benefiting their self-interests. As a result, the logic of appropriateness, namely the legitimacy of trade union rights, often clashes with the logic of consequences, as states fear that strong compliance with trade union rights norms will have negative economic effects.

This book argues that while states may be less motivated to provide strong protections for trade union rights because of changing economic and political conditions, trade union rights norms can still shape state behavior. The pressures of globalization have changed many states' incentives, closing domestic political channels and forcing trade unions to adopt transnational strategies.[24] Like many other contemporary transnational activists,[25] trade unions and other advocates use the status of trade union rights as international norms as a point of normative leverage. States, in turn, may argue with trade unions and international institutions over the extent of their obligations. The effectiveness of this discursive process relies on trade unions' ability to construct trade union rights disputes as valid human rights violations, and, in turn, to link the protection of these rights to state interests. This process is demonstrated within the book's three case studies: South Korea (Chapter 4); United Kingdom (Chapter 5); and British Columbia, Canada (Chapter 6).

This interaction constitutes what I term a *normative negotiation process*, an exchange in which states, trade unions, and international organizations construct and challenge a broader understanding of the international trade union rights norms, to determine whether a labor dispute constitutes a human rights violation. Even though states may have incentives not to provide strong legal protections for trade union rights, their disputes with international institutions do not concern the legitimacy of these norms, but rather whether the disputed law constitutes a norm violation.[26] Because international institutions have historically promoted a broader understanding of trade union rights, one that recognizes power imbalances and the importance of solidaristic workers' action, this attempt to renegotiate the state's normative obligations does not always work. Therefore, the state's engagement in the normative negotiation process can be an important first step toward promoting stronger protection of trade union rights.

Uncovering Mechanisms for Change: Normative Negotiations and Compliance

While international institutions may criticize a state's interpretation of trade union rights norms, the state may ignore international institutions' counter-interpretations, as most of these institutions lack strong enforcement mechanisms. While many human rights campaigns have successfully shamed states into changing their policies, advocates' arguments in support of stronger trade union rights protections do not necessarily "[fit] well or resonate with widespread pre-existing understandings."[27] Unlike anti-sweatshop or anti-torture campaigns, trade union rights campaigns deal with neither issues of bodily integrity nor issues of fairness, which scholars have noted strongly resonate with transnational and domestic audiences. Appeals to solidarity and social and economic justice are not as persuasive as they may have been in the past.

In this book's case studies I investigate the extent to which trade unions can use trade union rights norms to defend their interests. Most of the time, arguments themselves did not lead to legal changes. Instead, these case studies demonstrate that under contingent political conditions, these normative negotiations can set in motion a process that politicizes trade union rights and thus makes compliance more likely. In these cases, changes occurred through two causal pathways: (1) when activists were successful at linking trade union rights issues with a state's interests (either political or economic) and (2) when the normative negotiation process persuaded powerful judicial institutions. In both instances, states would reform trade union rights laws to better comply with international institutions' interpretations of these norms. States, however, did not seem to "learn" or internalize a stronger understanding of trade union rights norms.[28] Rather, in the three cases, states were compelled, either in pursuit of existing political interests, or because of rule of law obligations, to change their laws. In the South Korean case, the political conditions influenced changes, while in the Canadian case, the judicial process led to changes. In the United Kingdom, a combination of political and judicial processes led to changes.

The political conditions that granted greater expediency to trade union rights norms were highly contingent, and often had little to do with trade union rights. In these cases, states' elites had specific internationally focused goals that made them vulnerable to trade union rights, and the normative negotiation process helped link trade union rights with state interests. The presence of such an internationally focused political interest created vulnerabilities that trade union activists and allies could exploit to pursue their interests. Likewise, when a government, such as the Conservative government in the United Kingdom and the Liberal government in British Columbia, lacked an internationally focused goal, this made trade union rights advocacy more difficult. In Canada, the Supreme Court's internalization of a broader, more solidaristic understanding of trade union rights norms was necessary for the legal change to occur.

These political incentives worked differently in each case study. For example, in South Korea, trade union rights concerns became politicized by South Korea's attempt to join the Organization for Economic Cooperation and Development (OECD), and, later, by the 1997 Asian financial crisis. In the United Kingdom, New Labour's attempts to bring the country more in line with "Europe" created new political pressures to follow a broader understanding of trade union rights. In the case of British Columbia, the provincial government was largely uninterested in conforming to international human rights standards, doing little other than issuing public statements dismissing the validity of the United Nations' or ILO's opinions. In this instance, however, change occurred after trade unions and international institutions persuaded the Supreme Court of Canada to adopt a broader interpretation of trade union rights, more in line with international standards.

The Normative Negotiation Process and State Behavior

In all the cases, a normative negotiation process helped counter the state's position and legitimize the trade unions' claims. International institutions provided an additional support for trade unions' interpretation of human rights law. Even though the political, economic, and ethical conditions that led to the establishment of trade union rights norms have changed, the fact that trade union rights are incorporated into international law provides international institutions interpretive authority which prevents states from engaging in brazen "self-serving auto-interpretation."[29] In addition, creation of an international consensus challenging the state's understanding of trade union rights norms proved useful. Such international attention can give a trade union rights violation greater saliency.[30]

International opinion enjoyed greater influence when multiple institutions made similar recommendations. As international trade union rights have many different supervisory regimes, with no single institution claiming authority over another, international institutions do not always agree about a trade union rights dispute. Rather, "it remains entirely possible that one institution will condemn a course of conduct while another will not. These differences have the potential to undermine the 'authority' of particular supervisory bodies and their conclusions."[31] Similar recommendations from multiple institutions strengthened trade union rights advocates' political and legal arguments, while a lack of consensus weakened their claims.

Learning vs. Coercion: Analyzing the Depth of State Compliance

As I will explain in more detail in Chapter 3, there is a significant range of obligations and entitlements included within trade union rights. Trade unions in these case studies brought a diversity of complaints to international institutions. Some involved general shortcomings in the law that affected large groups of workers, while others involved more specific issues. While support from international institutions strengthened the trade unions' claims, it was not sufficient to create change. Another factor affecting compliance was whether the dispute focused on protecting the rights of individual workers or collective rights of organizations. While the states discussed in this book all made some legal changes, they mostly complied with the recommendations of the international institutions in a shallow manner. Rather than internalizing stronger interpretations of trade union rights norms, the states seemed to act on instrumental logics.

The evidence for this shallower compliance can be found by determining the type of trade union rights laws that states were more likely to comply with. In these case studies, those laws that directly affected the ability of an individual to engage in basic trade union rights were more readily amended than those laws that protected trade unions' collective rights. Individuals' rights to freely form and join unions were more readily protected than a trade union's right to exist freely and pursue its members' interests. As a result, states privatized workers' collective rights in a way that reflected dominant neoliberal interpretations of human rights commitments.

On the other hand, states were less likely to reform their violations of collective bargaining and strike rights. States constructed workers' human rights as individualistic, and they especially resisted protecting groups and their collective interests. Even after a multiyear negotiation process, the case countries in this book offered fewer additional protections for effective collective bargaining and organizational survival. Provisions allowing for collective protections for trade union activities were often highly circumscribed. This was especially noticeable in the case of public sector workers, in which the state served as both an employer and the legal arbiter. In each of these three cases, there was at least one dispute involving public sector workers; even when the states made changes, they failed to protect their workers' rights to strike and to take other forms of collective action.

Case Selection

The case selection in this book follows the specificity of its research question. While social scientists who seek to make generalizable claims about state behavior and political phenomenon usually recommend a research design with decisive variation on the dependent variable,[32] this book's focus on the complex struggles surrounding trade union rights necessitated a less elegant research design. On initial inspection, the cases in this book seem to share a similar dependent variable: each state in question changed its domestic laws to better comply with recommendations from international institutions. However, this seeming lack of variation in the dependent variable allows a researcher to identify the necessary, though perhaps not sufficient, causal conditions to explain the dependent variable.[33] Because this project focuses on revealing the political conditions under which the transnational normative negotiation process may lead to changes in state behavior, choosing cases with significant variation in the dependent variable would not be fruitful. Specifically, many such "noncases" can be attributed to key structural conditions within a state, such as a weaker trade union movement, authoritarian regimes, or problems with the rule of law. Exclusion of such countries allows the analysis to focus on contingent, and not structural, reasons for compliance or noncompliance. Therefore, the three countries' similarity in the dependent variable helps to focus on the contingent political factors that may empower international interpretations of stronger trade union rights. By examining the different political and economic factors that interacted with the normative negotiation process in each case, this research design provides a way to generalize about how and when this process can be effective.[34] In this way, the general research design most resembles John Stuart Mill's Method of Agreement.[35]

Though the transnational normative negotiation process in each country did lead to some improvement in legal protection of certain trade union rights issues, not all of the complaints brought by trade unions resulted in successful legal changes. Furthermore, not all of the legal changes were considered satisfactory implementations of strong trade union rights norms. Therefore, variation exists in the dependent variable within the cases. As these cases span several years, division of the cases into multiple parts allows for longitudinal analysis.

While South Korea, the United Kingdom, and Canada[36] are quite different countries, they share several common characteristics that make a comparison between them appropriate. Specifically, they share characteristics that could reasonably predict protection of trade union rights, based on both the international law and labor rights literatures. These case studies are limited to countries with active trade union movements because, as Cook argues, strong trade unions are necessary for effective protections of labor rights.[37] While trade union density is not necessarily comparable, labor movements in all three cases have significant political influence.[38] The scholarship also suggests that "liberal states" are more likely to follow international laws and norms.[39] In addition, the multiyear case studies in this book involve countries that have strong state capacities and received clarification about norms from international institutions over a period of several years.[40] Therefore, noncompliance in these case studies cannot be explained by managerial theory, which argues that state compliance is often the result of a lack of state capacity, timing, or clarification. Despite these similarities, these countries' degree of compliance with trade union rights recommendations varies.[41]

There are also a number of variables in these case studies that international relations and international legal scholars have argued could affect an international institution's influence on a state. The first "control" variable is partisan coalitions. Specifically many scholars have noted the strong electoral connection between left-governing coalitions and organized labor,[42] and this would suggest that left-governing coalitions would be more willing to protect trade union rights than right-wing governments. However, in the following case studies, the political orientation of the ruling partisan coalition is insufficient to explain why states did or did not comply with an international organization's recommendations.

The second control variable is the state's legalization of trade union rights' obligations. The degree of legalization is determined by whether a state's participation in an institution creates harder or softer obligations on a state party. According to a rationalist perspective, a state is more likely to commit to harder international legal obligations if the state was already likely to comply with the norm. Likewise, a state would likely commit to softer international legal instruments if it were less likely to comply.[43] However, compliance in these case studies follows neither the state's degree of legal commitment nor the specific trade union right's degree of legalization. In addition, the international recommendations themselves mostly constitute soft law, as the institutions' decisions were not binding on states. In these cases, the level of legalization did not have a clear effect on states. Both the OECD, which has minimal legal authority, and the European Court of Human Rights, which creates binding legal rulings, influenced state compliance. In fact, though the "softest" recommendations came from the OECD, they still influenced significant compliance in South Korea.

The third control factor is the level of development. Theoretically, a country with a lower level of economic development would not comply either for economic reasons or a lack of state capacity. Empirical studies of multilateral human rights and environmental treaties demonstrate that states with higher levels of development are more likely to comply.[44] Because of this finding, the case studies in this book are limited to industrial, Global North countries, which the World Bank considers "high income countries."[45] Canada and the United Kingdom have comparable per capita incomes, and though South Korea's income is lower, it is still quite high by global standards. Yet South Korea complied more readily in some instances than Canada and the United Kingdom. And while income levels within each state remained relatively constant, state responses to international institutions' recommendations changed over time. Therefore, in these cases, a state's level of development did not provide a sufficient explanation for compliance or noncompliance with trade union rights.

To isolate the influence of the control variable, the case studies largely consist of within-case analyses. Because these cases all span multiple years, and in South Korea and the United Kingdom, multiple governments, the case chapters are divided by key years. The South Korea case is divided between the period before the 1997 financial crisis and the period after this crisis. Given the political significance of the financial crisis in South Korean politics, this division allows one to compare how the different political incentives aided and hindered compliance with trade union rights. The chapter also compares changes between various presidential administrations. In the United Kingdom chapter, the case is divided between the two governments. While New Labour claimed to be more supportive of trade unions than the Conservative government, its statements to international institutions about its labor rights obligations were almost identical to its predecessor's. Finally, the Canadian case compares the response of the government before and after the 2007 Canadian Supreme Court decision regarding collective bargaining rights. While this decision did not ameliorate all the legal issues brought by unions to international organizations, it did lead to legal redress. These comparisons within cases provide a means to isolate and compare a state's behavior and rhetoric during its participation in the transnational normative negotiation process over time. This reveals how the interaction of normative, material, and political interests can influence state behavior.

Methodology

My primary method of inquiry is comparative historical case analysis, relying heavily on process tracing to uncover the various mechanisms influencing state compliance. Process tracing allows researchers to discover the "intervening causal processes—the causal chain and causal mechanisms" between independent and dependent variables.[46] As this book studies three countries, across long periods, with certain factors (such as partisan governments) changing over time, this is also a dynamic comparative study.[47] The cases link local-level political contestation over the legitimacy of trade union rights claims with the transnational process by which states defended and defined their obligations within legal contexts. These interrelated processes led to changes not only in domestic policies and practices, but also in the international interpretation of trade union rights norms.

Process tracing provides a means to link key variables and theoretical claims to processes that occur within cases. While political conditions and material interests of states, political or otherwise, seem to explain why certain changes occur, process tracing opens up the "black box" of the case. It is difficult to understand the relationship between these factors without careful attention to historical sequences and consequences of earlier factors. For example, successful legal changes in some of these cases seemed to correlate with changes in government. In both the United Kingdom and the South

Korea cases, the government changed trade union law after partisan shifts to a more left-center government. However, this could not explain the changes in British Columbia, where a change in government did not occur. This also could not explain the timing, variation, and depth of legal changes. While South Korea, under President Kim Dae Jung, made significant changes, many problems remained. And despite its center-left partisan identity, the New Labour government in the United Kingdom resisted the pressure from the International Labour Organization (ILO) and other institutions to change certain laws, citing the same arguments the Conservative government used to defend its practices. Process tracing helps to uncover how such factors relate to the successes and failures of the transnational normative negotiation process. Qualitative and historically rich, process tracing methodology provides necessary tools to understand the political and normative dynamics present in these interactions.

To evaluate this negotiation process between unions, states, and institutions, this book draws on a number of different primary sources. Written sources include the proceedings of the ILO's Committee on Freedom of Association, published biennially in the ILO's *Official Bulletin*. This book also uses the OECD Economic Surveys of Korea, which include recommendations on labor laws, and the proceedings and communications of the Committee on Economic, Social and Cultural Rights (CESCR) and the United Nations Human Rights Committee. From the Council of Europe, this book draws on texts from the European Court of Human Rights and the Social Charter's Committee of Independent Experts. The proceedings of the ILO, CESCR, and the European Court are useful as they contain communications from the institutions, the trade unionists, and government representatives, and thereby allows for analysis of the changing rhetoric and actions of each state. The case studies also rely on campaign literature, government reports to international organizations, public statements, press releases, speeches, and parliamentary proceedings.

The cases also build on semi-structured interviews with key actors and representatives from important organizations, particularly trade unionists and NGOs. Interview subjects were selected from the actors listed in the reports of complaints brought to the ILO Committee on Freedom of Association, as this institution provided the most information about individuals involved. I contacted representatives from all the unions and governments that participated in the relevant ILO committee's complaints. In addition, interviews were conducted with civil society representatives that participated in the transnational negotiation process. While not all government representatives consented to interviews, most were cooperative and provided documents relevant to the cases. The interview subjects included representatives from trade unions, national union federations, bureaucrats, a former labor minister, and representatives from civil society groups such as business organizations and human rights organizations. The interviews provide insights about the changes in domestic law and the role that international institutions played in influencing these changes. Follow-up phone interviews provided additional information about the effect of the case outcomes.

While interviews were not the primary source of the case materials, they did provide information on the way these interactions with international institutions affected trade unions' campaigns. As most of the interview subjects were trade union representatives, these interviews were important in creating the historical narrative on how the transnational normative negotiation process resulted in changes on the ground, including policy and legislative changes. Trade unions were the initiators of the transnational normative negotiation process, and, therefore, it was important to make their perspectives central to the narrative. These interviews also clarify how legal outcomes from the normative negotiation process fell short of trade union expectations. In addition, the interview subjects provided information about the relationships between local unions and parties, international federations, and broader civil society organizations. The South Korean interviews contextualize the government's claims about the illegality of trade union activities. In the Canadian case, interviews with a broader range of union and civil society actors provide insights on the inaccessibility of political institutions under the Liberal government. In addition, former and current government officials were interviewed in South Korea and Canada both to determine whether the governments interpreted the narrative differently from the trade unions and to determine whether the governments felt obligated to follow international institutions' recommendations. In the United Kingdom, the interviews provided technical legal background, as this case was more characterized by legal activism.

Outline of the Book

Chapter 2 details the foundational conditions for the institutionalization of trade union rights. The Great Depression pressured dominant state elites to propagate many new social and economic norms, of which trade union rights were one part. This narrative highlights the shortcomings of trade union rights today. Although these rights have a long history and are inscribed into multiple legal documents, their initial institutionalization was the result of specific material, political, and ideological conditions. Trade union rights, as well as many other social and economic rights, were codified into international law not because there was a strong consensus on the inherent value of industrial democracy and social justice, but because state elites recognized the instrumental importance of such rights. Even within the drafting of the Universal Declaration, the inclusion of trade union–specific rights was highly contested.

In addition to this history, Chapter 2 also examines the ways that different international institutions within the cases have codified protections of trade union rights. Chapter 2 also analyzes how and why trade union rights are challenged under the current political, economic, and ideological contexts of neoliberal globalization. As mentioned earlier, although neoliberalism uses the rhetoric of "non-intervention" and "free markets," neoliberal states actually promote new norms of employment. Instead of protecting workers' organizational rights, states and other actors have promoted new norms of labor flexibility. Often, these flexible labor policies include direct attacks on the freedoms and rights of trade unions.

Chapter 3 first explains the many sub-rights and principles included in trade union rights norms, drawing on the 2006 International Labour Organization Committee on Freedom of Association's *Digest of Cases*. This is a compendium of the many specific principles that the committee has decided in the course of its more than sixty-year history. In addition, Chapter 3 explains the institutional design and mechanisms for compliance and monitoring. This section compares these institutions' different interpretations of states' trade union rights obligations, demonstrating that even international institutions lack a clear consensus on trade union rights obligations. These institutions include: the ILO's Committee on Freedom of Association; the United Nation (UN) Committee on Economic, Social and Cultural Rights; the UN Human Rights Committee; the OECD's Employment, Labour and Social Affairs Committee[48]; and the two human rights bodies of the Council of Europe: the European Social Charter and the European Court of Human Rights.

Chapter 4 analyzes three major trade union rights violations in South Korea that received sustained attention from the ILO's Committee on Freedom of Association; the OECD's Employment, Labour and Social Affairs Committee; and the UN Human Rights Committee. When South Korea finally joined the United Nations in 1990, it also joined the ILO and ratified both the International Covenant on Civil and Political Rights and the International Covenant on Economic, Social and Cultural Rights. Unlike many other recently democratic countries, South Korea resisted reforming its trade union laws, prompting South Korean trade unions to bring their complaints to an international audience. While international institutions issued many strongly worded critiques to South Korea, the country claimed that its practices did not constitute human rights violations. When South Korea found itself under international scrutiny upon joining the OECD, trade unions and international institutions used this opportunity to hold South Korea responsible for its human rights aspirations. However, the resulting legal changes fell short of the strong protections recommended by international institutions. A similar dynamic occurred when trade unions were able to threaten South Korea's reputation immediately after the 1997 Asian financial crisis. South Korean elites feared negative consequences from trade union activism during the financial crisis, which provided political leverage for trade union rights claims. While trade union rights reforms resulted, many collective trade union rights issues remain unaddressed.

Chapter 5 focuses on a specific trade union rights legal question in the United Kingdom. Trade unions sought to use domestic and international institutions to challenge Thatcher-Major policies that undermined basic trade union rights. The British state, under different Conservative governments, claimed that the trade union rights dispute in question constituted a justifiable employer practice. This dispute, beginning in 1988, involved employers' use of individual contracts. These contracts promised workers a raise in pay conditioned upon giving up union membership and the right to collective bargaining. After domestic courts declared this illegal, the Conservative government passed a bill that specifically allowed the practice. Complaints were brought to the ILO Committee on Freedom of Association, the UN Human Rights Committees, the European Social Charter, and the European Court of Human Rights. The ILO argued strongly in favor of the trade unions, claiming that such laws undermined the ability for unions to exist and the security of trade union members. With the 1997 election of Tony Blair, some trade union rights reforms occurred, but these new laws did not prohibit employers from offering individual contracts as an incentive to abandon collective bargaining. When the European Court of Human Rights asked for information about the trade unions' case, Blair's government responded to the Court using the same rhetoric and justifications as the Major government. The European Court of Human Rights ruled against this law in 2002, overturning some of its prior decisions. The resulting 2004 U.K. legal changes claimed to close the loophole, although some British labor experts have criticized the new law for its shortcomings.

Chapter 6, the final case study, analyzes a recent dispute involving public servants' trade union rights in British Columbia, Canada. This dispute, which was the subject of multiple complaints to the ILO, focused on the provincial government's legislation, which replaced existing public-sector collective agreements. This case is somewhat different from the others because a subnational level of government was responsible for the laws in question.[49] When the Liberal government came to power in 2001, it broke its campaign promises by legislating over the existing collectively bargained agreements. The government justified these new unilateral agreements by claiming these developments were fiscally responsible, as they imposed pay cuts and mass layoffs. The government defended its practices, suggesting that it did not feel constrained by the ILO's recommendations. The British Columbia unions continued to contest these laws in domestic courts. While the provincial-level courts rejected their case, the Supreme Court of Canada ruled in their favor, citing the ILO and other international institutions in their decision. While the Supreme Court did not accept all of the trade union's complaints, it did agree that the government had violated basic trade union rights and required the provincial government to pay compensation and change the relevant laws. Yet despite this legal action, the resulting law was unsatisfactory to a number of observers, specifically because it did not address the vulnerability of public-sector trade unions during times of fiscal austerity.

Chapter 7 compares these three cases, examining how the original disputes and the eventual legal changes compare to the recommendations of the international institutions. This chapter shows how these different states engaged in a similar, economically justified process of normative negotiation. In all three cases, there is a consistent pattern of states privileging employers' desire for flexibility over workers' rights. The human rights commitments did sometimes constrain state elites and thereby provide the "hook" by which advocates made claims for legal changes. However, the success of these changes was dependent on a number of political conditions. While South Korea was most amenable to change when it felt pressured to protect its international reputation as a human rights-abiding country, the United Kingdom and Canada were more likely to change when domestic political conditions were aligned. The election of New Labour and its human rights, pro-European politics, and the influence of international institutions on the Supreme

Court of Canada created the conditions for change. In addition, this chapter also discusses whether or not these changes provide evidence for "post-neoliberalism" and the effectiveness of international trade union activism.

The cases of South Korea, the United Kingdom, and Canada illustrate the complicated task of promoting trade union rights as labor rights within the contemporary transnational context. As the case studies demonstrate, the human rights framework has been somewhat effective in changing trade union rights laws, but it is unclear whether other frameworks would be more effective. The goals of promoting workplace democracy and pursuing social justice through labor rights may be less relevant in a globalized and competitive economy. While transnational advocacy has led to piecemeal victories for trade unions against unsympathetic states, it is less clear whether it has effectively challenged the dominant ideology of neoliberalism, which understands trade unions and collective rights to be inflexible relics.

CHAPTER 2

Negotiations and Norms

The Development of Trade Union Rights in International Law and Institutions

Trade union rights include three related norms: the right to freedom of association; the right to collective bargaining; and the right to collective action, including the right to strike. These rights developed as a result of popular political contestation and an emerging, though fraught, social consensus regarding the necessity of allowing workers to organize and act collectively.[1] In doing so, trade unions can bargain for better working conditions and protect the interests of their workers. While states can provide workers with some of the same tangible benefits (individual-level protections such as minimum wage, job security, layoff protections, health and safety standards) as trade unions' collective agreements, trade union rights have intrinsic value because they provide a means of voice and representation for workers.[2] As the ILO has stated, these rights provide trade unions "the means to promote and defend the interests of their members, constitute a source of social justice and one of the main safeguards of sustainable peace."[3] In other words, trade union rights are valued not only because they are a means toward redistribution of resources and power, but also because they create industrial democracy within workplaces.

The history of trade union rights norms, however, reveals that there was never a clear consensus over the exact scope of states' responsibilities to trade union rights. Despite the claim of some human rights theorists that the Universal Declaration of Human Rights represents an overlapping universal consensus,[4] labor rights, including trade union rights, have always been contested[5] because they seek to constrain capitalist production. While trade unions and some states preferred precisely codified protections for workers, other states and employers resisted such protections. This resulted in softer, more flexible codifications of trade union rights norms in many international treaties. Because of this lack of consensus, states deliberately created softer legalization to deal with various political and coordinative problems, as well as the potentially high costs of international legalization.[6] In addition, the political consensus surrounding these norms was precarious even at the moment of their codification. Because many of these rights are codified imprecisely, states, trade unions, and international institutions contest each others' interpretations of these rights.

Yet if trade union rights are so contested, how did they become recognized as international norms? Their incorporation required three different foundational conditions, reflecting the interests of powerful Western states and different workers' organizations. These conditions included the political urgency of the Bolshevik Revolution, the fear that uneven labor standards would lead to trade disadvantages, and the prominence of functionalist ideologies that linked peace with economic prosperity. Unions and advocates of labor rights effectively promoted these rights because they resonated with contemporary ethical, economic, and strategic political circumstances. The development of these foundational conditions will be further elaborated in the discussion of the ILO's development.

This chapter will explain the historical emergence of trade union rights, and their legal codifications within several international institutions that protect them. The incorporation of international trade union rights into various treaties and institutions was a contested process, made possible by the political expediency given to the "labor question." The Cold War, the political power of trade unions, and the postwar economic order allowed for the creation of these norms. However, when the initial foundational conditions changed, states often decided to pursue labor flexibility goals, privileging employers' interests over collective trade union rights. The third part of this chapter analyzes the way support for trade union rights has changed over the years.

Trade Union Rights: From National to International Norms

The rights for workers to form organizations and act collectively to protect their interests emerged during the early period of industrialization. The new employment relationships that emerged under early industrial capitalism lacked protections and entitlements for workers, disrupting the social arrangements of the pre-industrial economic regimes. At a time when democratic and human rights did not exist, workers began a long fight for representation and protection of their interests in both industrial and political contexts. Many scholars have demonstrated the close relationship between the struggle for workers' rights and the struggle for universal (male) suffrage.[7] Historical evidence suggests that workers began to come together to promote their interests in the eighteenth century, but this activity was not legally protected.[8] As national protections for trade union rights began to emerge, both popular movements and political elites sought to create a regulatory regime on the global level. The global labor protection regime was established more than twenty-five years before the creation of the global human rights regime.

Local struggles for workers' rights to organize and act collectively helped create new domestic norms and laws. As more workers moved from traditional forms of labor to paid "free" employment, workers faced precarious new material conditions and tried to protect their interests through associations. While some privileged groups of workers did enjoy certain rights and protections, these benefits were often limited to members within exclusive trade guilds. These early protections were not rights of workers *as* workers, and they included neither political freedoms (to make demands as workers) nor rights to collective action. These privileges were more exclusionary than our modern universal conceptions of workers' rights.[9]

Organizations advocating more universal and solidaristic conceptions of workers' rights emerged around the turn of nineteenth century, but they typically did not seek protection from a central state. Instead, these workers' organizations drew on local authorities, lords, parishes, or municipalities to protect their rights.[10] States often saw these workers' organizations as subversive, and quickly passed statutes outlawing their existence and activities. For example, the Combination Acts of 1799 in England banned any type of collaborative activities by workers for twenty-five years, although workers often found creative ways to circumvent these limitations.[11] Another significant setback was the French Le Chapelier Law of 1791. This law outlawed all workers' organizations, even friendly societies, during the height of the French Revolution.[12]

Despite this repression, workers continued to form and act through organizations. In addition, academics, clergy, industrialists, and statesmen began to advocate for changing the employment relationship. This group included utopian socialists such as Robert Owen, doctors such as Daniel Mareska, businessmen such as Jacques Necker, and revolutionaries such as Karl Marx and

Friedrich Engels.[13] In addition, local churches provided important organizational resources to budding workers' organizations. For example, the Church of England and Methodist churches were instrumental in organizing workers in England; many British trade unions still call local unions "chapels" and union leaders "fathers." As a result of both elite and mass-level support, legal allowances began to emerge. National laws protecting the rights of workers to organize became implemented in the first quarter of the nineteenth century. These laws either protected a positive right of workers to form associations or decriminalized their activity. According to Bernhard Ebbinghaus's study on European trade unions, Western European states began to recognize and protect workers' rights to form and join unions at these times (Table 1).[14]

While many European states began to protect workers' organizing rights by the mid-nineteenth century, support for an internationally based norm of workers' organizing rights was disorganized and disparate. Some national leaders took initiatives to create a more international formulation of the norms. The underlying motivation was to prevent a competitive race to the bottom between trading European states. For example, Bismarck's Germany took leadership in establishing international conferences to promote an international regime of labor standards in 1876 and 1890, in Switzerland and Berlin, respectively. In the United States, lawyers established the International Association for Labor Legislation in 1890.[15] A major normative breakthrough occurred with Pope Leo XIII's issuing of 1891 *Rerum Novarum* in 1891. This statement expressed the Pope's support for workers' rights to form and join organizations for self-help purposes, and articulated the obligation of states

Table 1: Trade Union Rights: Year of First Protection

United Kingdom (including Ireland)	1824
Belgium	1830
Norway	1839
Switzerland	1848
Netherlands	1855
Denmark	1857
Sweden	1867
Germany	1869

to allow such a right. *Rerum Novarum* can be seen as the first nonbinding ("soft law") declaration of trade union rights. Workers in Europe began organizing in greater numbers, although prohibitions on organizing whole segments of workers, such as the "unskilled," women, and agricultural workers, remained.[16]

In addition to statesmen and leaders, workers and other grassroots organizations also sought transnational promotion of these rights, aided by the greater ease of communication and travel due to the Industrial Revolution. Workers found additional strength through new transnational organizations, such as the newly created international trade secretariats (ITS). The international trade secretariats[17] provided organizational support and created linkages between different countries' trade unions. This became the backbone for the International Workingmen's Association, or the First International, in 1864. At this society's meetings, radical trade unionists demanded political and economic rights for workers, seeking these rights through socialist revolution[18] This initial transnational effort was followed by the creation of the more organized and successful Second International in 1889. The Second International was a political network of trade unionists, academics, and activists dedicated to Marxist ideology and politics.[19] In addition to the secular organizing of the two internationals, Catholic unions also held international conferences during this time.[20] Trade union–led organizations sought to promote and protect workers' economic and social rights through solidaristic and social movement means.

Professional legal and reform organizations dedicated to promoting the international regulation of labor also emerged around this time. These organizations, which approached labor rights issues from an "economic standards" perspective, sought to pass international labor standards that would harmonize the protection of workers and help prevent a race to the bottom. Their early efforts to bring together like-minded reformers resulted in the first International Congress on Labor Legislation in 1897 and the follow-up intergovernmental conference of the International Association for Labor Legislation in 1905. These organizations began drafting early international labor conventions, particularly regarding health and safety measures, in the early 1900s. The 1905 conference, mostly involving academics and legal experts, was supposedly the first real "international labor conference." The first two international labor standards, banning night work for women and using white phosphorous in the manufacturing of matches, "passed" at the 1905 conference. These conventions were easily adopted because they were relatively uncontroversial; the more controversial questions, particularly trade union rights, went unaddressed.[21] These early attempts of Western European countries to set up legal protections of workers' rights were difficult, and demonstrated the reluctance of states to commit to strong international legal provisions.

Secular trade unions were instrumental in solidifying transnational demands for the modern regime of international labor rights. They created the first international trade union federation in 1913, the Berlin-based International Federation of Trade Unions, which survived the war. The first worker-led demands for international trade union rights emerged during the 1916 international trade union conference in Leeds. This Leeds conference, which included the International Federation of Trade Unions and a number of representatives from various national union federations, formulated a list of demands that later became a blueprint for the ILO. World War I, while often considered a failure of international solidarity because of workers' willingness to fight each other for their respective nations, was still helpful for trade unions' efforts. Soldiers' contributions to war efforts increased workers' bargaining power vis-à-vis states. It became harder for states to ignore the demands of workers in the war's aftermath. The labor leaders from the victorious powers of World War I, such as Samuel Gompers of the American Federation of Labor (AFL), were also instrumental in the ILO's establishment.[22]

The ILO was formed in 1919, during the Peace Conferences in Paris and Versailles following the World War I. This was the culmination of transnational efforts to institutionalize labor standards and rights, including trade union rights. Such an effort was possible because of the cooperative and self-reflexive "liberal moment" shared between states at the end of the war. During this period, functionalism guided the design of international organizations. Functionalism was the ideological commitment to creating a working peace system through strong international relationships and the domestic promotion of economic development, social justice, and welfare.[23] Gompers led the constitution-writing project, which also included representatives from Belgium, Cuba, Czechoslovakia, France, Italy, Japan, Poland, the United Kingdom, and the United States.[24] The ILO's establishment was not a smooth process, emerging from the harmonious interests of different actors. Some states rejected the social justice emphasis of the organization, while others accepted it only "grudgingly."[25] The establishment of the ILO resulted from a protracted compromise between the competing demands of pragmatic statesmen, fearful liberal capitalists, socialists, idealistic reformers, and trade unionists.

World War I victors United States, Britain, and France sought to include social provisions in the peace treaties both to reward worker-soldiers and to ensure against the growing threat of communism post-1917.[26] Powerful states feared workers' revolutionary power, and responded by creating of an international liberal regime of rights for workers. Robert Cox, who worked in the ILO for twenty years, argues that the ILO "offered labor participation in social and industrial reform within an accepted framework of capitalism."[27] The ILO was created after many rounds of negotiations as a tripartite body with the authority to draft and monitor international labor standards. Its constitution, which emphasized the importance of the trade union rights in its preamble, was incorporated into the Treaty of Versailles in 1919. The ILO's establishment, including its protection of trade union rights, was the result of a political bargain between workers and states at the end of World War I. The importance of trade union rights was reaffirmed toward the end of World War II in the 1944 Declaration of Philadelphia.

Therefore, there were three *foundational conditions* leading to the establishment of the ILO and international labor rights regime. The first was the moral/ethical concern: increasing labor standards was seen as an ethical good, relating to human rights and dignity. The second condition related to politics and security. At the end of the war, there was an international consensus recognizing a relationship between industrial peace and international peace. This concern was also supported by deep fears of the Russian Revolution. The third concern was economic, as some states feared that a lack of international regulation of labor standards would lead to "social dumping," which could economically hurt the positions of high standard countries.[28] International labor standards would be necessary to prevent unfair trade practices and disadvantages to those states that protected the interests of workers.[29]

After the ILO's work was interrupted by World War II,[30] the organization held a meeting in Philadelphia for member states to re-commit themselves to the organization's principles. The resulting document, the Declaration of Philadelphia, reestablished the ILO, and designated trade union rights as one of its four fundamental principles.[31] As in the 1918 constitution, the Declaration of Philadelphia stated that trade union rights, called "Freedom of Association," were "essential to sustained progress."[32] State and labor leaders at this event also promoted the idea, developed by the Irish economist John Kells Ingram in the late nineteenth century, that labor should not be considered a commodity. This general principle sought to protect conditions of work from negative market pressures. It was directly incorporated in the 1944 Declaration of Philadelphia, which read:

> The [International Labour] Conference reaffirms the fundamental principles on which the organization is based and, in particular, that—
> (a) labour is not a commodity;
> (b) freedom of expression and of association are essential to sustained progress;
> (c) poverty anywhere constitutes a danger to prosperity everywhere;
> (d) the war against want requires to be carried on with unrelenting vigor within each nation, and by continuous and concerted international effort in which the representatives of workers and employers, enjoying equal status with those of governments, join with them in free discussion and democratic decision with a view to the promotion of the common welfare.[33]

The Declaration of Philadelphia not only established the fundamental importance of rights for workers, but also aided the inclusion of trade union and other labor rights within the broader international human rights regime.[34]

In addition to reestablishing the mission of the ILO, the end of World War II also marked the beginning of a new normative global regime. This included new norms about economic regulation and also the creation of a global human rights regime. Many international actors recognized the social and political importance of state intervention into national economies, resulting in a new political economic system called "embedded liberalism" by John Ruggie. Embedded liberalism was a compromise between the reigning free market ideologies and the political demands "by land, labor and capital upon the state to reimpose broader and more direct social control over market forces."[35] This intervention included capital controls, the creation of welfare states, and social protections for workers and citizens. In addition to the new economic protection regime, trade union rights were incorporated in the new international human rights regime, although its inclusion into the Universal Declaration was contested.[36] This postwar overlap between old liberal economics and the emerging global human rights regime also supported the further institutionalization of labor rights and trade union rights.

Therefore, during the initial post–World War II era, most democratic states accepted trade unions, and their rights, as necessary actors in democratic societies. Unions provided a means to "offset the economic and organizational dominance that employers had over individual employees" and generally promoted peaceful means of dealing with labor-management conflicts.[37] While internationally, trade union and other labor rights were often subsumed under larger Cold War struggles, trade union rights mostly enjoyed protection at the national level.[38] But even during this period, the position of trade union rights was not clear. The next section explains how various international institutions codified and interpreted trade union rights norms.

International Institutions' Incorporation of Trade Union Rights

Trade union rights have since been formally included within international legal treaties with varying degrees of precision and obligation. While the inclusion of trade union rights in the ILO's Constitution at the Declaration of Philadelphia illustrates their importance to the postwar audience, the declaration did not have strong binding force. This section analyzes the institutions included within this book's case studies.[39] The incorporation of trade union rights within international legal bodies was a contentious process hampered by Cold War concerns, which produced a wide range of legalization outcomes. Socialist and Western states fought over the inclusion of the right to strike within these laws. Workers also worried about the codification of highly circumscribed strike rights, which could limit their activities in the future. As a result, this right is the least explicitly legalized right, although two of the institutions included an explicit right for workers to strike.[40]

Because trade union rights were politically difficult to codify, they were embodied in general terms; thus, although they are legally binding, they are somewhat ambiguous. Compared to other institutions, the ILO's conventions include the most specific obligations, but even they do not include explicit protections for all aspects of trade union rights (such as the right to strike). As a result, states in these case studies interpreted these laws in a limited manner, claiming that they only had the responsibility to *allow* workers to associate and attempt collective bargaining. States understood their primary obligation as noninterference in this process. Some international institutions, on the other hand, have read stronger positive state responsibilities into the laws, such as an obligation to *establish* collective bargaining and consultation mechanisms, collective rights and protections for unions, and the right to strike. As international legal documents often do not explicitly state these provisions, states can claim less responsibility. As a result, the debate over the extent of state responsibilities is quite significant. The following section traces the development of labor rights institutions and their legal provisions for protecting trade union rights.

The International Labour Organization Conventions and the Universal Declaration of Human Rights

The ILO recognized trade union rights[41] as a fundamental founding principle in its constitutional preamble, but these rights were not institutionalized until 1947. Part of the reason for this almost thirty-year gap related to the contestation over these norms, as states, employers, and workers could not reach a consensus on how to best codify trade union rights. The ILO first attempted to legalize trade union rights in 1928, but this failed because of disagreements. Trade unions wanted a freedom of association convention to explicitly include the right to strike, but states and employers resisted this, fearing it might overly empower workers. Employers and some states wanted to include the negative right not to join unions, an issue on which trade unions did not want to compromise. In 1928, a proposed convention for the freedom of association failed by a vote of 66 members against and 28 members in favor. This failure to pass a convention was considered a "debacle."[42]

Attempts to codify trade union rights were tabled during the tumult of the Great Depression and the World War II. However, these rights were reaffirmed by their inclusion in the 1944 Declaration of Philadelphia. The declaration, which became an addendum to the 1919 ILO constitution, specified workers' rights to organize as "essential" to sustained progress.[43] As a result of this reaffirmation, workers' organizations again began to advocate for a convention on freedom of association, although Cold War tensions divided the trade unions' efforts. The AFL and the World Federation of Trade Unions submitted separate requests to the United Nations Economic and Social Council to consider guarantees to protect trade union rights. The World Federation of Trade Unions was a left-wing postwar international trade union federation made up of European trade union federations, North American federations such as the Canadian Labour Congress and the U.S.-based Congress of Industrial Organizations, and additional representatives from Latin America, Asia, and Africa.[44] While the World Federation of Trade Unions preferred a United Nations–based labor committee, the AFL preferred ILO leadership. Despite their differences, both groups wanted trade union rights to be considered during the next International Labor Conference in 1948.[45]

In 1947, the ILO began to prepare for the creation of its freedom of association and collective bargaining conventions. Two key preferences were excluded from the final conventions: workers' preference for including the right to strike and employers' preference for freedom *from* association (the freedom for workers not to join a union or engage in collective bargaining and action).[46] Even though the Universal Declaration had a provision on freedom of association (in general, nonlabor-specific terms), this preference of employers was not included in the final drafts. The Socialist Bloc countries expressed concerns over the lack of protection for striking workers, but their protests did not change the wording of the final documents.[47] These drafts became the basis of Conventions 87 and 98, which protect the freedom of association and right to collective bargaining, respectively.[48]

Despite the pioneering work of the ILO, the inclusion of trade union rights in the Universal Declaration of Human Rights was not a smooth process. Even the socialist leader John Humphrey did not include explicit mention of trade unions in his initial drafts. As a result, the World Federation of Trade Unions lobbied the UN Economic and Social Council in March 1947. These communications linked trade union rights to democracy, connected the right to collective agreements to peace and prosperity, and stressed the importance of trade unionists and workers in winning World War II. The AFL sent a similar statement. In addition, the Latin American representatives lobbied to include specific mention of trade unions, instead of presuming sufficient protection within the general rights to assembly and association. These communications prompted the Economic and Social Council to urge the Commission on Human Rights to include these rights.

Though the inclusion of trade union rights was contested, state representatives did eventually include trade union rights language in the final version of the declaration. Article 23(4) states, "Everyone has the right to form and to join trade unions for the protection of his interests."[49] However, some states found this language insufficient to cover all necessary trade union rights. For example, the Swedish delegation, pointing to the lack of collective action allowed under Nazi Germany (where trade unions were allowed to exist), sought inclusion of a right to strike. The Swedish delegate stated that the basic right to form and join trade unions was worthless if trade unions could not use the right of work stoppages to protect members' interests. The commission, however, did not include this right within the final document.[50] Despite the Swedish delegation's support of the trade union position, workers' collective action rights did not seem as pressing as the basic association rights.

The United Nations Human Rights Covenants Protecting Trade Union Rights

The International Covenant on Civil and Political Rights (ICCPR) and the International Covenant on Economic, Social and Cultural Rights (ICESCR) are fundamental human rights texts of the United Nations. These documents were adopted in 1966 and came into force in 1976, after they received an adequate number of state ratifications. They are the legalized version of the nonbinding 1948 Universal Declaration of Human Rights, but their legalization was delayed for almost twenty years because of the political conflicts of the Cold War.[51]

The two covenants followed the Council of Europe model of splitting human rights into two different categories: one for political and civil rights and one for social, economic, and cultural rights. These two conventions were also differently legalized. This difference in legalization is not surprising, however, based on the debates over the different types of human rights law. While the original Commission on Human Rights wanted a single covenant with strong legal provisions, in 1951, the General Assembly voted to draft two separate conventions—one for civil and political and the other for social, economic, and cultural rights. This was justified based on the claim that civil and political rights were more enforceable, creating protection "against the unlawful and unjust actions on the part of the state, while social and economic rights were rights that the state would have to take action to promote."[52] The differing level of legal obligations created by this separation is discussed in Chapter 3.

Trade union rights are protected within both the ICCPR (Article 22) and the ICESCR (Article 8).[53] Unlike the Universal Declaration and the European Convention, Article 22 in the ICCPR designated freedom of association (for workers) as separate from the more general freedom of assembly. Article 22 specifies the civil and political elements of trade union rights, protecting workers' associations from state and private interference and oppression. In addition, it protects a very broad understanding of workers' interests, which can include political interests.[54] Article 8 of the ICESCR protects the rights to form and join trade unions, including the right to strike. Some state representatives debated whether to include Article 8 in the ICESCR, because of its inclusion in Article 22 of the ICCPR. Other actors argued that trade union rights were not human rights because they only relate to a specific group of people. These difficulties led to a purposefully vague articulation of Article 8. While the ICESCR includes collective rights for unions (freedom from interference, right to collective bargaining), the right to strike, usually exercised collectively, is framed as an individual right.

The articles protecting trade union rights in both covenants included similar references to the special place of ILO Convention 87. This reference states that "nothing in this article shall authorize State Parties to the International Labour Organisation Convention of 1948 concerning Freedom of Association and Protection of the Right to Organize to take legislative measures which would prejudice, or to apply the law in such a manner as to prejudice, the guarantees provided for in that Convention." Yet while referencing the importance of the ILO, the ICESCR goes an additional step and includes the right to strike. No ILO convention to this date has specified a right to strike. Article 8(d) of the ICESCR urges states to ensure "the right to strike, provided that it is exercised in conformity with the laws of the particular country."[55] The proponents for an international codification of the right to strike "learned" from the failures and silences within the ILO conventions. Specifically, the Socialist countries wanted to include the right to strike during the debates on the ICESCR, but the United States and France objected. However, when South American countries joined the Socialist Bloc countries, Western countries finally agreed.[56] While the right to strike was incorporated into the ICESCR, the provisions were weakened by a qualification. Article 8(d) specifies the right to strike, but limits this to the national laws of each country. Despite this proviso, the Committee on Economic, Social and Cultural Rights, the ICESCR's monitoring body, has generally evaluated a country's strike rights in comparison to universal norms, not in the context of a country's law.[57]

Council of Europe

The Council of Europe, like the OECD, was a liberal Cold War institution with the mission of promoting peace among Western states.[58] It was established in 1949 in London with ten founding members—Belgium, Denmark, France, Ireland, Italy, Luxembourg, the Netherlands, Norway, Sweden, and the United Kingdom—and currently includes 47 member states. This organization was limited to European countries, was more political in its membership criteria, and promoted human rights and democracy. The council has two regional human rights documents with corresponding monitoring and enforcement bodies: the European Convention on Human Rights and the corresponding European Court of Human Rights, and the European Social Charter and its monitoring body the Committee of Independent Experts.[59] These bodies played an important role in the United Kingdom case. While the European Convention is dedicated to civil and political rights, the Social Charter is dedicated to economic and social rights. Like the UN covenants, these institutions have different levels of legalization and adjudication, but unlike the UN covenants, they are not institutionally referential to the ILO and thus have had different historical interpretations of labor organization rights.

European Convention and European Court of Human Rights

As one of the primary organizing principles of the Council of Europe was promoting freedom and human rights, the council quickly adopted the "Convention for the Protection of Human Rights and Fundamental Freedoms" in 1950, which entered into force in 1953. While this legal document was based on the UN's Universal Declaration of Human Rights, the Convention only covered civil and political rights. Social and economic rights were specifically not included in the earlier convention on Human Rights because of political difficulties. According to the records of the debates around the Convention, only civil and political rights were seen as "essential" for democracy. The British representative to the council claimed that a strong legalized document protecting economic and social rights would be "too controversial and difficult [for] enforcement even in the changing state of social and international development of Europe."[60]

Although the European Convention is quite clear, there has historically been differing interpretations of the Convention's trade union rights provisions. Article 11 states that:

1. Everyone has the right to freedom of peaceful assembly and to freedom of association with others, including the right to form and to join trade unions for the protection of his interests.
2. No restrictions shall be placed on the exercise of these rights other than such as are prescribed by law and are necessary in a democratic society in the interests of national security or public safety, for the prevention of disorder or crime, for the protection of health

> or morals or for the protection of the rights and freedoms of others. This article shall not prevent the imposition of lawful restrictions on the exercise of these rights by members of the armed forces, of the police or of the administration of the State.[61]

While this article precisely states which categories of workers may be excluded from these rights, it does not clearly identify the kinds of state behaviors that constitute a violation of workers' trade union rights. For example, the provision allowing states to restrict these rights as "necessary in a democratic society" is a very vague parameter. Instead of a proscribed rule, one of the standards for strongly legalized norms, Article 11 seems more like a general principle. In addition, the standard of restrictions as "are necessary in a democratic society" is also quite general. Because of this indeterminacy, the European Court of Human Rights has interpreted this article very differently from other institutions, especially the ILO.

European Social Charter

The European Social Charter is the second part of the Council of Europe's mission to protect rights and democracy in Europe. The process to create a separate document for protecting social rights began as early as 1951, when the Committee of Ministers established a subcommittee, the Social Committee, to create a highly legalized document to set policies in the "social field," similar to the European Convention. But when representatives of member states in the Social Committee could not agree to a highly legalized document protecting social rights, the Committee instead adopted the "quasi-legal" structure of the Social Charter.

The Social Charter was therefore created with two sections, one of general principles and another of more legalized obligations. In part I, states committed themselves to general, "hortatory" goals, with "the aim of their policy, to be pursued by all appropriate means, both national and international in character, [so that the principles can] be effectively realized."[62] Part II was legally binding, creating more specific obligations for states based on the principles outlined in Part I. In order to be party to the Social Charter, a state had to accept five out of the seven "hard core" articles of Part II, along with several other articles so that the total number of commitments equaled ten out of the nineteen articles, or forty-five of the seventy-two numbered clauses. These hard-core articles were considered especially significant and were thus given more emphasis, although not all states committed to them.[63] Articles 5 and 6 related to the right of workers to organize and engage in collective bargaining and collective action. The United Kingdom, the only country in this book that is a member of the Council of Europe, ratified the charter in 1962 and included both Articles 5 and 6 in its legal commitments.[64]

Changing Foundational Conditions

As the previous section demonstrates, the various international institutions that include trade union rights in their mandates have a variety of legal embodiments, and have likewise interpreted differently state responsibilities to these laws over the years. For the most part, the ILO Committee on Freedom of Association, the European Social Charter, and the two UN human rights committees have promoted stronger responsibilities for states than their legal documents literally specify. The European Court of Human Rights has been more reticent to read more explicit protections than those in the European Convention on Human Rights.

However, independent from these legal developments, the international political climate has grown more hostile to trade union rights norms in recent decades. Trade union rights were grounded in political (Cold War), economic (ethical trade and social dumping), and moral (human rights) conditions. However, the political/security concerns of the Cold War are gone. Embedded liberalism, and its support for social protection of individuals and national economies from market forces, has been replaced with new normative regimes. As the economic pressures and interests of states have changed, so too have domestic public sympathies toward trade unions, and these newer attitudes challenge the idea that workers benefit from such representation at all. As a result, the foundations of trade union rights have shifted.

In the national Fordist production regime under which many democratic countries had strong trade and financial regulations, trade unions were often considered a necessary aspect of a stable national economy. Trade union rights were part of a larger regime of economic and social rights associated with the social citizenship of postwar welfare states. However, since the last quarter of the twentieth century, structural transformations within the global economy have significantly changed incentive structures for states. These shifts include such developments as the "new international division of labor"; the shift to tertiary industries in the Global North; capital flight to lower labor cost places (particularly in production of labor-intensive industries such as textiles); and the newer, more volatile monetary regimes.

A significant challenge to the old embedded liberalism was the new market-oriented ideology, or neoliberalism, that promotes workfare, greater competitiveness, and the rhetoric of minimal intervention into markets such as labor markets.[65] Neoliberalism, also called the "Washington Consensus," promotes individual freedoms, competitive free-market values, and privatization as the best practices for strong economic outcomes.[66] While the political reasoning behind the establishment of the international labor protection regime in the early twentieth century assumed that "labor is not a commodity," neoliberalism has sought to "make market functioning (and the openness of national economies to global market forces) the overwhelming priority for social organization."[67] The end of the Cold War and the diffusion of state neoliberal practices, adopted under the competitive pressures of "globalization," have largely guided these shifts in priorities. The pressures for states to deregulate, including taking a hands-off approach to labor regulations, have come from a number of different sources. They include the labor-related conditions of the IMF and the World Bank, and the spread of Anglo-American employment practices through the creation of a transnational management consultant industry (a new "epistemic community" that disseminates "best practices").[68]

Most states now ascribe to the dominant neoliberal ideology, which, according to David Harvey, seeks to promote the following: entrepreneurial activities, free-market mechanisms, free trade, free financial flows, and privatization of public services in the name of promoting individual freedom.[69] States continue to intervene in the economic sphere, but they do so to promote competitive deregulation and labor market flexibility policies rather than distributive and solidaristic goals.[70] Neoliberalism can be understood as both an intellectual movement and specific policy outcomes. The intellectual movement includes philosophical and economic communities, operating in universities, intellectual organizations, and think tanks. At the policy level, neoliberalism results in measures taken by economic, political, and sometimes cultural and military elites to "destroy . . . Fordist compromises and restructure power relations, institutions, [and] overall orientations . . . towards more capitalist interests."[71] The widespread diffusion of such economic liberal policies has been widely observed by scholars.[72] State practices, however, do not always match their ideological commitments, as popular protest and counterpolitics can also disrupt neoliberal policies, practices, and claims.[73]

The normative foundations of labor and trade union rights have been challenged by the increasingly important labor flexibility regime. In the past, while many states may not have completely subscribed to the labor protection regime, labor market regulations were at least rhetorically recognized as a necessary remedy to the vulnerability of workers in a capitalist society. While any meaningful system of labor rights requires the active involvement of the state in regulating labor relations,[74] neoliberal prescriptions recommend minimal regulation of economies. A host of research claiming to find definitive links between regulation of labor markets and economic growth has emerged in recent years. For example, Besley and Burgess's controversial and often-cited study of labor law reforms in India argued that "pro-worker" legal changes in various provinces led to lowered economic productivity, reduced output, decreased manufacturing jobs and investment, and increased urban poverty.[75] The work of Botero and colleagues, commissioned by the World Bank, argued that labor regulation was associated with higher unemployment, especially among youth.[76] A study by Forteza and Rama, also of the World Bank, found that labor market regulations resulted in "rigidity," and led to deeper recessions and longer recovery periods.[77] Many governments have adopted these labor market flexibility policies as appropriate to promote growth and investment.[78]

While economic scholarship does not clearly demonstrate whether labor flexibility reforms are financially beneficially,[79] such policies remain politically relevant. State leaders, as illustrated within this book's case studies, claim that labor flexibility will cut costs and attract capital. Such policies are seen as a necessary response to the competitive pressures of globalization and increased international trade. This is a politically accepted argument in most countries, and had led to expedient changes beginning in the 1980s.[80]

In addition, a wealth of scholarship has also emerged challenging the utility of trade unions rights, especially collective bargaining. Neoclassical economists thus champion formal models that demonstrate the distortionary and suboptimal effects of trade unions (and trade union rights). For example, freedom of association could lead to higher unemployment rates, "above market" wage premiums, and lower economic efficiency due to the "rent-seeking" behavior of trade unions.[81] This in turn could have inflationary effects and lead to suboptimal economic outcomes. In contrast, the OECD argued in its 1996 report that state respect for trade union rights was not detrimental to attracting foreign direct investment. Interestingly, the OECD published works promoting labor flexibility and labor rights just a couple years from each other.[82] Yet despite this evidence, state leaders still often choose to curtail trade union rights in an attempt to promote economic growth and competitiveness.[83]

The dominance of the market-oriented ideology has changed the ways in which many states understand their obligations to protect trade union rights. States now often seek to minimize labor costs, either to private employers or to themselves, in order to increase their competitiveness. This includes not only curtailing protections for workers' trade union rights, but also curtailing workers' individual protections. Even though such individual workers' protections are often separate from trade unions rights law, the political support for state intervention for both has eroded in many contexts. While these laws are often separate, changes to individual labor protection laws have increased the precariousness of workers' employment, which in turn harms the ability of trade unions to advocate for workers' interests.[84]

Though international organizations have influenced (and sometimes coerced) states into promoting labor flexibility policies, political and business leaders within states have also been at the forefront of pushing such reforms.[85] The changing normative and material conditions of neoliberal globalization have transformed the way state elites understand their social and economic obligations to their citizens. Strong promotion and protection of workers' trade union rights are perceived as having negative effects similar to labor regulations, such as hurting a country's productivity, reducing the competitiveness of its exports, and scaring off foreign investment. Collective bargaining and other trade union activities have been lumped together with minimum wage protections, unemployment insurance programs, and employment protection policies as distorting labor market forces.[86] As a result, states have reconstructed their responsibilities toward trade union rights to fit neoliberal ideologies. Outright oppression of trade unionists is considered illegitimate, but states may avoid providing strong protections for trade unions. While some of the earlier foundational conditions are absent, the fact that these trade union rights exist within international (and often domestic) law remains important. Thus, these norms are *contested*, as actors with different interests continue to argue about the legitimate understanding of states' obligations.

Neoliberalism and its key proponents (including multilateral lending institutions) do not explicitly encourage trade union rights violations. Rather, as a result of engagement with trade unions and the ILO, these institutions have publically endorsed trade union rights as part of the body of core labor standards.[87] In fact, in 2002, World Bank President James Wolfensohn responded to criticism of the bank's handling of the 1997 Asian Financial Crisis by announcing that "the Washington Consensus is dead."[88] But the World Bank and the International Monetary Fund (IMF) continue to prescribe greater prerogatives to capital and employer needs, while providing far less attention and using fewer resources to promote labor rights.[89] In doing so, these organizations and other economic actors claim to support trade union rights while acting as norm entrepreneurs for labor flexibility. This labor market flexibility regime seeks to reinforce labor as a commodity, in opposition to the principles of the ILO's Declaration of Philadelphia. Proponents of labor market flexibility endorse the idea that a state's primary responsibilities are to ensure that labor markets are free from constraints. While the labor market flexibility regime does not directly contradict trade union rights norms, it does exclude the consideration of workers as rights-bearing people. The labor flexibility regime provides employers wide latitude (free from state interference) over hiring, firing, work hours, benefits, work conditions, and other terms of employment. In addition, labor flexibility often undermines the legal framework that allows for meaningful exercise of workers' basic organizing rights.[90] Since they often undermine the stability of the labor contract, labor market flexibility reforms hurt the practical ability of workers to form unions and engage in collective bargaining and action.

Despite the ascendancy of the labor flexibility regime, there are still some articulations of the economic foundational basis of trade union rights. These economic foundations sought to promote higher standards of labor rights for all countries as a way to protect the economic interests of high-standard countries, and also to provide consumers with ethically made goods. In the past, states worried that other states' lower labor rights protections would hurt their economic interests. Today, states also worry that other states' more flexible labor markets might hurt their own economic interests. Despite a strong push from the United States and other industrial states, as well as the historic actions of civil society at the Seattle Ministerial Meetings in 1999, the World Trade Organization (WTO) has not created protections for workers. While the WTO has created rules that allow interventions into the "free market" to protect intellectual property and investment rights for business, no such rules for labor rights have emerged. Some state leaders claimed at the 1996 WTO Singapore negotiations that lower labor standards were the competitive advantage of less-developed countries, and thus an enforceable system of labor standards would lead to suboptimal trade outcomes for all, especially for developing countries.[91]

The labor flexibility regime lacks the legal power of codification, but enjoys institutional support. With the problems of unemployment and slowed growth in the 1970s and 1980s, richer industrial states tried to create policies for recovery. Perhaps one of the most significant proponents of labor market flexibility has been the OECD, in its groundbreaking 1994 *Jobs Study*. The key finding of the *Jobs Study* was that many OECD countries suffered from persistent unemployment because of their labor markets' inability to adapt to changes created by technology, increased trade, and increased competition.[92] The *Jobs Study* offered a number of policy recommendations to its member states, emphasizing the importance of promoting labor market flexibility. These recommendations included policies that promoted greater flexibility on labor costs, work hours, and wages. The report also urged states to balance social policy with growth-oriented labor market policies. Several years later, the Economic and Development Review Committee of OECD published the 1997 *Implementing the OECD Jobs Strategy: Member Countries' Experience*. This document praised the United States for its flexible labor markets and Japan for its flexible work-time institutions. Countries such as New Zealand, the United Kingdom, and the Netherlands were also commended for reducing their structural unemployment rates through policies that matched the OECD Jobs Strategy.[93]

Beginning in the 1990s, the IMF and World Bank made labor flexibility policies a loan condition for developing countries.[94] Though the IMF and World Bank claimed a new focus on social concerns, with their shift toward "country driven" poverty reduction in the 2000s,[95] both institutions continue to promote labor deregulation. For example, the World Bank's most widely circulated publication is its *Doing Business* report, which ranks economies based on "ease of doing business." One of its most controversial indicators was the Employing Workers Index, which measured labor flexibility. Countries were ranked on the following criteria: difficulty of hiring, rigidity of hours, difficulty of firing, rigidity of employment, nonwage labor cost (percentage of salary), and firing costs (weeks of wages).[96] States with stronger legal protections for workers received lower rankings. While these protections do not directly or legally infringe upon trade union rights law, they can hurt unions' bargaining position and ability to organize new members, as contingent workers are more difficult to organize.

This index was so controversial that trade unions, academics, legal experts, and some economists advocated for the World Bank to end the index.[97] For example, Peter Bakvis of the International Trade Union Confederation reported that the World Bank ignored the requests of local trade unionists and human rights groups in 2005 to pressure the Nepalese king to return to democratic rule and civil rights. Instead, the World Bank staff in Nepal used the *Doing Business* data to push the king to pass further labor flexibility measures, threatening to cut off financial aid if certain reforms were not made. These reforms included changing laws to privilege individual contracts over collective bargaining agreements.[98]

As neoliberal policies are not immune to political criticism, the campaign successfully convinced the World Bank to amend the Employing Workers Index in April 2009. The World Bank released a statement claiming that while it had prioritized business climate in the past, with the current challenges of the economic crisis, its new priorities would include "political stability, social safety nets to shield vulnerable parts of society from intolerable levels of risk and protection of rights for workers and households as well as for firms. . . . It is important that government actions focus on the needs of the labor force and lower income households as well as those designed to help businesses to survive and grow."[99] The World Bank stated it would create a new index on employment protection, using collaboration from trade unions and other experts. The bank also promised to reevaluate its index on "Social Contributions and Labor Taxes." This index has been criticized for penalizing countries that tax companies in order to fund welfare and worker protection policies. This decision was welcomed by critics of the Employment Workers Index, including the International Trade Union Confederation and certain pro-labor U.S. political leaders.[100] The reform suggested that the dominance of the neoliberal labor market flexibility regime could be successfully challenged.

It is unclear to what extent civil society activism has challenged the dominance of labor market flexibility. Some labor scholars and bureaucrats have touted "flexicurity," which allows employers flexibility but provides security for workers at the national level as the appropriate solution.[101] However, the neoliberal economic regime, though strongly challenged in recent years, remains prominent, enjoying support from a significant body of economic literature. Much damage has already been done, as trade union rights have been negatively affected.[102] As a result, the scope of issues allowed for collective bargaining is limited; whole sectors of the labor force (especially workers in export processing or other "special economic" zones) are often denied basic organizing rights, and the right to strike is often curtailed. In addition, even if states do not change their trade union rights law, they may often fail to enforce and protect them. This curtailing of trade union rights is not limited to developing countries, as it also occurs within industrialized national contexts. Trade union rights become unacceptable if they interfere with the flexibility and competitiveness imperative. As Harry Arthurs argues, "Few, if any, national governments in the industrialized West have concluded that the strengthening of collective labor laws is the best strategy for enhancing their global competitiveness."[103]

Given the challenges that trade union rights have faced with changing political and economic conditions, why do states and nonstate actors publicly declare commitment to these rights? While the political (Cold War) and economic (embedded liberalism) conditions are gone or weakened, the moral/human rights elements remain strong. Trade union rights, despite the inconveniences they may present to states seeking to minimize economic regulation, have maintained their position within the international human rights regime.[104] States do not question the legitimacy of these rights, but instrumentally seek to narrow their obligations to them to reconcile their economic and political interests. Trade union rights remain so important that states not only sign and ratify treaties with such provisions, but they also push for labor rights in other countries. Still, unions and NGOs claim repression of their basic rights.[105] The dynamics between these competing state claims has resulted in a number of fascinating exchanges between the states and international institutions. These continuing problems, states' justifications for the violations, are presented in the following chapters.

CHAPTER 3

International Institutions and Their Protections of Trade Union Rights

This chapter introduces the mechanics of the trade union rights institutions discussed in this book and the extent to which they protect these rights. The first part of the chapter reviews the range of "sub-rights" that international law defines as specific protections of trade union rights. The second part of the chapter explains the processes within each international institution involved in the cases studied and analyzes how these institutions have interpreted their legal commitments over time. This chapter also evaluates whether institutions codify trade union rights under harder or softer legalization, using the Abbott and Snidal framework of legalization: obligation, precision, and delegation.[1] The harder or softer legal status of an institution could determine its ability to influence a state's protection of trade union rights.

These institutions have often interpreted a more expansive understanding of trade union rights than what is literally written within the relevant legal documents. This suggests that the interpretation of trade union rights adopted by international institutions recognizes the inherent power inequalities and social justice aims of trade union rights norms. Because many of their interpretations refer to existing decisions and recommendations, international institutions' evaluations of trade union rights problems are often based on an established tradition of interpreting expansive protections for these rights.

International Trade Union Sub-Rights

Although they include individual and civil rights aspects, trade union rights include many specific sub-rights and principles within the more general precepts of freedom of association, the right to organize, and the right to collective action. International institutions have recognized that the range of activities and protections included in these rights are expansive. Scholars have identified three major components of trade union rights: (1) rights of individual workers, (2) collective rights of workers' organizations, and (3) positive obligations of states. While many scholars of human rights recognize that rights include both negative and positive inducements for states, the collective aspects of many human rights are typically less emphasized.[2] The classical view of human rights understands rights as protections for individuals against absolute and arbitrary state power. Yet trade union rights are based on a different assumption: the necessity of protecting workers from the vulnerability of employment relations, which can potentially be exploitative. The state must both intervene into this employment relationship and refrain from repressing trade unions and other workers' activities. Yet since the foundational conditions of labor rights have changed, many states no longer see protecting the vulnerabilities of organized labor to be important. While human rights do recognize and seek to reconcile inequalities of power and wealth, many states interpret the international human rights regime as only obligating the protection of individual rights. This limited understanding can undercut trade union solidarity and activities.

The specific obligations international norms create for states are not always clear, as norms often guide rather than define appropriate state behavior. But unlike many international norms, trade union rights have been adjudicated, interpreted, and widely discussed by a number of competent actors. The relatively high number of laws and institutions protecting such rights means that some specific provisions have been incorporated into the international trade union rights law. A number of scholars have detailed the specific standards included within trade union rights. The most extensive scholarly list of possible trade union rights violations has been compiled by Dave Kucera of the International Labor Institute, an educational unit of the ILO. His list specifies a range of state behaviors that might constitute norm violations.[3] Another publication by Verité, an international socially responsible auditing firm that produces reports for union retirement funds, includes criteria for its quantitative evaluations of workers' organizing rights. The following is a condensed list of key trade union rights principles, based on Kucera and Verité as well as international legal documents and jurisprudence. The legal instruments include the European Social Charter, European Convention on Human Rights, the International Labour Organization Conventions, and the United Nations Covenants on Human Rights. The legal source, including the article and clause number, of each of the rights is listed in the column on the right.

Table 2: International Legal Obligations of Labor Organization Rights

1. Individual Rights	**Legal Source**
a) Right to civil liberties as union members (speech, assembly, privacy, bodily integrity)	ICCPR-22.1,2 ICESCR-8.1c ESC-5 ECHR-11
b) Right of all workers without distinction whatsoever* to form and join organizations of their choice, without previous authorization (*armed services may be excluded)	ICCPR-22 ICESCR-8.1.a ILO C87-2 ESC-5 ECHR-11
c) Right to be protected against discrimination at work for trade union membership or activity	ILO C98-1 ILO C98-2a, 2b
2. Collective Rights	
a) Right of organizations to make their own constitution and rules, to elect representatives, to organize their own administration, and to formulate their own program (including freedom over finances, political program, and activities including the right to strike)	ILO C87-3.1 ILO C98-2.1 ICESCR 8.1a, a
b) Right to protect their interests from domination or interference by employers or public authorities, including suspension/dissolving	ICESCR-8.1a C87-3.2, 4 C98-2.1
c) Right to affiliate with any national or international labor federation/confederation	ICESCR-8.1b C87-8.1 ESC-5
d) Right to have legal personality with minimal preconditions	C87-7
e) Right of all workers to engage in collective bargaining, with minimal exclusions (of workers) and restrictions on scope of bargaining issues	C87-11 C98-3 ESC-5

3. Obligations of the State	Legal Source
a) Take appropriate steps to encourage and promote the development and utilization of machinery for collective bargaining between employers and workers' organization with the goal of creating collective agreements with minimal exclusions and interference	ESC-6.1 ESC-6.2 ILO C87-3, 8, 11 ILO C98-3, 4
b) Protect the right to strike by law with minimal prior requirements and minimal exclusions (such as essential public services, police, or military)	ESC-6.4 ICESCR-8d

KEY: ICCPR: International Covenant on Civil and Political Rights; ICESCR: International Covenant on Economic, Social and Cultural Rights; ESC: European Social Charter; ECHR: European Convention on Human Rights; ILO C87: ILO Convention 87; ILO C98: ILO Convention 98.

The list above is long and by no means comprehensive, as institutions such as the ILO and other human rights bodies have derived a much larger body of protections from existing laws. The next section will outline the full range of trade union rights protections that the ILO Committee on Freedom of Association has created over the years. It is important to note that not all international institutions that seek to protect trade union rights norms share common interpretations of state obligations. For example, the European Court of Human Rights has historically disagreed with the ILO committee and the European Social Charter's Committee of Experts about certain protections and rights for trade unions. In fact, prior to the case explored in Chapter 5, the European Court of Human Rights had not ruled in favor of collective trade union rights activity.[4] Just as international institutions sometimes disagree, states likewise disagree, typically claiming that trade union rights claims brought by unions are partisan, frivolous, or not tantamount to rights violations. The case studies illustrate this dynamic process of rights negotiations.

The ILO Committee's Principles of Trade Union Rights

This section briefly introduces the full range of rights, protections, and activities that the ILO Committee on Freedom of Association (the "ILO committee") has defined over the period of 60 years. Because it both takes complaints from workers' associations and hears responses from member governments, it is uniquely positioned to consider trade union rights disputes from multiple perspectives. While not every labor lawyer would agree with the full range of protections and sub-rights presented here, the committee's findings, published regularly in its *Digest of Cases*, provides a comprehensive introduction to the various entitlements, principles, and protections included within "Freedom of Association." There are three major categories covered in this section: trade union individual rights, trade union collective rights, and obligations of states.

Individual Rights and Liberties of Union Members

Trade union rights include individual-level civil and political rights, such as prohibitions and protections from arbitrary arrests, murders, disappearance, and violence against trade union members. Individual trade union rights also include the rights of trade unionists to due process, free assembly, free speech, free movement, demonstration, and political activities.[5] States must both refrain from violating these rights and protect workers from employer violations of these rights.

Fundamental to trade union rights is the right of workers, without distinction whatsoever, to join and establish organizations of their own choosing, without prior authorization. A workers' organization must not be required to first obtain permission from state authorities or another trade union organization to exist. However, states may create reasonable legal formalities for the establishment of a union or workers' organization, although minimum membership requirements, such as 30 percent of a workplace, may be too high (60). The right also allows for the existence of multiple trade unions. The right to form and join organizations applies to a wide scope of workers, regardless of occupation, which according to the ILO committee, includes all public and private employees, with the exception of police and armed services.[6] In addition, workers must be able to form organizations without discrimination based on race, political opinions, or citizenship status (46, 47).

Another major component of individual trade union rights is protection from discrimination. The ILO Committee on Freedom of Association's *Digest of Cases* calls anti-union discrimination "one of the most serious violations of freedom of association, as it may jeopardize the very existence of trade unions" (155). States must protect workers from discrimination based on current or past trade union membership or engagement in trade union activities.

Workers must be protected against discrimination in hiring, dismissal, and other punitive actions short of dismissal, such as harassment, intimidation, withholding of bonuses and raises, transfer, and demotions. The committee has also found blacklisting of union members, blocking them from further employment, to violate trade union rights principles. These protections must extend to membership and activities within both recognized and unrecognized unions (156–160).

The mere existence of laws that outlaw anti-union discrimination is insufficient; the state must also create effective protections with timely enforcement mechanisms. To prevent employers from engaging in anti-union discrimination, the ILO committee has ruled that states are responsible for preventing "all acts of anti-union discrimination and . . . must ensure that complaints of anti-union discrimination are examined in the framework of national procedures which should be prompt, impartial and considered as such by the parties concerned" (163). This includes reinstatement of workers dismissed for anti-union discrimination (168).

Collective Rights

In addition to individual rights for workers and trade union members, trade union rights include collective rights for unions and workers' organizations. These rights are necessary to protect the union's activities and interests, including the interests of its individual members. According to the ILO committee's decisions, unions have the freedom to make their own constitutions and rules, to elect representatives, to organize their own administration, and to formulate their own program of action. This includes unions' control over their finances and political programs. A significant component of collective trade union rights is the right of workers' organizations to have legal personality with minimal preconditions. A set of national regulations necessary for the legal personality of trade unions is permitted under the ILO committee's standards. However, these regulations may not create such difficult legal preconditions or other obstacles as to make the formation of unions virtually impossible (58).

The ILO has determined that collective bargaining is an important right because it provides a means for workers to help determine their wages and conditions of work. This entails two provisions. First, all workers, public and private, have the right to engage in collective bargaining, with only minimal exclusions. The only acceptable exclusions are armed forces, police, and public servants directly engaged in the administration of the state (179).[7] There should be minimal restrictions on the scope of bargaining issues. Unions should be able to freely bargain on a wide range of issues relating to their workplace interests, working conditions, and terms of employment. Laws should allow negotiations over certain workplace issues, such as wages, work time, leave, redundancy, and other working conditions. Government authorities may not dictate working conditions in a way that disrupts existing collective agreements. Finally, collective bargaining rights include workers' freedom to choose their bargaining representatives and freely draw on outside parties for assistance (183–185, 197).

The ILO committee's jurisprudence has remained neutral about union security clauses. Union security clauses are provisions either in law or collective agreements that allow for some kind of compulsory union membership or union dues payment for employees. While recognizing that trade unions have the right to engage in collective bargaining with employers over union security clauses, the committee recognizes that national systems may either allow or forbid union security clauses and still conform to trade union rights principles, as long as the law does not mandate a union monopoly system. In addition, any law that makes union membership a condition for employment is only considered discriminatory if the conditions for gaining membership are "unreasonable" (77).

While the freedom to join and form unions includes the right to join any union of a worker's choice, the ILO committee has recognized that different national industrial relations systems may create different privileges and collective bargaining rights. Therefore, the committee has concluded that both systems that grant collective bargaining rights to multiple unions in one workplace and systems that grant such rights to only the most representative union may fulfill the ILO's understanding of trade union rights requirements. This also applies to national labor relations systems that grant exclusive bargaining rights to the most representative organization at the industrial or national level (190). The committee has also decided that industrial relations systems, such as the U.S. system, which requires a representative union to be certified for it to have exclusive collective bargaining rights, may conform with international trade union rights as long as the following conditions are met: an independent body administers the certification process, the representative union is chosen by a majority vote, the union that fails to win an election may request a new vote after a period of time, and a challenging union organization may request a vote for certification when a reasonable time period has lapsed since the last election. To protect all workers' associational rights, however, the ILO's Committee of Experts declared that minority unions must also be allowed to represent their members (193, 195).

Trade unions must be able to engage in a broad range of legitimate activities. The Committee on Freedom of Association has recognized that trade union movements exist to promote the economic and social interests of their members. While this may include normal political activity, it should not compromise the objectives of a trade union movement. Unions have the right to petition, protest government decisions, engage in public campaigns (such as minimum wage laws), and protest legal decisions relating to trade union members. States may not prohibit political activities by trade unions, as this limits their actions (107. 104).

Another aspect of collective rights includes the right for trade unions to autonomously run their organizations. This includes the right to create their own rules, elect their own leaders, and operate without government interference. While governments may require certain formal procedures to ensure that trade unions operate lawfully and under democratic principles, such laws should not be so overly restrictive as to infringe upon a trade union's right to freely operate and exist. For example, authorities cannot be allowed to protest the establishment of a union after it has already been registered. Trade union elections should be governed by the trade union's rules, with little government regulation of the proceedings, although the authorities may create election schedules and set term limits for executive bodies (84). Trade unions have the right to control their finances. This includes controlling union officers' compensation and the spending of dues (96, 98). If trade unions are required to be audited, such audits should be done by qualified independent professionals, not state authorities (101).

If public authorities challenge the outcome of trade union elections, these challenges should be limited and taken to judicial authorities (92). In addition, trade unions cannot be required to provide minutes of meetings, names of trade union members present, or a treasurer's report (79). The committee has also decided that trade unions, not governments, should be able to decide workers' eligibility for membership and leadership, in terms of the following qualifications: a worker's employment status, nationality (citizenship), criminal record, or political orientation. For example, if a union member or leader is dismissed, the trade union, not the government, should be able to decide if he or she retains membership (87). Governments are also not permitted to replace union leaders. Rather, reorganization of trade unions should be carried out by the trade union organization itself, and if the authorities remove corrupt leaders, the union should elect their replacements (94).

A final major collective right for trade unions, including public sector and agricultural unions, is the right to affiliate. This includes the right to establish federations and confederations, and to affiliate with international organizations. Unions must be able to freely join and create higher-level organizations without government interference or need for approval. Governments may not prohibit multiple federations, at the national or industrial level, from existing in a country. This is meant to prevent governments from controlling the national labor movement. However, the workers in a country may voluntarily choose to belong to a single national trade union confederation, in conformance with international trade union rights standards (67).

Obligations of the State

The ILO committee regards the state as obligated to protect collective bargaining and strike rights. Governments are expected to create mechanisms to aid and encourage collective bargaining, including independent dispute settlement bodies, but the ILO's committee has ruled that bargaining should be a good faith, voluntary activity by both employers and workers. Governments should encourage but not interfere in the process of creating a collective agreement. While governments are not to interfere with the bargaining process, states should help enforce the final collective agreement (185–187). This means that governments cannot impose compulsory bargaining if employers and trade unions cannot reach a satisfactory agreement (197). Likewise, governments are not permitted to legislate over existing collective agreements, even to fulfill an economic policy. Rather, to respect workers' rights to collective bargaining, the government should attempt to persuade unions and employers to voluntarily adopt changes (200). This also means that governments may not claim the right to approve of freely negotiated collective agreements, even in the public sector (201). Restrictions on the collective bargaining process must be agreed to by all parties (210).

The ILO committee regards the right to strike as an "intrinsic corollary right" to workers' basic associational rights. The state is obligated to protect this right with minimal requirements and minimal exclusions. As long as they stay within the parameters of the law, workers must be protected against dismissal, discrimination, penalty, or liability for the peaceful exercise of their right to strike (135–136). Workers may legitimately strike over both economic/industrial interests as well as broader social and economic policy issues relevant to their members' interests. This can also include strikes for union recognition. The ILO committee has argued that a state may not limit legal strike activity only to those involved in collective agreement disputes. This includes a ban on national strikes, provided certain minimum basic services are maintained (112). The state may justifiably limit certain kinds of strike activities (like sit-down strikes, wildcat strikes, tools-down strikes, slowdown strikes, and work-to-rule) if they are no longer peaceful (113). The committee has argued that the right to strike does not protect strikes of a "purely political" nature (110).

The state has several key obligations in terms of protecting trade unions' right to strike, based on the ILO committee's principles. The state should protect the right to strike by law with minimal prior requirements and minimal exclusions. Those workers who exercise authority in the name of the state (police and armed services) may have their right to strike restricted (118). Preconditions to calling a strike, such as voluntary arbitration or conciliation, should not be so burdensome as to prevent a strike. Requirements of prior notice, include a longer period for public employees, are acceptable. Authorities may suspend a strike in order to allow mediation, conciliation, or negotiation of a solution, but any such process needs to be impartial, adequate, and speedy (114).

While states should refrain from restricting strike rights, the ILO Committee has recognized that the state may justifiably curtail strike rights for workers in "essential services." These services are defined "in the strict sense of the term, namely those services whose interruption would endanger the life, personal safety or health of a whole or part of the population." Workers in these services[8] must have appropriate "compensatory measures" if their strike rights are restricted. This could include limited strike rights and the provision of "adequate, impartial and speedy conciliation and arbitration proceedings" with impartial bodies to promote the interests of the parties involved (122). Limited strike rights would allow certain services the ability to strike while maintaining minimum operational services to prevent harm to public health and safety (125). The range of minimum services required should not render strike activity ineffective, and should be determined by state authorities, employers, and trade unions (126).

States should also refrain from declaring strikes illegal. If a strike is to be declared illegal, it should be done by an independent body that enjoys the confidence of employers and employees, especially when the government is party to the dispute (such as in public services) (128). Strikes should not be broken by the military or through back-to-work orders, unless public health or an acute national emergency is at stake (129). Likewise, police may not intervene or break strikes except in "grave situations where law and order is seriously threatened" (131). The committee has found that the right to strike includes protections for workers' reinstatement after the strike. Specifically, if employers refuse to rehire workers at the end of a strike, workers should have to right to challenge this decision at an independent court or a tribunal. The committee has recognized that in some instances, such as strikes that harm public safety, employers cannot be compelled to reinstate striking workers (169–170).

International Institutions: Mechanisms for Protecting Trade Union Rights

The following section reviews the international institutions that participated in normative negotiations within this book's case studies. As each of these institutions is affiliated with different organizations and legal instruments, each institution has slightly different policies for accepting trade union rights complaints. Because they are independent, these institutions occasionally disagree with each other about the scope of trade union rights. For instance, even though the European Social Charter and the European Court of Human Rights are part of the Council of Europe, they have developed different understandings of states' trade union rights obligations.

International Labour Organization and the Committee on Freedom of Association

After creating the relevant trade union rights conventions, the ILO wanted to create an accessible body to which workers' organizations could bring complaints and violations of freedom of association. While the ILO already had the Committee of Experts on the Application of Conventions and Recommendations (CEACR), it only accepted reports from member states that had ratified conventions. The International Labor Conference asked the Governing Body to consult with the United Nations' Economic and Social Council on how to better monitor trade union rights.[9] The Governing Body, which serves as the ILO's executive committee, is elected from the conference and is tripartite in its structure, with representatives from governments, workers, and employers' groups.[10]

As a result of this recommendation from the International Labor Conference, the governing body set up a Fact-Finding and Conciliation Commission on Freedom of Association in January 1950. This commission was authorized to investigate alleged violations of freedom of association against only those member states that had ratified Conventions 87 and 98. The consent of those countries that had not ratified the relevant conventions would be required prior to being investigated by the commission. However, because of this legal prerequisite, few cases of trade union rights violations were reported to the Fact-Finding and Conciliation Commission in its first years. To make the process more accessible, the governing body set up its own committee to act as an initial screening point for the complaints, called the Governing Body Committee on Freedom of Association, created in late 1951. This Committee on Freedom of Association would examine written documents from the complaining workers' organizations and responses from the government prior to sending the complaint to the Fact-Finding Commission. Like the governing body, this committee was tripartite in its structure, with an independent chair and nine titular and nine substitute members; it would meet three times a year.[11]

The Committee on Freedom of Association was originally meant to serve as a type of complaints clearinghouse, the initial examining point for complaints brought to the Fact-Finding and Conciliation Commission, but it evolved into a more prominent institution. While the Fact-Finding Commission has only examined six cases in over fifty years (as of 2001), the Committee on Freedom of Association has examined over 2,300 cases. The Fact-Finding Committee still exists, but its original functions are served by the Committee on Freedom of Association, since the latter is more accessible to workers' organizations. Because a country need not have ratified the relevant conventions for the committee to examine its cases, the committee became the primary institution for investigating trade union rights violations.[12] As a result, it is an often-used and well-known committee among certain state's trade unions.

In 1954, the ILO committee established the principle of reviewing cases against member states that had not ratified the core conventions. This case, number 102, involved a complaint against South Africa regarding a 1953 law that prohibited strike rights for African workers only. The South African government claimed that since it had not ratified Conventions 87 and 98, it was neither bound by the principles of the conventions nor to the ILO committee's investigations. In response, the committee claimed that the ILO's Declaration of Philadelphia, as part of its constitution, created obligations for all member states to protect trade union rights by virtue of membership. This established the precedent for the Committee on Freedom of Association to review complaints brought against non-ratifying member states.[13]

The process by which the committee examines possible violations of trade union rights is very simple. First, the committee receives complaints about a possible violation from a workers' organization. This can come from a workers' organization from the country in question, an organization from another country, or an affiliated international or national trade union federation. The trade union does not need to be certified or even have legal status to make a complaint. Next, the committee forwards the complaint to the member government, which in turn, provides a response. Then, during the next regular meeting of the Committee on Freedom of Association, the committee members examine the documents related to a case and make a consensus-based decision for recommendations. Since the committee is not a court, the recommendations are not intended to make accusations or condemnations, but instead to create "constructive" and "non-oppressive" discussion to bring about more secure promotion of freedom of association rights and principles.[14] This makes it a "softer law" adjudication mechanism, according to the Abbott and Snidal matrix. The important element of this process is that the investigation and recommendations cannot begin unless it is initiated by workers' organizations.

Because of the somewhat vague language of Conventions 87 and 98, and the vast volume of cases the committee has heard in the past 60 years, the committee has defined a broad range of situations as violating trade union rights. Often, the committee will refer to prior recommendations and principles in determining whether a complaint constitutes a violation. At other times, the committee will make an original decision. For example, the committee has established a clear list of the public industries that qualify as "essential services" for which strike rights may be restricted (such as health care), as well as those which do not qualify as essential services (such as education). The committee has applied its categories throughout its cases. The committee has been influential in specifying the extent of member states' responsibilities in protecting basic trade union rights. These interpretations are nonbinding but have been important for various legal understandings of the conventions and norms. These international standards have been developed and applied independently of the actual national-level definitions and standards.[15]

In addition to interpreting state responsibilities with regard to the actual language of the trade union rights conventions, the Committee on Freedom of Association has developed a rich jurisprudence on the right to strike. This was in spite of the fact that the right to strike is not an explicit provision within the conventions' language. The committee's jurisprudence regarding the right to strike has varied by case. In its first strike-related case (number 102), the committee strongly supported the workers, finding the denial of African workers' right to strike in violation of South Africa's responsibilities as a member. The ILO Committee decided to promote a universal international norm of the right to strike, regardless of national laws in question, beginning with their decision in case 148 (Poland) in 1956. The committee has used Convention 87 as the implicit legal basis of the right to strike. Article 3 of Convention 87 states that workers and employers' organizations have the right to "organize their administration and activities and to formulate their programmes." The committee has included strikes within trade unions' protected programs and activities. The right to strike has also been derived from Article 10, as it articulates that workers' organizations must be able to act with a view to "furthering and defending the interests of workers."[16] The Committee on Freedom of Association has defined strikes as an "essential" tool for workers to further their interests. Both the ILO Governing Body and the Committee of Experts on Applications of Recommendations and Conventions have accepted this Committee on Freedom of Association interpretation, although employers have criticized the Committee of Experts for adopting the Committee on Freedom of Association's principles.[17]

There are few enforcement provisions for the ILO's various bodies, including the Committee on Freedom of Association. The ILO promotes compliance through information gathering and monitoring and offering technical assistance, communications, and moral suasion. Under Article 29 of the ILO constitution, a state can refer a conflict with the ILO to the International Court of Justice, based on the outcome of a Commission of Inquiry; this, however, has never been used. The ILO could also request member states to engage in sanctions against a specific norm-violating member state.[18] In addition, the ILO could also expel a member country for failing to adhere to basic principles. However, the ILO took such a measure only once, in 2000, calling for sanctions against Myanmar because of continued problems with the use of forced labor. Sanctions and threats to remove states would hurt the ILO's claims about the universality of its principles.[19] Yet despite this lack of real "teeth," the ILO considers the Committee on Freedom of Association to be a successful and effective body. Though it does not keep strict statistics on its successes, the committee began to note "cases of progress" in 1970, and has since recorded cases of progress in over 60 different countries between 1970 and 2001. Most of these cases have occurred since the 1990s.[20] In some countries, there are multiple cases of progresses. The absolute number of cases brought to the committee has increased over the years, which means that the percentage of cases of progress has gone down.

Table 3: ILO Committee Cases of Progress

	Cases	*Countries*
1970–1979	26	24
1980–1989	33	23
1990–1997	60	51

Source: Geraldo von Potobsky, "Freedom of Association: The Impact of Convention No. 87 and ILO Action," *International Labour Review* 137, no. 2 (March 1998): 207

While the committee has certainly been prolific in its examination of cases, its recommendations are not binding and enjoy only soft legalization status. Although the ILO Conventions create binding obligations, the ILO Committee plays an advisory role. Since the Committee on Freedom of Association examines cases even in countries that have not ratified the relevant conventions, the committee has less legal authority. Compared to other international institutions, the committee's recommendations have a lower level of legalization, according to the Abbott and Snidal framework of obligation, precision, and delegation.[21] For a country that has ratified the relevant ILO conventions, the obligation is medium-high, as the conventions are quite explicit about the scope of state obligation. In terms of precision, the designation is medium/medium-low. Finally, the delegation of the Committee on Freedom of Association is medium-low because although it represents a kind of soft dispute resolution mechanism, its methods are more geared toward "conciliation and mediation" than toward arbitration.[22] Therefore, ILO committee recommendations do not create a strong enough legal obligation to effect changes in state behavior.

The United Nations Human Rights Covenants and Committees

The United Nations High Commission on Human Rights created two committees to review and monitor state compliance with the ICCPR and the ICESCR Currently, there are 158 state parties that have ratified ICESCR and 161 state parties to the ICCPR.[23] The state parties are obligated to engage in a regular monitoring process with the Committee on Economic, Social and Cultural Rights (CESCR) and the Human Rights Committee. The CESCR was established in 1985 by the United Nations Economic and Social Council, as per the instructions of part IV of the ICESCR. Similarly, the Human Rights Committee engages in a periodic monitoring process with its state parties, although this committee was established earlier than the CESCR. Both the Human Rights Committee and the CESCR require that state parties submit an initial report within two years of ratification; state parties then submit follow-up reports every five years. The two committees are made up of eighteen independent experts elected by state parties to the covenants. The CESCR meets twice a year in Geneva.[24] The Human Rights Committee meets three times a year, once in New York and twice in Geneva.[25] Each committee examines a state's report, engages in open dialogue with the state party representative at meetings, and then issues recommendations in its Concluding Observations document. In recent years, the Human Rights Committee and the CESCR have allowed nongovernmental organizations (NGOs) to make submissions regarding the status of human rights in their countries.

The interpretations of the Human Rights Committee and the CESCR have, like the ILO Committee, typically been both expansive and substantive. This is likely due to the clause in each covenant that references ILO Convention 87. The committees have generally interpreted this clause to mean that both covenants must be interpreted in a way that is harmonious with Convention 87. As a result, these UN human rights committees have adopted broad interpretations over the extent of state obligations to trade union rights. For example, while neither covenant includes an explicit right to collective bargaining, both committee bodies have interpreted such a responsibility and thus monitored their member states' protection of collective bargaining. This may be because the ILO has interpreted Convention 87 (which does not explicitly mention collective bargaining rights) to implicitly protect such rights. The CESCR has also followed the jurisprudence of the ILO in interpreting the protection of the right to strike more broadly than the explicit provisions in Article 8. As a result, even the Human Rights Committee has now begun to read freedom of association, collective bargaining, and the right to strike under Article 22, despite original reticence to do so.[26] It now monitors its member states' progress and compliance on these three issues.[27] Both committees now refer to ILO principles in creating their recommendations to states on labor rights.

There are problems with the reporting and monitoring system. For example, even though the covenants require periodic reports from state parties, they lack a means to enforce this requirement should states fail to provide them. For example, the CESCR publicized that in May 1996, there were 97 overdue reports from 88 state parties, and 17 states had not submitted a report in ten years (two reporting cycles).[28] The participation of NGOs is also fairly recent, and has not yet become a widespread phenomenon. Furthermore, while the

ICCPR has an optional protocol that accepts individual complaints of rights violations, the ICESCR lacks this petitioning process, and must rely solely on the monitoring and self-reporting process. Finally, the recommendations of the committees, although based on their interpretations of the International Covenants, are not binding and also lack enforcement mechanisms.

Both the ICESCR and the ICCPR are hard law instruments that bind ratifying state parties. But according to the Abbott and Snidal matrix, they are "softer" binding instruments, and the ICESCR creates less determinate obligations to states than the ICCPR. To understand this, one needs to look at the wording of the covenants themselves. Abbott and Snidal designate the ICCPR as high in terms of obligation (because it creates binding obligations on state parties), medium-low in terms of precision (because they are standards as opposed to strict and specific rules), and medium in terms of delegation (because it has a regular monitoring process).[29] While the ICCPR obligates states to respect and ensure the rights of the covenant, the ICESCR only obligates a state party, according to Article 2(1), "to take steps, individually and through international assistance and co-operation, especially economic and technical, to the maximum of its available resources, with a view to achieving progressively the full realization of the rights recognized in the present Covenant by all appropriate means, including particularly the adoption of legislative measures."[30] While the ICESCR does bind state parties, it does so in an ambiguous and highly conditioned manner. The trade union rights clause, Article 8, may have slighter higher legal obligation, however, because it requires immediate implementation; the article compels states to "ensure," not just "recognize" these rights.[31] ICESCR has a lower-medium level of obligation, because its language specifically creates more "contingent obligation and escape clauses."[32]

Council of Europe Instruments: European Convention on Human Rights and European Social Charter

EUROPEAN COURT OF HUMAN RIGHTS

After the creation of the European Convention on Human Rights in 1950, the European Commission of Human Rights was established in 1954 to make friendly settlements and determine whether violations of the convention had occurred. In 1959, the European Court of Human Rights was established to create binding adjudication on complaints against states. If a case was found to be admissible by the European Commission, and a friendly settlement had not been reached, the case would go to the European Court. However, a state party must submit itself to the jurisdiction of the Court. This country then had three months to make submissions to the Court, which the Court would use to make a binding decision and possibly mandate monetary compensation. The Committee of Ministers of the Council of Europe, made up of each member state's Minister of Foreign of Affairs, had the mandate of overseeing the execution of these decisions.[33] The convention allowed both other contracting states and individuals to bring complaints against member states.

However, as the number of case applications began to increase, the Council of Europe decided to amend this process in the 1990s. Caseloads increased from 404 in 1981 to 4,750 in 1997. This was partly due to the increase in the number of states in the post–Cold War Council of Europe. The adjudication procedures were streamlined and made more accessible. This resulted in Protocol 11 in 1998, which replaced the commission and the temporary court with a permanent court that both determined admissibility and made decisions. This change also made compulsory new rules that allowed individuals to bring complaints against all contracting state parties and gave the new court jurisdiction over all state parties to the convention. As a result of this greater degree of openness, the number of case applications has further increased, from around 6,000 in 1998 to 13,858 in 2001.[34]

While thousands of applications are made to the Court every year, cases brought before the European Court must fulfill strict requirements prior to submission. First, the applicant must have been personally victimized by the state, not by private actors. The violation can be an act of omission, as well as a positive action. General complaints about unjust laws or practices are not a sufficient basis of complaint. Although the individual need not be a national of a state party to the convention, the individual needs to have been a victim within the territory or jurisdiction of a state party. Furthermore, the individual must have exhausted all appropriate national-level remedies, including all appeal processes, prior to submission, and the submission to the Court must occur within six months of the final decision of the highest domestic court. Individuals must also specify whether the complaint has been submitted to any other "international investigation or settlement." This is quite different than the ILO Committee or the Committees for the United Nations human rights covenants, which have no prior domestic legal requirements; these institutions do not require the incidence of individual harm, but will examine cases of general complaints about law or practice.

The European Court is the most highly legalized institution in this study.

The European Convention on Human Rights creates binding and precise obligations. Unlike the other institutions, the European Court of Human Rights is authorized to adjudicate on state obligations to the convention. The chamber, a group of seven judges, decides the outcome of the case. This decision need not be unanimous. The dissenting opinions of judges have had influence in the decisions of later cases. Unlike a domestic court, decisions of the European Court are not self-executing within member states. According to the convention, state parties are legally bound to cooperate with the decisions of the Court and take necessary steps to follow the decisions.

However, while the decision-making procedures of the European Court are quite formal, the enforcement mechanisms remain weak, like the other institutions in this study. The Council of Ministers has the mandate to supervise this process, but there are no real means of enforcement. The president of the chamber (of judges) may take appropriate steps in cases of noncompliance, but it is unclear what this entails for a state's obligations to the European Convention.[35] While Articles 52, 53, and 54 of the convention make the Court's decision final and legally binding, they still provide member states wide latitude on how to implement the decision. The Council of Ministers is authorized only to request information about the state party's implementation and to decide if a state's actions are satisfactory. The Council of Ministers could decide to expel a member for failing to implement a decision, under Articles 3 and 8 of the Statute of the Council of Europe, but this has not yet occurred. Instead the most significant problem in terms of compliance has been insufficient "depth" of domestic remedies for Court decisions. Remedial legislation often occurs, but some legal scholars have claimed that such changes do not adequately address the requirements of the Court rulings.[36]

The European Court of Human Rights and the former European Commission of Human Rights adhered to uniquely meager interpretations of states' responsibilities to protect trade union rights. Historically, the Court has been most influential in undercutting the bargaining power of trade unions by ruling that union security clauses violated workers' human rights. These decisions did not contradict the ILO Committee on Freedom of Association's interpretation either of "negative trade union rights" or the right *not* to join and associate with trade unions. However, the Court has done little to protect those trade union activities that *do* fall under the human rights framework. The Court has also read limited protections for trade unions' right to collective bargaining as well.[37] As of 1999, no trade union had successfully used Article 11 in the Court to defend its interests. The Court, however, has consistently protected the interests of those individuals who suffer because of their status as non-union members. These decisions have resulted in jurisprudence clearly favoring the *freedom not to associate.*[38]

EUROPEAN SOCIAL CHARTER

The original mechanism for the Social Charter's monitoring was the Committee of Independent Experts, made up of seven members elected for a six-year term. While the monitoring body has since changed its name to the European Social Committee, which is more open to individual complaints, this new committee was not yet operating during the time period this book covers. According to the old rules, these experts, all from different member countries, were to serve in their capacity as individuals, not national representatives. The Committee of Independent Experts received and reviewed biennial reports by states' parties. The committee then determined whether a state's laws and practices complied with the obligations of the Social Charter.[39] Next the reports and recommendations went to the Governing Committee, which was made up of representatives of each the contracting parties (members). The Governing Committee then adopted a report in response to the Committee of Experts' recommendations and observations. These documents were next forwarded to the Committee of Ministers, which then decided if the state was in violation of its Social Charter obligations.[40] In its decisions, the Committee of Independent Experts generally tried to apply and refer to other international instruments, especially the ILO or European Union standards.[41] Thus, even though the Committee of Independent Experts might have argued that a state had violated the Social Charter, the Governing Body or the Council of Ministers might not have concurred, because these other bodies were more political in nature. This earlier monitoring process was similar to the monitoring process of the UN's human rights conventions, although with a generally lower level of legalization.

In terms of interpreting trade union rights, the Committee of Experts has referred more to the ILO Committee and its interpretations than the European Court. Even though Article 5 is quite general in its provisions for workers' rights to organize, the Committee of Experts has interpreted a high level of protection for workers and unions, as well as strong obligations for states. For example, the actual language of Article 5 obligates states to make sure that national law does not impair the freedom of workers to form local, national, or international organizations to protect their interests. Despite its wording as a "negative right," the Committee of Experts has interpreted a number of positive obligations for states from this article, stating that "the Contracting

State is obliged to take adequate legislative or other measures to guarantee the exercise of the right to organize, and in particular to protect workers' organizations from any interference on the part of employers."[42] This included corollary protections such as a union's access to the workplace, strong protections against discrimination and reprisal for trade union activities, and rights for civil servants. The committee has also historically read a higher standard of the right to strike than those allowed by national laws, establishing general principles to protecting striking unions and their members.[43]

In terms of Abbott and Snidal's legalization framework, part I of the European social charter is a classically soft law instrument. The norms are not specific, and states are committed but not legally bound to them. However, depending on the state's choice, the part II provisions are more legalized. If a state commits itself to an article, then the legalization of that particular rule is as follows: medium-high obligation, medium precision, and medium-low delegation. This is because Part II of the articles of the European Social Charter have the force of a political treaty, even though the charter itself creates only contingent obligations and allows escape clauses. Part II articles are also a medium level of precision, because they are general principles, but do set some limits and clear expectations of behavior. Although the Committee of Experts can publicize in its proceedings whether a state has complied with its obligations, this is still a fairly weak, nonbinding instrument.

Organization for Economic Cooperation and Development

The Organization for Economic Cooperation and Development (OECD), unlike the other institutions in this book, is not primarily a human rights–promoting institution. It lacks a legal basis that articulates a human rights or labor rights mandate. However, like many other international organizations, the OECD has numerous subdivisions that do not necessarily focus on their original mandates. The OECD was established in 1961 to promote "democracy and market economy" around the world. Its original members were leaders aligned with the United States (the "West") during the Cold War, including Austria, Belgium, Canada, Denmark, France, Germany (West Germany), Greece, Iceland, Ireland, Italy, Luxembourg, the Netherlands, Norway, Portugal, Spain, Sweden, Switzerland, Turkey, the United Kingdom, and the United States. The Convention on the OECD, signed in Paris in 1960, declared that "economic strength and prosperity are essential for the attainment of the purposes of the United Nations, the preservation of individual liberty and the increase of general well-being"; therefore, the continued economic cooperation of Europe was seen as a necessary condition to help maintain lasting peace. Cooperation would include freer trade, cooperative pursuit of development and sustainable growth, financial stability, and multilateral engagement.[44]

Like the ILO or the UN Human Rights Organizations, the OECD creates norms, but is not primarily concerned with human rights norms. Instead, the OECD sets standards for economic growth, cooperation, and development, with the ultimate goal of ensuring harmony among countries through economic interactions, free market principles, and development. As stated in its foundational convention in 1960, the member states are committed to integrate and expand economic cooperation between all states, in an effort to "make a vital contribution to peaceful and harmonious relations among the people of the world."[45] But unlike other economic organizations, it lacks resources for grants, loans, and a legalized dispute resolution mechanism. Instead, the OECD serves as an international clearinghouse of economic data, organizing a large database of economic and social statistics of both member states and 100 other countries that participate in reporting and sharing data. The OECD takes this data and "monitors trends, analyses and forecasts economic developments and researches social changes or evolving patterns in trade, environment, agriculture, technology, taxation and more."[46] These activities provide the OECD with the necessary expertise to create standards, develop best practices, and give advice to both Global North and Global South countries. The OECD and its different subagencies publish around 250 reports and books every year on a variety of subjects.

Because the OECD is more restricted in membership than a universal organization, its rules and norms lack the consensus and universal applicability of United Nations or ILO documents. However, depending on the type of norm, the OECD's developments can be binding on its member states. For example, the OECD's Code of Liberalisation of Capital Movements and Code of Liberalisation of Current Invisible Operations are legally binding on member states, although they are enforced by peer pressure, not a court.[47] In addition, the OECD Council, made up of all its member states, can make either nonbinding recommendations or binding decisions on member states. As a result of the greater ease of adoption (and lower level of legalization), the OECD Council more frequently uses recommendations. These are typically intended to influence changes in domestic economic, financial, and social policies.[48] As per Article 6 of the OECD Convention, recommendations and decisions require the consensus of the OECD membership.

Because membership is limited to the largest economies in the world, the OECD has accordingly been called the "rich nations club." Prestige is the primary "benefit" of OECD membership. An estimated two-thirds of all goods and services are produced in the OECD's member states. Countries, in order to join, must have free market economies and the unanimous approval of all current members. Compared to its higher profile fellow economic institutions like the WTO, the OECD is a largely "overlooked" organization, and it is generally understudied within political science and international law.[49] It would thus not be an obvious subject for an analysis of international institutions' effects on labor rights. Yet the OECD's involvement in the social aspects of international economics is not a new development. For example, the OECD created the first multilateral code of conduct for multinational corporations in 1976, positing rules for ethical corporate behavior. These rules included respect for freedom of association, collective agreements and collective bargaining, labor standards, nondiscrimination, and some minimal job security provisions.[50]

The OECD not only urges companies to respect labor and human rights, it also institutionally includes input from workers of OECD member countries. The Trade Union Advisory Committee (initially called the Trade Union Advisory Council) was established as an advisory body to represent workers' interests during the Marshall Plan and was later incorporated into the OECD. The committee is currently made up of 58 national trade union federations from the 30 OECD member states, representing 68 million workers. Its purpose is to "ensure that global markets are balanced by an effective social dimension."[51] The Trade Union Advisory Committee has representative and advisory status to the OECD Council, secretariat, other directorates, and individual member states. It is an independent organization entirely funded by its constituent members. In addition, the council engages in non-OECD activities such as representing trade union interests at Group of Eight (G8) meetings, and works with other trade union organizations such as the European Trade Union Council and the Council of Global Unions.

In addition to the consultative input from trade unions through the Advisory Committee, the OECD also has a directorate, the Directorate of Employment, Labour and Social Affairs (ELSA), with the mandate to deal with labor market issues related to economic growth and policy. The directorate of the ELSA is mostly focused on policy research and development. An important publication by the ELSA was the 1996 *Trade, Employment, and Labour Standards: A Study of Core Workers' Rights and Labour*

Standards, which challenged the long-standing idea that high labor standards disadvantaged a country in terms of trade and investment. The controversial report argued instead that the maintenance of low labor standards does not benefit an economy, nor does it provide comparative trade or investment advantages. The report also claimed that trade liberalization does not necessarily worsen labor rights.[52]

The OECD institution studied in this book, the Special Monitoring Process, was a temporary body set up by the OECD Council in 1997 following South Korea's accession to the OECD membership. The timing of South Korea's attempted entry, and the inherently political process of OECD membership, allowed this institution a unique degree of soft leverage over South Korea's labor rights. The monitoring was done under the authority of the ELSA Committee; recommendations for changes then came from the OECD Council. The ELSA Committee was established by the OECD to contribute knowledge about employment issues.[53] The Labor Monitoring Process was a temporary institution and ended in summer 2007; it has not been applied to any other country. This unique ten-year interaction between South Korea and the OECD's Monitoring Process influenced South Korean labor rights reform. This will be discussed more in Chapter 4.

Based on the Abbott and Snidal criteria, the OECD is the least legalized of all these institutions in terms of trade union rights, and its recommendations create the lowest level of obligations on states. Its human rights concerns have not been mandated based on binding law, and the OECD lacks a nonbinding legal mandate from which it can extract explicit trade union rights responsibilities. While some of the OECD's standards are binding international law, the OECD's labor rights recommendations do not have such force. Therefore, the obligation of the OECD Council's recommendations is quite low. Because there are no explicit trade union rights standards by which the OECD made its recommendations, the legalization level of the OECD's recommendations is low in obligation, precision, and its adjudication. The OECD never explicitly defined South Korea's obligations in terms of ILO Conventions 87 and 98, although these were generally assumed to be the standard. Finally, the delegation was medium/low. The Employment, Labour and Social Affairs Committee engaged in monitoring and investigation, while the OECD Council would thus make recommendations. The diversity of institutions and their legal documents are compiled in Table 4.

Table 4: International Laws and Institutions on Trade Union Rights

Institution	*Membership*	*Legal Basis*	*Complaint or Report?*	*Legalization*
ILO Committee on Freedom of Association	Universal	ILO Constitution	Complaint: Any worker or employers' association	Obligation: low; Precision: medium; Delegation: medium-low
OECD ELSA	Political, economic, and development based	None	Mostly reporting/monitoring (but TUAC and BIAC can make representations)	Obligation: low; Precision: low; Delegation: medium-low
UN Human Rights Committee	Universal	ICCPR	Reporting process, but NGOs can submit counter-reports every 4 years with scheduled state report	Obligation: high; Precision: medium; Delegation: medium
UN Committee on Economic, Social and Cultural Rights	Universal	ICESCR	Reporting process, but NGOs can submit counter-reports every 4 years with scheduled state report	Obligation: medium; Precision: medium; Delegation: medium-low
European Court of Human Rights	Regional (Council of Europe)	European Convention of Human Rights and Fundamental Freedoms	Complaint process, but very strict preconditions	Obligation: high; Precision: medium; Delegation: high
European Social Rights Committee	Regional (Council of Europe)	European Social Charter (1961)	Biennial reporting process, but certain trade unions could consult	Obligation: medium-high; Precision: medium; Delegation: medium-low

CHAPTER 4

South Korea

International Ambitions and the Postdevelopmental State

Unlike the United Kingdom or Canada, South Korea is a recently developed country. Within the last few decades, Korea has transitioned from a repressive dictatorship to a high income, industrialized democracy. Political space for independent trade unions opened up in 1987, when the ruling party announced plans for direct elections, following weeks of civil society contention. The state immediately restored certain human rights, such as freedom of the press and freedom for political parties.[1] Yet unlike Latin American countries such as Argentina and Brazil, or its neighbor Taiwan,[2] South Korea did not reform its labor rights practices in a timely manner following democratization. While the South Korean state liberalized its political institutions and allowed greater freedom to its independent trade union movement, reforms of its trade union rights and labor laws, in general, have been piecemeal and controversial.

As a result of remaining shortcomings in South Korea's trade union rights laws, its trade unions brought their concerns to various international organizations. Between 1987 and 2007, different governments made incremental changes to these laws. While South Korean trade unions had many concerns about the country's labor laws, this case study focuses on the following three major violations of basic labor rights norms: the maintenance of a trade union monopoly, the ban on "solidarity activities,"[3] and limitations on the basic rights of teachers and civil servants.[4] These legislative restrictions prevented entire sectors of workers from forming unions and engaging in collective activity; they also provided a legal basis for arrests. This chapter will demonstrate how external events, such as the 1997 financial crisis, in conjunction with the normative negotiation process, made the South Korean state more likely to change its trade union rights laws. As a result, the state passed considerable trade union rights legal reforms. South Korea, however, has still not addressed long-standing problems regarding collective action rights, such as strike and assembly rights, the legal status for certain trade union organizations, and ongoing mass arrests of trade union activists.

In this case study, South Korea engaged in transnational normative negotiations about its trade union rights issues for over fifteen years. During this time, it became more secure in its status as a democratic state. A process of political learning resulted from South Korea's extended engagement with international institutions. South Korea began to use more sophisticated arguments to justify the complaints and concerns that were voiced in this later period. While some scholars stress how states learn and internalize international norms as a result of prolonged interactions with international institutions,[5] such a process may also socialize states on how to best interact with international institutions. Over time, South Korea learned to justify its practices by appealing to the practices of other industrialized democratic states and by interpreting international norms in ways that justified its shortcomings in trade union rights protection.

This chapter covers the following four periods: (1) South Korea's initial interactions with international organizations (1991–1994), (2) South Korea's successful campaign to join the OECD (1994–1997) (3) the 1990s financial crisis and its aftermath (1997–2003) (4) the ending of the OECD labor-monitoring process (2003–2008). During these different periods, there were different government and political-economic conditions. The state allowed for certain concessions on trade union rights laws as a result of its extensive participation in the normative negotiation process. This chapter will uncover how specific, contingent political conditions helped to empower trade union rights' positions within South Korean politics at certain moments.

Korea's Trade Union Rights Obligations

Unlike Canada and the United Kingdom, South Korea's international legal commitments are relatively new, and therefore South Korea's prior experience in engaging with international human rights was limited. Because of geopolitical constraints involving North and South Korea, South Korea had not officially joined the United Nations until 1991.[6] South Korea signed and ratified the ICESCR and the ICCPR on December 10, 1990. Ratifying these treaties created moderate legal obligations to trade union rights.[7] South Korea also joined the International Labour Organization in October 1991, but did not ratify any conventions. Compared to the United Kingdom and Canada, South Korea has ratified fewer trade union rights legal obligations.

However, South Korea ratified the ICCPR with a reservation on the trade union rights Article 22, stating that it would interpret Article 22 in accordance with its national laws and constitution. South Korea's reservation provoked objections from countries such as Germany, the Netherlands, and Czechoslovakia.[8] This considerably weakened South Korea's trade union rights obligations, although Korea did ratify the ICESCR without reservation. Therefore South Korea's only unconditioned legal commitment to trade union rights is the ICESCR, which has a softer form of legalization than the ICCPR. For this reason, South Korea has only a medium level of commitment to international trade union rights norms.

South Korean Industrial Relations: Remnants of an Authoritarian Tradition

Unlike in Canada or the United Kingdom, South Korean workers have had constitutional protections of their basic labor rights since its independence from Japan in 1948. However, because of the political concerns of the military dictatorship since the end of the Korean War, these rights have been curtailed to curb political resistance and to encourage economic growth through lower labor costs. Both the constitution (Article 33) and labor legislation passed in 1953 guaranteed labor's "three basic rights": the right to organize, the right to collective bargaining, and the right to collective action. As a result, South Korean workers were granted many de jure protections for their trade union rights, but they lacked the ability to practice these rights under the authoritarian regime. South Korean workers belonged to trade unions, but these organizations were outside of workers' control. Subsequent amendments to basic labor laws allowed for a high degree of government interference.[9] The key objective of the industrial relations system prior to 1987 was to encourage labor market conditions ideal for rapid export-oriented industrialization. The South Korean state believed that a good business environment required labor repression to keep labor costs low, thus making exports competitive.[10] As the South Korean state's legitimacy was based on high rates of economic growth, state leaders understood this repression to be a politically necessary trade-off.[11] While wages did increase, they lagged behind increases in productivity, as the government often intervened in wage settlements to keep South Korean exports competitive abroad.[12]

The South Korean industrial labor relations system prior to democratization and political liberalization in 1987 mixed paternalistic job security protections with a lack of trade union rights; workers were simultaneously disempowered and protected. In contrast to the neoliberal approaches today, the South Korean state did not see labor market flexibility as a key to growth. Largely influenced by its economic exemplar, Japan, South Korea's industrial relations system included norms of lifetime employment and a seniority-based wage system. This emphasis on labor security was supported by strict legal regulations on dismissals. Unlike the United States, where layoffs are common and employers may freely fire employees, South Korean companies generally avoided dismissals, even in cases of over-staffing. Instead, companies typically pursued other cost-saving measures to deal with financial problems.[13] These practices were particularly important as South Korea lacked social insurance and public unemployment provisions common in most developed economies.[14]

In addition to economic development goals, the South Korean government, motivated by an anti-Communist ideology, also repressed the independent trade union movement. The state particularly feared political collaboration between anti-regime organizations and trade unions. Unlike many Latin American dictatorships or European social democratic states, in which labor was co-opted and incorporated, Hagen Koo argues that the South Korean state engaged in unfettered repression: "The Korean state's labor control had been more repressive than corporatist, more direct and physical than bureaucratic or ideological, and more blatantly anti-labor than subtle or disguised. Workers who participated in labor disputes rarely failed to confront state repression and see the true nature of the relationship between capital and state power."[15] The North Korean military threat created a militarized authoritarian state in the South with political justifications for repressing the independent labor movement.[16] Various presidents, who maintained strong military ties, suspended collective bargaining rights, criminalized collective action, and empowered the government to arbitrate solutions in industrial disputes.[17] In addition, unions' and workers' activities were carefully monitored by the South Korean Central Intelligence Agency. While some independent and democratic unions did exist, their activities were often suppressed by rival company unions or security personnel.[18]

Political space for union activities opened in 1987 after Roh Tae Woo, the ruling party's candidate for president, announced in his June 29 declaration that the state would no longer intervene in labor disputes. The June 29 declaration followed two weeks of heavy civil society demonstrations against the regime's announced cancellation of direct presidential elections. The regime accepted most of the civil society demands, allowing for direct presidential elections.[19] Following this democratic opening, workers engaged in the largely spontaneous Great Workers' Struggle, between July and September 1987. In this explosion of labor conflicts, during which the state did not intervene, South Korean workers demanded wage increases and greater protection of labor rights.[20]

The struggle resulted in a rapid increase in union membership as well as increases in wages.[21] Unionization rates rose from 12.3 percent in 1986 to a high in 1989 of 18.6 percent.[22] In the period between 1987 and 1989, wages increased on average at an annual rate of 15 to 20 percent.[23] However, this struggle did not lead to legal reforms of trade union rights.[24] Workers could now more freely form independent unions at the enterprise level, as long as they did not compete with existing unions, and unions now had greater autonomy over internal policies and leadership. However, the state began to intervene in industrial disputes again after the government passed the "Special Announcement on Maintaining Civic Security and Law and Order" in December 1988.[25] As the South Korean transition to democracy did not decrease labor repression, workers began to organize to change the law.

Trade Union Rights Disputes and Their Contention

As stated earlier, there were three major trade union rights–related disputes that workers brought to international institutions. This section explains the history of these controversies, which various international bodies later condemned as violating trade union rights norms. These rights violated both the individual rights of workers to join unions and the collective rights of workers to act within organizations of their own choosing. This chapter focuses on these particular disputes because they received attention from multiple international institutions.

Ban on Trade Union Rights for Teachers and Civil Servants

Teachers and civil servants were historically prohibited from basic trade union rights and the state repressed any attempts to exercise these rights. While teachers and civil servants were not initially barred from such rights, national security concerns prompted the government to curtail these rights, because of the important role of teachers in promoting anti-communist political ideology and the proximity of civil servants to the state.[26] Section 53(4) of the Public Education Servants Act and section 55(1) of the Private School Act prohibited public and private school teachers from creating organizations and engaging in union activities.[27] The 1963 revisions of the Public Officials Act and Trade Union Act excluded all civil servants' labor relations from the general industrial relations law.[28] This excluded all civil servants from basic trade union rights protections. During the Cold War, the government prevented the formation of radical teachers' organizations by establishing a state-sanctioned professional organization. Teachers attempted to organize during periods of political liberalization. Prior to the democratic transition, 800 teachers publicly signed the Declaration of Educational Democratization in 1986, which demanded both full trade union rights and participation in curriculum development.[29]

Trade Union Monopolies

South Korean industrial relations law only allowed the registration of one trade union within an enterprise, an industry, or a national federation.[30] As the government had decades earlier registered the historically anti-communist, state-sanctioned Federation of Korean Trade Unions (FKTU), any other national labor federations were automatically illegal. Local unions not affiliated with the FKTU were also illegal. The 1971 Law Concerning Special Measures for Safeguarding National Security established a monopoly union system, which allowed only those unions approved by management or the government to operate at the plant, industrial, and national levels.[31] South Korean law referred to this policy as the ban on "multiple unionism." As mentioned in Chapter 3, legal registration requirements for unions may not constitute a violation of basic trade union rights norms, as long as the registration process is a formality and not a hindrance.[32] However, South Korea's laws were designed as a means to curb the political threat of trade unions outside of government control. It was originally passed following the near election of the opposition candidate in 1971, when President Park declared a state of emergency and curbed possible opposition in the trade union movement.

After the 1987 Great Workers' Struggle, newly formed independent unions worked together to change the labor law, through demonstrations and petition drives.[33] Although the campaign was unsuccessful, workers decided to create an alternative trade union federation. A number of local workers' organizations coalesced into a nationally based labor law reform committee starting in August 1988. Their efforts eventually led to the establishment of the new Korean Trade Union Congress (hereafter called the Congress) on January 22, 1990. The Congress included 456 local unions and 165,000 members.[34] The harassment and state repression of this new union federation, which held critical views of the South Korean government, became an issue for international institutions.

Ban on Solidarity Activities

In their activities, trade unions have long relied on collaboration with allies, whether they are other trade unions, civil society organizations, or individuals. However, many countries have restricted the extent to which trade unions may involve outside parties in their disputes. In South Korea, the law regulating the role of outside, or "third-party," actors was quite strong, curtailing even the freedom of speech of any individuals who were not directly involved in a labor issue. Section 13(2) of the Labor Dispute Adjustment Act forbade anyone other than an employee, officially recognized trade union, or employer from "interfering" in the operation of a trade union or a dispute. The South Korean government called this "third-party intervention," and considered any public support for an industrial dispute to constitute "interference."[35] This law led to many arrests, including the suspicious death of the Congress's vice president during his detainment for "illegal" solidarity activities in 1991. The vice president had been arrested for publicly declaring support for a different union's strike.[36]

Early Domestic Attempts at Reform: 1987–1993

Trade unions tried using domestic political institutions after the 1987 elections. Teachers and civil servants successfully lobbied the opposition parties for a bill granting them trade union rights in late February 1989. The National Assembly also passed a bill amending the "solidarity activity ban," which allowed trade unions to collaborate with labor advisers and labor lawyers to advise trade unions.[37] While these reforms would have made South Korea's protection of trade union rights more aligned with international standards, President Roh vetoed the bills.[38] Soon afterward, in 1990, the moderate opposition party joined the government's coalition, making reform through the National Assembly more difficult.[39]

As unions' advocacy for reforms at the legislative and executive branches failed, they turned to the newly formed Constitutional Court to challenge labor rights shortcomings.[40] Trade unions contested the solidarity activity ban and the ban on teachers' unions in this case. However, the Constitutional Court ruled in favor of existing laws. In January 1990, the court argued that the solidarity activity ban did not constitute a violation of labor rights, as the law still allowed workers to receive assistance from their trade union or trade union federation. The Constitutional Court argued that the law was intended to protect the sensitivity of industrial disputes from the "manipulation, instigation, and obstruction" of outside forces, which could in turn "distort and hinder" labor and management's ability to make independent decisions.[41] In response to a case challenging private school teachers from forming unions, the Constitutional Court upheld the law, referring to the special position of education within South Korean culture and society, which was codified in the South Korean Constitution. The decision stated that teachers still had opportunities for representation and association within their professional organizations. For purposes of nondiscrimination, the Constitutional Court ruled that private and public school teachers receive the same treatment under the law.[42]

While these constitutional challenges did not overturn laws limiting rights for certain groups of workers, independent trade unions successfully used the courts in other ways. In 1992, the court decided to allow non-FKTU-affiliated trade unions to be granted legal status. While only one trade union could still be recognized at a workplace, it no longer had to affiliate with the government-sanctioned national federation. After this decision, the Labor Ministry began to recognize independent trade unions among white-collar hospital workers, journalists, and office workers at construction firms and government research institutes. This decision broke the FKTU's official monopoly on workplace unions, even though other national trade union federations were still illegal.[43]

International Opportunities

This section analyzes the communication between South Korean trade unions, relevant international institutions, and the South Korean state about the shortcomings in the country's trade union rights protections. This analysis demonstrates the norm negotiation process: trade unions and international institutions argued that these laws violated international human rights law, while the state responded that the laws were justified for political, economic, and cultural reasons. This negotiation process sought to clarify South Korea's obligations to international trade union rights. The South Korean state communicated its intention to reform trade union rights practices toward better compliance with international norms, but its statements were often unspecific. The narrative presented below will show how mere interaction between the state and the international institutions was not sufficient to influence reforms, but still put this issue on the international agenda. This provided opportunities for change later, when the state connected international concerns over its trade union rights protection to its own self-interests.

Initial Communications: Roh Tae Woo and the ILO

After South Korea joined the ILO, the newly formed Korean Trade Union Congress, the "illegal" independent national trade union federation, created the "Joint Committee for Ratification of ILO Basic Conventions and Labor Law Reform" with other independent unions.[44] Soon afterward, the Congress filed its first complaint with the ILO's Committee on Freedom of Association in March 1992. Additional unions supporting this case included the Korean Teachers' Union, the International Federation of Building and Woodworkers, the World Confederation of Organizations of the Teaching Profession, the ICFTU, and the International Federation of Journalists.[45]

This complaint dealt with several key issues relating to the legal shortcomings and the resulting trade union repression: the prohibition of solidarity activity,[46] the trade union monopoly system, and the lack of basic labor rights of civil servants and teachers. In addition, the first communication included reports on direct government repression resulting from these legal issues. For example, the Korean Trade Union Congress complained of several problems: the arrest of 177 of their leaders, the use of police violence to break up its inaugural meeting in 1990, and the impunity toward companies that engaged in unfair labor practices against its members.[47] The union also complained about the dismissal of 1,500 school teachers who had joined the Korean Teachers' Union, the random police search of the teachers' union office, and the continued dismissal of current teachers discovered to be union members.[48] Trade unions claimed that the authorities had arrested 1,634 trade unionists since 1988.[49]

The outgoing Roh Tae Woo government, which was generally unsympathetic to trade unions, responded to these allegations in October 1992 by dismissing the complaints and defending South Korea's labor rights position. Yet the state responded to the accusations while still reaffirming the legitimacy of international trade union rights norms. In its communications to the ILO committee, the South Korean government claimed it already protected labor rights norms because of its constitutional guarantees and ILO membership.[50] The communication even claimed that South Korea's industrial relations system was culturally unique and nonconfrontational, and therefore "western" models of human rights were not applicable.[51] The government justified union members' arrests by citing their illegal activities and radical politics,[52] accusing the Korean Teachers' Union and the Congress of conspiring to overthrow the democratic government.[53] While the government recognized that there were a few problems remaining from the authoritarian period, it argued that existing domestic institutions would remedy these deficiencies.[54]

In response to the unions' complaints, the government gave specific excuses. As many South Korean trade unions were less than three years old, the South Korean government justified the trade union monopoly system as a necessary means of protection. The solidarity activity ban was also justified as a way to protect weak and "young" trade unions and to ensure autonomous settlement of industrial disputes.[55] In response to teachers' and public servant's trade union rights, the government claimed that teachers had "high esteem" in the eyes of parents and students because of the emphasis on education in a Confucian society, and thus it would be inappropriate to give them the same rights as manual laborers.[56] Therefore, the report claimed that teachers and public servants already had sufficient special versions of representational and associational rights, as they enjoyed professional organizations and dispute resolution processes.[57] The government also justified trade union rights limitations by citing the "volatile" Korean peninsular situation. Public officials and teachers needed to be "pillars of stability for the society" and hence were exempt from labor organizing rights.[58]

In response to concerns about repression, the government claimed that it had arrested trade union leaders because of their "violent demonstrations" and prosecuted them for violating criminal laws rather than labor laws.[59] According to the government's report, unions used firebombs and other violent means in their pursuit of radical political goals such as the "breakup of the [ruling] Democratic Liberal Party."[60] The government's communication also claimed that the Congress and teachers' unions engaged in collective action not for "trade union purposes," but to overthrow the government.[61] The government also claimed that the Korean Trade Union Congress was led by old university radicals with revolutionary politics and that the KTUC had engaged in costly, disruptive, and illegal strikes in pursuit of unreasonable wage increases.[62] The government also noted that the 177 arrested Congress leaders had received a fair trial and were convicted; 84 had since been released because they had finished their prison terms or because their sentence was suspended. The other 83 trade unionists were finishing their sentences.[63]

Despite the government's justifications, the ILO committee found these laws and actions in violation of South Korea's trade union rights obligations. The committee stated that as a result of the trade union monopoly system, "employees may be denied the right to join the organizations of their choice, contrary to the principles of freedom of association," and urged the government to change the relevant law.[64] The committee rejected the government's cultural claims about public servants and teachers' special place in society. Citing the ILO principle that "workers, without distinction whatsoever and notwithstanding their particular status under national law . . . [should be] able to form and join organizations of their own choosing to protect their interests," the committee recommended that the government allow organizational rights to teachers and public servants.[65] In regard to the lack of strike rights for teachers and public servants, the committee noted that "the right to strike . . . [is one of the] fundamental rights of workers and organizations, [and] the right to strike can only be restricted and even prohibited . . . in essential services in the strict sense of the terms," but the committee did not regard teachers or education workers as a part of this category.[66] Finally, the committee rejected the rationale for the solidarity ban, as it did not allow trade unions to benefit from advisers. The committee called for a repeal of this law, as it constituted "a serious restriction on the free functioning of trade unions."[67]

The committee rejected the government's justification of trade unionists' arrests, as "no evidence was presented to prove the charges of arson, anti-State crimes, forgery and obstructing a public official in his duty."[68] The committee noted that if the trade unionists engaged in certain trade union activities, then their arrests constituted a violation of trade union rights. Citing its previously established principles, the committee stressed that "the arrest and detention of trade unionists, even for reasons of internal security, may constitute a serious interference with trade union rights." Since the government did not provide any evidence that the trade unionists were not engaged in the exercise of their legitimate rights, the committee called for their release.[69] The committee also stated that the 1,500 members of the Korean Teachers' Union were dismissed for engaging in legitimate trade union activities, a situation that the committee "deplore[d]." The committee recommended their immediate reinstatement.[70]

New President and New Opportunities

This report was the only communication between the ILO committee and the Roh Tae Woo administration. In late 1992, Kim Young Sam, the moderate candidate, became president. Kim Young Sam's government claimed an electoral mandate of political and economic liberalization, with the goal of further solidifying South Korea's position within international society.[71] This "New Korea" would be a country with a healthier democracy and greater respect for the rule of law and human rights.[72] After his inauguration in 1993, Kim Young Sam reaffirmed his call for a "new leap towards a new economy . . . to make Korea more competitive," which in practice meant deregulating industries and finance and reducing barriers to foreign investment.[73]

While Kim Young Sam claimed that economic and political reforms were necessary to purge the country's old authoritarian habits,[74] his election did not make the government more conducive to trade union rights. While Kim Young Sam's administration initially supported labor rights reforms, it soon rejected these plans as it became concerned about the country's slower economic growth in 1993.[75] While strikes had tapered off by the early 1990s, many blamed labor's rapid gains in wages during the late 1980s for the "decreased competitiveness" of the economy. Workers' gains were blamed for South Korea's decreased competitiveness. The Great Workers' Struggle had resulted in significant economic gains for workers, who saw their wages increase more than other workers in East Asia (and the industrial world) in a short period of time. Workers also "won" shorter work hours and stronger benefits, such as better work conditions, pensions, and holidays. South Korea had the lowest average compensation costs for manufacturing production among the "Asian tigers." After 1988, it was second in compensation costs only to Taiwan. These wage increases were significant, as profiled in Table 5, based on data from the Korea Labor Institute in 1997. Because of his dedication to economic stability, Kim Young Sam felt that he could neither politically nor economically afford to grant South Korean workers better rights.[76] According to South Korean labor experts, Kim Young Sam's approach was still a "traditional authoritarian labor policy to control and circumvent the militant labor movement."[77]

Table 5: Strike Days, Wage Increases, and Productivity in Korea

	Strike Days	*Nominal Wage Increase (%)*	*Production Losses (100 million won)*	*Losses in Imports (million $)*
1985	7.9	9.2	n/a	n/a
1986	8.5	8.2	n/a	n/a
1987	755.8	10.1	27,782	537
1988	562	15.5	32,020	732
1989	611.4	21.1	41,995	1,363
1990	409.8	18.8	14,387	314
1991	288.2	16.9	12,317	238
1992	132.1	15.2	19,586	260
1993	111.3	12.2	20,872	564
1994	120.7	12.7	15,026	550
1995	30.8	11.2	10,757	200
1996	68.5	11.9	17,983	386

Source: Kim, "Industrial Reform and Labor Backlash in South Korea: Genesis, Escalation and Termination of the 1997 General Strike," *Asian Survey* 38, no. 12 (1998): 1148.

While the Kim Young Sam government's interactions with the ILO committee were conciliatory, they did not lead to legislative changes. In a late 1993 communication to the ILO committee, the ICFTU reported further repression of strikers, including dismissals, arrests, and physical brutality. The ICFTU stated that the Ministry of Labor delayed implementation of the planned August 1994 labor law reform, despite its earlier promises to the ILO and other international trade unions. The Kim Young Sam government's response to the ILO's inquiry was slightly more cooperative than former President Roh Tae Woo's, but it still insisted upon the impossibility of respecting trade union rights reform during periods of economic hardship. Although these communications no longer characterized the trade unionists as political extremists, they still justified the repression by appealing to economic constraints.

Unlike the previous government, the Kim Young Sam administration did express an explicit commitment to changing the labor laws during its initial communication to the ILO committee. The administration gave clearer timelines for change as well as more detailed responses and more thorough justifications for its current violations. For example, this communication included a full explanation of the events surrounding the suspicious death of the Congress' vice president, who died while in police custody, information the previous government had withheld.[78] Although this communication repeated some of the prior government's justifications for trade union rights problems,[79] it also claimed that "a considerable amount of time and effort would be required to harmonize South Korea's legal structure, social ethics and traditions with the ILO's Conventions."[80] The government pledged that it would bring the recommendations of the "Founders Committee," a domestic committee investigating the need for labor law reform, to the National Assembly in late 1993 for public hearings.[81] The government also reported the release of 64 jailed trade unionists, who were granted amnesty by the new president.[82]

Yet by its next report, in March 1994, the government admitted delaying labor law reforms, agreeing with the ICFTU allegations that the delay was due to concerns about the country's economic performance. The communication also blamed disagreement between employers and trade unions for the delay. However, the government claimed that labor law reform remained a top priority, explaining that certain procedures had been established to ensure the appropriate changes. This delay was necessary, as the South Korean government claimed that labor "amendment[s] should not be made in a hectic way, but by taking into account . . . interests of all the concerned parties and those of the nation."[83] The Kim Young Sam government again claimed political hardship and the need for more time to properly implement their labor rights commitments.

It seems unlikely that the government was in fact "unable" to make these reforms. The government's communications expressed a willingness to respect labor laws, but also contended that the special circumstances of 1994 (the gridlock between social partners and South Korea's disappointing economic performance) were primarily responsible for the delay.[84] The communication claimed that a commitment at the upper levels of government was present, but that the correct political and economic circumstances were not. The evidence, however, suggests this was not the case. While certain immediate positive changes occurred, such as the release of some trade unionists, the South Korean state was not actually hampered by economic conditions or a lack of social consensus. Within two years, the same government would unilaterally institute wide-ranging labor reforms that ignored social partners' preferences and addressed few trade union rights problems. More changes would later occur during a time of even worse economic performance. Rather, the government's claim of economic hardship was an amiable-sounding cover for a lack of political will to institute changes.

Furthermore, the Kim Young Sam administration did not even reduce its direct labor repression, a change that would not have been hindered by political or economic difficulties. In 1993, the first year of Kim Young Sam's administration, arrests of trade unionists decreased from several hundred a year to only twenty-three, but this number later increased again to 142 in 1994 and 113 in 1995.[85] The continuation of state repression of trade unions may be due to institutionalization of such practices. Hathaway argues that repressive behavior can have a path-dependent effect. Long after the political impetus for the repression, individuals and institutions become entrenched within these patterns, normalizing these behaviors. Even if top-level officials change their positions, this may not automatically trickle down to the lower level of government. In South Korea, long after the threat of communist takeover passed, the political oppression of independent and militant trade unions continued. The administration recognized on some level that the international norms of trade union rights were important, but lacked a strong incentive to follow through.[86] While the engagement with the ILO in the early years of Kim Young Sam's government made labor law reforms a possibility, neither the international recommendations process nor the current political conditions were sufficient to pressure legal changes.

"Globalization," the OECD, and New Opportunities for Trade Union Rights

Between 1994 and 1997, three events occurred that made trade union rights reform possible. First, Kim Young Sam began to pursue a *segyehwa* (globalization) policy aimed at gaining OECD membership. Second, the struggling KTUC reorganized as the Korean Confederation of Trade Unions (KCTU) and initiated a new series of communications between the ILO and the South Korean government: ILO committee case number 1865. Third, a network of European, American, and international trade unions made the recommendations of the ICESCR and the ILO committee the basis of an OECD-related transnational political campaign to promote better labor rights in South Korea. In collaboration with the Trade Union Advisory Committee (TUAC), this movement helped make South Korea's labor rights problems a key bargaining issue in the debate over OECD membership. As a result, the South Korean government made a public, though nonbinding, commitment to the OECD to reform its labor laws according to international standards. When the government later passed a major labor law reform that largely ignored international recommendations, a nationwide general strike erupted. The ILO, the OECD, and international and foreign trade unions expressed support for this strike and condemned South Korea's new law. This transnational pressure minimized the state's repression of the strike and forced the government to reform the earlier bill. For reform to occur, trade union rights demands needed to be linked to a more politically expedient issue.

In 1994, President Kim Young Sam announced a new global economic integration policy to support economic recovery. This was called the "Grand Idea of Globalization," which the president developed after participating in the Asia-Pacific Economic Cooperation Forum in 1994.[87] To realize this goal, the president restructured government agencies, creating several new executive bodies to recommend reforms necessary to integrate South Korea into the global economy. [88] Internationally, the Kim Young Sam administration sought leadership roles at both the World Trade Organization and the Asia-Pacific Economic Cooperation Forum and sought an active role in UN peacekeeping operations.[89] This policy agenda prompted domestic complaints that the government was more beholden to promoting South Korea's participation within the global economy rather than the interests of the citizens. For example, South Korea's 1994 concession to the World Trade Organization, its decision to open its rice markets to international competition, was met with domestic opposition. This bill passed in the National Assembly in spite of a long civil society campaign against the dislocation of South Korean farmers that included the presentation of a thirteen-million-signature petition drive.[90]

These engagements were eclipsed, though, by the most important economic and international goal of Kim Young Sam's administration: membership in the Organization for Economic Cooperation and Development (OECD). In 1994, President Kim Young Sam announced South Korea's desire to join this club of rich countries. This was to be the "crowning achievement" of the president's globalization agenda.[91] OECD membership was both an opportunity to increase South Korea's sense of international esteem and a means to institutionalize South Korea's role as a high-income, industrialized country. By 1995, South Korea boasted a per capita income of $10,000 and the status of the eleventh largest economy in the world, surpassing Australia and other existing OECD members.[92] South Korea would become the second

East Asian country to join this exclusive club, second only to Japan. Mexico, another newly industrialized economy, had gained OECD membership in 1990 with the strong endorsement of the United States. However, unlike Mexico's smooth entry, South Korea's path would not be so easy.[93]

As mentioned earlier in Chapter 3, OECD membership is a political process requiring the consensus approval of existing member states. A country seeking membership must demonstrate commitment to three principles: an open market economy, democratic pluralism, and human rights. The country must also declare its position on more than 160 OECD legal instruments. These positions can be immediate adoption, intention to adopt, or reservations regarding the different rules established by the OECD. Once the OECD council decides that a sufficient number of these preconditions have been met, the member states invite the applicant country to accede to the OECD Convention.[94] Before considering South Korea's membership application, the OECD required South Korea to make macroeconomic and financial reforms,[95] opening up South Korea's financial markets, loosening controls on foreign investment, and increasing trade liberalization.[96]

During South Korea's OECD membership process, an unusual amount of attention was paid to its labor rights legislation. Advocates brought their concerns about the labor situation in South Korea to the Employment, Labour and Social Affairs (ELSA) Committee of the OECD, a standards-setting group. Its two constituency groups, a labor and a business group, both sought to condition South Korean membership on labor law changes. The business group, the Business and Industry Advisory Council (BIAC), sought greater labor market flexibility, which South Korean employers supported, given the recent decline in economic growth.[97] As mentioned earlier, the OECD often promoted labor market flexibility reforms. In contrast, the TUAC expressed concern over the state of workers' rights in South Korea. The lack of basic respect for labor organizing rights contradicted the democratic and human rights values of the OECD. The TUAC's attempt to link OECD membership to labor and human rights was surprising, as the OECD did not historically involve itself in the domestic politics of its members or potential members.

As a result of the trade union and TUAC concerns, member states, including the United States, France, Germany, Austria, and the Scandinavian countries, expressed labor rights–related reservations. In addition, human rights NGOs such as Human Rights Watch and Amnesty International began campaigning OECD members to condition South Korea's membership on better protection of labor rights.[98] Although the OECD lacks either an international legal basis or an official mandate on which to condition admission on human rights, a consensus vote of the Council of Ministers is required to allow the entrance of any new member state, making membership procedures inherently political. Since the OECD was established as an organization of democracies, its concern with human rights practices was perhaps not surprising, although it was unprecedented. These concerns were not raised regarding Mexico, Hungary, the Czech Republic, or Poland, which were also newly developed and newly democratic.[99]

In addition to the ILO committee's recommendations, the UN Committee on Economic, Social and Cultural Rights (CESCR) made its first set of recommendations regarding South Korea's human rights situation, including trade union rights, during this OECD accession period. This provided another legal authority supporting the transnational actors' push for labor rights conditions. South Korea, like other ratifiers to the ICESCR, participated in the review process outlined in Articles 16 and 17. The initial set of communications between the CESCR and South Korea, between 1994 and 1995, paid special attention to labor rights. The CESCR's concluding remarks were similar to the ILO's recommendations. They recommended that the government "immediately amend its laws and regulations concerning the freedom to form trade unions and the right to strike in order to bring them into compliance with the Covenant and with other applicable international standards." The report particularly emphasized granting teachers, civil servants, and other excluded groups the rights to form trade unions and engage in collective action.[100]

During the OECD accession process, the South Korean government continued to engage with the ILO's Committee on Freedom of Association. The disputes of the prior case were incorporated into the new case 1865, which included complaints from the newly formed KCTU, the organization that succeeded the prior Korean Trade Union Congress.[101] The government's refusal to grant legal status to this newer, larger, and more powerful national-level trade union federation became the basis of the new complaint to the ILO committee.[102] The government responded that the new KCTU was illegal for three reasons: one, it violated South Korea's multiple trade union ban (as the FKTU was an existing national trade union federation); two, some of its affiliated unions lacked legal recognition; and three, its officers and members included workers who were disqualified for trade union membership.[103] The report also justified the arrest of a KCTU leader under the third-party intervention ban law.

In spite of these justifications, however, the government did commit to making significant labor law changes in the near future. Rather than citing economic performance, the government blamed the delay on the ongoing disagreement between social partners. In Report 304, dated May 22, 1996, the government claimed that, as a result of South Korea joining the ILO in 1991: "[A] common understanding is now being reached on a broad spectrum of issues regarding the fundamental necessity of institutional reform in industrial relations. [The Government] will implement necessary follow-up measures to improve and develop the system of industrial relations and practices in order to achieve full compliance with international labour standards including ILO Conventions."[104] This statement suggests that political pressure and criticism from international institutions influenced the South Korean government's political calculations.

The ILO committee, after considering both the unions' and the government's reports, reiterated its support for the unions' concerns, urging the government to reform the Trade Union Act to allow for multiple trade unions. In evaluating the government's justifications for refusing to register the KCTU, the committee rejected the claim that the presence of non-recognized affiliate unions or non-employee union members or leaders in the KCTU disqualified the KCTU's application for recognition. The committee stated, "the Government's arguments for not registering the KCTU because it violates national laws are not persuasive since these laws are not in conformity with the principles of freedom of association."[105] The report urged the South Korean government to make these reforms without delay.

The OECD officially conditioned South Korean membership on improving labor rights in April 1996. The OECD's ELSA Committee and the TUAC held a special meeting in Seoul to discuss the growing concerns about South Korea's labor rights situation. At this meeting, the ELSA Committee recommended labor law changes that emphasized trade union rights concerns.[106] These recommendations drew heavily on the ILO committee's recommendations and standards. During April 1996 meetings in Seoul, OECD legal counsel Christian Schricke stated, "The OECD has no specific standards with respect to labor rights. However it is relevant for members of the OECD to note that there are certain basic values shared by all member nations with respect to human rights, and labor rights are a part of human rights."[107] The standards for these labor rights were understood to be ILO Conventions 87 and 98, although this was never explicitly stated.[108]

To demonstrate his commitment to reforming labor laws, President Kim Young Sam announced in April 1996 the creation of a new thirty-person presidential advisory committee, with representatives from labor, management, academia, and "public interests,"[109] which would make recommendations for labor law changes. He stated during OECD negotiations that "the excessively restrict[ive] laws and institutions of the past must be . . . revised in a way compatible with international standards and practices."[110] Although some member states continued to harbor skepticism, this nonbinding commitment for future change seemed sufficient. However, the South Korean government continued to stall on trade union rights reforms. In late August, the presidential adviser for judicial and civil affairs announced the government's intention to use the National Security Law against "'leftist revolutionary forces' engaging in illegal labor activities or instigating labor unrest when the economy is faltering."[111] In response to these developments, the International Herald Tribune stated on August 20, 1996, that "now the government [of South Korea] cites the pressures of globalization as a reason for restricting workers' rights," instead of Cold War political arguments.[112]

On October 6, 1996, just prior to South Korea's OECD accession vote, the South Korean Foreign Minister sent a confidential letter to the OECD's secretary-general Don Johnson, promising to protect relevant labor rights. No labor law changes had occurred at this time. The letter reiterated Kim Young Sam's earlier commitment to reform South Korea's labor laws toward international standards, claiming that the Presidential Commission on Industrial Relations Reform would aid this change. South Korea promised to follow up on its "commitment to reform existing laws and regulations on industrial relations in line with internationally accepted standards, including those concerning basic rights such as freedom of association and collective bargaining" in a democratic manner. In response, the ELSA Committee expressed an expectation for such changes within a year, and the OECD Council publicly welcomed South Korea's new commitment.[113] The OECD Council of Ministers soon approved South Korea for membership in October, which would be official on December 12, 1996.[114]

South Korea passed sweeping labor legislation soon after its official entry to the OECD, which President Kim announced as fulfilling South Korea's obligations to the OECD as a member state.[115] Yet in contrast to its earlier commitments, this law worsened some trade union rights protections. The new law, the Trade Union and Labour Relations Adjustment Act (TULRAA), consolidated previous laws on industrial relations. While the law made some positive changes, it also restricted trade union rights and gave greater control to employers.

When the initial bill TULRAA was announced on December 3, 1996, it was controversial among the opposition parties and trade unions. The government had promised the OECD labor reforms in accordance with the Presidential Commission on Industrial Relations Reform. However, this commission broke down as a result of dissatisfaction between both labor and business representatives, despite strong pressure from the government to draft a bill by November.[116] The Ministry of Labor quickly drafted its own labor bill without consultation from social partners.[117] Trade union representatives accused the bill of favoring management interests. Both the FKTU- and KCTU-affiliated unions threatened to strike if the bill passed.[118] The initial bill provided labor market flexibility measures, such as enabling layoffs and flexible working hours, establishing a temporary employment system, and creating a new no-work/no-pay strike procedure. These addressed some of the concerns of the OECD business interest group, which felt that South Korea's rigid labor markets were inefficient and discouraged foreign investment.[119] This included measures allowing for layoffs, the freedom to assign more flexible work hours, and the ability to hire substitute workers during industrial disputes. In addition to layoff procedures, employers were allowed to seek subcontractors.[120]

The proposed TULRAA bill consisted mostly of labor law changes preferred by employers, although it did include some trade union rights protections, as recommended by the ILO, the CESCR, and the OECD. The proposed bill legalized multiple unions, but delayed their implementation. National- and industry-level multiple unions would be permitted in 1999, although permission for multiple enterprise-level unions was delayed until 2002. The bill mostly decriminalized solidarity activity, although unions and employers were still required to register their supporters with the Ministry of Labor prior to receiving support.[121] There were no provisions allowing teachers or civil servants' rights to unionize.

The proposed bill was controversial among the opposition political parties in the National Assembly. Yet opposition parties avoided openly supporting or opposing the bill, for fear of alienating business and labor. The National Congress for New Politics, the largest opposition party, tried a number of means to prolong the debate to avoid a vote.[122] As a result of this disagreement, "physical scuffles broke out almost daily in Korea's single-house legislature."[123] Controversy over the bill transformed the National Assembly into a place of confrontation and deadlock. Sensing the difficulties surrounding the bill, the New Korea Party government passed the bill through questionable means. The bill passed on December 26, 1996, during a secret, seven-minute, unpublicized predawn session of the National Assembly, of which the opposition parties were neither invited nor present.[124] Some labor union critics considered this final bill even more pro-business than the original proposed bill in its allowances for greater labor flexibility.[125]

In response, both the KCTU and the FKTU mobilized their members for a general strike. This strike primarily protested the bill's infringement on job security, but it was also a political strike protesting the government's undemocratic practices and failure to address labor rights. This mobilization was so impressive that the *Guardian* newspaper remarked that it "makes Britain's Winter of Discontent in 1978/79 look like an experiment in suburban repertory."[126] The two union federations sustained a high level of worker participation for a three-week strike, disrupting production in key industries including automobile manufacturing, ship building, heavy manufacturing, health services, and public transportation. An estimated three million workers participated.[127] In addition, the strike received a broad base of domestic public support, including from the middle class, which since the 1987 Great Workers' Struggle, had begun to distance itself from labor unions. Even moderate South Koreans felt outrage at the undemocratic manner in which the government had implemented these reforms.[128]

In addition to broad national support, international institutions and actors supported this strike and condemned the new law. Michael Hansenne, the secretary general of the ILO, sent a letter to President Kim Young Sam requesting greater respect for labor rights, as an obligation of its membership in the ILO.[129] The OECD's TUAC called it a "slap in the face to both [South Korea's] workers and international public opinion."[130] The secretary general of the TUAC requested that Kim Young Sam veto the bill and bring it back to a parliamentary debate in January 1997.[131] The OECD leaders and member states saw the bill as violating the October 1996 promise to reform labor laws, and as a result, the Council of Ministers asked the ELSA Committee to assess the situation. OECD members worried that if a new member state reneged on its membership commitments, it would set a bad precedent for other countries joining the OECD and other international economic institutions in the future. TUAC pressured the OECD leadership to take formal action against South Korea.[132] An OECD official expressed embarrassment over how the South Korean government had used the OECD's support of flexible labor practices to push through the law, stating, "it makes the OECD appear [as if] it encouraged (Seoul's) crackdown on striking workers, which was obviously not [our] intention."[133]

As a result of the new bill, the OECD Council established a new Special

Monitoring Process, granting the Secretariat the unprecedented mandate to monitor the development of labor relations within a member country. The ELSA Committee began a periodic assessment of South Korea's progress in regard to freedom of association, collective bargaining rights, and other labor-related issues.[134] In addition to the Special Monitoring Process, the OECD member states discussed the possibility of censuring the South Korean government, and South Korean officials began to respond publicly. South Korean leadership first claimed that the new law had brought South Korea into full compliance with its OECD commitments, referring only to the labor market flexibility changes. But in January, Labor Minister Jin Nyum claimed that while immediate compliance with the OECD's standards was not possible, South Korea was "moving in the right direction."[135] This rhetorical shift reflected the South Korean government's recognition that the law did not in fact fulfill its OECD commitments.

Concerns about the law were also brought before the ILO's Committee on Freedom of Association, in two reports dated December 29, 1996, and January 28, 1997. In the first report, the ICFTU claimed that these legislative changes further undermined freedom of association, despite South Korea's "solemn commitment" to the OECD to bring its laws in line with international standards. International labor groups, such as TUAC, the ICFTU, and International Metalworkers' Union, also gave their support for this report to the ILO.[136] The ICFTU, after examining the situation in South Korea, complained to the ILO about the incompleteness of the major reforms, such as the remaining trade union monopoly issues.

Despite their hard line, South Korean officials expressed apprehension about a possible censure. For example, the South Korean Foreign Ministry announced that any rebuke from the OECD would constitute a "national disgrace."[137] Following news that the OECD would likely censure South Korea, President Kim Young Sam announced on January 22, 1997, that the government would revise TULRAA. This was considered a "surprise move," as he had earlier expressed an unwillingness to reconsider the legislation.[138] In negotiations with the opposition party, President Kim agreed to suspend the arrest warrants for labor leaders.[139]

Despite President Kim Young Sam's pledge, the OECD censured South Korea on January 23, 1997. The Employment, Labour, and Social Affairs Committee delivered a carefully worded statement claiming that South Korea's "reform, as it stands, does not fully meet the commitments made by the Korean government concerning freedom of association and collective bargaining."[140] The release of a public statement about a new member's labor laws was unprecedented, as the OECD typically relied on peer pressure, not censure, to influence member states. The South Korean delegation supposedly fought "bitterly" to prevent the release of any such statements.[141] In response, the South Korean Foreign Ministry announced on January 24 that the labor law was a "domestic issue"; a spokesperson stated, "We were skeptical whether it was appropriate for the OECD to discuss the labour law, which is in principle a domestic issue . . . [although] the OECD press release was [a] balanced and objective observation."[142] The South Korean Foreign Ministry representative also questioned the right of the OECD to examine the labor laws of South Korea, but did not deny the validity of the OECD's evaluation.

Despite its attempts to defend its sovereignty, the South Korean government was affected by the international pressure. The National Assembly reconsidered the bill in light of trade unions' and international institutions' demands. The parties in the National Assembly agreed to reopen debate and make appropriate changes to the law on February 17, 1997.[143] While not all the trade union rights problems were addressed, several important changes were made. The timing of the international intervention and the visible display of both transnational and domestic political pressure limited the government's range of possible choices, forcing it to take a more conciliatory stance.[144] Specifically, the immediate public transnational scrutiny likely influenced the government to release many of the trade unionists arrested during the general strike.

South Korea's communications with the ILO during this time demonstrate a reluctant acceptance of the ILO committee's expertise. In late January 1997, the South Korean government responded to the ILO committee's inquiry, arguing that the labor law bill constituted a "considerable step forwards towards respecting ILO standards, at the same time reflecting the Republic of Korea's economic needs and its socio-political particularities."[145] As the South Korean government would now reopen the bill in response to democratic protest, the government requested the ILO committee adjourn the case.[146] The ILO committee noted this request but stated its intention to continue examining trade union rights problems in South Korea. The committee expressed "great regret" over the remaining trade union rights problems and recommended urgent revisions of outstanding legal issues.

The committee also disagreed that South Korea had made sufficient changes. For example, the committee found the three-year delay before allowing legal recognition to the KCTU unsatisfactory, stating "the free choice of workers to establish and join organizations is so fundamental to freedom of association as a whole that it cannot be compromised by delays."[147] While noting that unions could now enjoy solidarity support, the committee expressed concern that unions had to provide the Labor Ministry with the names of supporters, prior to receiving their support. This was unsatisfactory, as the committee argued that "workers should have the right to choose, without any hindrance, the persons from whom they wish to seek assistance during collective bargaining and dispute settlement procedures."[148] The committee expressed "serious concern" about the labor rights situation in general, particularly in light of the trade unionist arrests and detentions, and it offered to send a high-level mission to South Korea so that the government could hear specific views on how to fully implement freedom of association.[149]

Soon after this communication, the government adopted the mildly revised TULRAA on March 10, 1997. The labor flexibility measures remained, but the revised law suspended these layoff provisions for a two-year grace period. The only major labor rights change involved a new provision allowing for the immediate recognition of multiple unions on the national and industrial levels. In other words, there could now be more than one national trade union federation, and there could now be more than one trade union federation per industry (such as automakers or transportation). However, only one trade union was allowed at each individual workplace. Teachers and civil servants were not granted labor organizing rights.[150]

The revised TULRAA maintained a number of shortcomings. Public-sector employees, especially teachers and civil servants, benefited the least from the 1997 act. While these issues received a significant degree of attention from all three institutions, there were no legislative changes. The other major legislative issues also remained unresolved. The revised 1997 act included de jure provisions for the immediate legalization of multiple trade unions. But these rules were written in such a way that the KCTU could not qualify for legal personality. The KCTU was organizationally strong and sought to use collective action for both employment and political grievances. Under the law, the KCTU could not be certified because several leaders had been fired, and because of the illegal status of the Korean Teachers' Union. Given the organizational strength of the KCTU, this shortcoming seemed to be a deliberate attempt to undercut the power of an independent trade union. This also made all KCTU collective actions illegal, which would serve as the legal basis for arrest in the future. The lifting of the solidarity action ban was incomplete; "solidarity" actors could face stiff criminal penalties if they did not notify the Labor Ministry prior to giving support.

Table 6: Changes to Trade Union Rights Laws, Korea 1997

Trade Union Rights Problem	*Recommendation*	*Revised Trade Union and Labor Relations Adjustment Act (March 1997)*
Ban on solidarity activity	ILO, OECD, CESCR: Lift ban on solidarity activity and allow workers to receive and give solidarity, advice, and aid	Solidarity action now allowed, but requires Labor Ministry notification; some trade unionists released (partial compliance)
Trade union monopolies at the enterprise, industrial, and national level	ILO, OECD, CESCR: Immediately recognize the rights of independent unions to organize and right for unions to affiliate with organizations of their choice	Multiple unions allowed at national and industrial level; no multiple unions allowed at enterprise level, but legal requirements keep KCTU illegal for three years (partial)
No basic trade union rights for teachers and civil servants	ILO, OECD, CESCR: Immediately recognize the rights of teachers, civil servants, and independent unions to organize	No change for teachers or civil servants; ongoing repression of KCTU (no compliance)

In addition, President Kim Young Sam, even though he did issue warrants for the arrest of labor leaders, was constrained by international pressure. He warned companies not to fire striking workers, even though the new law allowed employers to fire illegally striking workers.[151] This international pressure also led the president to release jailed trade unionists on January 21, 1997.[152] According to KCTU officials, the combination of pressure from the OECD Director General and the ILO Director General "held the Korean government's hands a little. It's an issue of timing, choices became limited; without international intervention, they could have arrested strike leaders. But with pressure from the international institutions, the Korean government could not arrest, which put out the sign [to strikers] to negotiate [an agreement]."[153] This international attention held Kim Young Sam's government accountable to his public statement promising to improve labor rights. Even though the amendments to the revised bill did not address all the issues, the combination of international institutional and domestic pressure shaped the choices of the South Korean state.

The 1997 IMF Crisis

New opportunities for trade union rights changes emerged in late 1997, when the Asian financial crisis hit South Korea. What started out as a local Thai currency crisis in the summer of 1997 soon turned into a full-blown regional financial crisis. When the South Korean stock market fell by 7 percent in one day in November, it became clear that contagion had spread to South Korea, making emergency intervention necessary. However, Kim Young Sam's government denied the need for an IMF rescue package, as it wanted to avoid the stringent demands of an intervention before the presidential election. Yet with a lack of sufficient foreign reserves,[154] and a failure to secure bilateral emergency funding from Japan and the United States, President Kim Young Sam announced South Korea's request for IMF intervention on November 22, 1997. While foreign investors believed that only an IMF package could address the "fundamental problems" responsible for South Korean finance problems, the rescue package did little to restore investor confidence and stabilize South Korean economic indicators.[155] The final agreement, including a $57 billion bailout,[156] was signed on December 3, 1997, but consumer and investor confidence showed few signs of recovery. A regional economist from ING Barings Hong Kong claimed that these poor economic indicators were evidence that foreign investors did not believe that South Korean politicians would deliver on their commitments to the IMF.[157] Fear of South Korean default became a significant concern by December 14, during the height of a very close presidential election campaign.

The IMF rescue package included many policy requirements, such as implementing financial reform,[158] checking inflation, restoring market confidence, slowing the devaluation of the *won* (South Korean currency), minimizing economic slowdown, and building international reserves.[159] The documents also required labor market flexibility and social security reforms. The Memorandum on the Economic and Financial Program and the Letter of Intent stated that "the capacity of the new Employment Insurance system will be strengthened to facilitate the redeployment of labor, in parallel with further steps to improve labor market flexibility."[160] This particular single-line clause became the point of contention between labor, employers, and the government. Surprisingly, this requirement empowered domestic unions to pressure greater compliance with the international institutions' labor rights recommendations.

On December 19, 1997, Kim Dae Jung was narrowly elected with 40 percent of the popular vote. Kim Dae Jung was the only candidate to take a tougher stance against the IMF conditions, promising to fight layoffs. While

Kim Dae Jung sent a letter on December 13 to Michael Camdessus, expressing his support for the IMF package, his campaign also placed newspaper ads the day before the election that pledged to renegotiate the IMF.[161] Kim Dae Jung had a long history of opposing the past military government and maintained close ties to unions. Financial analysts and foreign investors, frightened by his pro-labor sympathies and alarmed by his campaign rhetoric,[162] worried that his presidency would worsen economic instability. Soon after his election, the won fell by 11 percent, and the stock market fell by 5 percent. Kim Dae Jung attempted to reassure foreign investors that South Korea was economically credible, changing course and supporting liberalizing reforms. During an impromptu press conference on December 20, 1997, he pledged to implement free market principles and to restore investor confidence by following the specifications of the IMF rescue package. Kim Dae Jung pledged to make South Korea a "paradise for business," even telephoning the IMF director to reiterate his support.[163]

Attempting to maintain his promise of no layoffs, Kim Dae Jung's transition team announced the creation of a Tripartite Commission, a forum for business and labor interests charged with achieving a "grand national social contract." Businesses would pledge to avoid layoffs, and trade unions would pledge to moderate their demands and accept wage cuts. However, this strategy shifted on December 22, when Kim Dae Jung announced that as more companies went bankrupt, some South Korean workers would have to lose their jobs. The president-elect announced to labor union audiences that layoffs were inevitable.[164] Fear that the economy was worsening prompted the transition team to call for drastic and expedient labor flexibility reforms, and Kim Dae Jung's election team announced that his campaign's advertisements against the IMF plan had been a mistake. The South Korean government communicated its newfound commitment to labor flexibility in its reports to the IMF, promising to introduce bills allowing for temporary employment and a public employment insurance system to the National Assembly by February 1998.[165]

Provisions of the Tripartite Agreement

In early February 1998, after months of deliberations, the Korean Tripartite Commission recommended domestic labor policy changes. The Tripartite Commission, a stronger reincarnation of Kim Young Sam's 1996 Presidential Commission, consisted of representatives from the KCTU and the FKTU, two representatives from business interests, two representatives from the government, and four representatives from the major political parties. The key objective of this commission was to outline how the social partners would share the responsibility of resolving the economic crisis. The February document, which outlined the goals and policy prescriptions of the commission, endorsed granting teachers organizational and collective bargaining rights, but not strike rights. It also established limited associational rights for civil servants. In exchange, trade unions were to restrain bargaining and accept layoffs and the dispatch worker system.[166]

Based on the events of the previous year, the government recognized that unilaterally adopting the labor flexibility reforms would be difficult. To prevent a return of the previous winter's public protests, the Tripartite Commission sought to create a consensus through social partner bargaining. The commission began negotiations with social partners in early January 1997. During their sixth meeting, on February 6, 1998, the commission adopted and released the *Social Agreement to Overcome the Economic Crisis*, also called the "Great Compromise." This agreement, which was to form the basis of upcoming legislative changes, consisted of 90 clauses covering a broad range of economic policy changes. These included provisions on corporate governance and transparency, strategies to improve exports and the balance of payments, financial regulation, price stabilization, and implementation of new management policies.

The Korean Tripartite Commission's directive introduced both layoff procedures and some beneficial policies for displaced workers. The most significant reforms were the provisions for creating a category of dispatch (temporary/short-term contract) workers and a layoff system outlined in a section titled "Enhancement of Labor Market Flexibility." Section 7, clause 76 articulated standards and provisions designed to ease the layoff process for businesses. Provisions for laid-off workers included the following expansions of unemployment benefits: medical insurance benefits, job placement programs, tuition assistance, and job retraining services. Additional measures, such as emergency loan provisions to bankrupt companies (to support the workers whose wages were in arrears), were also proposed to ease the transition for workers.[167]

Gains in basic labor rights were elaborated in section 6. These granted workers some new trade union rights and provided timelines for legislative changes that would move South Korea toward compliance with the international institutions' recommendations. The laws prohibiting teachers from forming unions and engaging in collective bargaining were scheduled for amendment in September 1998. The agreement also allowed civil servants the right to form workplace councils beginning in January 1999. While falling short of granting civil servants trade union rights, this law was the first step in that direction. In addition, this directive recommended allowing trade unions full political rights immediately, following revisions of the Elections Law and the Political Funds Act. Since the agreement granted employers greater latitude to lay off workers, this section included a clause granting unemployed workers the right to maintain their union membership, a provision that would help the KCTU gain legal status. Finally, the agreement gave trade unions greater financial freedom and tax benefits.[168]

The exchange of labor rights for flexibility was a domestic bargain made possible by the political conditions created by the IMF. Dong-Eung Lee, senior managing director of the Korean Employers Federation, stated, "in order to get the labor movement [to agree to] labor market flexibility, [we] had to grant more labor rights."[169] Dr. Kiu-Sik Bae, the director for industrial relations research at the Korea Labor Institute (an independent government-funded research institute), agreed, arguing that the February agreement "was an exchange. The unions conceded to allow workers' layoffs; in exchange, they can have legalization of the teachers unions and other freedom of association [measures]."[170] Chang and Chae's study of labor relations since the financial crisis also characterized this event as a "fair exchange" of difficult layoff and dispatch labor provisions for better basic organizing and social welfare rights.[171]

The Influence of International Institutions

The Tripartite Commission's recommendations helped legitimate trade union rights claims. Though its recommendations lacked legal status, the government soon followed them. The dire economic situation turned the commission's advisory role into an almost self-executing one. Its labor recommendations were adopted in their entirety, despite domestic opposition to various provisions. The negotiation process between labor, management, and the government helped to make the international institutions' recommendations politically expedient. Trade union representatives promoted labor rights within the Tripartite Commission. In addition, the state's recognition that it would continue to engage with international institutions made it likely that the recommendations would become law.

In many ways, this exchange between trade union rights and labor flexibility seemed an entirely domestic one. However, the transnational normative negotiation process profoundly influenced the likelihood of trade union rights changes in a number of ways. For example, the government, in the midst of the crisis, accepted the ILO committee's offer of a high-level tripartite mission.[172] The ILO initially offered to send a high-level mission in late December 1996, but the South Korean government responded ambivalently. It agreed and invited the high-level Tripartite Mission, however, during the crisis. This mission visited February 9 and 10, 1998.[173] South Korea was not obligated to accept the ILO's offer of this investigatory mission, because it had not ratified Conventions 87 and 98. The government's decision to go beyond its legal obligations to trade union rights suggests that it felt more vulnerable to international standards during the crisis.

Another way in which the international institutions' recommendation process influenced the domestic legal changes was through the creation of the Tripartite Commission. Dr. Ho-Guen Lee, the 2006 expert adviser to the Korean Tripartite Commission, claimed that "the ILO and other international institutions recommended and demanded that the Korean government upgrade the level [of protection] of basic rights . . . the biggest result was the creation of this organization." Lee also argued that the creation of the commission was a decidedly political move by the president-elect, Kim Dae Jung.[174] The government had relied on similar tripartite-styled organizations in the past, but they had not succeeded in creating consensus between social partners.

The exchange of labor rights for labor flexibility was not inevitable, as other options were possible. For example, in an *International Herald Tribune* interview given during the Tripartite Commission's negotiations, Kim Dae Jung stated that he favored retraining and unemployment insurance programs as a way to deal with increased unemployment. Even as late as January 31, Kim Dae Jung promised workers who would lose their jobs increased social safety net provisions, without mentioning better rights.[175] During national public debates over which policy options could convince workers to accept the new layoff provisions, the suggestions largely included better welfare and social safety net benefits.[176] The debates did not include the idea of a trade union rights trade-off in exchange for labor flexibility reforms, nor did the president-elect suggest such an exchange. Almost all other policy options, labor-related or otherwise, were presented publicly as part of a larger attempt to reassure the skittish international economic audience that these reforms would be accepted by labor unions.

International institutions' recommendations also influenced the actual composition of the Tripartite Commission. Specifically, their recognition of the KCTU likely influenced the South Korean government's decision to include the KCTU in the commission, which in turn influenced the outcomes. In fact, the South Korean government even told the ILO during the special Tripartite mission that its illegal status was "not such a problem in practice in terms of its organizational status or activities."[177] This process led to de facto state recognition, and the KCTU in turn advocated for trade union rights changes. Although the legally recognized trade union federation, the FKTU, would have advocated for better rights even without KCTU participation, it lacked the same vested interests in expanding trade union rights, as it lacked the need for legal recognition.

Additionally, the influence of international actors on the South Korean labor rights situation had been demonstrated during the 1996 strikes. International institutions, including the OECD, helped legitimize the demands of the general strike the previous winter, thus boosting the bargaining position of workers, granting labor unions the power of a credible threat. The international attention and criticism directed at the South Korean government during the general strike made future state repression difficult.[178] The South Korean state was in a delicate bind: the need to appease both international investors and international labor rights institutions required South Korea to *peacefully* adopt unpopular labor reforms. Further labor unrest would only lead to additional international criticism and further weakening of investor confidence.

Finally, South Korea's domestic politics also suggest that international pressure influenced the "rights for flexibility" exchange. Powerful opposition political parties did not want to grant these rights and would continue to protest them afterward. The Grand National Party walked out of negotiations in the Tripartite Commission because it did not want to grant teachers rights. Therefore, without the external influence of the international institutions, the "rights exchange" may not have occurred. There was nothing "inevitable" about this exchange. Dr. Young Lee Goh, the deputy senior manager of the labor and welfare department of the Korean Federation of Industries, one of the social partners at the Tripartite Commission, claimed that this negotiation in 1998 was neither peaceful nor clear: "[It did] not go smoothly. Actually, it was like a combat field."[179] Had the bargaining by the labor representatives been less convincing or less politically expedient, these labor rights reforms may not have occurred.

Furthermore, the government's own portrayal of how South Korean trade union rights evolved emphasizes the role of international institutions. This demonstrates that the labor rights and labor flexibility changes of 1998 were neither purely a domestic compromise nor just a function of Kim Dae Jung's policy preferences. The Labor Ministry's 2006 *Labor Administration* pamphlet provides the following narrative explaining how these changes occurred. It claims that in light of the 1997 financial crisis, a domestic political demand emerged: "from the [civil servants] themselves that they should be given a channel by which they could make themselves heard about their working conditions or the environment of their work. In addition, international organizations, including the ILO and OECD, had continued to call on the Government to make institutional improvements to guarantee [civil servants] basic labor rights."[180] The subsequent 2004 law was satisfactory, according to the Ministry of Labor publication, because these "rights . . . are guaranteed for [civil servants] to the extent that it is recommended by the ILO and OECD."[181]

The same publication uses similar rhetoric to explain the change in teachers' trade union rights. The document states that the Act on Establishment and Operation of Teachers' Unions "provides for basic labor rights of teachers to the extent that is recommended by the ILO and OECD."[182] Interestingly, this document uses the language of international norms to limit the state's responsibilities to labor rights reforms. The Ministry of Labor publication characterizes the recommendations of the ILO and the OECD as providing important standards for what constitutes necessary labor rights.

A Social Democratic President and Trade Union Rights Changes

One could maintain that these rights emerged mostly because of the partisan change resulting from the presidential administrations. It is possible that international recommendations on labor rights bolstered the existing policy preferences of the Kim Dae Jung government, which used ILO recommendations to extract concessions out of reluctant social partners (such as business representatives) and the stronger opposition Grand National Party. During his presidency, the National Assembly passed the "Act on Establishment and Operation of Workplace Associations for Public Officials" in late 1998 (made effective in January 1999) and the "Act Establishment and Operation of Teachers' Unions," in January 1999 (to be put into effect July 1, 2009), despite opposition party protests.[183] This would be similar to the way that other state leaders have used IMF conditionality to push through otherwise difficult liberalizing economic reforms.[184] Prior to his election, Kim Dae Jung had, in speeches and publications, stressed the importance of basic labor rights for workers as necessary for sustained long-term economic growth.[185] Yet if the labor rights reforms were merely a function of partisan change, and the new government had internalized labor rights norms, it would have acted and spoken differently with regard to the remaining trade union rights problems. For example, the state could have consulted more with the ILO and reduced direct repression (i.e., arrests) of trade unionists. Even if further labor rights law reform was politically difficult, Kim Dae Jung's commitment to labor rights should have been evidenced through its reports and communications to international institutions.

An example of the lack of norm internalization under Kim Dae Jung's presidency was the state's repression of new civil servants engaged in preparatory activities prior to the implementation of the new civil servants workplace council law. The Ministry of Government Administration and Home Affairs sent a directive to local government offices, entitled "Countermeasures in response to the Public Servants' Works Council Preparation Committee" on April 3, 1998, instructing that municipalities disrupt any display of civil servant collective activity. The directive stated that until the new civil servants workplace association bill became law on January 1, 1999, "these activities shall therefore be dealt with strictly in accordance with the law."[186] As a result, two civil servants who attempted to organize exploratory committees on civil servant unions in 1998 were fired for engaging in "collective action."[187]

The Kim Dae Jung government justified direct state repression of workers' freedoms by claiming economic hardship, just as Kim Young Sam's administration did in 1994.[188] The government repressed collective trade union activity, including curtailing demonstrations and strikes.[189] The number of arrested trade unionists increased under Kim Dae Jung's administration, although this may have been due to the increased number of industrial disputes.[190] Amnesty International reported a minimum of 850 trade unionists arrested between February 1998 and October 2002.[191] Trade unionists found Kim Dae Jung's Nobel Peace Prize ironic and unfair. Dan Byung Ho, the president of the KCTU during much of the Kim Dae Jung administration, spoke out about Kim Dae Jung's lack of support for workers' rights in an interview with the International Metalworkers Federation: "Korean workers don't consider [President Kim Dae Jung] to be a positive figure . . . although he is called the 'human rights president' in some Western countries. . . . The number of workers jailed in his first three years in office has been greater than that of the previous president's total four-year term. He is an oppressor, not a human rights president. And his economic policies have brought a great deal of suffering to the workers."[192]

International institutions continued to find problems with the South Korean trade union rights situation, but the government responded with justifications, rather than recognition of shortcomings. For example, the international institutions continued to express concern over mass arrests of striking workers, whose activities were criminalized under the "obstruction of business" laws.[193] The ILO committee did not agree with South Korea's justification that the mere illegality (unauthorized status) of strikes justified the South Korean state's response. Although the strikes were not legally sanctioned, they were peaceful and occurred on workplace premises; the committee condemned the arrests and argued that national law and order were not harmed during the relevant sit-down strikes. The committee noted that South Korea's "heavy emphasis on the security and stability of the country . . . only serves to aggravate industrial disputes."[194] It observed that these tactics, especially mass arrests, had "increased dramatically in comparison to previous years," and it urged a more conciliatory approach.[195] The OECD's recommendations in 2000 similarly stated that "legal provisions, which are often used to arrest trade unionists for what other OECD countries consider legitimate trade union activities, need to be revised or used with utmost restraint."[196]

Yet despite this international condemnation, the South Korean state continued to justify its practices. For example, Mr. Hwang, a delegate of the South Korean government, responded to the UN Human Rights Committee's concerns during a November 1999 meeting, that while the South Korean government sought to guarantee basic labor rights, it was obligated also to "punish [the] violent and destructive action" that was present at many of the post–financial crisis protests and strikes.[197] Hwang also claimed that the government wanted to allow strike rights, "but it intended to suppress illegal strikes accompanied by violence and destruction, acting within the law and in conformity with internationally recognized standards . . . Authorities were determined to improve the labor relations [and] to turn the economy around."[198] These claims by the government representative to the UN Human Rights Committee demonstrates the hard line that the Kim Dae Jung government took against striking workers, and how the government had shifted from the solidarity action ban to "obstruction of business" as a means to criminalize trade union collective action.

In response to the problems with the civil servants bill, the ILO committee, the OECD, and the UN Human Rights Committee urged South Korea to grant full union rights to a broader range of civil servants. The ILO committee stated that these new rights were discriminatory to government workers and violated international trade union rights principles granting workers "without distinction whatsoever" basic organizational rights.[199] In its concluding observations to South Korea's second periodic report to the ICCPR, the Human Rights Committee expressed "concern that the remaining restrictions on the right to freedom of association of teachers and other public servants do not meet the requirements of article 22, paragraph 2, of the Covenant," and urged further trade union rights protections.[200] While the OECD conceded that not all of its member countries conformed to ILO standards, it recommended that South Korea change its laws and practices because South Korea's violations were so fundamental. The OECD stressed that South Korea's failure to recognize the basic right of civil servants to join unions was out of sync with other OECD countries.

The establishment of the Korean Tripartite Commission also lessened the influence of international institutions. After the first temporary Tripartite Commission issued the February Agreement in early 1998, the newly inaugurated Kim Dae Jung government established a more permanent body in June, with the mandate to monitor the provisions laid out in the February Agreement.[201] Soon afterward, the government's reports to the Committee on Freedom of Association referred to the Tripartite Commission's plans as a generic response to the committee's concerns. For example, when the ILO committee expressed disappointment with the lack of progress in South Korea, the government merely responded that the second Tripartite Commission would adequately address all remaining issues.[202] The South Korean government claimed that the presence of this new permanent, domestic labor institution was sufficient to respond to the ILO's concerns. Likewise, the South Korean government responded to the concerns of the CESCR by referencing the Tripartite Commission and its agenda. The government justified its limitations on civil servants' and teachers' basic rights by claiming that these laws were currently under discussion by the Tripartite Commission, which was "moving towards greater readiness to accord such rights to both groups."[203]

The Roh Moo Hyun Administration: New Forms of Institutional Engagement

By the next presidential election in 2002, South Korea was no longer facing economic crisis. It was a more confident state, a more institutionalized democracy, an OECD member, and a well-established member of international society. Roh Moo Hyun, the victor, was a center-left candidate who had suffered personal persecution for his political activities under the military regime, including arrest and disbarment for supporting an illegal labor protest.[204] Roh Moo Hyun's campaign focused on economic growth and the lofty goal of economic leadership in Northeast Asia.[205] Although he did promise to legalize trade union rights for civil servants, labor rights were not a major part of his platform. In fact, during the campaign, Roh stated, "labor-management problems are what foreign investors doing business in Korea are concerned about most." Roh Moo Hyun called for "dialogue and compromise" to forge "a cooperative labor-management culture."[206]

As Roh Moo Hyun's government lacked a clear international goal that could have created domestic vulnerabilities vis-à-vis trade union rights, these international institutions' recommendations became less influential. The South Korean state's communications toward international institutions shifted in this period. Though initially conciliatory, the communications between the Roh government and the ILO, OECD, and UN human rights bodies later became more confident and defiant, using new frameworks to respond to these institutions. Roh Moo Hyun's government questioned the institutions' legitimacy and authority for making recommendations on certain laws. The communications also co-opted the language of international standards and rights as a means to justify South Korea's actions. The state compared South Korean practices to other states, and constructed an interpretation of trade union rights norms that was contrary to the international institutions' understandings. In addition, the government questioned the accuracy of the unions' submissions, accusing the institutions of providing recommendations based on false information. Finally, the South Korean government repeated its earlier claims that the appropriate forums for such legal changes were domestic institutions (national courts and the Tripartite Commission) as a way to render the international institutions' recommendation processes less important.

The administration's more confident attitude may have been related to South Korea's emerging international leadership on labor issues. Under Roh

Moo Hyun, South Korea adopted a significant leadership role at the ILO. South Korean representatives were elected to serve on the ILO's Governing Body in 2002 and 2005, and a South Korean representative served as the chair of the governments' group at the 2002 International Labor Conference meeting. South Korea also began to engage in cooperative ventures with the ILO. Since June 1998, the ILO and South Korea had worked on collaborative programs in different technical workplace areas, such as re-employment training, the creation of a social safety net for temporary and agency workers, and the general improvement of unemployment benefits.[207] In addition, South Korea began to regularly donate to the ILO budget. According to the director of the Ministry of Labor's International Policy Team, South Korea gave approximately $800,000 to the ILO in 2006.[208] South Korea even hosted the 2006 Asian Regional Meeting of the ILO in Busan. The meeting was moved from its usual location in the Philippines as a result of heavy lobbying by South Korean representatives.[209] According to former Labor Minister Kim Dae Hwan, Roh Moo Hyun's labor minister during the planning process, the regional meeting was moved to Busan because the Labor Ministry felt that this might help change the ILO's negative perception of South Korea's labor rights situation.[210]

The Roh Moo Hyun government's initial communications were conciliatory. In the February 2003 report, the new government told the ILO committee that it was "firmly committed to building industrial relations for social integration. . . . The government will reform the labor laws to meet global standards and harmonize with domestic reality."[211] This communication promised to legalize civil servants' unions, but only in a manner sensitive to domestic concerns.[212] The government even requested the ILO's consultation on this bill. In addition, the Roh government promised a "new era" in labor relations, promising to pardon many jailed trade unionists and pledging the creation of task forces and joint committees to improve industrial relations cooperation.[213] The ILO committee welcomed the change in tone, and expressed its desire to deal with the unresolved issues.[214] The government stated the need for further "reasonable" labor rights reforms and deferred to the ILO's authority over certain issues.[215]

South Korea did not communicate again with either the ILO or a UN agency until 2006. In a June 2005 OECD Council meeting, the OECD secretariat proposed ending the labor rights legal monitoring process in South Korea by 2007. The OECD secretariat argued that with the creation of its Industrial Relations Roadmap, South Korea was fully addressing all the outstanding concerns of the OECD. These outstanding concerns had included problems with civil servants' unions, the ban on solidarity activity, and multiple unions at the company level. While the council members did not reach an agreement at the meeting, some member states agreed that the OECD should end the monitoring system soon. The BIAC strongly advocated ending the monitoring, but the TUAC urged it be maintained. The OECD Council publicly noted the progress of labor law reforms in South Korea and invited South Korea to report on its continued progress to the ELSA Committee by spring 2007. According to a follow-up South Korean Labor Ministry publication, many OECD members believed that the Industrial Relations Roadmap constituted compliance with international standards on labor rights.

Between the 2005 OECD meeting and the 2006 ILO committee communication, South Korea's law allowing civil servants' trade union rights came into effect. The new Public Officials Trade Union Act, passed in late 2004 (to become law in 2006), gave civil servants the rights to organize and collectively bargain. However, the law did not include political or strike rights, and only applied to certain categories of civil servants.[216] The KGEU refused to register under this law because of the lack of collective action rights. In response, the government continued its harassment and direct repression of KGEU members in 2006.[217] Trade union's communications to the ILO committee included concerns about the shortcomings of the civil servants law and continued repression of the KGEU. For example, the government used riot police at major universities to prevent a series of KGEU rallies in October 2004. When 1,500 KGEU members attempted to enter Kunkook University, the police responded violently, injuring ten union members, and detaining 40 union members for twenty hours. At another rally in October 2004, 6,000 riot police converged on a rally of 10,000 striking public-sector and civil service workers, preventing workers from reaching their rally destination. This action led to 44 strikers being detained for about one day.[218]

The government justified both its repression and any shortcomings within the new civil servants' trade union law with the new language of international standards. This demonstrated that the South Korean government had "learned" how to justify its trade union rights violations. In its 2005 report to the ILO committee, the South Korean government began justifying its shortcomings by appealing to "international standards." In contrast, the government had used economic and cultural justifications in the past. For example, the government responded to concerns about the new civil servants trade union law (and the subsequent arrests of KGEU members) by stating:

> [The] Government considered that the Public Officials' Trade Union Act which did not recognize the right to collective action (right to strike) for public officials, was in conformity with international standards, such as the International Covenants on Human Rights and ILO Convention No. 151 and Recommendation No. 159, which did not contain any provision clearly prescribing public officials' right to strike. Thus, KGEU leaders and members were not arrested arbitrarily and their human rights and basic freedoms were respected in accordance with the Declaration of Human Rights and Human Rights Conventions ratified by the Republic of Korea.[219]

The South Korean government justified its behavior by citing the Committee on Freedom of Association's own past decisions. The government quoted an ILO Committee on Freedom of Association principle, which recognized that trade union rights principles do not protect a right to strike that includes criminal activities.[220] Therefore "punishing the abuse of the right to strike according to national law was not considered to be counter to the principle of the freedom of association as long as punishment was not excessive."[221] This response by the South Korean government demonstrated its new strategy of using ILO committee principles to justify its trade union rights issues.

Despite these new rhetorical moves, the ILO committee responded in 2006 with recommendations strongly favoring the unions' complaints, asking the government to respect the basic rights of civil servants in all grades and categories.[222] In addition, the UN Human Rights Committee, in its November 2006 review, also recommended granting full trade union rights to those civil servants who had been excluded from trade union rights (grades 5–9) and also urged the South Korean government to recognize the extra-legal KGEU.[223]

The South Korean government responded to this next set of reports with indignation and disbelief.[224] The South Korean representative expressed "grave regret" in response to the 2006 committee recommendations at the ILO Governing Body meeting.[225] In its 2007 response, the government included a special section responding to the ILO committee's 340th report on the South Korean case, questioning the legitimacy of the committee. The government's key claim was that the ILO committee was acting outside of its appropriate bounds and had been misinformed by South Korean trade unionists.[226] The government was "greatly disappointed" at the "biased" ILO decision, which "unilaterally" took the unions' position, without clear evidence.[227] As the government's report insisted, "the Committee's prejudgment that KGEU members are public officials whose right to strike should be recognized is wrong in the factual and legislative contexts."[228] The government also pointed to the many domestic political institutions that it had created to deal with these labor rights issues, such as the Korean Tripartite Commission, the High-Level Tripartite Representative Meetings (separate from the ILO mission), and newly established labor-management workplace councils, as sufficiently addressing the ILO's concerns.[229]

This 2007 communication also argued that South Korea's practices fit with other states. For example, the South Korean government justified limiting strike rights for civil servants, as the "United States, Australia, Japan, Germany, etc." also did so.[230] The government's report pointed out that South Korea's use of "obstruction of business" laws to criminalize illegal strike behavior was also a practice in other states, claiming that "in other countries, in case a trade union obstructs nonunion workers and replacement workers in performing their jobs or forces its members to participate in industrial action, it is punished on charges of coercion, etc. This is the same logic and mechanism that the provision on an obstruction of business charge in the Republic of Korea follows in its application."[231] To justify its practices, the government also cited the text of ILO Convention 87 that trade union activities "shall respect the laws and regulations of the land."[232] Claiming South Korea's status as a divided state created special security needs, the government stated that public officials' unions must be held to a different standard. Since the KGEU was often critical of South Korean government policies, South Korea argued that its limitation of civil servants' trade union rights were justifiable under international standards, citing paragraph 502 of the 1996 Digest of Freedom of Association Decisions.[233]

The government expressed similar concerns in its response to the NGO submission to the UN Human Rights Committee. The KCTU had invited the ICFTU, TUAC, and the Global Union Federation to undertake a joint mission to observe the trade union rights situation in South Korea prior to the 2006 ILO Asian Regional Meeting. The joint mission's report urged the South Korean government to fully reform its labor legislation to bring it in line with the ILO recommendations from March 2006 and ILO principles on trade union rights.[234] The Human Rights Committee's concerns echoed this counter-report. In response, the South Korean government wrote its own counter-report in October 2006, providing its version of the narrative. This counter-report claimed that the trade union submission was one-sided and false. The report also claimed that "Since its accession to the OECD in 1996, the Korean government has continuously devoted itself to reforming labor laws in line with internationally-accepted standards and has experienced a great deal of progress in many fields. The South Korean government has guaranteed the freedom of trade union activities and thus it would be impossible to say that, either in practice or in legal terms, the freedom of union activities has been suppressed in any way or form."[235] The government also claimed that it had such a favorable attitude toward labor that employers and businesses claimed they felt disempowered in such a labor-friendly environment. The report also reiterated South Korea's reforms, especially the passing of the recent Industrial Relations Roadmap, and evidence for its long-standing respect for international labor union solidarity.[236] This response to the UN Human Rights Committee may have been a calculated public relations move, because the government had to emphasize its progress in order to convince the OECD to end the labor monitoring process.[237]

In its 2005 meeting, the OECD had praised the provisions of the proposed Industrial Relations Roadmap. This roadmap was created from negotiations within the Tripartite Commission, of which the KCTU had refused to participate. The agreement had many provisions. First, it pushed back the introduction of plural unions from the beginning of 2007 to December 31, 2009. In addition, the roadmap included some provisions to protect recall rights for laid-off workers. Finally, the requirement for prior notification for "solidarity action" in an industrial dispute was removed.[238] The government reported to the ILO committee in February 2007 that the removal of the prior notification requirement was one of the "highlights" of the September 2006 compromise. The roadmap's policies were supposed to address the concerns of the ILO and other international institutions. This framework was passed into law during a plenary session of the National Assembly on December 31, 2006.[239] The South Korean government likely thought that the ILO would be as supportive in its response to the roadmap as the OECD had been.

On June 12, 2007, the OECD Council in Paris decided to end the ELSA Committee special labor-monitoring mandate. The South Korean government, in anticipation of the OECD meeting, had prepared a progress report on South Korea's labor law reform in April 2007. The ELSA Committee's report argued for a termination of the monitoring process, noting the progress of South Korea's labor law reforms, especially the legalization of public officials' trade union rights and the new roadmap legislation. The South Korean government claimed that almost all the OECD issues had been dealt with, except multiple unions at the enterprise level, which was to be resolved within a three-year timeline. Therefore, no further monitoring was necessary, and further monitoring might even be counterproductive. The ELSA director stated in his report, "I also detected a consensus to the effect that the OECD's peer-group pressure had contributed to the South Korean reform process. At the same time, it was clear that compared to the 2005 review, there has been a noticeable shift in the Committee's view about the wisdom of continuing with the special monitoring process."[240] Only one OECD member country (unnamed in the report) and the TUAC wanted to continue the monitoring process. As a result, the OECD Council decided to end its official monitoring but welcomed continued information about future labor law reforms.[241] This marked both the official end to an historic labor monitoring system and a break in the ten-year-old international consensus about South Korea's labor rights situation.

Conclusion: Influence, Engagement, and Remaining Issues

The multiyear recommendation process brought international attention to South Korea's trade union rights problems and forced South Korea to address its legal shortcomings. However, the transnational normative negotiation process became more influential when South Korea had political vulnerabilities, either influencing South Korea's international position or affecting a domestic bargaining situation. The first set of legal changes occurred after the international trade union movement politicized South Korea's trade union rights situation, as Kim Young Sam attempted to join the OECD. However, South Korea's soft commitments to the OECD were insufficient to create substantive changes in trade union rights. Rather, this commitment constrained Kim Young Sam's government in the face of strong international and domestic pressure. The OECD accession process created new vulnerabilities in 1996.[242] The sustained strike action of winter 1996–1997 attracted international focus to South Korea's labor issues, and countries such as Australia, the EU countries, and Canada pressured South Korea to change its laws. International media outlets also covered the strike action thoroughly.[243] Therefore, the legitimizing effects of the ILO and the incentives of OECD membership, in conjunction with strong domestic and transnational civil society organizing, brought about an incomplete and highly contingent compliance. The legal changes in early 1997 included some trade union pluralism and greater freedom for solidarity actions.

During the IMF crisis, the transnational normative negotiation process worked more indirectly. Specifically, South Korea felt vulnerable to international concerns about its creditworthiness and its ability to follow through on the IMF rescue package policy requirements. However, in order to do so, the state required cooperation from trade unions. International institutions' criticisms legitimized the complaints about the KCTU and complaints about trade union rights. This transnational normative negotiation process and the role of domestic unions advocating for greater rights within the Tripartite Commission influenced difficult changes, namely trade union rights for teachers and limited associational rights for civil servants. This was surprising because states often complain that economic problems make protection of trade union rights difficult. South Korea managed to pass sweeping reforms during a severe economic crisis.

The final period of change occurred as Roh Moo Hyun attempted to end international monitoring of South Korea's trade union rights situation, focusing on the OECD. By this time, South Korea was more confident and experienced in its participation in the transnational normative negotiation process. South Korea's changes during this time included the passing of the 2006 Industrial Relations Roadmap, which dealt with the solidarity action pre-requirements. The state also passed a law granting limited trade union rights for civil servants. However, as the civil servants laws and other laws fell short of strong trade union rights protections, international institutions continued to criticize South Korea. But as the OECD considered these changes sufficient, this marked a shift away from the international institutions' consensus on South Korea's trade union rights situation, which further weakened the influence of international institutions on South Korea's labor practices.

South Korea complied with several more of the international institutions' long-standing recommendations. Although these legal changes did not necessarily result in the full degree of compliance that the institutions recommended, there was a trend toward increasing compliance. Table 7 demonstrates the extent to which the concerns of international organizations were addressed by the South Korean state.

With the exception of the lifting of the ban on solidarity activity, South Korea did not fully comply with the other legislative recommendations despite an extensive period of engagement. However, while South Korea fixed the solidarity ban problem, it did not address the underlying problem with the law, as international institutions originally criticized how the solidarity ban provided criminal liability, allowing for the arrest of trade unionists. The law was abolished, but the practical problems remained, as trade union arrests are still an issue in South Korea. The state shifted to using the "obstruction of business" law as a means to arrest striking unionists. Likewise, teachers were given the right to form unions and bargain collectively, but they were not allowed to strike or bargain over nonwork conditions, such as control over educational curricula. The Civil Servants law only provided rights to about 330,000 of a total of 920,000 (nonmilitary) civil servants in South Korea (according to 2006 estimates), and does not provide them with collective action rights.[244] Finally, the lifting of the ban on multiple unions at the enterprise level was still being postponed to December 30, 2009, according to South Korea's 2009 report to the ILO.[245]

Although international institutions' recommendations constrained state behavior, domestic civil society also played an important role in maintaining political pressure. As the policy representative from the KCTU stated, "There is a gap between the Korean and international labor standards. Korean labor unions do a lot to change things. If we don't do this, nothing will happen. But Korea doesn't care so much about its labor unions . . . even though it lies [to these institutions] it still cares [more] about the OECD and the ILO."[246] According to a former international organizer for the Korean Metalworkers Federation, "they [international institutions] keep the issue in focus, by [constantly] asking the government for updates and explanations. But the unions [must] fight for implementation."[247] The expert adviser of the Korean Tripartite Commission expressed a similar sentiment, claiming, "It's good that international institutions ask the government for responses in these cases . . . the communication process somehow positively advanced the rights in Korea, practically and legally, but the government doesn't always do what the ILO [and other institutions] want."[248] Therefore, one major conclusion from the South Korean case is that sustained political pressure, both domestic and transnational, was very influential.

One clear pattern emerges from the chart above: strike rights are the most readily curtailed and the least likely to be protected. There were no improvements in protections of strike rights, as unionists engaged in strikes could now be charged with "obstruction of business" charges and possibly arrested. Teachers and civil servants never received a right to strike. This difference cannot be explained by legal commitments, however, as South Korea has a legal commitment to protect strike rights under the ICESCR. Rather, South Korea's reluctance to protect strike rights, or "collective action" rights, suggests a concern that collective protections for unions may lead to economic and political disadvantages.

Table 7: Changes in Labor Rights Law and Practice, Korea, 1998–2007

Violation in Question	*Recommendation from International Institutions*	*Legal Changes, Post-1998*
Arrests ("solidarity actions," members of "illegal unions," disruption of business); disruption of mass arrests	Stop arresting workers for normal union activities	Some curbing of arrests, but large scale arrests of trade unionists still continue under "obstruction of business" laws; use of civil suits against striking workers
Teachers and civil servants could not join unions	Immediately recognize the rights of teachers and civil servants to form and join unions	Teachers (1999) and civil servants (2004) granted right to form unions; KCTU granted legal status in 1999; strict limits on trade union rights of civil servants
Workers could not form alternative unions at the national, industrial, and enterprise level	Immediately recognize the rights of workers to form and organize independent unions at national, industrial, and enterprise level	Multiple unions are now allowed at the national or industrial level (1997), but company-level multiple unions are continuously delayed
Ban on "solidarity activity" limits ability of a union to receive outside assistance	Lift the prior requirement for solidarity activity	Lifted requirement of prior notification for solidarity activity (2006)

The South Korean case illustrates both that international institutions' recommendations can influence compliance, but that the length and frequency of interaction and recommendation matters. A state's extended interaction with an institution may not always strengthen a norm. Instead, it can result in institutional engagement "fatigue." While initial recommendations may damage a state's esteem, the fifteenth may be less important. This institutional fatigue seems to have been exacerbated by South Korea's successful attempt to end OECD monitoring, which gave the government the confidence to question the ILO. South Korea engaged less with the UN

Human Rights Committees because the UN committees review countries' human rights compliance less frequently, typically once every four years. There is also less evidence that the UN Human Rights Committee had influence, as neither the labor unions nor the government mentioned them as being significant. Therefore, a great deal of contact with the ILO (up to three times a year) might have led to fatigue, but too infrequent contact might have made the institutions less relevant to the domestic political context. By contrast, in Canada and the United Kingdom, the ILO made far fewer recommendations.

CHAPTER 5

United Kingdom

New Labour and New Labor Rights?

This examination of trade union rights in the United Kingdom, like the South Korean case, considers whether the change to a social democratic government was a sufficient political condition to explain better trade union rights compliance. The Conservative government in power from 1978 until 1997 was hostile to trade union rights. Some legal changes in this case could be attributed to the shift in government, when the historically pro-union Labour party came to power in 1997, under Tony Blair. The Labour government made several trade union rights changes within its first five years. However, partisan efforts alone cannot explain this change. Blair's Labour Party sought to distance itself from trade union interests, and its interactions with international institutions regarding this case's specific trade union rights disputes mirrored those of the prior Conservative government. But New Labour's embrace of a human rights identity unintentionally compelled it to consider the human rights aspects of trade union rights. This chapter argues that Blair's commitments to European norms created an unforeseen domestic political vulnerability, which strengthened the arguments of international institutions that advocated reforms.

This chapter focuses on a legal challenge to a private-sector employment practice. Private employers in the United Kingdom offered pay increases to workers who relinquished their trade union rights by accepting individual contracts. British courts ruled that this practice violated the United Kingdom's laws, prompting a legislative response from the British state. This local labor dispute became a transnational normative conflict as international actors criticized the state's responses.

Though British labor laws existed to protect workers from antiunion discrimination, employers were allowed to offer individual contracts compelling employees to give up the benefits of union representation and the right to collective bargaining. This practice was challenged through a lengthy series of litigations, referred to here as the Wilson/Palmer cases. The United Kingdom and the employers argued that the right of an individual worker to have union membership was different from the right to trade union representation, which included the right for a worker to have his or her work conditions determined through collective bargaining. Unlike in South Korea, this situation in Britain, and the related Palmer case, concerned only employer practices, not direct state repression. The state, however, sided with employers, and trade union claimed that the state had violated its responsibility to protect trade union rights. This process began in 1990 and culminated in 2004 with reforms to the United Kingdom's employment law. This case study spans fourteen years and three administrations. It includes the dismissal of several litigants, recommendations from multiple international institutions, three major changes to British labor law, and a landmark ruling from the European Court of Human Rights.

A major difference separating the United Kingdom case from the South Korean and British Columbia/Canadian cases is the absence of an organized mass protest supporting this particular legal campaign. Yet this lack of public mobilization did not preclude compliance, due to the strong legal status of the European Court of Human Rights and the European Convention on Human Rights. However, legalization did not do all of the "work" in the United Kingdom case. As in the South Korean case, the litigants made creative use of different institutions' recommendations in presenting their legal arguments. As the Labour government had made specific electoral promises about human rights, the European Court of Human Rights' pro-union decision a created a political vulnerability for the state. The timing of multiple institutions' recommendations and the government's attempts to include human rights promotion as part of its "modernization" policy agenda empowered the European Court of Human Rights' decisions and made reform more likely.

United Kingdom's Commitments to Trade Union Rights and History

Historically, trade unions in the United Kingdom pioneered many important political demands. Likewise, the United Kingdom was a founding member of the ILO and is an established member of the European Union and the Council of Europe.[1] The United Kingdom has a unique trade union relations system and a long history of trade union contention. A strong trade union system enjoying broad domestic support, though lacking strong statutory protections, existed throughout Britain's postwar "Golden Age" of 1950–1973. This period was marked by strong economic growth, generous welfare benefits, and government policies aimed toward full employment.[2] The subsequent deterioration of labor rights in the United Kingdom under the Conservative governments of Margaret Thatcher has been well documented by a number of legal and industrial relations scholars.[3] The next section will give a brief background on the industrial relations system of the United Kingdom and explain challenges to trade union rights since 1978.

United Kingdom Commitments to International Trade Union Rights Norms

Of the countries examined in this book, the United Kingdom has the strongest commitments to international trade union rights legal obligations in terms of ratified treaties. The United Kingdom has ratified both ILO Conventions 87 and 98, which protect the rights of workers to organize associations and to engage in collective bargaining. By contrast, South Korea has ratified neither, and Canada has only ratified Convention 87. The ratification of both conventions obligates the state to protect trade union activity and membership from discrimination. The United Kingdom, like the other countries considered in this book, has ratified both the ICCPR and the ICESCR, but, unlike South Korea, without reservations. Finally, the United Kingdom has ratified strong regional human rights commitments through the Council of Europe's two human rights documents, the European Convention for the Protection of Human Rights and Fundamental Freedoms and the European Social Charter. By contrast, Canada has not signed the relevant regional human rights document, the American Declaration of Human Rights.

The Development of the British Industrial Relations System

Until the late 1970s, the United Kingdom's trade union rights laws and practices were based on a system of "collective laissez faire." Because of its earlier experience with industrialization and its common-law tradition, British unions lacked positive statutory legal protections. Rather, common-law tradition provided "negative" protections, meaning that laws provided cert ain immunities for trade unions and their activities.[4] Canada and South Korea, in contrast, experienced later industrial economic development and therefore followed other more established industrial relations practices. While Canada and South Korea have a more American-style system, with a minimum "floor" of basic protections and provisions for collective bargaining, the United Kingdom has historically lacked these minimal protections and relied instead on collective bargaining to provide workers protections.[5] This meant that basic protections, such as antidiscrimination and safety rules that were part of a statutory regime for individual workers in Canada and South Korea, were determined by collective bargaining in the United Kingdom. Such a model was preferred by industrial relations scholars such as Otto Kahn-Freund, who argued that workers' rights would be more secure and more adaptable if they were protected by unions, not law.[6] The British state also encouraged collective bargaining through such measures as creating wage councils (which set local minimum wages), nationalizing industries (creating monopoly industrial unions for hospitals), adopting union wages in all government contracts, and acting as a major employer.[7]

In the United Kingdom, employers voluntarily recognized unions at high rates after the passage of key laws in the late nineteenth century.[8] Most U.K. employers voluntarily recognized unions and engaged in collective bargaining.[9] British employers and the state tried to maintain generally harmonious relations with trade unions. Collective agreements, because they were negotiated voluntarily by employers and workers, were not binding in the United Kingdom and could be ended at will by either the employer or the union, while collective agreements in Canada and South Korea were legally binding contracts. Labor rights associated with industrial relations were "negative rights" under British law, enjoying strong support from business, the state, and citizens. Instead of provisions protecting and encouraging collective bargaining and strike rights, British law granted unions certain immunities and protections from liability.[10]

Individual Rights and a Breakdown of the Domestic Consensus

Beginning in the 1960s and 1970s, the British government (under the leadership of both political parties) passed a series of industrial relations laws that provided some statutory protections for unions and individual workers.[11] Due to the perceived economic need to regulate the inflationary effects of trade unions on wages and prices, governments sought to legally limit their activity. For example, the Industrial Training Act of 1964 created industrial tribunals, a first-instance dispute resolution mechanism between workers and employers. This gave workers and employers a specialized court in which to air their grievances in exchange for bargaining restraint. In 1966, the Labour government also attempted to limit wage increases by setting price and wage ceilings.

The 1970s, a period of slow economic growth, saw other legislative attempts to curb trade union activity. The Conservative government passed the Industrial Relations Act of 1971, which created standards and procedures for strikes and tried to control unofficial strike activity, limiting the range of legal strike actions.[12] The incoming Labour government of 1974, which was politically successful largely because of the failure of the Conservative government to deal effectively with the miners' union strikes of 1972 and 1974, embarked on a campaign of compromise with trade unions. The Labour government promised the continuation of full employment policies and welfare benefits despite slower economic growth, on the condition that trade unions commit to real income restraint, a political deal called the "New Social Contract." To combat inflation, unions also agreed to limit their wage increases to 5 percent in return for the Employment Protection Act of 1975. This act provided the first statutory provisions for union recognition, compelling employers to bargain with a union under specified conditions.[13] While these laws may have limited the range of collective action, they were not generally understood to significantly curtail trade union rights.

However, this social contract, and the domestic support of trade unions and their rights, broke down by 1978 or 1979, during the historic "winter of discontent." Following a £4 billion IMF emergency loan in 1976, the government was forced to cut expenditures and could not meet the wage demands of public sector employees. In response, strikes broke out in many sectors, leading to the disruption of public services. An estimated one million public sector workers were reputed to have gone on strike that winter. The U.K. Employment Department estimated that in 1979, there were approximately 1,291 working days lost as a result of work stoppages, per 1,000 workers. These included both official work stoppages and lock-outs.[14] National polls reflected a change in public opinion toward trade unions that year, as a higher percentage of respondents claimed that unions were a "good thing" as claimed they were a "bad thing." This was a significant shift in public opinion. Remarkably, the Gallup Poll announced a similar shift that year in public opinion toward unions in the United States.[15]

The unpopularity of these strikes was largely responsible for the defeat of the Labour Party, bringing Thatcher and the Conservative Party to power in the elections of 1979. This new government was the most stridently antiunion Conservative government ever, the first to outright dismantle the corporatist (union-supporting) public sector institutions. Trade unions were seen as suffocating economic growth and competitiveness. Conservatives used the Winter of Discontent to warn against the excesses of trade union power and the undesirable consequences of a Labour Party government.[16] Yet prior to the public relations disaster of the Winter of Discontent, Thatcher went on record claiming that she would include trade unions in her plan to build a prosperous new Britain and vowed to neither "bash" unions nor "bow to" them.[17] After the strikes that winter, however, she changed position, publicly declaring that solving Britain's problems required curbing the power of unions.[18]

Thatcher/Major: A New Approach to Trade Unions

Starting in 1978, the Thatcher government began imposing strong restrictions on unions in a larger effort to dismantle the previous system that had granted wide latitude to trade unions. Rather than responding to economic challenges through cooperating and consulting with trade unions, the Conservative government passed economic deregulations that heavily favored employers. This was a sharp departure from the policies of previous governments from both parties, which had regulated trade union activity while working within the collective bargaining framework.[19] The Thatcher government, and that of John Major, who succeeded her, worked to change this system by both lowering the "floor" of rights and making collective bargaining and action increasingly difficult. Fundamental to this policy was the goal of promoting *individual* employment relationships at the expense of the *collective*.[20] This was a marked shift away from the reliance on collective labor activities as a means to protect workers' interests.

Thatcher's political and economic goals were a significant departure from the postwar social contract that sought to promote full employment and economic equality. Rather, Thatcher claimed that high unemployment was a "price worth paying" in order to engage in promoting economic growth, which called for lowering labor costs and privatizing assets.[21] The government sought to change the dominant opinion about trade unions in British society, from the belief that unions were legitimate representatives that improved workers' lives and economic outcomes, to the idea that union leaders were

selfish, radical, and out of touch with their members. The Conservative government had three union-related policy goals. First, its leaders sought to curb all union security (closed shop) clauses to reduce the unions' power. Second, the Conservative government wanted to curb the right to strike. Third, the government wanted to limit the power of union leaders, whom the government believed were more radical and strike-oriented than their rank and file members.[22] The legislative changes toward these goals were gradual, and complicated. These laws passed in a series of piecemeal reforms between 1980 and 1992, culminating in the passage of the 1992 Trade Union and Labour Relations Consolidation Act.[23]

The Conservative attack on British trade unions was carefully framed to emphasize general principles of fairness. For example, both Conservative governments claimed that their policies were democratic because they provided strong protection for individual workers against the power of trade unions. Yet the political justifications for these laws contradicted their actual provisions. The government claimed to promote democracy and shop floor interests through measures such as the 1984 strike ballot initiatives, which would supposedly "give unions back to their members." Yet the Conservative government did not protect workers who wished to engage in collective action *against* the wishes of trade union leaders. Rather, these new laws increased the penalties for wildcat strikes, which were member-initiated strikes not sanctioned by union leadership.[24] In addition, workers who went on a strike without their leaders' approval were not protected against dismissals.[25] The Conservatives' claims about democracy and protecting the interests of individual workers were merely justifications for their political attack on the power of unions.[26]

Despite its rhetoric of democracy and fairness, the government did not pass laws to protect workers against the power of employers. While strong penalties existed for trade unions that might discriminate against nonunion members or union members who refused to participate in collective action, no recourse was provided to protect workers from discrimination by employers for their trade union membership. For example, the laws gave workers the right to compensation if they had been either excluded or disciplined by a union, but did not provide measures to protect trade union members who had been blacklisted or discriminated against for their trade union membership.[27] Furthermore, in cases of unfair dismissal, the government changed the law to shift the burden of proof from employers to employees.[28] The Conservative government considered the power asymmetries between individual workers and the union to require more intervention than the asymmetries between employers and employees. In addition to laws that hurt the bargaining and political power of trade unions, the Conservative government mandated mail-only union executive and strike ballots, which depleted trade union resources and limited their ability to self-govern.[29]

The government also temporarily suspended collective bargaining for some public employees, despite the fact that collective bargaining and consultation between public servants and the state had been in place since 1925, and British civil servant trade unions had existed since 1947.[30] For example, the government unilaterally imposed a collective agreement overturning a past civil servants' pay law in 1981.[31] In 1984, the government suspended the rights of unionized employees at the Government Communications Headquarters (GCHQ), a state intelligence and information service. GCHQ employees could either willingly give up their membership, transfer to another sector of the civil service, or be dismissed. This action contradicted the provisions of a 1978 law, which protected workers from dismissal or action short of dismissal for trade union membership or activities.[32] The government also passed the 1987 Teachers' Pay and Conditions Act, which blocked teachers in England and Wales from collective bargaining. This act determined the terms and conditions of teachers' employment for three years. It was similar to Bills 27, 28, and 29 in British Columbia, which supplanted existing collective agreements. The ILO's Committee on Freedom of Association claimed that these laws violated the United Kingdom's commitments under ILO Conventions 87 and 98.[33]

During this period, the government also weakened protections for the right to strike and made it cumbersome to designate an industrial action as a legal strike. The Conservative government established stricter requirements, such as requiring election certification, limiting ballot rules, and requiring prior notification. Strikes were no longer legal against a secondary employer, and workers could not strike unless it was specifically over work conditions or pay. This was similar to the way the South Korean state attempted to limit legitimate strike action only to pay and work conditions. In addition, it became easier for an employer to get an injunction against a union's collective actions, granting employers greater legal latitude to interfere with workers' strikes and other collective activities. The ILO's Committee of Experts criticized these legal changes, as they no longer provided strong protections against for workers' collective action under common law liability.[34]

The government also prohibited all secondary collective actions and boycotts, such as sympathy strikes or secondary pickets, which had been commonplace in the 1960s and 1970s. The ILO Committee on Freedom of Association condemned these limitations on strike rights in 1989.[35] The Council of Europe's Committee of Independent Experts also argued that these changes to the United Kingdom's labor law violated its European Social Charter obligations. Because the European Social Charter designated trade union rights as part of its "hard core" articles, the United Kingdom had formally committed itself to both of the trade union rights articles, Article 5 and Article 6. The Committee of Experts, which evaluates every member state on its Social Charter obligations, said that Britain had violated eleven out of the sixty-two provisions in the Social Charter. To avoid more embarrassment for failing to follow legal obligations, the government announced that it would deratify Article 7(8) of the 1961 European Social Charter, the clause that forbids night work for children.[36] The United Kingdom did not commit itself to the 1989 Additional Protocol to the European Social Charter, which specified additional protections for workers.

Conservative Policy Positions on Labor Unions

The Conservative government published a number of policy papers reflecting its continued anxiety over the negative economic effects of regulation, especially labor regulation, on business and profits. The government's publications openly criticized collective bargaining. The 1992 February White Paper,[37] called *People, Jobs and Opportunity*, specifically categorized collective bargaining as an example of "outdated personnel practices" that had become "increasingly inappropriate." As a result, the White Paper said, the "government . . . will continue to encourage employers to move away from traditional, centralized collective bargaining towards methods of pay determination which reward individual skill and performance."[38] This paper ignored the status of trade union rights as basic human rights, and framed labor relations concerns only terms of "efficient" economic outcomes.

In 1991, the Employment Department published a document entitled *Industrial Relations in the 1990s*.[39] This publication both praised the changes of the 1980s and projected future needs. The paper claimed that the British industrial relations system was "generally acknowledged as the fundamental cause of the weakness of the British economy," and "damag[ed] . . . the reputation of the British economy abroad."[40] The paper claimed that the 1980s had successful reversed this trend in a number of ways. First, the reforms decreased the number of lost strike days, from an annual average of 13 million in the 1970s to an average of less than 3.4 million in the last half of the 1980s. Second, the restriction of such trade union activities as secondary and solidarity actions meant that they no longer could "depress productivity." As a result, the government believed that foreign opinions about British trade unions and industrial relations had changed for the better. The paper cited a 1987 survey of 300 foreign firms in the United Kingdom, of which 96 percent claimed that industrial relations had improved since the 1970s.[41] Here, the British government clearly privileged its reputation as a good location for foreign investment over trade union rights.

The Conservative government claimed to have successfully reigned in the permissive legislation of the prior Labour government through the achievement of major legislative goals, both "safeguard[ing] the democratic rights of trade union members within their unions" and "establish[ing] a fair balance of bargaining power between employers and trade unions." The document stated the need to protect employers and workers from "abuses of trade union power such as the closed shop and the flying picket which both damage the economy and are offensive in terms of personal freedom."[42] The flying picket was a type of industrial action that involved mobile picket lines that would show up unannounced at any of a business's many facilities and had the potential to be very disruptive. The government had established the following safeguards for employers and employers: "free choice" for workers over whether to join trade unions by ending closed shop provisions, employee choice over participation in strikes through a new pre-strike election system, the "free choice of employers to decide whether to recognize or negotiate with a trade union," and the prohibition of secondary (solidarity) collective actions. These "democratic" measures were established to create "safeguards against intimidation and irregularities." The prior notification requirement for strikes was intended to protect "businesses and jobs from the damaging effects of industrial action and to safeguard the community."[43] The need to protect workers from union power was repeated throughout the White Paper. The Conservative government's legislation would provide remedy for employees and employers and their interests, while stripping arbitrary power from unions, which were susceptible to fraud and corruption.[44]

The government predicted the continued obsolescence of the collective bargaining model under new economic conditions, which sought greater labor market flexibility, faster response rates, and attention to local needs. The White

Paper claimed that the failure of industrial relations laws and practices to keep up with current changes could even "threaten the prosperity of society as a whole."[45] It asserted that the workers knew this better than the unions, as "many employees now recognize that the old, traditional forms of collective bargaining are no longer in their own best interest." As overseas investors continued to seek stability and strike-free workplaces, more typically "modern" collective agreements were emerging. Given the new economic trends of service and technology-related employment, the government characterized trade unionism and collective bargaining as Luddite relics of an industrial and nationally based economic past.[46] The White Paper stressed that "they [workers] should also consider whether negotiating directly with their employees on an individual basis . . . [will] serve both the needs of the company and the interests of their employees better than persisting with traditional collective bargaining." As workers now sought "careers, not jobs," this made direct consultation between employers and workers more relevant than collective bargaining.[47] The absence of these burdensome third-party unions would allow an open and democratic relationship between employers and employees.

The Question of Individual Contracts: United Kingdom's Contested Trade Union Rights Violations

Domestic Legal Activism

This case study concerns two related legal cases that were eventually considered together in a number of domestic legal institutions. These included the Industrial Tribunal and the Employment Appeal Tribunal, which were labor bodies, and two general courts, the Court of Appeals and the House of Lords. Internationally these cases were examined by the ILO Committee on Freedom of Association, the UN Human Rights Committee, and then the European Court of Human Rights. They were originally called *Associated Newspapers v. Wilson* and *Associated British Ports v. Palmer and Others*; as they were later consolidated into a single case, it will herein be referred to as the *Wilson/Palmer* case. Both involved similar legal challenges by trade union members who were denied raises and eventually fired for refusing to sign individual contracts. Under these contracts, workers surrendered their collective bargaining rights in exchange for raises.[48]

David Wilson, a newspaper reporter, had worked since October 1977 in London for the *Daily Mail*, an influential conservative newspaper, and had served as the union chapel father (the British term for a local union representative).[49] There had been a long-standing in-house collective agreement between the *Daily Mail* and the National Union of Journalists, although this agreement was not legally enforceable through the statutory provisions of the time.[50] Despite the very high percentage of union members (98 percent of the workplace),[51] the employer de-recognized the National Union of Journalists in 1990, as it was legally entitled to do, and terminated the in-house agreement. The employer would no longer engage in collective bargaining with the union, but the union was allowed to meet with the employers over health and safety issues. The *Daily Mail* offered 4.5 percent raises, including backpay, to those workers who signed individual contracts before January 1990. These contracts required that workers agree to give up their rights "to be represented by a union and the right for the union to engage in collective bargaining."[52] Those who signed the collective agreement would also become eligible for future merit-based pay increases.[53] However, workers who signed the contract did not have to give up union membership.

Wilson and other trade union officials at the National Union of Journalists decided to challenge this practice under the existing antidiscrimination provisions.[54] Wilson took this issue to an industrial tribunal, which ruled in his favor in October 1990. The tribunal ruled that Associated Newspapers' refusal to grant an employee the 4.5 percent raise unless that employee signed a new individual contract did in fact constitute an "action short of dismissal" with the "purpose of deterring him from being a member of the National Union of Journalists and/or penalising him for being a member" or "taking part in [the union's] activities." The Industrial Tribunal agreed that the choice offered to the *Daily Mail* employees constituted a breach of the protections of trade union membership and activities found in the Section 23(1) of the 1978 Employment Protection (Consolidation) Act.[55] The tribunal found that the stated goal of the employer, to end collective bargaining, sought "to reduce the power of the union as to negate it totally." Such conditions would thus discourage individual journalists from union membership, and this was illegal within the scope of Section 23(1)(a). The tribunal also argued that the employer had tried to use its right to de-recognize a trade union as a way to prevent individual journalists from being trade union members.[56]

The positive ruling was surprising, even to the legal representatives of the union. John Hendy QC, the lead counsel who represented Wilson (and later Palmer) throughout this case, explained that "we relied on an indirect argument. Section 146 [the newer version of Section 23] protects against discrimination. That was quite difficult to fit; [it was] a very tricky legal argument to make."[57] In other words, the team used a creative legal strategy to locate the protection of collective bargaining rights under an antidiscrimination clause. Despite the upholding of Wilson's complaint, the *Daily Mail* filed an appeal.

A related case involving the use of individual contracts and financial inducements came soon afterward to an industrial tribunal in January 1992. The employers at Associated British Ports offered personal contracts to their employees in February 1991 as a replacement for a collective bargaining agreement with the National Union of Rail, Maritime and Transport Workers. According to the company's offer, workers who accepted the individual contract also agreed to give up "the right to be represented by a trade union," and to have their pay rates negotiated by the union. Those who did not want to sign individual contracts could continue to have their terms of employment determined by the union-negotiated collective agreement. The incentive to sign an individual contract was an increase in basic pay and new overtime calculators that allegedly worked in the employees' favor. These included a 10 percent wage increase as well as an offer of private medical insurance. By signing the individual contract, however, employees lost their rights to trade union representation and all other pay increases and conditions negotiated by the union in the collective agreement. Future pay increases would be determined by merit evaluations.[58]

The communication from the employers specifically claimed that signing the individual contract did not preclude workers from trade union membership. However, the workers who did not sign these individual contracts continued their employment under the terms of the old collective agreement. They received lesser raises (8.9 percent instead of 10 percent) and were not offered private medical insurance. Several of the resistant employees, including Terrence Palmer, Brian Stedman, and Arthur Wyeth, complained to the local Industrial Tribunal that this action violated section 23(1)(a) of the 1978 Employment Protection (Consolidation) Act. They claimed that they received £150 less than coworkers doing the same work because they had not signed the individual contract. The National Union of Rail, Maritime and Transport Workers had not yet been de-recognized, but in 1992, the employer sent a communication that it was ending the collective agreement and would no longer recognize the union.[59]

The tribunal accepted that the purpose of Associated British Ports may have been to encourage benefits for those employees who signed the individual contracts, but the goal of greater flexibility required the "purpose" of persuading employees to abandon their right to union representation. Therefore, the employer's actions constituted an action short of dismissal under Section 23 of the Employment Protection (Consolidation) Act of 1978 and the applicants thus were qualified for compensation.[60] The key decision was that the employers' denial of the pay raise to those employees who did not take individual contracts was intended to *penalize* them for choosing not to give up union representation, an action that contravened the provisions of the Employment Protection (Consolidation) Act of 1978, Section 23(1)(a).[61] Both the Wilson and the Palmer cases ruled unanimously in favor of the trade unionists' positions.

In response, both Associated Newspapers and Associated British Ports appealed the decisions to the Employment Appeal Tribunal, the judicial institution for appealing Industrial Tribunal decisions. The Wilson case, decided on June 25, 1992, ruled in favor of Associated Newspapers for a number of reasons. The employers' failure to give a 4.5 percent pay raise to those employees who did not sign individual contracts did not constitute a violation of section 23(1)(a) of the Employment Protection (Consolidation) Act. According to the Employment Appeal Tribunal, individuals that signed the contract could still hold union membership and the trade union could advocate on certain issues to an employer on the member's behalf.[62] Therefore, signing an individual contract did not infringe upon an individual's right to union membership. Since the employee was not faced with the choice between accepting an individual contract and leaving employment, Section 23(1)(a) did not apply in this case, as the law only protected *individuals* from actions "short of dismissal." The Employment Appeal Tribunal also disagreed with the Industrial Tribunal's claim that allowing these contracts "reduce[s] the power of the union as to negate it totally." Rather, the appeal tribunal stated that the issuing of individual contracts would not render the National Union of Journalists powerless, as it still had the power to provide legal, financial, and health and safety advice services.[63]

In the Palmer case, decided on October 13, 1992, the Employment Appeal Tribunal also reversed the prior Industrial Tribunal's decision. While Section 23(1)(a) protected workers from action short of a dismissal "taken against him as an individual for the purpose of preventing or deterring him from being or seeking to become a member of an independent trade union," the Employment Appeal Tribunal argued that "flexibility was the [employers'] purpose, [while] ending union representation the means of achieving it."[64] Therefore, the employer's offer of the individual contracts did not fall under the terms of Section 23(1)(a) of the 1978 act. The action was neither individually oriented nor did it constitute a genuine threat to trade union membership. Section 23(1)(a) did not provide an employee the right to be represented by a trade union in negotiations with an employer with regard to pay. Therefore, the tribunal ruled that there was no statutory right for union representation in Section 23(1)(a).[65]

After these reversals by the Employment Appeal Tribunal, the cases were considered simultaneously by the Court of Appeal, a general judicial appeals body, in April 1993. At this point, the prior 1978 law had been included within section 148 of the new Trade Union and Labour Relations Consolidation Act of 1992. [66] The Court of Appeal upheld the original decisions of the Industrial Tribunals, overturning the decisions of the Employment Appeal Tribunals. The Court of Appeal ruled that the employers' purpose in introducing the individual contracts was indeed to "penalize" those who did not sign them and to create disincentives for union membership. As a result, the court upheld the original decisions that the employers' actions violated what was now section 148 of the 1992 act. Although the Employment Appeal Tribunals had ruled that the employers had merely engaged in "*omission*," the Court of Appeal argued that an omission to provide the same benefits to trade union members was in fact discriminatory.[67] This ruling in favor of the trade unionists elicited strong reactions from the employers' barrister, who in violation of decorum of the court clenched his visibly white fist and stated that the judge had made a mistake.[68]

The Court of Appeal argued that trade union membership was not limited to merely having a union card and one's name on a union member registry.[69] This ruling concurred with a dissenting opinion of the Employment Appeal Tribunal that the employers had made individual contracts so attractive that the union would thus "wither on the vine."[70] The Court of Appeal rejected the Employment Appeal Tribunal's majority claim that de-recognition, change in terms of employment, and the conditional 4.5 percent wage increase did not deter journalists from maintaining union membership. According to the testimonies from the trade union chapel and a major editor at the *Daily Mail*, the trade union would prove irrelevant within two years of the issuing of individual contracts.[71] The Court of Appeal noted that if Associated Newspapers had merely de-recognized the union and changed conditions of employment, this would not have qualified under the protections of Article (23)(1)(a). But because the employer had conditioned individual 4.5 percent pay raises on the signing of individual contracts, this constituted an individual "action short of dismissal."

This unanimous Court of Appeal decision in favor of the workers was rendered on April 30, 1993. But the Conservative government seemed unwilling to accept it. On May 6, the Conservative-dominated Parliament engaged in the scheduled third reading of an employment bill, the Trade Union Reform and Employment Rights Act of 1993.[72] Despite established legislative procedures, an amendment was published as late as possible (on Thursday, May 20), soon after the recent Court of Appeal decision in the Wilson/Palmer case. It passed on Monday, May 24.[73] This amendment, called the Ullswater Amendment (section 13) of the Trade Union and Labour Relations Reform Act of 1993, added a new subsection (3) to Section 148 of the 1992 Trade Union and Labour Relations Consolidation Act. The amendment altered Section 146 (which protected workers from action short of dismissal for trade union membership and related activities), allowing employers to engage in actions as long as the employer's purpose was "to further a change in his relationship with all or any class of his employees."[74]

This controversial amendment met significant opposition, although not strong enough to stop its passage. Many key Labour MPs, such as Tony Blair, Gordon Brown, and Robin Cook, voted against the amendment. A number of Labour MPs went on public record stating that this was a violation of basic civil liberties, and even the antithesis of democracy. One MP charged the new law with turning back the clock on the earliest laws protecting trade union rights in Britain.[75] The Trades Union Congress (TUC), the largest national trade union federation in the United Kingdom,[76] described the hasty addition of the Ullswater Amendment as being "in open conflict of normal parliamentary procedure."[77] The speedy passage of the Ullswater Amendment resembled the passage of both British Columbia's contested Bill 29 and South Korea's first draft of the Trade Union and Labour Relations Adjustment Act of 1996. These other laws were rushed through in nonstandard, stealthy procedures.

The Ullswater Amendment was exceptional not only because it clearly violated the United Kingdom's international labor rights obligations, but also because it happened just five working days after the Court of Appeal ruled that the use of such inducements was illegal. The amendment was introduced even before the transcript of that decision had been made publicly available. John Hendy QC stated that "[while] the 1993 Court of Appeal was not considered controversial, [it was] politically controversial because of the subsequent amendment. The Ullswater [amendment] was unique and unprecedented. Amendments usually take a much longer period of time."[78] The amendment, to Section 13 of the bill, considerably limited the ability of an employment tribunal to examine whether an employer's actions prevents or deters a worker from being or becoming a member of a trade union and "thus practically compels a tribunal to reject a victimization complaint."[79] According to the government, this amendment was a necessary clarification that would allow an employer to act freely to change their negotiating situation. The unanimous Court of Appeal decision was legally overturned by this law without "due consideration." As a result, under the new amendment, an Industrial Tribunal could not hold an employer responsible for actions that would have the consequence of preventing an employee from being a trade union member, if the tribunal determined that such an outcome was not the employer's primary intention.[80]

Despite the legal protections from the Ullswater Amendment, the employer appealed to the House of Lords, Britain's highest court after the Court of Appeal judgment. The resulting House of Lords' decision, dated March 16, 1995, reversed the Court of Appeal's decision on *Wilson v. Associated Newspapers Ltd.* and *Palmer v. Associated British Ports.* The Law Lords ruled 4 out of 5 in favor of the employers. The decision was based on two main arguments. The first argument—the *construction issue*—dealt with whether the employers' behavior constituted the kind of action short of dismissal covered by section 23(1)(a) of the Employment Protection (Consolidation) Act of 1978.[81] The Law Lords held that the Court of Appeal's decision did not recognize the issue in question as an *omission*. When employers withheld a benefit from an employee, it was an "omission," whereas the 1978 law sought to protect workers from antiunion discriminatory *action*. Secondly, the Law Lords claimed that there was insufficient evidence at the original Industrial Tribunal to establish that the employers' purpose was to "deter" or penalize trade union *membership*, although arguably the employers may have acted to discourage the use of some union services or to make union membership less attractive. Since in both the Wilson and Palmer cases the employee litigants were able to maintain their trade union membership, the Law Lords argued that the primary "purpose" of the pay raises was to ensure individually negotiated contracts, not to deter union membership.[82] The Lords reasoned there was insufficient evidence to show that the employers had sought *primarily* to discourage union membership, which would have been a clear violation of the Employment Protection (Consolidation) Act of 1978. Therefore, the evidence suggested that the employers in each case were primarily concerned about getting rid of collective bargaining to promote greater employment flexibility, not to discourage trade union membership.[83]

International Criticisms of Rights Violations: The United Kingdom and the Normative Negotiation Process

Given that it had almost exhausted every domestic legal and legislative institution, the Trades Union Congress filed a complaint with the ILO's Committee on Freedom of Association following the passage of the 1993 Act (prior to the Law Lords' decision), under case 1730. The TUC claimed that the amendment to Section 13 of the Trade Union Reform and Employment Rights Act of 1993 violated Conventions 87 and 98. The government argued that the allegations were untrue. While British law explicitly prohibited discrimination against workers who wanted to be in labor unions, the government claimed that this did not include a protection for workers who seek to engage in collective bargaining. The government's communications to the ILO insisted on the maintenance of a distinction between an individual's *right to be a member of union* and the idea that a "union should be entitled to insist that an employer bargains (or continues to bargain) with it over employees' terms and conditions of employment."[84] The government communicated that the United Kingdom encouraged voluntary collective representation, but maintained that "if the employer withdraws recognition from the union, or takes steps to encourage workers to cease being collectively represented by it, that act does not prejudice the worker by reason of his or her union membership. The worker is exactly as free to belong to the union as would be the case if the union had never been granted collective representational rights in the first place."[85]

The government's report maintained that there was a clear distinction between trade union membership and access to collective bargaining. In other words, collective bargaining was an activity of trade unions and, therefore, was unrelated to whether the state effectively protected workers from discrimination based on trade union membership. The government also defended its eleventh-hour change to the 1993 Act as being in no way related to demands made by the employers involved in the Wilson or Palmer cases.[86] In its communications with the ILO, the government reiterated: "Section 13 of the TURER was not introduced as an attack on trade union membership rights, but rather was intended to ensure that there was no fetter on the ability of employers to change their negotiating arrangement and to make clear that the right not to be discriminated against on trade union membership grounds did not include or imply a right to have one's terms and conditions negotiated by collective bargaining."[87]

The government supported these claims, despite how Parliament acted against established legislative procedure. The date of the bill's third reading, May 6, 1993, was the eighth and typically final step of the legislative process. New additions or amendments to bills are usually not made at this stage. Yet the addition of the Ullswater Amendment was announced on May 6, even though it had not even been mentioned in the government's prior White Paper. This meant that there could be no discussion among or consultation with social partners, such as trade unions or business representatives. The amendment was made public on Thursday, May 20, and passed on Monday, May 24. The TUC argued that the urgency of the amendment did not make sense if its introduction was not connected to the recent Court of Appeal decision. If in fact Ullswater had been a pressing point of law requiring clarification, the TUC pointed out that the government could have changed it at any time since 1979 or included the issue within the White Paper.[88] Its absence from the White Paper and its close proximity to the court decision made the Ullswater Amendment seem like a political response to the Court of Appeal's protection of workers' rights.

In its recommendations regarding this case, the ILO committee found that the introduction of the amendment at the third reading of the bill, just five days after the Court of Appeal's crucial judgment, suggested "unusual alacrity."[89] Such a late-stage amendment did not allow for serious discussion. The ILO committee argued that if employees who refused to give up their right to collective bargaining were denied a pay increase as a result, this was incompatible with the principles of freedom of association, especially Article 1(2)(b) of Convention 98, and Article 4. The committee argued that section 13(3) of the 1993 Act was so "wide and vague" that "in virtually any situation . . . the tribunal would then be practically compelled to reject a victimization complaint, save the extraordinary circumstances."[90] It rejected the government's argument regarding the separation between the right to trade union membership and the right to collective bargaining, and it found the new amendment to "emasculate" the provisions in the ILO conventions. As a result, the committee recommended that the government reconsider the amendment of section 13 of the 1993 act, and cooperate with both employers' and workers' associations regarding this legislation.[91]

After the Law Lords' 1995 decision, which further went against ILO recommendations, the TUC presented this development to the ILO committee, under case 1852, and claimed that the ruling removed protections intended to keep workers from being victimized because of their union membership.

David Wilson had since been fired because of his trade union activity, and the TUC brought forward a new case in which an employer attempted to persuade employees to give up their rights to a collective agreement.[92] In its response to the ILO committee, dated November 8, 1995, the government reiterated its position: Amendment 13 was not an attack on trade union membership rights but rather a way to ensure that there were no limitations on an employer's ability to "change their negotiating arrangements." The amendment was therefore necessary to clarify that the right not to be discriminated against based on trade union membership "did not include or imply a right to have one's terms and conditions negotiated by collective bargaining."[93] British law already protected individuals from refusal of employment, dismissal, or action short of dismissal on trade union membership grounds. According to the government, employers' offers to workers of incentives to enter into contracts with terms and conditions that had not been negotiated collectively did not take away their opportunity to be a union member. Rather, this represented a prerogative of an employer to change the nature of the employment relationship.[94] Here, the British government was maintaining the distinction between the right to be a union member and the right for unions to engage in consultation and collective bargaining.

The Law Lords' case and the continued problems of employer tactics to discourage collective bargaining became an important concern for both the ILO Committee on Freedom of Association and ILO's Committee of Experts on the Application of Conventions and Recommendations (CEACR). The CEACR, which monitors state compliance with ratified conventions, noted that the 1995 House of Lords' judgments had "reinforced [the CEACR's] apprehensions that the legislative protection to be afforded to workers against acts of anti-union discrimination by virtue of Article 1 of Convention No. 98 seems to be insufficient."[95] The Committee on Freedom of Association reiterated that the Ullswater Amendment, in protecting employers' prerogatives, violated the United Kingdom's obligations under Convention 98 to encourage collective bargaining, as the law allowed a "situation wherein collective bargaining is easily and effectively discouraged instead of being encouraged."[96] The committee once again called on the government to amend the Ullswater Amendment.

These cases also received attention from the United Nations human rights monitoring bodies. For example, in November 1997, during a meeting of the Committee on Economic, Social and Cultural Rights, members raised concerns about the *Wilson/Palmer* case and the British domestic court rulings. Referencing the ILO committee's 1996 recommendation that the United Kingdom change its laws and practices accordingly, the Economic, Social and Cultural Rights Committee members expressed the view that the use of inducements to compel workers to give up collective bargaining was a violation of their freedom of association. The committee also asked why the government had not committed to changing Section 13 of the 1993 Trade Union Reform and Employment Rights Act. The British representative said that the use of inducements would be dealt with in an upcoming White Paper (produced by the new Labour government) on fair employment.[97] The committee found this practice of discrimination, related to the conditional granting of pay increases, a violation of Article 8 of the Covenant on Economic, Social and Cultural Rights. In its "Concluding Observations," the Economic, Social and Cultural Rights Committee recommended "that the right of employers to grant financial incentives to employees who do not join unions be abolished."[98]

The Committee of Independent Experts (COIE) at the Council of Europe also considered the recommendations of the ILO and UN committees in its own evaluations. The COIE, the body charged with monitoring member states' compliance with the European Social Charter, found the United Kingdom to be in breach of Articles 5 and 6(2).[99] The violated rights included both the right to organize and the right to collective bargaining. In 1995, the Committee of Experts examined Section 13 (the Ullswater Amendment) of the 1993 Act and stated that while an employer could "legitimately" seek to change his bargaining position, in the *Wilson/Palmer* case, employers "had the obvious intention of persuading their employees to relinquish trade union activities and collective bargaining." Therefore, the COIE found this amendment violated the Social Charter. The clause was so general that "only in exceptional cases would a tribunal be able to rule that the action taken by the employer was unlawful." The COIE further argued that collective bargaining was a "fundamental trade union prerogative" and that restricting collective bargaining could "amount to an infringement of the very nature of trade union freedom."[100] According to the COIE, the United Kingdom needed to amend section 13 of the 1993 Act to fulfill its obligations with the charter. The Committee of Ministers later endorsed this recommendation, and the COIE reiterated its criticism in both 1997 and 2000.[101]

Yet despite this consensus among a number of international institutions, these recommendations seemed to have little effect on the Conservative government. Breen Creighton, a labor lawyer, wrote that the ILO's observations had no impact at all on the government. The government refused to bring British law into compliance with international standards. In fact, it even went so far as to claim that there was no breach of international obligations.[102] An employment rights officer from the TUC believed that "the ILO [recommendations] had no direct impact."[103] John Hendy likewise stated, "the [ILO] decision did not result in any government response. They [government leaders] flouted the situation."[104] The explanation for this lack of influence is simple: the Conservative governments did not see compliance with international institutions as relevant to their goal of a more individualist and economically efficient Britain.

The Conservative government's behavior toward international institutions suggests a "go it alone" attitude. For example, during the Conservative governments, the United Kingdom denounced thirteen ILO conventions (although one had been declared obsolete by the ILO itself). In addition, the government refused to participate in a number of European-based initiatives. For example, it did not ratify the two protocols on expanding the Council of Europe's European Social Charter. The government also refused to join the European Union's (EC) 1989 Community Charter of the Fundamental Social Rights of Workers and the Social Chapter of the 1993 Maastricht Treaty.[105] International engagement on human and social rights was not an important element of the Conservative governments' political agenda.

New Labour and New Opportunities

The New Labour government under Tony Blair came into power in May 1997 after eighteen years of Conservative rule.[106] One might expect that a social democratic party with historic ties to trade unions would better protect trade union rights. As it won a significant majority of parliamentary seats, Labour could have fixed trade union rights problems to better comply with international standards without compromising with the opposition party.[107] However, it did not do so.

By the early 1990s, Labour began to distance itself from trade unions in response to Conservatives' successful attacks on them. The shadow cabinet[108] began to deliberately detach itself from trade union issues. Tony Blair, who served as the shadow Employment spokesman between 1989 and the 1992 election, mostly accepted the Conservatives' changes to labor rights and other industrial relations laws.[109] He publicly stated his support for the Conservative ban on closed shops and claimed that a Labour government would also protect workers' rights not to join unions.[110] Labour continued to weaken its historic ties to trade unions during the 1992 election. Although trade union donations historically provided around 90 percent of the party's funding, and union representatives received significant voting blocs at Labour Party conferences, the percentage of funding by trade unions continued to fall, to 50 percent in 1995 and 33 percent in 1996.[111] The party began to rely more on individual and business donations. The year 1992 was also the first year that the Trades Union Congress did not formally endorse Labour candidates. Although trade unions still favored the Labour Party, they had decided that silence might work in Labour's favor, given unions' political marginalization.[112]

As the Labour party began to build toward a fourth electoral challenge in 1997, it continued to distance itself from trade unions. In November 1994, "No Favours" Blair, as the opposition leader, stressed that Labour's new strategy was to show the British public that it would not "buckle" under trade union pressure. Instead, New Labour promised a policy of modernization, flexibility, and growth. Blair stated in his speech that "Unions, working intelligently and flexibly, can back up the efforts of individuals in the workplace." Unions were to continue to be subsumed under a larger framework of the primacy of the individual and flexibility, and Labour would curb their activities, just as under the Conservative government.[113]

This cautious approach to trade union interests and rights was expressed in the Labour Party's 1996 Road to the Manifesto document, entitled *Building Prosperity—Flexibility, Efficiency and Fairness at Work*. This document stressed the importance of labor market flexibility, legal restraints on trade union action, and the system of minimum standards encapsulated in the EU social model.[114] This reflected Blair's "prudent" economic management strategy, which he cautiously presented to allay the fears of the business community.[115] Like Kim Dae Jung, who identified himself with Tony Blair, Blair himself had to convince investors and employers that New Labour was independent of trade unions.

According to the pre-manifesto document, New Labour adhered to the following three principles: (1) the guarantee of minimum standards for all workers, (2) the promotion of labor market flexibility, and (3) job security. New Labour sought to promote job security through "employability," meaning that it would help British workers maintain secure jobs through training and skills development. This was a rejection of the historic use of collective bargaining as the best means of protecting workers; Labour instead sought to establish individual employment rights, to create a "partnership" between employers and employees.[116] Labour's subsequent manifesto for the 1997 election included a platform on trade unions and industrial relations law, but this platform did not criticize past Conservative governments' violations of trade union rights.

During the 1997 campaign, Conservative party members and other business leaders began to criticize Labour for its stance toward both the European Union Social Chapter and the proposed compulsory union recognition laws. This put Labour on the defensive, forcing it to tone down its commitments to trade unions.[117] In addition, Tony Blair and other Labour leaders articulated their support for many of the changes to labor law that had been made during the Thatcher/Major period, reiterating their pledge for "fairness not favors," and promising that "there will be no return to the trade union laws of the 1970s."[118] Blair stated that New Labour was new precisely because of its commitment to promoting business interests and fiscal moderation, its movement away from public ownership, and its status as wholly independent of trade union interests. This strategy was so effective that the business-friendly *Financial Times* endorsed Blair in 1997.[119] Like the Conservative government, Blair used rhetoric that suggested that British trade unions were coercing the nation and distorting its economy. He told the *Sun* newspaper in the month before the election that "we will not be held ransom by unions. We will stand up to strikes. We will not cave in to unrealistic pay demands from anyone."[120] These statements, both during the campaign and afterward in policy papers, demonstrated that even the historic ties between Labour and trade unions did not *guarantee* the protection of their basic rights. In addition, they parroted the earlier rhetoric of the Conservative government that trade unions bullied employers.

This is not to underemphasize the institutional links between Labour and trade unions in the United Kingdom. Labour and the trade unions were now less connected in three ways: institutionally, with fewer representatives at Labour meetings; economically, as more funding for the party now came from nonunion contributions; and politically, as Labour moved away from the political interests of trade unions. Yet a relationship between the party and unions still existed. It is comparable to the relationship between liberal Democrats and large trade unions in the United States. During their time as the opposition, Labour leaders still held regular meetings with trade unionists. For instance, Tony Blair and other Labour leaders met with National Union of Journalists' representatives during the 1990s to discuss the reorganization of media industries and unfair labor practices. According to a former secretary general of the NUJ, Blair willingly met with union leaders every six months or so, but he was "scared of [Rupert] Murdoch [president of Fox/Sky News] and the newspapers because you can't win elections without them."[121] Regardless of the personal ideological commitments of Labour's leaders, their official distance from the issue of trade union rights was a matter of political strategy. The NUJ representative stated, "the biggest challenge was to get Labour on board. . . . [They] were frightened to be associated with a trade union."[122] According to Stephen Cavalier, solicitor for the National Union of Journalists and David Wilson, "collective bargaining rights [were] not a priority of the government. Labour would claim to support collective bargaining but most legislation [was focused] on individual labor rights."[123]

The Labour government did offer some weak commitments to the ILO during the International Labour Conference immediately after the 1997 election. However, the newly elected government did not commit to complying with all of the ILO's recommendations. In fact, the Labour government steadfastly maintained some of the prior Conservative government's legal provisions, despite their condemnation by the Committee on Freedom of Association.[124] According to Employment Minister Andrew Smith, the "UK [had a] wholehearted commitment to human rights and . . . the ILO's efforts to promote internationally recognized core labour standards," but the government primarily sought to "promote the employability of our people and the economic responsiveness of both employers and employees . . . [and though] every person has the right to decent minimum standards . . . we must guard against excessive regulation."[125] Mr. Smith stated certain commitments of the United Kingdom with regard to its core labor standards. He pointed to the lifting of the ban on GCHQ workers' trade union rights as an example of the government's intention to follow through on its pledge.[126] The government also communicated in December 1997 that its upcoming White Paper on employment reform would address long-standing problems such as blacklists[127] and the issue of trade union discrimination in case 1852.[128] This change in tone toward the ILO committee suggested a change in the United Kingdom's approach to its international labor rights obligations, yet these communications continued to emphasize the importance of flexibility.

Yet the follow-up legislation did not represent either a commitment to the ILO's recommendations or to international norms in general. The first real evidence of the Labour government's response to trade union rights claims was contained in its May 1998 White Paper, *Fairness at Work*. This document outlined the Labour government's plan to make *some* changes to the Conservative government's overhaul of the industrial relations system. Instead of returning to the old system of rights and protections for trade unions, the

White Paper called for a "third way" in industrial relations. This approach would include some protections for union activity, such as a system for statutory trade union recognition, but would mostly promote individual-level labor protections. Such a compromise would supposedly "match rights with responsibilities." *Fairness at Work* declared that "the days of strikes without ballots, mass picketing, closed shops and secondary action are over" and assured British citizens that "even after the changes we propose, Britain will [still] have the most lightly regulated labour market of any leading economy in the world."[129] This statement demonstrates how the new "center-left" government was reluctant to regulate labor markets to better protect trade union rights. In return for new rights, "we will demand that employees in return accept their responsibilities to co-operate with employers. There will be no return to the days of industrial conflict."[130] The government's proposals were justified under the rubric of fairness and decency in the capital-labor "partnership" but made no reference to international standards, legal obligations, or rights.[131]

Labour's 1998 White Paper did include modest proposals for "collective rights," including some trade union rights. Although these proposals did not include specific references to the international institutions' recommendations, they did mention the legislative problems that emerged with the results of the Wilson case. The paper condemned the House of Lords' decision in the *Wilson/Palmer* case and vowed to get rid of discriminatory antiunion practices. The government pledged in its White Paper to "make it unlawful to discriminate by omission on grounds of trade union membership, non-membership or activities."[132] However, the White Paper did not make strong commitments to protect collective bargaining rights, continuing to separate individual's rights to union membership from the protection of trade union activities.

Employment Relations Act of 1999

The legislation resulting from the prescriptions of the *Fairness at Work* White Paper was the Employment Relations Act of 1999. As promised, this Act amended the prior 1992 Trade Union and Labor Relations Consolidation Act. It included provisions for statutory recognition procedures for trade unions, based on elections overseen by the Central Arbitration Council, with strict voting requirements.[133] Although in the past collective bargaining was only possible if the employer voluntarily recognized a union, the new statutory recognition procedure compelled employers to engage in bargaining over holidays, work hours, and pay.[134] The law also outlawed an employer's use of blacklists (against trade union members and activists) and unfair dismissals.[135] In addition, the law restored the right to trade union membership for workers at the GCHQ. Both the Trades Union Congress and the Confederation of British Industries, the major employers' organization, expressed some degree of satisfaction in a later review of the final bill, although the TUC also expressed the need for deeper reforms to protect trade union rights, especially with regard to Wilson case–related issues.[136]

Many of these changes did address the ILO committee's recommendations, as had been promised in the White Paper. The issue of blacklists had been the subject of a long-term ILO Committee on Freedom of Association case (no. 1618) dating back to 1992. The committee had found the justifications of the Conservative government to be insufficient. The Conservative government had claimed that the Economic League (the creator of these antiunion blacklists) had been dissolved and that the 1993 Trade Union Reform and Employment Rights Act gave greater freedom for workers to litigate against antiunion dismissals. The Labour government had pledged to outlaw the blacklists and pass stricter privacy laws in 1997, and these commitments were fulfilled in both the 1999 Act and the earlier 1998 Data Protection Act.[137]

The Employment Relations Act also dealt with the ongoing issue of GCHQ workers' trade union rights, which had been a subject of ILO examination starting in 1984. In response to serious of strikes, between 1979 and 1981, GCHQ workers were informed they had to either relinquish trade union membership or their employment. The government defended its practices based on state security needs to the ILO because the GCHQ workers were engaged in sensitive, confidential, and intelligence-related work. The ILO committee had argued that this violated workers' basic rights, and the ILO Committee of Experts suggested that the case be brought to the International Court of Justice. The United Kingdom refused. In 1988, the Council of Europe's European Commission of Human Rights rejected the case on the grounds that GCHQ workers were engaged in "administration of the state" that was similar in nature to the work of the armed forces.[138] The ILO committee continued to examine the details of this case and urged the government to amend the laws, but the British government would mirror the European Commission of Human Rights' decision. In the meantime, the remaining trade union members at GCHQ were dismissed.[139] In 1997, Tony Blair made this a campaign issue, and their rights (but not their strike rights) were restored with the 1999 Employment Relations Act.

Yet while the 1999 Act was intended to address the concerns about the GCHQ and blacklist cases at the ILO, the new law did not sufficiently deal with the legal loopholes exposed by the Wilson case. The government claimed that its recent changes, schedule 2 of article 146(1) of the Trade Union Labor Relations Consolidation Act, was a direct response to the House of Lords' ruling on the Wilson case. The Law Lords decision argued that the law did not protect against "omission" and therefore if employers withheld benefits, this did not constitute a legal violation. The 1999 Employment Relations Act now granted workers the right not to be "subjected to any detriment as an individual by any act, or any deliberate failure to act, by his employer."[140] In addition, Section 17 authorized the Secretary of State to protect workers who were dismissed or otherwise penalized for refusing to enter into an individual contract that had terms different from those in the collective agreement. Such an offer of an individual contract was considered a "detriment" under the new law.

However, employers were allowed to offer individual contracts with "financial incentives,"[141] as long the workers who signed the individual contracts were allowed to remain trade union members. Such financial incentives could include the payment of higher wages, improvement of overtime, or better rates of pay.[142] In other words, the bill continued to allow employers the ability to offers workers individual contracts, forgoing collective bargaining, as long as workers were not coerced into signing the contract. The law understood coercion as the threat of detriment or penalty.

Therefore, the provisions of the Employment Relations Act of 1999, in terms of the *Wilson/Palmer* case, were confusing. The government sought both to protect workers from the offer of individual contracts that differed from the terms of the collective agreement if it were a detriment by "omission" while still allowing the employer freedom to offer individual contracts, if said employer sought to reorganize the business. The Trades Union Congress, in its report of the 1999 Act to its members, stated that it was unclear how this might be interpreted in an Employment Tribunal. A tribunal would have to figure out if "favourable treatment, permissible under the law, in fact [also] constituted detriment by omission, [which] was not permissible under the law."[143] Likewise, labor scholars agreed that these provisions did not sufficiently deal with a *Wilson*-like situation. For example, Keith Ewing argued that it remained "possible for an employer to discriminate against trade unionists (by commission and omission) on questions of pay and otherwise; indeed it will continue to be possible to do so after the regulations are made except to the extent that certain forms of conduct are expressly forbidden."[144]

The politics during the drafting of the 1999 Employment Relations Act reflects the government's reluctance to provide stronger provisions to prevent another *Wilson*-type scenario. While some protections were extended to prevent limited cases of antiunion discrimination, no further protections were extended for workers to actually enjoy trade union benefits such as collective bargaining. In other words, the 1999 Act did not deal with the Ullswater Amendment, despite heavy petitioning from the TUC. Within the debates in the House of the Lords, the Government Minister Lord McIntosh stated that "the right to belong to a trade union is separate from any rights to collective bargaining . . . the existing law makes that distinction and we wish to preserve it."[145] A TUC report stated that at the last minute of the debate, the Conservative party introduced an amendment that reinforced Ullswater, continuing to allow the practice of providing individual contracts to convince workers to forgo collective agreements.[146] The 1999 Act failed to address the primary concerns raised by the *Wilson/Palmer* case, as it would still be legal for an employer to offer incentives as a means to get workers to give up their rights to trade union representation and collective bargaining.[147]

European Court of Human Rights

In September and October 1995, individual applicants Wilson, Palmer, Wyeth, and later Doolan, Farrugia, Jenkins, and others, with their unions the National Union of Journalists and National Union of Rail, Maritime, and Transport Workers, brought applications to the European Commission of Human Rights under Article 25 of the European Convention for the Protection of Human Rights and Fundamental Freedoms.[148] They alleged that British law did not adequately protect workers from discrimination by employers based on their representation (or seeking of representation) by a trade union and that it did not protect a worker from discrimination if he or she did not want to accept the removal or denial of trade union representation. The Trades Union Congress and the applicants' representatives also presented an update regarding their problems with the 1999 Act to the European Court. The unions claimed that the 1999 Act did not contain protections for workers who are either threatened by discrimination or offered some type of incentive to give up the benefits of union representation. Unions had no legal recourse against employers who tried to convince workers to give up their rights to collective bargaining.[149] It remained possible for employers to get workers to *contractually opt out of a basic human right.*

The applicants sought protection under Articles 10, 11, and 14 of the European Convention. These articles protected Freedom of Expression, Freedom of Association, and Freedom from Discrimination. Their applications were accepted in February 1997, but after the Court changed the composition of its sections in November 2001 (as explained in Chapter 2), the case was reassigned to the Court's Second Section. The public hearing took place in January 2002, and a decision was given in July of that year. The applicants, Wilson, Palmer, and others, had argued in their initial written communication to the court that despite the government's recent employment law changes, the law still did not protect workers from the relevant problems.[150] Moreover, the law protected "trade union membership as such" but not "the use of trade union services," including access to collective bargaining. This distinction had led to substantial limitations on the ability of trade unions to protect the interests of their members.[151] The applicants also referenced the findings and recommendations of the European Social Charter's Committee of Experts and the ILO's Committee on Freedom of Association.

The Blair government responded to the inquiries of the European Court of Human Rights with an almost verbatim repetition of the Conservative government's prior responses. The Labour government submitted its communication to the Court in September 1999, arguing that British law did not violate its European Convention of Human Rights commitments. First, the government strongly defended the Law Lords' ruling in the Wilson case. Specifically, the government claimed that the employers had not offered personal contracts with the *primary purpose* of deterring applicants from being members of a trade union. The government repeated the Law Lords' distinction between membership in a trade union and the use of union services for collective bargaining purposes.[152] Second, the government claimed that the changes to the law contained in the 1999 Employment Relations Act sufficiently dealt with the legal questions that the controversial cases had raised. An employer who denied a worker a pay increase because of his or her trade union membership would be in violation of the revised section 146 of the Trade Union and Labour Relations Consolidation Act.

The government also cited past case law of the European Court of Human Rights, which did not privilege trade unions' collective rights and gave states a "wide margin of appreciation" on protecting trade union freedoms, particularly given the sensitive and political nature of national industrial relations systems. These principles came from the *Belgian Police, Gustafsson,* and *Swedish Engine Drivers* cases, which established that Article 11 was not meant to regulate or encourage state intervention in specific industrial relations disputes.[153] The government also argued that the rights to trade union representation, collective bargaining, and trade union recognition were not "inherent" in Article 11 of the Convention.[154] In addition, the government claimed that trade unions had many other means to protect the interests of workers beyond collective bargaining, such as training, services, legal support, and political work. Trade unions were also free to advocate on a member's behalf regardless of their recognition status, as allowed under British law. Therefore the relevant statutory provisions were not in violation of Article 11's language protecting workers' rights to form and join trade unions for the protection of their interests.[155] The government also defended the spirit of the Ullswater Amendment, stating that the employers' actions were justified if they were protecting their own interests. The government's communication stated: "Employers may have an interest in being free from the obligation to recognise trade unions or to make collective agreements with them; and workers may wish to exercise their freedom to belong to a trade union whilst retaining their right personally to negotiate their own contract terms."[156] The government's claim suggested that the offering of these individual contracts was a mutually beneficial situation that, therefore, did not constitute a rights violation.

The U.K. government's choice to defend its practices and laws to the European Court of Human Rights represents a political decision. The Court process is lengthy and governments can sidestep it entirely through negotiated settlement. When a case is brought against a state, the state does not need to challenge the application. After the Court (or, in the past, the Commission) decides whether or not a case is admissible, the case is then referred to the Chamber, which invites the state and the applicants to send evidence and written observations. A hearing may also be held. Instead of a court hearing, a state can choose to engage in negotiations between its representatives and those of the applicants to make a friendly settlement. This procedure allows a state to avoid a decision by the Court, and also saves time and resources. Yet, in this instance, the British government decided to contest the case all the way to a final decision, taking a firm stance against the claims of the applicants. Stephen Cavalier said in an interview, "it was disappointing that the new Labour Government did not close the legal loophole that allowed the discrimination suffered by David Wilson and others. It was equally disappointing that the Government chose to go on fighting the case."[157]

The European Court of Human Rights made its final decision in July 2002.

The Court, after hearing the arguments from both sides, ruled in favor of the applicants, Wilson et al. and the unions. The Court argued that if employees were to have the right to join unions for the protection for their interests, they "should be free to instruct or permit the union to make representations to their employer or to take action in support of their interests on their behalf." If this was not possible, the Court argued, then the rights protected by Article 11 "become illusory." The court also countered the government's claim that the state is not responsible for the action of private employers, which was significant given that the European Court only deals with states' violations of human rights. In response, the Court argued that the state is responsible for ensuring that "trade union members are not prevented or restrained from using their union to represent them in attempts to regulate their relations with their employers." The United Kingdom's law did allow employers to "effectively undermine or frustrate a trade union's ability" to protect their members' interests. Specific reference was made to the recommendations of both the ILO Committee on Freedom of Association and the European Social Charter's Committee of Independent Experts.[158] The Court granted some non-pecuniary damages (7,730€) to the individual applicants but did not agree to pay damages to the unions.[159] Of the seven judges, six were of the majority opinion. This included the United Kingdom's Lord Phillips, who was the Master of the Rolls.

Legislative Response: Employment Relations Act of 2004

After the publication of the European Court of Human Rights' decision in the *Wilson/Palmer* case, the government announced its plans to change the law. The initial goal was to change the Employment Relations Act of 1999 within the same parliamentary period. However, the draft bill was not introduced until 2003 and not passed until 2004. In the meantime, the government engaged in a series of consultations with trade unions, employers' organizations, and legal experts in drawing up the bill. Many different groups gave their opinions on how the law could best be changed. For example, lawyers from the Institute of Employment Rights, a labor-sympathetic think tank, argued for the need to radically change section 146. In their view this section required an amendment to clarify that "any act or deliberate failure to act by the employer which has the effect of preventing or deterring employees from instructing or permitting their union from making representations to their employer or taking action in support of their interests on their behalf violates section 146." The institute's 2002 paper argued that it would be necessary for both individual workers and trade unions to contest violations of this right. Since the European Court had explicitly rejected the House of Lords' claim that trade union membership could be equated with nothing more than the mere possession of a member card, the government needed to amend section 146 in order to prohibit action short of dismissal "with the effect of preventing or deterring an employee from union membership or taking part in union activity." The institute recommended either repealing the Ullswater Amendment or changing its wording under section 146 so any attempt by an employer to deter trade union membership or access to union services and activities would constitute a violation. In addition, they argued that section 17 of the 1999 law[160] was so broad that it would not prevent another Wilson/Palmer situation from occurring.[161]

The resulting Employment Relations Act of 2004 was not as comprehensive as the Institute for Employment Rights' proposal. Part 3, section 29 entitled, "inducements and detriments in respect of membership etc. of independent trade union," dealt with the issues involved in the *Wilson/Palmer* case, although the law is somewhat confusing. This section amended the 1992 Trade Union and Labour Relations Consolidation Act after section 145. The new act includes two major provisions. The first provision provides workers the "right not have an offer made to him by his employer for the sole or main purpose of inducing the worker" from becoming or being a trade union member, taking part in trade union activities, or using trade union services. Trade union services refer to "services made available to the worker by an independent trade union by virtue of his membership," but section 145(B)(4) specifies that "services" do include collective bargaining. In the second provision, a worker who is a member of a *recognized* union, or a union seeking recognition, has the right to be offered contracts that would end collective bargaining or protections of a collective agreement. However, it must be the employer's "sole or main purpose in making the offers" to end collective bargaining. Only an individual worker or a former worker may complain about an employer's violation of these protections to a tribunal.[162]

There are three major problems with the 2004 law. First, only individuals, not unions, may make complaints to the Industrial Tribunal. In some instances, this may not be the best way to protect a vulnerable worker's interest. Second, collective bargaining rights are protected *only* for those workers in recognized unions, or unions in the process of gaining recognition. A third major problem is the unclear "purpose" test. The language changed from "purpose" to "sole or main purpose" in the 2004 Act. Section 145D(2) of the law does place the burden on the employer to prove that his "sole or main purpose" was not to end collective bargaining or discourage trade union membership.[163] However, it may be more difficult under the new law to prove that an employer made an offer with the "sole or main purpose" to deter trade union membership, activities, or collective bargaining.[164] The offering of individual contracts would be legal if the primary purpose was to reward or retain these employees for their high value as workers.[165] Professor Lord Wedderburn QC, a eminent British labor law expert who served as the first junior during the *Wilson/Palmer* case at the European Court of Human Rights, stated in his analysis of the 2004 law that the "sole or main purpose requirement" was too broad. Allowing employers to convince their workers to give up their rights, even if unintentionally, was not in the scope of the European Court's decision.[166]

Understanding Compliance: The European Court and Partisan Shifts

According to an interview with an U.K.-based international law and labor rights scholar, "typically the UK government takes treaty responsibilities lightly, and sometimes not to the fullest extent."[167] So why did the British government decide to mostly implement the European Court's rulings? While the European Court is quite legalized with "binding" decisions, it lacks a strong enforcement provision that can compel state compliance.[168] According to Article 46(1) of the European Convention on Human Rights, the state must pay relevant compensation and take general measures to deal with any underlying problems in order to prevent the violation from happening again. The Committee of Ministers[169] is responsible for the execution of all decisions according to Article 46(2). But while the committee monitors progress, it does not enforce changes. The committee makes sure that the Court's decisions are respected and monitors the extent to which necessary remedial action takes place. The state needs to demonstrate that compensation and other changes (perhaps legislative) have been made to satisfy the Court's decision. Cases remain on the Committee of Ministers' agenda until its members decide that the issues have been resolved. The major force within the Committee of Ministers is political power. The ultimate sanction would be to expel a member state from the Council of Europe.[170]

While the British government seems to have been influenced by the stronger legal status of the European Court's decision, the normative negotiation process also determined the government's compliance. The many recommendations of other international institutions on the trade union rights issue mattered for the European Court's decision. Although in South Korea multiple recommendations led to great political support for domestic and transnational activists, multiple recommendations in the United Kingdom were more important to the final legal outcome. In the past, the European Court (or Commission) of Human Rights had not primarily concerned itself with other international institutions' recommendations. However, in this case, the barristers specifically included the recommendations of the ILO and the European Social Charter in their submissions to the Court. The Court's resulting decision referred to these prior decisions. While it is difficult to assess whether the presence of a consensus among international institutions on the *Wilson/Palmer* issue was important in explaining the change in the European Court's jurisprudence, it is notable that this decision did incorporate the opinions and recommendations of its fellow international institutions in this case.

In addition to the higher degree of legal obligation enjoyed by the European Court and the presence of multiple recommendations, the political conditions under which the Blair government came to power also impacted state compliance with the Court's decision. The "New Labour" identity limited the Blair government's range of action. The Labour government sought to wed the social values of Europe with the market-based policies of neoliberalism. This ambitious "third way project" created unforeseen human rights obligations for the British state. These identity commitments and multiple favorable institutional recommendations tied the Labour government's hands. These pledges created domestic political commitments to a liberal rights-based politics that made the Blair government vulnerable to the European Court ruling and compelled them to become more than simply a "Tory-lite" government.

The effect of international institutional engagement on the 2004 labor rights law was also due in part to the government's domestic political commitment to its "New Labour" identity. Unlike in the South Korean and Canadian cases, in which identity and reputational goals were related to specific economic outcomes, New Labour's goals were focused on domestic politics. Labour had succeeding in convincing the British public that it was no longer the party of trade unionists during the early 1990s. As the Labour and Conservative parties began to converge as parties of economic growth and fiscal responsibility, Blair had to convince the Tory-weary British public that New

Labour was in fact a better alternative in the 1997 elections. New Labour thus made certain domestic commitments that were internationally oriented, as a way to gain votes during the election.[171] There were three related strands to the New Labour political identity: "modernization," "Europe," and "human rights." These three goals created an unexpected political vulnerability for the government in 2002.

"Modernization" meant several concrete measures for Blair. The first was the "democratization" of governance, designed to contrast Labour with the more traditional, nationally focused Conservatives. Blair tried to adopt casual new practices within his office, and famously took on a "Call me Tony" demeanor. He asked his cabinet to drop formalities and titles. His Chancellor of the Exchequer Gordon Brown also established the policy of not wearing a white tie, tail, or top hat during official duties.[172] But beyond the more superficial governance style, this signified the modernization of old Labour into "new Labour" through the discarding of its strong relationships with trade unions.[173] Tony Blair spoke of the dangers of inflationary policies and warned against the "immediate punishment of capital markets" should Labour return to the antiquated policies of the past. These policies were rooted in misguided ideologies such as Keynesianism, corporatism, and the favoring of trade unions' special interests.[174] In addition, New Labour abandoned most of its socialist policy prescriptions, especially goals about public ownership. Ironically, Labour's attempts to get away from its traditional trade union ties, and move toward more economically liberal associations, created unforeseen obligations to labor rights through the European Court's decision.

Another related aspect of the New Labour platform, also under the umbrella of "modernization," was the push to integrate the United Kingdom more fully into Europe. The United Kingdom had long been an outsider within the European Community. As part of the goal of creating a "New Britain" with a "bridge into the twenty-first century," Blair pledged to bring the United Kingdom back into line with the other EU countries. The April 1997 party manifesto thus included a pledge to give "Britain the leadership in Europe which Britain and Europe needs."[175] The Labour manifesto emphasized a number of key provisions. Recognizing that the United Kingdom was no longer a "leader of nations" (a reference to the decline of its historic hegemony, which Labour attributed to the poor leadership of the Conservatives), the manifesto stressed the goals of strong national defense, human rights advocacy, participation in international institutions, and leadership in Europe. A Labour government would create a "fresh start" with "the credibility to achieve reform."[176] The Conservatives had been divided on the question of Europe. Some political commentators argued that the huge electoral mandate of the new Labour government reflected in part the public's desire to create strong ties with Europe.[177]

As early as 1990, the Labour Party had pledged to adopt the European Community's Social Chapter, a part of the Maastricht Treaty, which the Conservative government had uniformly opposed.[178] The proposed Social Chapter was the result of trade unions and other progressive political actors in the EU's original twelve members. It was side agreement that created minimum social standards during negotiations over the European common market.[179] The United Kingdom was the only member state that was openly opposed to the concept. Prime Minister Margaret Thatcher called the proposed Social Chapter a throwback to "a Marxist period, a class struggle period"[180] and also an "undesirable form of social engineering."[181] The Social Chapter was formally adopted in 1992 (to be operational in 1993), and was officially called Protocol 14 of the European Community Treaty on Social Policy. Through negotiations in 1991, the United Kingdom had been able to opt out of the Social Chapter, which became a politically prominent issue during the 1992 election.

During the 1997 election, the Labour Party pledged to opt in, as a way to raise the United Kingdom to the same the high employment standards of other European economies. Independent polls showed as early as 1989 that approximately 65 percent of Britons believed that the Social Chapter was a positive measure.[182] The 1992 Labour manifesto pledged that Britain would act as a leader within the European Community and play an active role within the negotiations around the Monetary Union. It even proposed locating the European Central Bank in Britain.[183] The role of the United Kingdom with regard to the Social Chapter—and with regard to Europe in general—remained a politically salient issue right up to the 1997 general election. The Labour Party, while distancing itself from domestic trade unions, sought to commit the United Kingdom to regulations that had been largely developed by European trade unions.

However, unlike South Korea, the British government did not feel internationally vulnerable. Labour's goal of closer integration with Europe was driven less by a desire to improve the United Kingdom's relations with European countries and the EU than by Labour's domestic interest in differentiating its agenda from the Conservatives. European and other foreign leaders were more likely to woo Labour than the other way around. The fact that European countries and institutions also desired a new relationship was evidenced by the European leaders' outspoken pre-election preference for

Tony Blair. Anonymous EU officials also told newswires that they preferred Blair because of his policies of constructive engagement with the EU. This was in spite of the fact that EU officials are prohibited from openly commenting on national political contests.[184] The European leadership's support for Tony Blair was expressed again during favorable meetings and optimistic statements following Labour's victory in May 1997.[185] The new government quickly followed up on its commitments. Labour's Minister for European Affairs traveled to Brussels only days after taking office to declare the United Kingdom's intention to sign the Social Chapter.

Human Rights

Human rights were central to Labour's election campaign, which the party included in its modernizing and internationalizing goals. Instead of the "go-it-alone" stance of the Conservative government, the Labour Party claimed in 1997 that it would protect human rights by adopting human rights–sensitive foreign policies abroad and by introducing a national human rights legal document into the British legal system. To do so, Labour pledged to codify the European Convention on Human Rights into domestic law, so British citizens could protect these rights within British courts. Labour's human rights policies abroad included the goal of being "respected in the world for the integrity with which [the United Kingdom] conducts its foreign relations [making] the protection and promotion of human rights a central part of our foreign policy."[186]

The idea of adopting the European Convention of Human Rights as domestic legislation was first suggested by John Smith, the Labour opposition leader, after the 1992 election. This policy plan was later incorporated by his successor, Tony Blair, as part of his platform to offer something new to the British electorate.[187] The Labour government followed up on its campaign promise by incorporating the European Convention on Human Rights into domestic law. It was the first major constitutional change in Britain since 1911 and the first codified attempt toward a written constitutional guarantee of basic human rights, countering the enduring tradition of "parliamentary sovereignty." This was a strategic move to finally convince the British public of New Labour's commitment to individual, rather than collective, rights.[188] The plan was included in the December 1996 Labour opposition publication *Bringing Rights Home*, which claimed that it would also "cut costs, save time and give power back to British Courts."

The Human Rights Act of 1998 gave domestic legal status to the European Convention of Human Rights, so that individuals and organizations could bring complaints about possible violations of human rights to domestic legal authorities. Applicants could bring complaints only against public authorities, as specified within the European Convention.[189] Higher-level British courts were granted the ability to judge whether future legislation was compatible with the European Convention. However, while British courts and public authorities *could* refer to the decisions of European Court of Human Rights' jurisprudence, British courts were not bound by its case law. Therefore the Human Rights Act did not self-execute the decisions of the European Court, but was primarily a domestic measure that committed public authorities, judicial and legislative bodies, to the European Convention of Human Rights.[190] As the European Convention of Human Rights focuses mostly on individual rights, the Human Rights Act was another step that Labour took to distance itself from its traditional trade union base.

The Human Rights Act created a public human rights commitment for the government. Unlike a general campaign promise—for example, Kim Young Sam of South Korea's pledge to integrate South Korea into the global economy—the passing of the Human Rights Act of 1998 created a domestic legislative commitment to various human rights principles never before included in British law. According to the Trades Union Congress's Employment Policy Rights officer Hannah Reed, "this was a key manifesto commitment. [New Labour] felt people should be able to defend their human rights in court. This was a real landmark constitutional change—it has allowed for greater access for a number of claims."[191] As John Hendy QC stated, "in the UK, human rights mean more than trade union rights. The Human Rights Act [more than the ILO] has embarrassed the UK government."[192]

Multiple International Institutions' Recommendations

Based on the prior jurisprudence concerning Article 11, the European Court of Human Rights' decision may have been different without the prior recommendations of the other international institutions. Labor unions had not been successful in their past attempts to defend collective bargaining at either the European Commission or the European Court of Human Rights. Perhaps this was why the new Labour government decided to contest the *Wilson/Palmer* cases when it could have chosen to settle the issue out of court. European trade unions' claims had not historically fared well under Article 11. For example, in *Young, James and Webster v. United Kingdom* (1981) the court upheld the Conservatives' ban on closed shops. Given that this case dealt specifically with trade union security protections that fall outside the human rights framework, it made sense that the British government expected a decision unfavorable to the unions. Even the January 2002 European Court of Human Rights case against the United Kingdom, *UNISOM v. United Kingdom,* another trade union Article 11 complaint, resulted in a decision against the union. This decision specified that Article 11 included neither the right to collective bargaining nor the right to strike.[193] The court protected a very individualist and limited understanding of freedom of association that sometimes undermined the goals of collective bargaining.[194] This may not be surprising, however, given the Cold War history of the European Convention of Human Rights, which sought to protect individual rights and liberties.

Therefore, the Wilson decision was unusual because it included the right to union representation and the right to collective bargaining within the interpretation of "freedom of association." Stephen Cavalier stated that the 2002 European Court decision was ground-breaking, as "Article 11 is quite abstract, and therefore the interpretation could have gone either way." The final decision had "massive significance, [as the] first ever successful application under Article 11 and led to direct changes in the law . . . [it has] also [been] influential in subsequent case law. It gave unions the right to be heard."[195] The employment office from the TUC also stressed the decision's importance, claiming that "this is the first time ever that a trade union won an Article 11 [challenge]. [It was] very hugely significant. Prior to this, we had not had success at the European Court."[196]

Why was the Wilson/Palmer case at the European Court of Human Rights decided in favor of the trade unions? John Hendy QC, who also served as counsel, admitted that the decision was unpredictable. Hendy suggested that the ruling could have been due to a long-awaited European "political tide . . . turning against the United Kingdom [and its exceptionalism regarding collective rights] and Thatcherism. It is hard to predict decisions [of the European Court of Human Rights because] there are 10 very different judges. The British judge presiding was quite influential." Yet a major difference between this Article 11 challenge and previous ones was the notable presence of other international institutions' recommendations in the final decision. This was a new development, as the Court had previously not considered the evaluations of other international institutions' decisions.[197] The prior recommendations of both the ILO and the European Social Charter were used as a way to "construct" the obligations of the United Kingdom in this particular case.[198] According to Hendy, the *Wilson/Palmer* case was a first for the European

Court of Human Rights, because it considered the opinions of other international institutions, rather than just the text of the European Convention.[199] According to one U.K. legal scholar, the other, less legalized institutions had important legitimizing effects, although minimal political effects: "The Economic, Social and Cultural Rights Committee [at the UN] and the ILO rulings aren't important to the UK government, but they are useful to use these findings in the [European] Human Rights court. [The influence] was indirect . . . the European Social Charter and ILO complaints aren't embarrassing. No one knows about it and media won't talk about it."[200]

Because of the successful use of the ILO and European Social Charter recommendations, the Wilson/Palmer barristers were able to create a strong argument for a favorable Article 11 ruling. This was not overdetermined, but like the South Korean case, the presence of multiple international institutions' recommendations had a strong legitimizing influence. Therefore, even though there existed neither strong political organizing by unions nor much political will on the part of the Labour government to change the law, the 2004 Act went into effect and was a significant improvement.

Conclusion: Depth of Compliance?

While the United Kingdom changed its trade union rights laws, the 2004 Act fell short of the European Court of Human Rights' decision. Like the other countries in this book, it appears that this change was less a case of learning than political calculation. If strong internalization and learning of trade union rights norms had occurred, one would have expected the implementation of strong, clear laws to protect against another Wilson/Palmer situation. However, in many ways the resulting Employment Relations Act 2004 was "grudging and minimalist."[201] As one representative of the NUJ argued, this was not a case of full compliance.[202] Rather than provide strong collective rights, the provisions in the new law remained individualist. There were no rights given to trade unions, even to make representations on behalf of a victimized member in an Industrial Tribunal.

In addition to the lack of collective rights, the law is also quite limited in its understanding of individual violations. For example, the "sole or main purpose" criterion remains a difficult legal burden to prove. An employer could, as in the Palmer case, claim that its sole or main purpose was to introduce greater flexibility.[203] In addition, the law specifically defines "union services" to exclude the right to collective bargaining.[204] As the law is currently worded, a worker can still be encouraged to give up his basic human right to collective bargaining. The idea of "legally selling" any other rights would seem quite outrageous. Yet this practice is not limited to the United Kingdom. Some public authorities in South Korea began to offer individual contracts to civil servants in 2006, with raises in exchange for the giving up their trade union membership, representation, and rights.[205]

Even the government's responses to criticism of the 2004 law demonstrate its commitment to neoliberal principles. For example, the United Kingdom's Joint Committee on Human Rights, a domestic British legislative committee with members from both the House of Lords and the House of Commons, found the law's shortcomings significant. The Joint Committee's report criticized the provision that did not protect workers against inducements in non-recognized unions. The committee argued that no worker should be put in such a position.[206] The Department of Trade and Industry responded by saying that the union recognition question was indeed a "complicated one," but that including a provision for unrecognized unions might dangerously upset the current balance of power achieved by current trade union laws.[207]

Yet even though the provisions of the 2004 Act fall short of fully protecting trade union rights, the fact that the neoliberal Labour government eventually acknowledged a violation, engaged in consultation, and finally made legislative changes demonstrates how governments can be vulnerable to demands for trade union rights. In fact, a recent 2006 Newcastle Employment Tribunal ruled in favor of workers in a dispute over individual contracts. Workers at Asda, the British subsidiary of Wal-Mart, had been offered individual contracts that, if accepted, would end trade union representation and collective bargaining. The Employment Tribunal ruled that this constituted a violation of Section 145(e) of the 1992 Trade Union and Labour Relations Consolidation Act, which had been changed by the 2004 Employment Relations Act. The Asda workers were awarded £2500 in damages.[208]

Despite this recent success, the outcomes in the U.K. case demonstrate the difficulty in reconciling the issue of a "substantive" versus neoliberal reading of basic labor rights. British governments of both parties have emphasized the "individual" aspects of trade union rights, arguing that their obligations did not include protecting collective elements, but such an interpretation reflects an unsophisticated understanding of human rights. The Labour government, in an effort to distance itself from its past associations with "collectivities," remained reluctant to pass substantive protections that would prevent another *Wilson/Palmer* situation from occurring.

CHAPTER 6

Canada

Federalism and Stalled Compliance

Criticism from international institutions prompted both South Korea and the United Kingdom to make a series of partial trade union rights reforms throughout the normative negotiation process, though both countries were initially unwilling to do so. However, the provincial government of British Columbia, Canada, was slower to respond positively to international trade union rights criticisms. Public-sector trade unions in the province of British Columbia brought multiple complaints against a series of related laws, and as in the U.K. and South Korean cases, international opinion supported the unions' call for legislative changes. Unlike in the United Kingdom or South Korea, though, these interactions did not lead to acknowledgment of trade union rights shortcomings for several years, despite sustained criticism from the ILO committee. This chapter argues that because the provincial government felt neither an external nor a domestic incentive to comply with international standards of trade union rights, the international institutions' recommendation process was not *politically* ineffective at the provincial level. International criticism did, however, prompt changes at the federal judicial level. Thus the strategic use of international norms helped foster a broader conception of workers' human rights in Canada.

As in the United Kingdom, trade unions in British Columbia launched simultaneous domestic litigation against one of norm-violating laws. Eventually, the Canadian Supreme Court ruled that the law in question was a violation of workers' human rights as understood within the Canadian Charter of Rights and Freedoms, Canada's constitutional bill of human rights. In June 2007, the Supreme Court of Canada ruled in favor of the trade unions, declaring the law in question unconstitutional. The Supreme Court determined that workers' freedom of association rights, as protected in the Canadian Charter of Rights and Freedoms, included protection of collective bargaining activities. The first reading of the follow-up bill in the British Columbia Legislative Assembly occurred on April 14, 2008, and the final outcome was announced in November 2008.[1] However, because some issues remained unaddressed, such as the "essential services" designation of public school teachers, the ILO committee considers this a "follow-up" case, and continues to request additional information about progress.[2]

One would expect that Canada, like many industrialized democratic states, would comply with international legal commitments and respect basic human rights, especially since Canadian workers have historically enjoyed a system of mostly state-supported collective bargaining.[3] Yet despite the federal government's self-representation of Canada as a country with strong rights protections, international organizations have repeatedly scrutinized Canada since the 1980s for violations of its own commitments to labor rights.[4] This chapter focuses on a series of cases at the ILO Committee of Freedom of Association that were brought against British Columbia. These cases regarded several pieces of controversial public sector labor legislation. In 2003, the committee published its recommendations regarding case numbers 2166, 2173, 2180, and 2196. These recommendations were remarkable for their strongly worded findings in favor of the workers' complaints.[5] Within the next two years, additional complaints regarding similar violations of labor rights resulted in criticism of nine laws passed by the government.

This chapter explains why the government of British Columbia resisted complying with international labor rights between 2001 and 2008. Unlike in South Korea and the United Kingdom, improving trade union rights law did not fit within the government's political interests in British Columbia. The government of British Columbia's neoliberal political ideology and policy agenda led to electoral successes in 2001 and 2005 and thus limited the impact of criticisms by an international institution and domestic activists. As the Liberal party government lacked any clear international human rights–related goals or interests, the recommendation and normative negotiation process with the ILO had little effect. However, despite the lack of political motivation, the government still engaged in the transnational normative negotiation process, agreeing with international human rights norms, even as it tried to interpret its trade union rights obligations as more limited and individualistic. While the British Columbia's government did not care about improving the rights of workers, it still sought to interpret its behaviors as compatible with Canada's domestic and international human rights commitments. The government's defense was based on the limited way that Canada's domestic courts had historically interpreted trade union rights. The British Columbia government was therefore able to claim that it respected the accepted Canadian interpretation of workers' freedom of association even as it sought to curtail trade union rights.

The British Columbia case is a compelling point of comparison for several reasons. First, the interaction between federal and provincial division of labor provides the additional factor of level of governance. While the international labor rights obligations are federal, most labor law and practices are protected at the provincial level, and therefore international labor commitments are less powerful. Secondly, the situation was considered notable both by Canadian labor unions and by the ILO. Derek Fudge, of the National Union of Public and General Employees, explained that "the most consistent attack on workers' rights in the current decade is in British Columbia."[6] However, unlike the other cases, the British Columbia case was only successful in getting supportive recommendations from one international institution. This allows one to evaluate the comparative effects of one institution's participation in the normative negotiation process. In addition, because the issues involved public-sector workers, the state had the capacity to influence outcomes more readily than in a private-sector setting, such as in the United Kingdom. Finally, this case provides insight because of the role that domestic legal institutions played. Unlike in the United Kingdom, the highest court in Canada ruled the disputed law unconstitutional, which went against the political interests of the provincial government.

Canada's International Legal Commitments to Trade Union Rights

While reforms in British Columbia stalled for several years, international legal scholars would have predicted that a country with Canada's characteristics would generally comply with international law. Canada is a democratic country that claims a strong human rights identity. It has ratified a significant number of international legal agreements on labor rights. This includes ILO Convention 87 (Right to Freedom of Association), as well as four of the other eight ILO core conventions (Conventions 100, 105, 111, and 182, which deal with Equal Remuneration, Abolition of Forced Labour, Discrimination, and

Worse Forms of Child Labour, respectively).[7] Canada has ratified both the UN ICCPR (including the first additional protocol) and the UN ICESCR.[8] While Canada has fewer legal commitments than the United Kingdom, it has a greater number than South Korea; South Korea has ratified none of the ILO trade union rights conventions.

Canada has also historically played a major role in promoting trade union rights in the international sphere. For example, Canada was a founding member of the ILO in 1919, and during World War II, Montreal served as the organization's temporary home.[9] Canadian representatives supported the adoption of Conventions 87 and 98 (the major ILO trade union rights conventions) and have even worked in leadership positions at the ILO. In both bilateral and multilateral settings, Canada has promoted the protection of trade union rights within its free trade agreements, negotiating labor side agreements, known as the "social clause," into its trade treaties. Examples of this include the Canada-Chile Agreement on Labour Cooperation, the Canada-Costa Rica Agreement on Labour Cooperation, and the Canada-Brazil Memorandum of Understanding on Labour Cooperation. In addition, Canada continues to participate in the North American Agreement on Labour Cooperation, the labor side agreement of NAFTA.[10] The Canadian government also works within the Inter-American Conference of Ministries of Labour, an organization that focuses on social and labor standards within the Free Trade Area of the Americas. In 2001, the Canadian government hosted and chaired the organization's twelfth conference. Canadian representatives also pledged $1.2 million to help promote the ILO's Declaration on the Fundamental Principles and Rights at Work within the Western hemisphere.[11]

The Canadian federal government generally claims a high degree of respect for and compliance with trade union rights. In its reports to the monitoring regime of the ILO's 1998 declaration, Canada claimed that its domestic "legislation (at the provincial and federal levels) generally promotes free collective bargaining and recognizes the right to strike or lockout."[12] Even though Canada has not ratified Convention 98, Right to Collective Bargaining, two Canadian Labour Department officials wrote in 1999 that "there is a high conformity to the major principles of Convention 98."[13] Given this history, one would imagine that international trade union rights norms would be well respected in Canada and predict its full compliance with an international institution's labor rights recommendations.

Yet despite this strong level of legal obligation and tradition of protecting trade union rights, there are well-documented problems with local trade union rights protections.[14] In fact, Canada has had more cases brought against it at the ILO Committee on Freedom of Association than the other case countries: 97 cases, of which all but twelve have been brought since 1980. This is approximately 5 percent of all cases brought to the ILO committee during this time, and the committee found violations against provincial and federal governments in about 63 percent of the complaints.[15] The high number of cases brought to the ILO committee does not denote worse trade union rights protection in Canada than other countries. Rather, it shows that many Canadian trade unions have perceived a lack of domestic recourse and therefore are inclined to "go international" to protect trade union rights.[16]

To understand why this democratic state with a respectable human rights record garners so much ILO attention, it is necessary to understand how Canadian federalism mediates the responsibility of international legal obligations. Like in the United States where states sometimes come into conflict with the federal government over questions of jurisdiction, conflict between the federal and provincial governments has weakened the influence of international law in Canada. The 1937 Privy Council's Labour Conventions Case established a fundamental separation between international legal obligations with regard to federal commitments and provincial jurisdictions.[17] In this important case, *Attorney General for Canada v. Attorney General for Ontario,* the Privy Council ruled on the jurisdictional applicability of ILO international labor conventions. The Canadian federal government, following the ILO constitution's provisions in the Versailles Treaty, had ratified certain ILO conventions and passed a number of related laws in 1935. The province of Ontario protested the legitimacy of three federal laws that legislated terms of work, such as weekly rest, minimum wages, and limits on work hours. The Judicial Committee of the Privy Council ruled in Ontario's favor, and in doing so curtailed the power of the federal government to pass national legislation making the country more compliant with its international obligations.[18]

The Privy Council argued that these federal labor laws were illegitimate because "property and civil rights" fell under the jurisdiction of the provinces, as specified in section 92 of the British North America Act (Canada's original constitutional document). The federal government was not authorized to pass such laws, even to fulfill its international obligations.[19] This decision curbed the possible effectiveness of the federal government's treaty-making and compliance abilities.[20] F. R. Scott, a prominent Canadian jurist, argued that the decision hurt Canada's activism in international labor issues: "every time Canada abstains from participating in multilateral conventions aimed at achieving good international standards, because of a lack of jurisdiction to implement them, she withholds her influence for peace and cooperation."[21] Therefore, even when the federal government strongly commits to a certain norm, it can only encourage, not force, individual provinces to comply. International law's direct influence on trade union rights are limited to a small number of federal labor laws, which cover about 10 percent of the total workforce.[22] If a province is not interested in following particular laws or institutions' recommendations, the federal government has little leverage to compel the province to do so.

The Politics of Trade Union Rights in British Columbia

To evaluate why British Columbia's provincial government remained noncompliant, one must consider the specifics of British Columbia's provincial politics. One of the key factors in the other cases was the importance of economic constraints. As in the South Korea and the U.K. cases, the British Columbia government expressed concerns that changing laws to better comply with international trade union rights norms would undermine competitiveness, growth, and employment levels. Similar to the "weakened state" thesis of globalization, the British Columbia government argued that economic circumstances forced them into taking measures against trade union rights. However, some scholars of public-sector trade unions disagree that fiscal crises make trade union rights violations inevitable. Although a government's economic challenges can limit the outcomes of collective bargaining in the public sector, fiscal constraints and austerity goals do not necessarily preclude the collective bargaining process. Rather, the curtailing of workers' collective bargaining rights is a specific political decision made by governments.

One could argue that based on the Liberal party government's electoral mandate, it had a political interest in repressing collective bargaining rights for public-sector unions. The Liberal government was elected in 2001, with a mandate to cut public spending and to increase economic growth, which had slowed since the late 1990s (see Chapter 6 appendix for economic data). This can be a difficult problem for government leaders who often seek to balance competing interests—supporters, recipients of public services, and public-sector unions—with limited resources during economic downturns.[23] Yet the British Columbia government could have engaged in some economic reforms while respecting trade union rights. According to Swimmer and Bartkiw, there are three different ways to cut public-sector labor costs.[24] In the first option, the government demands concessions from unions at the bargaining table and prepares for a possible strike if the bargaining process does not go smoothly. Strikes can be risky, though, because public opinion may turn against a government. In the second method, the government engages in transparent cooperative bargaining by opening its budget to unions and asking for cooperation in balancing the budget. These first two options represent ways in which governments can both cut costs and respect collective bargaining. Fiscal restraint and collaborative public-sector bargaining are not necessarily in opposition.

However, the British Columbia government pursued Swimmer and Bartkiw's third option, which does violate norms of collective bargaining. The third option for a government dealing with public-sector trade unions during economic challenges is for the government to legislate and unilaterally impose collective agreements as a cost-cutting strategy.[25] Between 1991 and 1995, eleven of fifteen Canadian provincial governments followed the third option, curtailing the bargaining process by extending existing contracts, imposing days off without pay, changing job security provisions, and threatening unions into concession. Yet even as deficits recovered in the later 1990s, the governments that had violated the collective bargaining rights of public service workers in the name of economic necessity made no concessions to these workers.[26]

Swimmer and Bartkiw's typology demonstrates that even a public fiscal crisis does not necessarily force a government to violate public service workers' basic trade union rights. Even if public-sector unions refuse to cooperate, a state is always free to engage in consultation and more transparent bargaining activity, as the ILO conventions encourage. The choice to respect labor rights norms is political. A labor relations and research analyst at the British Columbia Public Sector Employers' Council Secretariat stated during an interview that "even under a 0 percent [spending] mandate, we can still be responsive to needs." Employers and employees can come together to find savings and cost-cutting measures in different aspects of the collective agreement in order to preserve certain valued provisions.[27]

Political History of Trade Union Rights in British Columbia

Although trade union rights are part of the international human rights and labor rights regime, they have historically been associated with partisan politics in British Columbia. Due to its resource-based economy and strong union presence, British Columba historically had a strong labor-backed social democratic party.[28] As a result, British Columbia politics has popularly been characterized as a contest between "the left" versus "the rest," as the major choice had been between "free markets" and provincially based socialism.[29] The early social democratic party, the Cooperative Commonwealth Federation (CCF),[30] had received impressive support but never enough votes to form a government.[31] Business, media, and other interest groups historically organized against the "socialist" threat of the CCF and its calls for "provincialization," (a local version of "nationalization") or public ownership of key resource industries.[32]

While private-sector workers long enjoyed basic rights, public-sector workers' trade union rights were delayed because of the province's left/right divide. Industries such as timber, mining, gas, and manufacturing were the traditional strongholds of trade unions, starting in the 1930s. However, the CCF's broad appeal with organized labor influenced the policies of the center-right government, compelling them to adopt strong social services and public employment policies to counter the left's demands for even more radical policies.[33] Ironically, the growth of public-sector employment from 1952 to 1972[34] gave greater electoral viability to the left party, as many of these public employees gave support to the left.[35] The New Democratic Party (NDP, the 1970s successor to the CCF) was twice able to form a provincial government, in 1972–1975 and in 1991–2001, against a number of splintered right parties.[36] As a result, public-sector workers were given statutory protections for their trade union rights in the 1970s under the NDP government.

While public employees in British Columbia enjoyed legally protected trade union rights following the election of the first NDP government in 1972,[37] public school teachers in British Columbia were excluded from these rights. Like their counterparts in South Korea, British Columbia's teachers did not legally secure their associational rights until much later. Teachers secured their rights in 1987, as the result of a long campaign involving the ILO. The increasing public-sector trade union strength, which overwhelmingly represented women, people of color, and immigrants[38] in collaboration with the NDP government, led to innovative policies emerging from public-sector collective bargaining. Over time, public sector workers had gained strong job security, seniority, and other protections in their contracts, including pay equity provisions for women.[39] Such policies led to significant "union" and "public sector" premiums (wage differentials as compared to nonunion jobs) within the province.[40]

The perceived privileged positions of public-sector unions in the late 1990s, a period when the province experienced slower economic growth, led to strong support for the opposition party, British Columbia Liberal Party, which called for curbing the high costs of public employees' wages. Because of the recession, this became a key campaign issue during the 2001 provincial electoral contest between the Liberals and the New Democrats.

Election 2001: Landslide for Liberals

The narrative of the 2001 election is key to understanding the controversies surrounding the bills brought to the ILO. Starting in the 1970s, British Columbia began to transition away from a resource "staples" economy to a service- and tourism-oriented one. As a result, the labor force moved away from primary and manufacturing production to tertiary/service sectors, like many developed economies. This new set of employment opportunities in the "post-staples" economy resulted in unemployment, underemployment, and other economic frustrations and social dislocations.[41] In addition, the close relationship between British Columbia and East Asian economies resulted in a provincial economic slowdown in the late 1990s, following the East Asian financial crisis. As a result, renewing economic growth and expanding employment became important political issues. The NDP, in response to this structural change, saw new service sectors and government expenditures as a primary means of economic stimulus. The Liberal party, the newly consolidated party of the province's center/right and right-wing parties, favored the following neoliberal reforms: deregulation, privatization, reductions in taxes, and the promotion of private corporate interests.[42]

Prior to the 2001 election, it became clear that the ruling NPD government, in power since 1991, would lose. According to some accounts, the NDP government had been "rocked with scandal" and thoroughly discredited prior to the election.[43] The previous NDP premier had engaged in questionable uses of public funds, and the NDP government was blamed for failing to promote economic growth and to manage properly the province's finances.[44] As a result, most predictions showed the British Columbia Liberal Party winning the election.[45] However, the NDP attempted to prolong its influence by negotiating a number of public employee collective agreements prior to calling for an election. Because of the historic ties between unions and the NDP, the Liberal party considered these corrupt "sweetheart" deals.[46]

In its campaign, the Liberal party promised to curb public-sector trade union rights as part of its larger goal to "tame" public spending and "structural deficits." The Liberal's campaign literature promised it would "Pass *real* Balanced Budget legislation, to make balanced budgets mandatory by our third full budget and to hold all ministers individually accountable. Reduce the cost of government by increasing efficiencies and eliminating wasteful spending on government mismanagement, propaganda, and business subsidies."[47] To do so, the Liberal party promised several public-sector labor law changes. This included establishing education as an essential service and thereby legally prohibiting teachers' right to strike. The Liberal Party argued the measure was necessary because several public school teachers' strikes that occurred during the NDP administration were very disruptive. The BC Teachers' Federation had moved to a province-wide bargaining model, which had been contentious during the collective bargaining process.[48] Yet while these teachers' strikes were high profile, the British Columbia Federation of Labour claimed they were not so disruptive, pointing out that the number of strike hours translated to an average of twenty-seven minutes of lost instructional time per K-12 student per year between 1992 and 2001.[49] The Liberals also vowed to take away the strike rights of local urban transit workers and provincial ferry workers (a key public service given the geographic dependence of British Columbia's significant island populations). Centralized bargaining and fair wage legislation on public construction projects and gender pay equity were also to be eliminated.[50] The major platform of the Liberals' 2001 election campaign regarding public services and labor regulations made these promises explicit.

The Liberals criticized the NDP government's public-sector policies. They alleged that the NPD government had engaged in "wasteful," "job-killing," and "inflexible" wage and service policies. These policies had led to "deteriorating patient care" in health care. The NDP's "one size fits all" policies had also hurt education services and compromised student learning. The Liberals promised to solve these public service crises by making health care services more efficient and introducing new flexible programs to meet student needs. Educational reforms would grant "local school boards more autonomy and control over the delivery of education services," while also providing a number of better performance measures and outcomes.[51]

Yet despite its strong rhetoric against the NPD government, the Liberal Party promised British Columbia's unions during the campaign that if it were elected, it would honor all prior collective agreements, even those recently negotiated with the previous government.[52] Gordon Campbell, the leader of the Liberal Party who would become premier after the 2001 election, was quoted as telling the large Hospital Employees Union, "I'm not tearing up any agreements" and "I don't believe in ripping up agreements."[53] This expression of respect for trade unions prior to an election was similar to Margaret Thatcher's overtures to trade unions prior to the Winter of Discontent in 1976. Otherwise, the Liberal party's platform was almost entirely focused on instituting deregulatory provincial reforms, with the supposed goal of improving the economic competitiveness of the province.

The 2001 election resulted in the low showing of support for the governing NDP, which only won two of 79 seats in the Legislative Assembly, and only 22 percent of the popular vote. The Liberal Party won 77 seats. Because the NDP did not win enough votes for official opposition status, it lost public funding for research and staff.[54] The Liberal government interpreted this high electoral margin of victory as a mandate for its ambitious policy platform, including its public-sector union policies. As a result of its overwhelming majority, the government was free to make policy changes without an institutional opposition party to act as a check. This logic was evident in the government's justifications of the trade union rights violations. In its original response to the ILO committee's inquiry, the government claimed that the province approved its policies, as it was "elected with a wide mandate to improve fiscal accountability and reduce the public deficit and debt."[55]

Upon entering office, the government engaged in two related budget measures. As part of the general budget cut, the government first passed a $1.5 billion tax cut.[56] It justified this by claiming the public debt was unsustainable even though the province's level of debt (measured both as a ratio to GDP and as service costs as a percentage of public revenues) was among the lowest of all the Canadian provinces.[57] Second, after passing this tax cut, the government announced across-the-board budget cuts for all public agencies as a means to deal with the $400 million deficit in health care costs. The Liberal government began to impose unilateral changes to public-sector collective agreements. These unilateral changes legislated new collective agreements, ended strikes, and set new terms for collective bargaining. They became the subject of the ILO cases discussed in the next section.

In early 2002, the government drastically altered collective agreements for teachers and health services workers by passing Bills 27, 28, and 29. These bills were pushed through in an unusually rushed manner, and trade unions received littler prior notification, and therefore did not engage in any consultation.[58] On Saturday, January 26, 2002, the second day of a three-day "marathon anti-labour session, weekend" at the British Columbia Legislative

Assembly in Victoria, the Liberal government informed the two-person NDP caucus of its plan to debate Bills 27 and 28 on Sunday and Bill 29 on Monday. But on Saturday evening, a Liberal government minister told the NDP Caucus Director Clay Suddaby that the Liberal caucus had decided to debate all three bills on Sunday, even if this meant a late Sunday night session, with no dinner breaks. The bill was passed in the middle of the night, with almost no consultation with unions. According to then Labour Minister Graham Bruce, the bills were motivated by the government's desire to increase employment flexibility in education and health services. A reporter from a local magazine claimed to have heard "no fewer than 126 utterances of the word flexibility."[59]

This faster pace is did not allow for trade unions to protest or communicate with lawmakers about the bill. In response to these developments, teachers and health care workers organized a rally the next day, Monday, on the legislative lawn in the provincial capital.[60] Despite workers' last-minute mobilization against this set of bills, they were passed in the legislative assembly that Sunday. Trade unionists were angered by both the content of the bills and the rapid, back-room manner in which they were passed. These laws were passed in a way that was similar to the way in which the Trade Union and Labor Relations Consolidation Act (1996) was passed in South Korea and the Ullswater Amendment to the Trade Union and Labor Relations Adjustment Act (1993) that was passed in the United Kingdom.

Trade unions immediately recognized this was an unprecedented violation of their rights, as a Hospital Employees Union representative stated that no prior provincial government had "ever gone into the text of a collective agreement while it's in force and rewritten its provisions."[61] These laws were the basis of the ILO Committee on Freedom of Association complaints. In addition, just four months later, three local unions coordinated a constitutional challenge to Bill 29 under the Canadian Charter of Rights and Freedoms.[62]

Labor unions in British Columbia filed a complaint to the ILO Committee on Freedom of Association in December 2001. A total of four separate cases, numbered 2166, 2173, 2180, and 2196, were filed against six pieces of legislation. The parties to these cases included the following actors: national-level union federations, such as the Canadian Labour Congress;[63] international union federations, including the International Confederation of Free Trade Unions and Public Services International; national-level industrial unions, such as the Canadian Teachers' Federation and the National Union of Public and General Employees (NUPGE); and local unions, such as the

Health Sciences Association of British Columbia and the Canadian Union of Public Employees-British Columbia (CUPE-BC).[64]

Limited Normative Negotiations: The ILO Committee and the Trade Union Rights Violations

As the Liberal government's contentious legislation passed over several months, four different cases were brought to the ILO committee. The first of these cases, number 2166, regarded Bills 2 and 15, both laws that the government passed in response to public-sector strikes. The Health Sciences Association union[65] began bargaining for a new collective agreement in January 2001, as their old contract was set to expire at the end of March. After the parties failed to reach an agreement in April 2001, 90 percent of the union members voted to strike. Between May 18 and June 18, 2001, these workers engaged in an "essential services" strike, withdrawing some of their labor but maintaining basic levels of services. In response, the government tried to expedite the strike resolution, appointing a special mediator on June 19. Yet during an emergency session of the legislative assembly on June 20, the legislature passed the Health Care Services Continuation Act (Bill 2), ordering the health science workers back to work and back to the bargaining table. When the parties still could not come to an agreement, the health science professionals went back on strike again on July 23.

On August 9, the government passed the Health Care Services Collective Agreements Act (Bill 15), which unilaterally imposed a contract with differential wage increase schedules that the union had rejected. There was no consultation with the workers' organization before the legislation was passed, and the union was only informed about the existence of the bill five minutes before the legislation's introduction.[66] The ILO committee expressed concern about this process. While it did not find Bill 2 to be in violation of freedom of association principles (as it considered health care to be an essential service in the strictest sense)[67] the committee did find Bill 15 to violate trade union rights. According to the committee, Bill 15 had not "violated freedom of association principles inasmuch as it did not respect the autonomy of the bargaining parties and legislatively imposed working terms and conditions, without the workers being able to submit the dispute to mutually and freely chosen independent and impartial arbitration."[68] The committee recommended that the government consider amending key aspects of Bill 15.

The ILO committee found similar problems with Case 2173, which involved the nurses' and teachers' unions. The nurses had begun to bargain at the beginning of 2001, but they had not made significant progress toward an agreement. On April 13, 2001, they also started an essential services strike, maintaining minimum services, as they were allowed under the law. The nurses were legislated back to work under the conditions of Bill 2 on June 19. They returned to work while continuing negotiations, but when the Legislative Assembly passed Bill 15 in August, it imposed a contract on the nurses before a facilitator could even make recommendations. The nurses' collective agreement was unilaterally imposed by the legislature during their participation in a collective bargaining process, as had happened to the health science workers.[69]

Case 2173 and Case 2196 included similar complaints by the teachers and university professors. Teachers had begun their bargaining process in March 2001, as their collective agreement was set to expire at the end of June. There was little progress in the negotiations, but the government passed Bill 18, the Skills Development and Labour Statutes Amendment Act on August 16, 2001, before any industrial action had taken place. This bill made the categories of teachers and nonteaching employees in public schools "essential services," which heavily restricted their rights to strike. Teachers could now only engage in limited "essential services" strikes, and the Labour Relations Board would determine the scope of legal activities during such a strike. By late January 2002, still lacking a negotiated collective agreement, the government passed Bill 27 (Education Services Collective Agreements Act) and Bill 28 (Public Education Flexibility and Choice Act). Bill 27, like Bill 15, imposed a new collective agreement, and it included provisions that negated all the gains the teachers had won in prior agreements and also limited the scope of future agreements. This went against British Columbia's customary practice of successor rights, a public labor relations practice that honored the clauses of all prior agreements unless both parties negotiated otherwise. Workers were now prevented from bargaining over seniority rights, leaves of absence, and hours of work. Bill 28 also gave school boards the privilege to unilaterally change the school calendar, a decision that negated prior collective agreements. The bill also curtailed the possibility of future negotiations on this subject.[70] Case 2196 involved the University Teachers' Union, which presented a similar complaint regarding Bill 27, as it imposed a collective agreement on professors as well.

The ILO committee found the bills in question in Case 2173 and Case

2196 to constitute violations of trade union rights principles. Bill 18 was found to violate freedom of association principles, as the ILO did not consider teaching an "essential" service. The committee argued that workers needed the right to strike to protect their interests, and recommended that Bill 18 be repealed.[71] Bills 27 and 28 were also found to violate freedom of association principles because they were unilaterally imposed upon the bargaining process, and the committee argued that this action undermined the "autonomy of the bargaining parties."[72] The committee recommended a review of Bill 27, with added safeguards to protect workers' basic consultation and associational rights.[73]

The most controversial of all these laws was Bills 29, the Health and Social Services Delivery Improvement Act. Two national-level labor federations[74] filed the complaint against Bill 29, under the auspices of Case 2180, which also complained about Bills 27 and 28. These bills all overrode and invalidated prior collective agreements and even prohibited certain issues from inclusion in future collective agreements. However, Bill 29 was considered particularly damaging because it overrode an existing, already negotiated collective agreement[75] and negated provisions that the unions had "won" as the result of past bargaining and strikes. The bill dictated the terms of the following provisions: protections on job mobility and employment security, increases in wages, and schedules that allowed for privatization of the services provided by certain job categories. The government passed the law to reduce the province's health services expenditures and to provide management more control over labor costs. This was particularly devastating because it affected 60,000 public employees in the province, many of whom were female, immigrants, and people of color.

As a result of its review, the ILO committee also found Bill 29 to conflict with basic freedom of association principles. While noting and appreciating the political concerns of the provincial government, the committee argued that any legislation that could affect collective bargaining or employment conditions should respect trade union rights principles. To do so, the committee stated:

> the introduction of [such] legislation . . . should be preceded by full and detailed consultations with the appropriate organizations of workers and employers . . . which was not the case here. The Committee recommends that such full and detailed consultations be held with representative organizations in the health and social sectors; to be meaningful, these consultations should be held under the auspices of

> a neutral and independent facilitator that would have the confidence of all parties, in particular trade unions and their members whose rights are mostly affected by Bill No. 29.[76]

The committee urged the government to review the law and make appropriate remedies. In its concluding remarks, the committee recommended that the British Columbia government consult workers' representatives and refrain from legislatively imposing collective agreements in the future, regardless of the fiscal situation.[77]

The following chart lists the legal issues and the ILO committee's responses and recommendations regarding the cases shown in Table 8.

Table 8: Cases Brought to ILO Against British Columbia, 2001–2002

Case Number (Year)	*Bills in Question*	*ILO Decision*
2166 (2001)	Bill 2 (Legislates striking Health Science Association members back to work for a cooling-off period.) Bill 15 (Imposes a collective agreement on striking Health Science Association members.)	Bill 15 violates the bargaining process. Recommends the government amend Bill 15.
2173 (2002)	Bill 15 (Imposes agreement.) Bill 18 (Makes education an "essential service" and limits teachers' right to strike.) Bill 27 (Imposes collective agreement on teachers.) Bill 28 (Grants school board rights to unilaterally change provisions and voids any prior negotiated provisions that conflict with new changes.)	Bill 18 violates freedom of association, as teaching is not an essential service. Bills 27 and 28 violate freedom of association; committee recommends amending Bill 27, reviewing Bill 28.
2180 (2002)	Bills 27, 28 (see above) Bill 29 (Allows employers to override existing collective agreements and contract out to nonunion employers, interrupts already existing negotiated collective agreements.)	Bill 27, 28, and 29 violate freedom of association. Recommends reviewing and complete consultation regarding Bill 29.
2196 (2002)	Bill 28 (Imposed collective agreement on university professors.)	See above

Response of the British Columbia Government: Justifications and Minimal Normative Negotiations

While the British Columbia government did not admit that there was a need to change its laws, it still engaged in justifying its practices to the ILO committee. It engaged in the normative negotiation process less so than the United Kingdom and South Korea, sending in communications only five times during the nine-year period of 2001 to 2010.[78] However, the government did respond in a detailed manner to the ILO committee's criticisms, providing extensive political and economic justifications for its actions. Even the Liberal government, with few reasons to care for international opinion, did not completely ignore accusations of human rights violations. As in the South Korean and United Kingdom cases, the Liberal government's 2002 communications to the ILO justifying its recent legislation were very carefully worded. The government never denied the importance of basic trade union rights; rather, it claimed to follow a "Canadian" interpretation of those norms.

The government defended each of its laws as justifiable because of the Liberal government's political and electoral mandate to ensure labor flexibility and better-managed social services. However, the government also claimed, "Any restrictions on collective bargaining or on the right to strike were exceptional measures, [due to the] difficult economic and fiscal situation . . . [and] protracted and difficult labour disputes, which could have serious consequences in the health and education sectors." These included the province's dire, "structural" economic crisis, challenges such as "unsustainable pressures on the budget" from changes in the global economy, and rising debt driven by wages in the health and education sectors. The government listed many economic indicators as evidence for the crisis, including the largest health care labor costs in the country. It was only because of this "emergency" that collective bargaining rights had to be curtailed. The report claimed that the government had little choice but to pass the laws, given the economic contexts.[79] Interestingly, the government claimed it had not violated trade union rights, but also claimed that the laws were passed only for exceptional reasons. In many ways, the Liberal government's denial of human rights problems was similar to the U.K. Conservative government's responses to the ILO. Both governments had little incentive to care about international institutions and labor rights.

Most significantly, the British Columbia government countered with its own interpretation of trade union rights obligations. It argued that

Convention 87, which Canada had ratified, was not meant to provide trade unions the right to "bargain collective on each and every issues which arises in the context of employment," claiming that such an interpretation would impinge on a state's ability to set individual workers' rights.[80] Furthermore, the government claimed that international trade union rights should not interfere with a government's ability to deal with competing social interests "in a manner which best serves the public interest."[81] Questioning the ILO's competency, the British Columbia government argued that it was not appropriate for the ILO committee to "second guess" legislative matters, "so long as [the legislation] is made through a democratic political process and does not undermine the fundamental rights of workers to organize, to select their bargaining agent and to engage in collective bargaining."[82] By its standard, the government was respecting these rights.

The Liberal government's ability to ignore the ILO's recommendations is related to the ways in which trade union rights have historically been interpreted by Canadian courts. Not only did noncompliance with the ILO's specific recommendations fit with the stated political interests of the Liberal government, but it was also in accordance with the accepted "Canadian" interpretation of basic workers' freedom of association rights. Because of a history of controversies within the Canadian Supreme Court over the scope of labor rights under the Canadian Charter of Rights and Freedoms, the British Columbia government could claim with confidence that even if it did not comply with the ILO's recommendations, it was acting within appropriately established domestic norms.

The claims of the British Columbia government that the laws in question did not violate trade union rights drew on a series of "Charter challenges," or court cases that claimed possible violations of the Canadian Charter of Rights and Freedoms. Like the United Kingdom, Canada has lacked a written constitution, and as a result, has lacked constitutional guarantees of basic human rights. Therefore, all human rights, including labor rights, were determined by either common law or a patchwork of provincial and federal statutes. Canada had passed a Bill of Rights by way of federal statute in 1960, but this was a "quasi-constitutional" guarantee only. This changed in 1982, with the adoption of the Canadian Charter of Rights and Freedoms. The charter provided a constitutional guarantee of basic rights and freedoms for Canadians.[83] The Charter replaced the British North America Act as Canada's primary constitutional document. Unlike international law, the Charter, and its subsequent judicial review, trumps all contradictory provincial laws.[84] This document is similar to the United Kingdom's Human Rights Act of 1999; in fact, the Canadian Charter was a model for the British law. With regard to labor rights, the Canadian Charter of Rights and Freedoms, section 2(d), states "Everyone has the . . . fundamental: . . . freedom of association," although this clause does not explicitly mention trade unions.[85] Historically, Canadian courts have interpreted this clause as protecting the basic freedom of workers to join unions, but not the right of workers to collective bargaining or collective action. This jurisprudence was established by a series of 1987 Charter challenges called the Labour Trilogy.[86]

In this series of Charter challenges, the Canadian Supreme Court justices interpreted section 2(d) of the Charter as excluding collective bargaining and collective action rights.[87] This is very different from the jurisprudence of the ILO Committee on Freedom of Association (as well as the UN Human Rights Committee), which specifically recognizes the centrality of collective bargaining and action within workers' freedom of association.[88] The Canadian Supreme Court decisions preserved judicial deference, which gave legislative discretion over the scope of collective bargaining laws. Yet reserving the responsibility for legislatures to set the terms of collective bargaining rights is problematic for a number of reasons. First, it results in a great deal of heterogeneity among the provinces, which can lead to uneven economic results.[89] But most important, deference to provincial legislatures had the practical effect of stripping collective bargaining rights of their human rights character. This ruling interpreted the Charter against most international opinions, with the exception of the prevailing view at the European Court of Human Rights, by reducing collective bargaining and collective action (such as strikes and boycotts) to *politics*. As a demonstration of this logic, Justice Gerald Eric LeDain, who wrote the majority decision in the Alberta case (one of the Trilogy cases), argued that collective bargaining and action were "*modern*" rights, not fundamental ones. Collective bargaining rights were created by legislation because they required "specialized" knowledge of competing interests. Therefore, these rights were outside the constitutional guarantees of freedom of association in Article 2(d) of the Charter.[90] The history of collective bargaining for public servants in British Columbia reflects the political nature of workers' rights questions in Canada.

The Supreme Court, in the Labour Trilogy cases, limited its interpretation of freedom of association to a purely individualist, negative right. This was again affirmed in *Professional Institute of Public Service of Canada v. Northwest Territories (Commissioner) [1990]* (PIPSC). The unions in this case argued that collective bargaining protected the "essential or foundational collective activities of an association." But the majority opinion of the Canadian Supreme Court rejected this claim, ruling that collective bargaining was a "collective activity" belonging to unions, and thus unrelated to the exercise of Charter rights and freedoms.[91] The collective provisions of such rights were thus precluded from the constitutional protections of the Charter. The Labour Trilogy cases established a national consensus that understood trade union rights as limited.

This hard-line stance was challenged somewhat in *Dunmore v. Ontario (Attorney General)* (2001), in which the Supreme Court accepted the possibility that some collective elements were included in the right of freedom of association. The majority decision in that case argued that certain collective activities of a union are necessary for the proper enjoyment of freedom of association, and that governments are responsible for protecting vulnerable workers so that they may enjoy these rights.[92] It was not clear after the decision how the vague *Dunmore* ruling might influence future interpretations of Article 2d, although it did specify that "collective activities" do not include collective bargaining or the right to strike.[93] This is similar to the way in which the 2004 British Employment Relations Act did not include collective bargaining as a protected "trade union activity." However, despite Canada's claim to have a high level of support for the broad range of international trade union rights, the legal interpretation of Canada's human rights document has excluded collective bargaining and other more substantive and collective aspects of trade union rights from constitutional protection.[94] Because *Dunmore* did not explicitly protect collective bargaining rights under the Charter, there were no constitutional or other legal precedents to protect collective bargaining rights when the ILO cases were brought against British Columbia.

Although the British Columbia government made some rhetorical concessions recognizing the importance of trade union rights norms, overall it was neither cooperative nor respectful. In fact, in its initial responses to the ILO's complaints, the government claimed that the "complaints [were] fundamentally frivolous, vexatious, mostly driven by political motivation, and completely without merit." The government repeatedly questioned the legitimacy of the ILO committee as the institutional setting in which the laws should be examined, both because these laws had been passed through "democratic processes," and because the complaints had already been filed at the British Columbia Supreme Court.[95] The government's responses to the ILO were quite similar to the Roh Moo Hyun government's claims that domestic legal institutions, not an international one, were the legitimate arenas in which to investigate such questions. In fact, when the British Columbia Supreme Court later ruled in the government's favor, the Liberal government included this decision in later communications to the ILO.[96] After the reporting the British Columbia Supreme Court decision in early 2004, the Liberal government stopped follow-up communications with the ILO committee, despite repeated requests.[97]

Upon receiving the ILO's recommendations in March 2003, the unions began a coordinated public relations campaign, directed both to their large memberships and also to the broader public. This included newspaper advertisements, rallies, and communications with members, although media coverage of these events was very limited.[98] Premier Campbell publicly announced that he would not make the changes recommended by the ILO, arguing that "We said in the election we were going to do this and that is what we have done. I feel no pressure whatsoever. I was not participating in any discussion with the UN."[99] As a representative for the Labor Ministry stated in 2003, after the initial round of ILO recommendations: "As a government, we respect the ILO but we disagree with the interpretation of pieces of our legislation. The province doesn't feel it has violated any international agreements. The legislation was brought in to provide flexibility and choice and maintain core services to the public."[100] Unions also sent communications to the Minister of Labour in October 2004, urging the government to make reforms according to the ILO recommendations, but the ministry responded in a February 2005 letter that it had no intention of doing so.[101] These actions demonstrated a general lack of concern about the normative negotiation process.

The Liberal government, including the Ministry of Labour, former labor ministers, and the premier's office, declined multiple requests for interviews. During an interview in 2006, the press secretary of the premier shared a similar sentiment, claiming, "there was very little [government] response required [to the ILO recommendations]. It wasn't an issue. The ILO will do and say what they will and in [British Columbia] the government is in a great place and that's what we'll do. I don't recall it being a huge issue and to be totally frank it was not that big a deal."[102] During this time, the government had stopped sending communications to the ILO.

The legislature's public record also demonstrated a general lack of concern regarding the ILO recommendations. According to the legislative transcripts, Labour Minister Graham Bruce stated on April 29, 2003, that the ILO report "said a number of things," but despite the ILO's claims, education and health care were still "essential" in their society. He emphasized that labor relations were difficult for every government. Graham ended his remarks by reiterating that the Liberals had promised in their campaign "to put patients and to put students first." The Minister of Labor also emphasized that these laws, unlike the ILO's recommendations, were more legitimate as they had come from a democratically elected legislature.[103] This reflected some of the claims made by the government's 2002 communications to the ILO.

The only notable outcome of this normative negotiation process in British Columbia was the establishment of a special commission on the teachers' bargaining process in 2005.[104] The government responded only twice to this set of ILO recommendations, once in 2003 and once in 2004, despite the national public-sector union federation's attempt to elicit a response from the government for a third time in 2006.[105] The government claimed that its 2004 communication to the ILO committee was evidence of its willingness to revisit the issue. It had reached a new collective agreement with the health services sector within the confines of Bill 29, suggesting that since a recent collective agreement had been reached, the government had successfully respected the bargaining process.[106] There was no direct legislative response to the ILO's many recommendations. The participating unions, although they did not get the legislative changes they desired, continued to provide new information and developments regarding these cases to the ILO. The ILO, for its part, continued to review the situation and request updates from the British Columbia government.

The government's actions after the economic recovery suggested continuing disrespect for trade union rights. Instead of engaging in more consultation when the financial constraints were gone, the government continued to pass similar laws,[107] some of which became the subject of further complaints to the ILO. For example, the Legislative Assembly passed laws to end strike actions and impose collective agreements, including a retroactive agreement in 2004 that would override provisions of existing agreements. After the economy recovered and the government had a new budget surplus, the Liberal government passed a number of laws that infringed upon the rights of health services and ferry workers. These various 2004 bills became the subject of ILO complaint number 2324. However, instead of providing economic data to justify the new laws, the government now responded to ILO's criticisms by first admitting the new law had limited the scope of bargaining, but claiming, "this restriction [was] necessary to give private sector partners and contractors the discretion to decide on the most efficient and cost-effective manner of providing non-clinical services." Rather than claiming economic constraints, the government now justified its curtailing of collective bargaining by claiming that employers need more flexibility.

In addition, the government repeated its claim that curtailing collective bargaining did not infringe on workers' freedom of association. The government's communication claimed that these laws did not violate Convention 87, "since they do not restrict workers' rights to establish organizations of their own choosing, to draw up their constitutions and rules, elect their representatives, organize their administration and formulate their programmes."[108] This attempt to define international trade union rights obligations in a narrow way, limited to individual rights and union autonomy, was similar to the way that the U.K. government distinguished between individual trade union membership and substantive access to collective rights and activities, claiming that as long as the government did not interfere with basic trade union membership, no international trade union rights norm violation had occurred. The British Columbia government repeated these justifications for each of the laws in question, and a very similar justification was used in response to a 2005 ILO case regarding an imposed teachers' collective agreement.[109] The British Columbia government put forth its narrow, "Canadian" interpretation of trade union rights norms to justify its actions as completely legitimate, no longer using political or economic arguments to excuse its violations.

Judicial Game Change: The 2007 Canadian Supreme Court Decision

On June 8, 2007, the Supreme Court of Canada issued its decisions in the case of *Health Services Support-Facilities Subsection Bargaining Association v. British Columbia* (2007 SCC 27).[110] British Columbia trade unions had successfully appealed this case, as lower courts—the British Columbia Supreme Court in 2003 and the British Columbia Court of Appeals in 2004—had ruled in favor of the province. The case challenged the constitutionality of Bill 29 (the Health and Social Services Delivery Act). The provincial courts, drawing on the prior decisions of the Canadian Supreme Court, decided that collective bargaining rights were not included within the scope of section 2(d) of the Canadian Charter.

The Labour Trilogy established the precedent that while the Charter protected the right of individuals to join trade unions, it did not include the procedural right to collective bargaining. The question the Supreme Court examined here, like the one explored in the U.K.-based Wilson case, concerned whether protecting the rights of workers to freely associate and form trade unions necessarily included protecting the right to collective bargaining, or whether it was limited only to the right to hold a union card and an affiliation, as the British Employment Appeal Tribunal and the British Columbia government claimed.

The Supreme Court of Canada broke with the prior case law and ruled in favor of the unions.[111] The court found these past arguments unconvincing and historically uninformed, claiming that they did not "withstand principled scrutiny and should be rejected." The Court offered a more expansive interpretation of freedom of association, even though there was no explicit basis for this in the text of the Charter. In doing so, the Court overturned the Labour Trilogy decisions. In what the *Globe and Mail* newspaper called a "landmark decision," the Supreme Court ruled that the right to collective bargaining is in fact protected by the Charter and that Sections 6(2), 6(4), and 9 (in conjunction with Section 10) of Bill 29 violated workers' rights.[112] The majority opinion was held by six of the seven judges.[113]

There were several parts to this majority decision. The Supreme Court argued that prior rulings misunderstood the value of collective bargaining as an important and historically established procedural mechanism inherent in workers' basic rights to associate. In the 2007 *Health Services* case, the court dismissed the Labour Trilogy decisions, stating that these cases were based on a "decontexualized" interpretation of Section 2(d). The court instead proposed a "purposive" approach to interpreting the Charter, which considered the historical context of Canadian labor relations.[114]

According to such an approach, collective bargaining was *implicit* within the Charter, based on the fact that Canada has historically protected and recognized the right of collective bargaining as key to freedom of association. The Court argued in the *Health Services* decision that collective bargaining had long been an important part of Canadian society. The recognition of the centrality of collective bargaining existed prior to the establishment of its modern statutory protections, "emerging as the most significant collective activity through which freedom of association is expressed in the labour context."[115] The Court also cited early government publications[116] that stressed the importance of collective bargaining and the records from the debate on the wording of the Canadian Charter, which included questions as to whether to include collective bargaining in the text. One of the writers of the Charter argued that collective bargaining was implicit in freedom of association, but did not want it mentioned specifically as this might detract from the other nonlabor-related elements of the law. This decision to exclude specific mention of collective bargaining, according to the Court, was an implicit affirmation of its importance.[117]

The majority opinion also argued that including collective bargaining protections within freedom of association was consistent with the rights, freedoms, and values of the Charter. The justices stated that the Charter has underlying values; therefore, its provisions should be interpreted in such a way that maintains "internal cohesion." These values include "human dignity, equality, liberty, respect for the autonomy of the individual and the enhancement of democracy."[118] The Court ruled that the right to bargain collectively is necessary because it enhances the rights of workers and promotes these core values.

The final arguments of the Court related to the context of freedom of association, both within international law and the Charter itself. As the Canadian Charter is a "living document" that changes based on "the current situation and needs of Canadians," the Court argued that international law should guide the interpretation of section 2(4). Therefore, both "Canada's *current* international law commitments and the current state of international thought on human rights provide a persuasive source for interpreting the scope of the Charter."[119] The Court cited the language of ILO Convention 87, as well as the United Nations' ICCPR and the ICESCR. The Court stated, "The ICESCR, the ICCPR and Convention No. 87 extend protection to the functioning of trade unions in a manner suggesting that a right to collective bargaining is part of freedom of association. The interpretation of these conventions, in Canada and internationally, not only supports the proposition that there is a right to collective bargaining in international law, but also suggests that such a right should be recognized in the Canadian context."[120] While none of these three legal documents includes an explicit right to collective bargaining, the Court cited their jurisprudence, which has interpreted collective bargaining as inherent within the law. For example, the Court cited the 1999 Concluding Observations of the Human Rights Committee, which interpreted Article 22 as including the right to form unions and collective bargaining.[121] The Court did not, however, directly cite the recommendations of the ILO Committee on Freedom of Association with regard to Bill 29. Perhaps this was to avoid creating a precedent in Canadian law through which the Committee on Freedom of Association's recommendations might gain a privileged legal position. But the Court stated that ILO bodies, including the Committee on

Freedom of Association, the Committee of Experts, and the Commission of Inquiry, had provided good interpretations of the freedom of association, which (though not binding) were "cornerstones" of international trade union rights laws that "shed light on the scope of section 2(d) of the Charter as it was intended to apply to collective bargaining." The *Health Services* decisions cited a recent ILO article, published in the ILO's journal, *International Labour Review*, outlining basic principles of freedom of association that include collective bargaining.[122]

Having overturned prior rulings on the scope of the Charter's protection of "freedom of association," the court then evaluated whether the British Columbia government's Bill 29 had indeed violated the Charter. In order to do so, however, it was necessary to create a standard of violation, called "substantial interference."[123] The justices argued that Section 2(d) protects citizens from any "substantial interference," in which government actions discourage the collective pursuit of common goals, *regardless* of whether or not there was *intent.*[124] These actions must "seriously undercut or undermine the activity of workers joining together to pursue the common goals of negotiating workplace conditions and terms of employment."[125] This interference must be so strong as to hurt the ability of workers to engage in meaningful negotiations with their employers. Two conditions were deemed necessary (both had to be present) for substantial interference to take place. The first concerned whether interference in a particular matter affected the *process and capacity* of collective bargaining. An example would be if the state passed legislation to unilaterally negate the existing negotiated provisions of prior agreements. The second involved whether the interference would therefore affect the "collective right to good faith negotiation and consultation." In other words, the state (or province) may curtail some particular elements in the process of collective bargaining for emergency purposes (the first condition), but as long as the possibility remains for open consultation and good faith negotiation (the second condition), this does not then violate Section 2(d).[126]

The Court decided that sections 6(2), 6(4), and 9, in conjunction with section 10, fulfilled the requirement of substantial interference. Section 6(2) violated collective bargaining rights because it negated existing collective agreements that limited the ability of employers to contract out non-clinical services. Section 6(4) negated clauses of prior agreements requiring employers to consult with unions before contracting out. In conjunction with section 10, sections 6(2) and 6(4) gave no future voice or consultation to workers regarding the contracting out of services and reassignment/transfer.[127] Section 9 violated collective bargaining rights because it forbade future collective agreements from restricting layoffs. Thus, the court found that these clauses of Bill 29 limited workers' access to collective bargaining, which in turn sufficiently limited workers' freedom of association, constituting a violation of Section 2(d).[128]

In addition to "substantial interference," the Court argued that in order for a law to violate the Charter, it must violate the principles of Section 1 of the Charter. Section 1 of the Charter allows for "reasonable limits . . . [that] can be reasonably justified in a free and democratic society." To determine whether Bill 29 could be justified as necessary in a free and democratic society, the justices applied the four categories (from the 1994 Oakes case) to the relevant sections of the law. The Oakes test requires the following conditions. First, there must be a "pressing and substantial" need for the law. Second, there must be a "clear and rational" connection between the law's objective and "the means of the law to attain this goal." Third, the law must be "minimally impairing." Finally, the law must be "proportional"; the measures ("deleterious effects") of the law must be justifiable based on the objectives of the law ("salutatory effects").[129] The government bears the burden of proof in the satisfying of these conditions.

The Court decided that while the situation in British Columbia was indeed pressing, given the "unsustainability" that the provincial government attributed to the current health care system, the need for greater labor flexibility, and rising labor costs in British Columbia, the laws were not justifiable under Section 1 because they were not minimally impairing.[130] Although the pressing need, rationale, and proportionality requirements were covered, the laws were not minimally impairing because they clearly curtailed basic collective bargaining rights, and the legislative process lacked union consultation. The unorthodox speed with which Bill 29 was adopted was noted by the Court as evidence of this lack of consultation. The Court wrote in its decision:

> The only evidence of consultation is a brief telephone conversation between a member of the government and a union representative within the half hour before the Act (then Bill 29) went to the legislature floor and limited to informing the union of the actions that the government intended to take. This was an important and significant piece of labour legislation. It had the potential to affect the rights of employees dramatically and unusually. Yet it was adopted with full knowledge that the unions were strongly opposed to many of the provisions, and without

> consideration of alternative ways to achieve the government objective, and without explanation of the government's choices.[131]

The British Columbia government's use of irregular procedures in passing Bill 29 was an important reason that the Court found the law and the conditions of its passage unconstitutional.

As this decision in many ways went against the Labour Trilogy, it was considered an important development in Canadian human rights. Even the sole dissenter, Justice Deschamps, argued that this interpretation was a "major step forward in the recognition of collective activities."[132] To give the British Columbia government time to make the appropriate changes and compensations, the ruling was suspended for one year. The initial public response by Premier Campbell was typically unwavering. He stated, on June 11, 2007, that the process would be long and would require "legal remedies," and he defended Bill 29, claiming that the Supreme Court ruling "did not change the facts . . . that we inherited . . . politically driven contracts which cost literally hundreds of millions of dollars to taxpayers that weren't funded."[133]

Many observers found this decision surprising. The *Globe and Mail*, a national newspaper, called this decision an "astonishing about face," despite the fact that the current bench of justices had established itself as "conservative, pragmatic and uneasy about using the Charter of Rights to disturb the status quo."[134] According to Brian Etherington, not a single Canadian labor law specialist present at the Canadian Labour Law Casebook Group meeting in Montreal on June 7 and 8, 2007, predicted this outcome.[135] The Court decided that collective bargaining not only protects the act of making representations but also the "right to be heard in the context of a meaningful process of consultation and discussion."[136] This was in contrast to the United Kingdom's interpretation of the European Court, as the government's publications on the 2004 Employment Relations Law explicitly rejected the principle of the "right to be heard."

The British Columbia government reopened negotiations with the province's trade unions on January 10, 2008, in order to deal with the compensation and legal changes necessitated by the Supreme Court decision. By the end of the month, the unions (including the nurses, health sciences, and service employees) came to a tentative agreement. This agreement included a cap on future contracting out, better severance and retirement provisions, new job opportunities specifically intended for affected workers, the restoration of seniority and servicing rights, and greater provisions for consulting with workers on outsourcing and privatization.[137] These provisions were meant to improve the protection of collective bargaining rights for public-sector (especially health) workers. In addition, they were to compensate for damages suffered since 2002, including a $75 million lump sum, with some funds dedicated to retraining the 40,000 affected workers.[138] In addition, the final agreement included provisions to remove those parts of the law that violated the Charter protections.

British Columbia's Health Minister George Abbott told the *Globe and Mail* that this put the province in a difficult position, and he once again justified Bill 29: "When those changes were undertaken, it was a series of changes undertaken to try and preserve the sustainability of the health-care system in British Columbia. . . . We were really in a tough place. The Supreme Court, rightly or wrongly, said you should have consulted more before you made the changes." Yet despite having to change the law, Abbott expressed satisfaction with the final settlement, because it allowed the province "much-needed flexibility, continued flexibility" while clarifying procedures with unions.[139] Union members voted to accept the settlement, and on April 14, 2008, the British Columbia Legislative Assembly held the first reading of the Health Statutes Amendment Act (Bill 26), which would amend the problematic clauses of Bill 29. This bill was eventually passed on May 29, 2008.[140] Unions later reported to the ILO committee that the province had settled over 3,000 grievances related to Bill 29 in a May 2008 communication.[141]

However, it is important to note that the reparations made with regard to the 2002 Bill 29 did not address all of the issues brought up in the ILO complaints. In fact, the ILO committee considers case number 2173 to be in "follow-up," rather than "closed," because the government has not responded to several issues. In its communications to the ILO committee in March 2009, the British Columbia government not only spoke of the progress made with regard to the Supreme Court case, but also claimed to have "undertaken numerous measures to facilitate and support the collective bargaining process between teachers and school employers." [142] This included the Industrial Inquiry Commission in 2005, which released its report in February 2007. The commission's findings were also the basis of a five-year collective agreement, which started in 2006. As evidence of its good faith in promoting public-sector collective bargaining, the government also reported that by the end of 2006, it had settled 130 collective agreements, "securing unprecedented labour peace in the province."[143] While the ILO committee accepted this news with great interest, it regretted that the British Columbia government "had not shown any sign of willingness to search [for] resolution of grievances concerning the education sector," particularly the continued designation of education as an essential service, which limited teachers' strike rights.[144]

Theoretical Implications: Stalled Compliance and Political Outcomes

What is most notable about the Canadian case, in contrast to the South Korea and U.K. cases, is that the political process did not respond as readily to the normative negotiation process. In the United Kingdom, the government made changes prior to the ECHR decision by passing the Employment Relations Act in 1999, and the South Korean government admitted the need for reforms by establishing its commissions on labor relations and passing the Trade Union and Labour Relations Adjustment Act of 1997. However, there was very little response from the British Columbia government, until they were legally obligated to do so. This section will investigate this nonresponsiveness and stalled compliance.

In some ways, it appears that the normative negotiation process had no effect on the British Columbia government. It was not held accountable to international law, and it did not care what an international institution said about its trade union rights situation because weakening those rights was a key part of its platform. However, even an antiunion government such as the British Columbia Liberals still felt obligated to justify its practices within a larger normative framework. But there are interesting differences between the British Columbia case and the South Korean and the United Kingdom cases. First, unlike the other countries, the British Columbia government confidently contested the ILO's recommendations because it could rely on an emerging "Canadian" legal interpretation of trade union rights: a limited conception that matched the Liberal government's agenda. In addition, domestic actors were not able to secure recommendations from additional international institutions on British Columbia's violation of labor rights. NGOs brought concerns about Bill 29 to other UN human rights organizations, but these concerns were not mentioned in any of these committees' reports. While the presence of multiple international institutions' recommendations mattered in other cases, it is not clear whether more recommendations would have mattered to the Liberal government. Unlike the other cases, the Liberal government saw the protection of human rights and labor rights as working against its political interests. In contrast, the U.K. government followed the ECHR decision because of its larger "pro-Europe" agenda, and

South Korea responded to international pressure because of its ambitions to join the OECD and become a prominent actor in the global economy.

In addition to its subnational status, which shielded it from ILO Conventions obligations, the political and ideological orientation of the British Columbia government also limited the influence of human rights law. Strikingly, the British Columbia government during its first term dismantled existing human and labor rights institutions and protections. In addition to labor-related human rights, general human rights were seen as a hindrance to the province's economic goals. For example, the Liberal government shut down the independent, government-funded Human Rights Commission in 2002, after a recommendation by the B.C. Business Council that such a commission served no good purpose.[145]

Furthermore, the British Columbia government seemed equally unconcerned with the human rights recommendations of other international institutions. For example, the British Columbia government ignored the recommendations of the UN Committee on the Elimination of Discrimination Against Women (CEDAW).[146] The CEDAW's 2003 Concluding Comments regarding Canada's fifth periodic report included a special section on British Columbia's women's rights deficiencies. The CEDAW Committee specifically mentioned that cuts in social and welfare provisions within the province had disproportionately affected Aboriginal women, and it cited as evidence of such cuts the closing of the independent Human Rights Commission, the closing of courthouses, and changes in social programs for victims of domestic violence. The CEDAW report stated that "the Committee . . . urges the government of British Columbia to analyze its recent legal and other measures as to their negative impact on women and to amend the measures, where necessary."[147] Although this international report received a fair amount of media and public attention in British Columbia, there was still little response from the government.[148] While the Liberal government did not publicly reject human rights, as governments rarely do,[149] "the [British Columbia] government . . . act[ed] with extraordinary disregard [for the] Human Rights standard," according to a representative of the Poverty and Human Rights Centre.[150] Unlike in the cases of the United Kingdom and South Korea, at no time did the Campbell Liberal government declare itself dedicated to protecting and promoting human rights.

Not only did the Liberal government have little regard for women's rights and trade union rights, but its record on labor protections was also poor. According to Chuck Puchmayr, a member of the Legislative Assembly and the opposition NDP's Labour critic in 2006, labor standards under the Liberal government were among the worst in North America.[151] For example, under the Liberal government, British Columbia's child labor laws became the most permissive in Canada. Children as young as twelve years old could now work in British Columbia, as long as they had the consent of one parent. Previously, the employment of anyone below the age of fifteen required the consent of school officials, each parent in the household, and the director of the local Employment Standards Branch.[152] Similarly, the minimum wage was scaled back through the introduction of a "training wage" of $6 per hour for the first 500 hours worked by new employees of any age. Safety regulations and their protection regimes were also significantly scaled back. Between 2001 and 2005, the Employment Standards Branch had its budget cut by 16 percent, its staff cut by one-third, and its branch offices in the province reduced by 47 percent (from seventeen offices to nine). Additionally, workers who sought to complain about violations of basic standards now faced greater obstacles under the Liberal government, including possible fees. Instead of workplace complaints being investigated by the government, complaints were now resolved through in-house "mediation," with the goal of "settlement." The government's Employment Standards Officers could adjudicate only after the mediation process was exhausted.

Another troubling labor regulation retrenchment under the Liberal government involved a decrease in the "minimum floor" of standards.[153] This floor of minimum standards served as a baseline of protections for unions' collective bargaining, as well as minimum protections for nonunion members. Under the changes, however, standards lower than the baseline could be negotiated into a collective agreement. This could lead to managers only recognizing employer-sympathetic unions in order to reduce their labor costs. In addition, specific occupational groups, such as agricultural and construction workers, became excluded from some of the basic protections of the Employment Standards Act. For example, agricultural workers were excluded from hours of work, overtime, and statutory holiday provisions. The justification for these cuts in funding and relaxing of employment standards, according to former Minister of Labour Graham Bruce, was "to provide flexibility and encourage self-reliance so employees and employers can build mutually beneficial workplace relationships."[154] This simultaneous attack on both collective trade union rights and workers' individual labor protections shows how the Liberal government's economic goals were tied to a significant curtailing of general labor rights.

The open hostility of the Liberal government toward basic human rights demonstrates that the British Columbia government was not driven solely by economic needs to impose its collective agreements, but also by political motivations to undermine the power of trade unions. The Liberal government repeatedly claimed that the economic crisis tied its hands, necessitating the controversial legislation. The government told the ILO's committee that limitations on collective bargaining were passed only because of the exceptional economic circumstances of the time.[155] However, as many opponents and unions pointed out (and as the government failed to communicate in its statements to the ILO), the Liberals, upon entering office, enacted a large tax cut, prior to passing the controversial public-sector labor bills. In 2001, the government ushered in a gradual 25 percent income tax cut, which cost the province $2 billion in the following year (2002). In 2002, the year in which Bills 27, 28, and 29 were passed into law, the government claimed "structural budget problems," including a projected $2 billion deficit.[156] It seemed that the Liberal government, in fulfilling its promise of lowering taxes, exacerbated, or perhaps created, the budget problem that it had blamed on the high wages of public service workers.

Lack of Additional International Institutional Support

Given the domestic interpretation of trade union rights within Canadian courts, the Liberal government's confidence is not that surprising. As discussed earlier, there was a domestic legal consensus excluding collective bargaining from the Charter's freedom of association clause. Therefore, the British Columbia government likely felt free to curtail these rights in the name of economic needs. In the cases of South Korea and the United Kingdom, the national courts disagreed about the scope of obligations and possible collective protections accompanying trade union rights. In addition, multiple international institutions also criticized South Korea and the United Kingdom's trade union rights practices. However, in this case, only the ILO Committee on Freedom of Association made recommendations about the laws in question.

Domestic activists did bring the British Columbia labor right situation to other international institutions with the hopes that additional institutions might make similar recommendations. In 2002 and 2005, respectively, a coalition of NGOs, including the British Columbia Poverty and Human Rights Center, sent counterreports to the UN's Human Rights Committee and the CEDAW. These submissions sought to bring further international attention to the number of general human rights abuses resulting from the new Liberal government's laws. In their communications, the NGOs also mentioned specific violations of international trade union rights norms. This was especially relevant to the CEDAW, because the majority of workers affected by Bill 29 were women. Both the CEDAW in 2003 and the Human Rights Committee in 2006 noted the multiple violations of human rights commitments by the British Columbia government, but neither report mentioned the legislative violations of trade union rights.

It is unclear why these human rights institutions did not comment on the trade union rights situation in British Columbia, even though UN Human Rights organizations do concern themselves with such rights. The localness of these disputes may have played a role in the omission. Also, unlike the ILO committee, UN human rights treaty-monitoring committees do not take complaints, but instead only review reports. While UN Human Rights agencies may have strengthened the trade unions' cause if they had commented, it is unclear if this would have had a significant impact. The British Columbia government was clearly not interested in being perceived as protecting a human rights image, and the UN committee's recommendations on other human rights concerns did not lead to changes in British Columbia laws.

Despite international attention and domestic organizing, the British Columbia government did not change the relevant legislation. Yet even though the British Columbia government was not concerned with its international reputation and legal commitments, it was still accountable to the provincial electorate and other actors. No matter how antiunion the Liberals were, the British Columbia government could not seriously dismantle the public-sector union system. It still felt compelled to justify its practices to international organizations.

The fact that the government still perceived a need to pass the bills furtively suggests a tacit recognition by Liberal leaders that these laws were not entirely legitimate. The pieces of legislation, especially Bills 15, 27, and 29, were pushed through the Legislative Assembly without the normal consultation process, with a rushed reading, and with little notification of other political actors. Bill 2 was passed during an "emergency session" of the Legislative Assembly, during summer recess, in response to the strike action of Health Sciences Association's members. When Bill 15 was passed soon afterward, the unions were only given five minutes' notice before its introduction.[157] Bills 27, 28, and 29 were passed through the legislature in just one weekend. Joy MacPhail, one of the two NDP members of the BC Legislative Assembly, described the process as "ram[med] through over the weekend."[158] Teachers and health care workers only heard about Bills 27, 28, and 29 the day before they were introduced and yet they still managed to turn up in significant numbers to protest at the provincial legislature. The passing of these laws abandoned the ordinary consultation and legislative process. It is puzzling that the Liberal government felt compelled to pass the bills outside standard procedures given that it had an overwhelming legislative majority. The Liberals could have given proper notice and consulted with social partners and the small opposition before passing these laws. By contrast, the South Korean secret legislative session in December 1996 had a practical purpose as President Kim Young Sam lacked parliamentary support. This suggests that the Liberal government recognized that these laws would likely find popular resistance and simply did not want attract public scrutiny.

Conclusions

This case is difficult to analyze comparatively for a number of reasons. First, the "outcome" of the case was determined primarily by a domestic judicial outcome, rather than a transnational political process. The outcome was in many ways unforeseen. During fall 2006, about a year prior to the Supreme Court's decision, the trade union leaders and their lawyers were pessimistic in interviews about the possible Charter challenge. Some expressed the view that the ILO committee's agitation had been most helpful for the way it mobilized the unions' membership. Yet in an unexpected turn of events, the Court wrote a sympathetic decision in favor of a broad interpretation of freedom of association.

It is not within the scope of this project to explain why the Court ruled against years of prior jurisprudence on Article 2(d) in the *Health Service* case. Much like the European Court's decision in 2002 regarding the *Wilson/Palmer* case, the decision was surprising both to the trade unions and to the government. The British Columbia Liberal government and the Labour government in the United Kingdom both expected the courts to rule in their favor. Both courts endorsed a broader interpretation of workers' rights than what was explicitly written in the law. This was even more unexpected in the Canadian case, because Article 2(d) only protects the right of freedom of association generally, making no mention of trade union rights. In contrast, Article 11 of the European Convention specifically mentions trade union rights. Neither the Charter nor the Convention, however, mentions anything about collective bargaining rights.

Additional international institutions did not make recommendations to the British Columbia government about the labor rights situation. However, despite the influence of multiple institutions' recommendations in other cases, it is not clear whether additional institutions' recommendations would have helped the trade union rights situation in British Columbia, given how unconcerned the Liberal government felt about human rights or international law. Clearly, economic growth, flexibility, and reform of the public services were its priority. The CEDAW and the Human Rights Committee made recommendations to the British Columbia government concerning its many welfare rights retrenchments, but the government did not acknowledge these recommendations as important either. It seems that multiple recommendations and their political advocacy matter more if domestic political conditions are receptive.

In British Columbia, unlike in the United Kingdom, there were strong domestic trade union networks that advocated for these legal changes. Trade unions often helped create community-based coalitions to resist the welfare cutbacks of the Liberal government. There were an estimated thirty-two public rallies in 2001–2002 against these bills. In the period after the Liberals came to power, many local political actions were coordinated because citizens connected their right to public services with the unions' concerns about the privatization of public service jobs.[159] Yet because of their strong electoral mandate and their overwhelming majority of Legislative Assembly seats, the Liberals did not feel pressured by such public organizing between 2001 and 2005. The economic successes in the third and fourth years of their first term probably only emboldened the government to continue legislating collective agreements. Furthermore, the organizational power of labor unions and local communities was not sufficient to remove the Liberals from office. Although the Liberal government lost its super majority in the 2005 election, they still maintained a large majority of seats. Unlike in South Korea, the organization of trade unions did not present a sufficient threat to the government's interests, and therefore failed to promote compliance.

However, the Supreme Court's decision remains puzzling. Was there a relationship between the ILO's recommendations and this reversal of jurisprudence? The language of the decision refers to the Committee on Freedom of Association but not its specific recommendations to British Columbia. Perhaps this was a political move, one intended to avoid a legal precedent in which provinces could be held to specific recommendations in the future. Several Canadian labor scholars have speculated that the Supreme Court ruled in favor of a stronger interpretation of trade union rights in light of the political costs of the earlier, narrower version. Provincial governments, believing they had free reign due to the *Labour Trilogy* decisions, ran roughshod over trade union rights.[160] This decision has promoted a somewhat "thicker" interpretation of the norm, similar to the decision in the European Court of Human Rights. The contestation over trade union rights does not occur in a vacuum, and it is possible that the many "stronger" claims by the UN human rights agencies and the ILO influenced the Canadian Supreme Court justices. William Schabas argues that Canadian Courts have increasingly referred to international jurisprudence, and even to those bodies to which Canada is not a party, in their decisions.[161] Perhaps for a case as controversial as *Health Services*, the Canadian Supreme Court felt compelled to turn to the international legal interpretations. Even though the European Court had not traditionally supported the "strong" version of freedom of association, its 2002 decision may have added to the international legal consensus on the thicker interpretation of the norm, despite the absence of collective bargaining from the explicit wording of some international legal provisions.

Though this landmark case has become a topic of much scholarly debate, there is some agreement that the Supreme Court's decision is still limited and unclear. For example, the majority opinion in *Health Sciences* struck down the *Labour Trilogy* decisions that excluded the right to strike from Charter rights, but it did not clarify the scope of strike rights in the decision.[162] *Health Sciences* does not protect against all infringement of collective bargaining and trade union rights. Rather, the decision protects only against state action that "substantially interferes" with collective bargaining in the pursuit of common goals, and the threshold for such a violation is quite specific and high. However, the Supreme Court's decision does not clearly define what kinds of behavior might constitute such interference. The ruling argued that the Charter protects collective bargaining "as the right to a process . . . [but] does not guarantee a certain substantive or economic outcome."[163] Yet the decision also states that substantial interference in the bargaining process would only constitute a Section 2(4) violation if the specific issues were relevant to "the capacity of union members to pursue collective goals."[164] The Court specifies that interference in bargaining over cafeteria layouts, uniform design, or parking lots, for example, would not violate the Charter. The Court's argument that the Charter does not guarantee substantive outcomes while conditioning Article 2(4) protections on particular bargaining issues seems contradictory.[165] Judy Fudge, a labor expert, called this simultaneous focus on process and substantive outcomes a "confusing mishmash."[166]

Appendix

British Columbia Annual Growth, in Percentage of Provincial GDP

Year	*Percent of Provincial GDP growth*
1985	6.86
1986	5.95
1987	9.89
1988	9.84
1989	8.26
1990	5.03
1991	4.39
1992	5.25
1993	7.61
1994	8.05
1995	4.53
1996	2.81
1997	2.74
1998	1.29
1999	3.01
2000	4.50
2001	1.07
2002	3.19
2003	2.58
2004	4.129943
2005	4.298502
2006	3.588828

Source: British Columbia, BC Stats, "The BC Economic Accounts," accessed July 29, 2008, http://www.bcstats.gov.bc.ca/data/bus_stat/econ_acct.asp.

CONCLUSION

International Norms, Trade Union Rights, and Countering Neoliberalism

Trade unions have been on the defensive in recent decades. While most of the attention has been focused on the oppression of unions in nondemocratic and developing countries, trade unions in more developed, democratic states have also faced problems. The case studies in this book demonstrate how even wealthy democracies may resist political demands to improve trade union rights protections. Often, state laws that fail to protect trade union rights are not the result of an accidental oversight, but rather reflect explicit political goals and interests. As a result of economic pressures under globalization, many states have adopted a powerful narrative that conditions economic competitiveness on curtailing trade unions' activities.

Although the postwar period has been characterized by the hegemony of human rights,[1] trade union rights have been largely ignored. Trade union rights are also part of the international economic regime, but unlike most trade-related issues, they lack strong enforcement mechanisms. Therefore, the status of trade union rights as international norms raises critical questions for international norms theory, as their protection involves not only normative and human rights elements, but also a state's economic interests. These comparative case studies show how older, established norms can still influence contemporary state behavior, as constructivist norm theory predicts. This influence, however, is often secondary to states' material and political interests. The postwar shift in the global economy has resulted in new incentive structures for states. But rather than abandon their past commitments, states now construct their obligations to trade union rights in narrow and individualistic ways. Yet because of trade union rights' association within the human rights regime, trade unions and other actors have been able to use international institutions as platforms to critique rights violations and to influence positive reforms to domestic trade union rights.

Despite the fact that South Korea, the United Kingdom, and Canada have very different geographic positions, economic interests, and political leadership, the three countries had similar interactions with international institutions regarding their violations of trade union rights. While the legislative issues involved in these three cases may seem different, the underlying issues and legal questions were similar. For example, prior to the international institutions' inquiries about trade union rights violations, trade unions in each country lost domestic political support because of large-scale strikes. While Britain had the largest and most significant strikes during the Winter of Discontent in 1978–79, the Great Workers' Struggle in South Korea negatively affected the popular perception of unions.[2] Likewise, the comparatively small-scale but unpopular public-sector strikes in British Columbia in the 1990s created political support for curbing public-sector trade union rights. These strikes led to elections of antiunion governments in British Columbia and the United Kingdom. As trade unions engaged in unpopular strikes during economic downturns (or prior to economic downturns, as in the cases of British Columbia and South Korea), they became effective scapegoats for politicians who wished to connect organized labor to poor economic outcomes. It seems that in these three cases, unpopular strikes are an important political precondition for labor rights violating legislation.

As trade unions in these cases lost some public sympathy, it is also interesting that the anti–trade union rights laws in these cases were similar. In all these cases, the legislatures passed laws violating trade union rights using questionable and often undemocratic means. For example, in South Korea, the parliament passed the 1996 reform in a pre-dawn morning session without inviting the opposition party. In the United Kingdom, the Ullswater Amendment was pushed through the parliament quickly, without the usual consultation or discussion with social partners, or even an introduction in a white paper. In British Columbia, the passing of Bill 29 also did not adhere to normal communication and reading procedures. While the state later defended its respective laws to international institutions, these irregular methods suggest that the governments recognized that the laws were controversial. Furthermore, despite the partisan and political differences between and within each of these cases, the governments of all three states engaged in a similar process of norm contestation when responding to and interacting with the international institutions. Each government argued that its practices did not violate trade union rights and, in so doing, implicitly affirmed the importance of the norms. This demonstrates how international trade union rights, despite lacking strong enforcement mechanisms, might affect the behavior and rhetoric of even relatively powerful state actors.

These cases also demonstrate the stickiness of norms and rights and the ways that international institutions can constrain state behavior. Even though some of the foundational conditions present during the post–World War II period have changed, trade union rights are not likely to go away. No matter how strong a government's antiunion commitments, none of these countries would (or realistically could) overturn its system of trade union rights. Yet it also seems reasonable to assume that few states would immediately comply with the International Labour Organization's trade union rights recommendations, especially if governments believed that compliance would economically disadvantage the state. While change would, or lack of change, in the partisan orientation of governments mattered, it seems that even self-described human rights governments were reluctant to change their laws toward stronger trade union rights compliance, even when these obligations were made explicit through the clarifications provided by the various international institutions.

The interactions between the international institutions and the three countries revealed the process by which the states contested these norms. States justified their refusal to comply by counter-interpreting these norms in ways that allowed the practice. In addition, states affirmed their commitment to trade union rights, while disagreeing with the particular recommendations of the international institutions. Economic concerns were the primary justification for the states' refusal to comply with the international institutions' recommendations, even though the countries were wealthy and productive. If this is the situation for democratic and economically prominent states, it does not bode well for the possibilities of strong labor rights protection in less wealthy countries. However, even though economic fears made states reluctant to change their practices, each state did gradually make legal changes to comply with the international institutions' recommendations. This concluding chapter will summarize the findings in these different case studies and offer conclusions about the future of trade union rights as a continuously "negotiated" international norm.

The case studies show an interesting dynamic. These states were not inclined to protect trade union rights for a range of reasons, yet they still constructed their normative obligations in ways that reflected their interests.

Even the government most openly hostile to organized labor, British Columbia's Liberal government, responded to international inquiries about its protection of trade union rights. This communication process between trade unions, international institutions, and states constituted a negotiation over the scope of international norms that are often ambiguous. While states are the ultimate arbiters of their behavior, this communication process limited states' range of possible choices. In each of these cases, a number of factors mitigated states' neoliberal reluctance to protect such rights. The intersection between normative commitments and strategic motivations affected the possibilities for state compliance with more robust conceptions of trade union rights. When the contingent construction of economic and political interests coincided with these trade union rights changes, domestic legal reform was possible.

This book contests the claims of constructivist international relations scholars who might interpret the resulting legal changes from interactions between states and international institutions as evidence of social learning, persuasion, and internalization of a norm. Changes in law did not occur because of social learning on the part of these states. However, the Canadian case suggests that judiciaries, which remain relatively independent of the economic pressures of political leaders, may learn. In all three of these cases, states adopted better trade union rights protections for instrumental reasons, not because they were convinced of the legitimacy of the trade union position. Therefore, the normative negotiation process in this book was a political process that promoted changes based on a logic of consequences.

In some ways, the dynamic between states, trade unions, and international institutions illustrated in this book demonstrates the difficulties of protecting workers' rights in the absence of the strong Fordist welfare state.[3] The efficacy of these rights is based on their association with a human rights regime primarily understood to consist of individual, civil, and political rights—in other words, to those minimal rights that fit well within the ideological apparatus of the new economy. Material conditions affect states' interpretations of international norms. While the importance of trade union collective action and solidarity was at least begrudgingly acknowledged in the past, the states in this book sought mostly to protect individual legal rights for workers to form unions, but offered little protection for unions' ability to influence change. The Great Depression, World Wars I and II, and the Russian Revolution created a different set of incentives for states vis-à-vis economic and social rights, but the declining significance of these rights may not be overdetermined. Another significant event could affect this material interest balance, such as a prolonged economic recession leading to subsequent popular contention. While human rights are not necessarily limited or unable to deal with economic justice and power inequalities, these cases demonstrate that the *current* dominant interpretation of these human rights reflects this limited, individual discourse.

State representatives generally justified the laws in question in these cases by appealing to the need for labor flexibility. States claimed that flexibility was necessary to promote greater economic growth, greater competitiveness, and promote employment. While laws that failed to protect trade union rights were passed in the name of flexibility, labor market flexibility does not necessarily require such violations. It should be noted that although labor market flexibility reforms hurt job security, a traditional concern for unions, job security is not a formal part of the trade union rights regime. Perhaps the direct conflict of interest between employers' economic need for flexibility and workers' desire for stable long-term employment explains the relative lack of protection for job security under international labor rights law. Regardless, labor flexibility measures are left to the discretion of states. In these cases, states gave greater prerogative to employers' desires to institute more flexible work relationships. South Korea sought to introduce flexible employment policies as a move away from traditional job security norms that would help the economy regain a competitive edge. The United Kingdom supported individual contracts that empowered employers to pursue more flexible employment relations, even though this practice ended collective bargaining. In British Columbia, the government sought to introduce flexibility in public service workers' contracts, as unions had negotiated strong job security measures, which were seen as too costly.

These states all sought primarily to increase economic growth and to enhance economic competitiveness. Governments would sometimes exaggerate their economic problems to international institutions to justify their behaviors. While certain economic crises did require the state to take strong measures, such as the IMF crises in both the United Kingdom and South Korea in the 1970s and 1990s, respectively, governments used the presence of crisis to justify drastic action against trade unions and their rights. Even the British Columbia government used the east Asian financial crisis in its communications with the ILO committee as part of its larger justifications of the laws in question. These justifications were given four years after the crisis, which had occurred in a different hemisphere. The cases do suggest, however, that economic crises do not necessitate the curtailing of trade union rights or repression of trade unions' activities. Although the circumstances were unique, the state was able to grant significant concessions to trade unions in terms of organizing rights during some of the most severe times of the financial crisis.

In addition, states often misrepresented the severity of economic problems in order to justify curtailing trade union rights. For example, the Kim Young Sam government repeatedly told the ILO committee and even the UN human rights committees that it wanted to amend its trade union rights law, but such reform had to take a back seat to more pressing economic concerns. Specifically, the government cited disappointing economic growth. However, according to the World Bank indicators listed at the end of Chapter 4, South Korea's economy grew at a rate of about 8.5 percent in 1994 and more than 9 percent in 1995. Though in 1991 and 1992 it experienced less growth—about 5.8 percent and 6 percent, respectively—these are still impressive rates of economic growth. Likewise, British Columbia did not suffer from severely stunted economic growth after 2001, as growth rates quickly rebounded by 2002. However, the British Columbia government passed most of its offending laws in 2002, claiming they were economically necessary. While state leaders cannot accurately assess growth rates during a year in the way that economists can after the fact, these numbers suggest that the situation was not dire enough to justify such drastic changes. It is not clear whether these economic concerns are simply window dressing to undermine the power of trade unions or if these exaggerated perceptions of economic vulnerability reflect a genuine anxiety on the part of state leaders. High unemployment figures and an inability to attract foreign investment are genuine concerns for any state. But the fact that the leadership of the United Kingdom stressed the importance of radically challenging existing employment norms as way to "recover" Britain and increase its competitiveness is very revealing. That the New Labour government adopted similar language, despite a historical connection to trade unions, as the Conservative government's in justifying these laws suggests that there is something exceptional about contemporary political economic circumstances that make robust protection of trade union rights difficult.

Yet with some exceptions, human rights remain politically important within these neoliberal contexts. While the Liberal government in British Columbia felt less vulnerable about human rights for different reasons, many of the governments in South Korea and the Labour government under Tony

Blair made human rights an important part of their political platforms. This turn toward human rights within neoliberalism is a well-documented phenomenon. While critics argue that human rights have become the legitimizing ethical discourse of the current global economic context,[4] this criticism ignores the fact that human rights have multiple interpretations, origins, and effects. While human rights frameworks cannot solely counter the effects of neoliberalism, these cases show how the strategic use of this rhetoric can limit the state under certain circumscribed conditions.

Possibilities for Compliance

States in this book changed their trade union rights laws to better match the recommendations of international institutions because of a series of contingent conditions, often the unintended consequences of other policies. This was most likely to occur when economic or political goals temporarily aligned with the strengthening of trade unions. This book identified a number of important conditions in which this pressure on states could lead to trade union rights compliance. In South Korea, the necessity of bargaining with trade unions during the IMF crisis resulted in a state's economic goals and trade union rights reforms being rapidly aligned. However, in most cases, this was a slower process. The cases identified several factors as important for this dynamic norm and interest-creation process: the presence of recommendations from multiple international institutions, the types of disputes in question, and the vulnerability of various domestic political institutions to human rights considerations.

Multiple Recommendations

International institutions' recommendations by themselves had limited power to affect domestic trade union rights changes. As observers have often noted, these international institutions lack strong enforcement mechanisms. The ILO's Committee on Freedom of Association was the first organization to make a recommendation in each of these cases. This is likely because the cost of bringing a complaint to the committee is the lowest both in terms of resources and requirements. Getting this initial report from the ILO committee was an important first step that trade unions pursued when domestic avenues seemed closed. Receiving supportive recommendations is not guaranteed, however, as the ILO committee draws on its own jurisprudence when judging complaints from trade unions. For instance, some of the laws that the British Columbia unions brought to the ILO were not considered violations of trade union rights.

However, international institutions' initial recommendations mattered in a couple ways. First, they provided a symbolic victory for domestic trade unions, who would continue to press for better protections of their rights through various domestic means, including legal avenues. This external legitimation was particularly important in South Korea, as many of the unions lacked legal status. Even though these recommendations do not bind states, representatives and leadership of trade unions incorporated these recommendations into their legal or political arguments. Such arguments became stronger if other international institutions referenced each other when evaluating these laws. Typically, other institutions would cite the ILO's recommendations. In the case of South Korea, trade union and human rights supporters gave information about the ILO and other state representatives at the OECD, which in turn made the trade union rights issue salient to South Korea's admission criteria. In contrast, even though no additional international institutions made recommendations about the British Columbia laws, the Canadian Supreme Court adopted some of the ILO's standards, similar to the European Court of Human Rights.

Though a consensus among multiple international institutions could help trade unions, the states capitalized on the breakdown of this consensus. This can be observed in the United Kingdom under the Conservative government, and South Korea under Roh Moo Hyun. While the Conservative government resisted advice from international institutions, it did refer to the European Commission of Human Rights' decision when responding to the ILO about the GCHQ issue. In a way, the U.K. government used the favorable decision from the European Commission to vindicate its position vis-à-vis international trade union rights institutions. Likewise, when the OECD began to reconsider the need for labor rights monitoring in South Korea, the tone and even the frequency of communications between South Korea and the ILO committee began to change. For South Korea, ending the OECD monitoring process became an important goal in itself. South Korea seemed less concerned with complying with trade union rights than with disrupting the international "consensus" that it was violating these rights.

In the case of British Columbia, only the ILO committee made recommendations, and therefore trade unions could not cite an international institutional consensus on its trade union rights concerns. Rather, the government had the convenience of drawing on an existing body of jurisprudence to support its understanding of trade union rights norms. The British Columbia government used a domestic consensus on the limited nature of trade union rights to counter the ILO committee's recommendations. In doing so, the state was able to construct its trade union rights obligations to fit its neoliberal goals.

Type of Disputes in Question

Some trade union rights issues were more likely than others to prompt states to change their behavior. Based on the diversity of disputes presented in the book, it appears that states were more likely to address complaints regarding individual-level protections. While South Korea readily changed laws that allowed individual workers to join unions, some problems in protecting collective rights have not been addressed. For example, the scope of South Korean teachers and civil servants' bargaining rights remain limited. While the Korean Teachers' Union sought to improve curricula and change South Korea's educational culture, the Act Concerning the Establishment of and Operations of Teachers Unions (1999) limits their scope of bargaining to working conditions. Civil servants in South Korea are likewise only allowed to bargain about wages, welfare, and working conditions. In addition, the state continues to repress the KGEU, and as a result, this organization lacks official status.

South Korea also fails to uphold its obligations to protect strike rights. Both civil servants and teachers lack the right to strike. In addition, the South Korean state often intervenes in strikes and workers' collective actions. The state uses the "obstruction of business" law to arrest many striking workers, criminalizing their trade union activity. The Committee on Freedom of Association argued that these workers were engaging in legitimate collective action, but the South Korean authorities claimed they were involved in illegal activities.[5] The state allows private employers to bring suits for "damages" against trade unions for engaging in collective activities.[6]

In the United Kingdom, the New Labour government was more likely to respond to individual trade union rights issues. For example, New Labour was unambiguously committed to ending the blacklists, which violated individual rights. New Labour also vowed to end the ban on trade union rights for GCHQ workers, a goal that it communicated to the ILO committee. Under the 1999 Employment Relations Act, GCHQ workers were granted their individual rights to join a union. While GCHQ workers could engage in collective bargaining, they were not allowed the right to strike. The Labour government also responded to the Wilson/Palmer case by protecting individual workers from both omissions and actions that sought to discriminate against individual workers. However, both the 1999 and 2004 legal changes did not provide strong protections for unions themselves.

Likewise, in all of its communications to the ILO, the British Columbia government insisted that it did not violate trade union rights because it respected individual rights to trade union membership. While the unions complained about collective bargaining and strike provisions, the state insisted that these laws did not violate individual members' rights. Yet even after the Canadian Supreme Court's ruling, collective rights issues remained. For example, the province has maintained limited strike rights for British Columbia's teachers, justified because of their "essential services" status.

Human Rights Commitments

A state's legal commitment to trade unions mattered, but these case studies demonstrated that the degree of a country's international legal commitments did not predict compliance. The United Kingdom has the highest level of formal legal commitments to trade union rights, having ratified ILO conventions, the European Convention, the Social Charter, and the relevant UN human rights documents. In fact, since the United Kingdom has ratified Convention 98, the convention on collective bargaining, the United Kingdom has the strongest obligation to collective trade union rights, compared to the other countries in this book. However, the United Kingdom was reluctant to make changes to its trade union rights laws to protect collective bargaining. The Wilson case was first considered by the ILO in 1994, but the United Kingdom's reforms did not occur until 2004. Canada has the second strongest obligation to international trade union rights laws, as it has ratified the UN human rights documents and ILO Convention 87. However, because of Canadian federal arrangements, these obligations had little effect on the laws in British Columbia. In contrast, South Korea has the lowest level of obligations, with a conditional ratification of the ICCPR, a ratification of the ICESCR, and no ILO conventions. South Korea, though, moved more quickly and more comprehensively to protect trade union rights compared to other countries.

However, while formal legal commitments were not necessarily sufficient to promote change, informal commitments were sometimes influential. Often these informal commitments were linked to the presence of an international identity or reputational concern. One of the most effective points of leverage over South Korea was its labor rights commitments to the OECD. The OECD has little sanctioning power and no legal status. However, because OECD entrance was important for President Kim Young Sam, this commitment provided an effective means for trade unions and transnational supporters to apply pressure. Likewise, the Labour government pledged greater commitments to Europeanization and human rights. While this alone was not enough to bring about changes, the Blair government committed itself to the principles of the European Convention on Human Rights. Although the European Court had historically interpreted these trade union rights to be limited and individualistic, the United Kingdom's legislative commitments via the 1999 Human Rights Act made it difficult to ignore the results of the Wilson case. This, however, was not strong enough to pressure the government into instituting a legal remedy that would prevent similar infractions from occurring in the future.[7]

Depth of Compliance

The resulting changes in trade union rights laws have received considerable attention in these case countries. While almost all observers have welcomed these changes as good news, the question remains whether these reforms provide substantive protections for a wide range of trade union rights. In other words, legal ambiguities made these violations of trade union rights possible in the first place. Recommendations from international institutions confirmed the arguments of trade unions, but as the possibilities for trade union violations are disparate, scholars are still debating whether the resulting legal changes provide adequate protections for workers.

In the United Kingdom, even government agencies have argued that the 2004 labor rights reforms are not sufficient. Although the government claimed that provisions of the 2004 Employment Relations Act were meant to fix the shortcomings of the prior 1999 Act, various legal experts have argued that the 2004 Act fell short of obeying the European Court's rulings. Their key claim is that the provisions of the 2004 Act were so focused on protecting individual rights that they failed to consider broader protections. As a result, another Wilson/Palmer situation, in which an employer offered a discriminatory inducement for workers to give up their collective bargaining rights, could legally occur in the future. These concerns were well documented in the Joint Committee on Human Rights' "Scrutiny of Bills: Sixth Progress Report" in 2006. The Joint Committee on Human Rights is a domestic British legislative committee with members from both the House of Lords and the House of Commons. The Joint Human Rights Committee submitted a report including many objections to the details of the Employment Relations Act.

Lord Wedderburn QC presented objections to the 2004 Act in the Joint Human Rights Committee's report. He also found the lack of recourse for trade unions problematic. Wedderburn argued that the law allowed insufficient redress for violations by employers. Specifically, the offering of financial inducements for workers to give up their rights to union representation violated both the unions' and workers' rights. Yet the law only permitted redress for workers. However, the European Court of Human Rights' decision made clear that trade union membership included the ability for trade union members to ask a union to represent them and their interests. As a result, Wedderburn argued that not allowing the union the right to ask for recourse in the situation would make the right to trade union membership "illusory." An individual who receives such a contract could only seek redress through an Employment Tribunal, which requires an individual member's willingness to engage in litigation. A trade union is not allowed to litigate on behalf of its members to protect their rights to collective bargaining and representation.[8]

Likewise, scholars continue to debate the future effect of the 2007 Health Services decision from the Canadian Supreme Court. The decision of the Supreme Court specifies exactly when a public authority has overstepped its bounds and violated the limited right of collective bargaining. This is an important distinction, as this decision does not specify conditions for protecting collective bargaining rights for workers in the private sector.[9] The decision broadens the Canadian Charter's right to freedom of association from an exclusively individual right to a collective right, but it also makes clear that it does not protect the right to strike. However, the Court's decision did include a very broad statement that Article 4(d) protects "the right of employees to associate in a process of collective action to achieve workplace goals," which means that nonunion members do have the right to collective activity.[10] The Court was careful to argue that not all aspects of collective bargaining were covered by 2(d) of the Canadian Charter. This decision protects process, not outcome.[11]

One of the key concerns about Bill 29 involves the privatization of public services. While neoliberal political goals seek to weaken the organizational power of trade unions by eroding their rights, the Liberal government wanted to redistribute power in public employment relationships to public authorities who, in turn, sought to privatize and contract out certain services as cost-cutting measures. Trade unions were concerned that this bill was an attack not only on the process of collective bargaining, but also on the very existence of public services for citizens. A state authority could have legislated privatization measures similar to Bill 29 while still respecting the Supreme Court's decision on collective bargaining. Provincial authorities are still free to pursue privatization, even though this hurts the job security of many organized workers, as long as governments engage in the meaningful consultation and cooperation that the Court requires. In addition, a provincial government could legislate against an existing collective agreement in the same manner as the Liberal government in British Columbia. This is protected under Article 1 of the Canadian Charter, which allows governments to take measures necessary under a free and democratic society. The onus would be on the government to prove that its methods were not intrusive or drastic, and that it had engaged in consultation with unions.[12]

As Chapter 6 outlines, not all of the trade unions' concerns about Bill 29 were due to violations of Charter rights. The Canadian Supreme Court upheld certain clauses in Bill 29 that changed the conditions of health service workers' employment as acceptable because they did not directly override collectively bargained provisions.[13] In addition, the attorneys who represented the British Columbia unions interpreted this decision as allowing certain state interventions on the collective bargaining process. The interference needs to pass a two-pronged test for a situation to constitute a violation of Charter rights: First the interference must be considered an "important matter to collective bargaining." Second, the Court must determine whether the interference hurts the "collective right to good faith negotiation and consultation."[14] Just as the strict requirements in the United Kingdom's 2004 law makes it difficult for unions to protect workers from a Wilson/Palmer-type situation, the Canadian Supreme Court also established a high standard to determine whether an action constitutes a collective bargaining rights Charter violation. Lemieux and Barrett argue that is unclear whether the Supreme Court decision will substantively protect the collective bargaining process.

One critic of the strategy for using human rights frameworks to support trade union interests argues that the 2007 Supreme Court decision, at best, might protect public-sector workers from the "worst excesses of neoliberalism by confirming the public policy environment of the postwar compromise."[15]

However, Savage argues that instead of demonstrating labor's power, the decision demonstrates organized labor's weakness. The legal victories are largely symbolic as they have done little to challenge the economic inequalities in Canada and are largely elite-driven shifts away from mass mobilizing and political struggle.[16]

In South Korea, the country that made the most legal changes, it is clear from the controversies that continue to surround trade unions, especially the Korean Government Employees Union, that the state has not yet internalized respect for many collective trade union rights. While teachers' right to join unions and the ability for the KCTU to exist without government repression have been established, the key problem that prompted strong attention from international institutions and the human rights community persists: the pervasive arrests of trade unionists. Even though the OECD ended its labor monitoring program with South Korea in 2007, international human rights groups continue to be concerned about the arrests of prominent trade unionists. For example, Amnesty International continues its campaigns to end arrests of South Korea trade unions' members, including a March 2009 press release about trade union leaders from the media sectors arrested for "interference of business." The release also expressed concern about the many legal loopholes that allow the state and employers to engage in civil suits against workers engaging in collective trade union activities.[17] These arrests and other violations of workers' rights continue to be the subject of several ILO Committee of Freedom of Association cases. Case 1865, which began in 1994, is still pending as the government continues to defend its practices without making changes to satisfy the trade unions or the ILO committee.[18] While South Korea has instituted many positive changes since 1993, the year that the ILO recommendations began, there are still significant shortcomings in the state's protection and general respect for basic trade union rights.

Analysis: The Efficacy of Trade Union Rights as Human Rights?

One pattern that can be observed from these case studies is the chronology by which states began to soften their stance on the trade union rights disputes. While in the early 1990s (or the early 2000s, as in the British Columbia case), states were more draconian in their approach to trade unions; by the later 2000s, the states in this book accepted stronger obligations to trade union rights. The fact that the European Court of Human Rights and the Canadian

Supreme Court both went against their established case law on trade union rights by supporting stronger, more collective understandings of state's trade union rights obligations suggests the possibility of a changing global approach. It is possible that these two relatively independent judicial institutions were influenced by civil society critiques of neoliberalism. As neoliberal institutions such as the World Bank and IMF faced strong criticism by the late 1990s, these developments could have signaled a new approach toward labor rights norms.

However, it is unclear to what extent a broader, global shift toward labor rights may be affected by the recent financial crisis. With the widespread criticism of the neoliberal model, and the devastation of the 2008 financial crisis, a number of scholars speculated about the possibilities of a new political economic regime: "post-neoliberalism."[19] While political leaders and international institutions initially called for solutions sensitive to social concerns and the needs of workers, it is unclear whether the disruption of the financial crisis has significantly challenged the reigning free market ideology. In fact, by 2010, almost all of the major industrial democracies had embraced austerity as the preferred policy to deal with the continuing economic effects of an extended recession. This included significant cuts to public employment, entitlements, and a political environment less sympathetic to workers' rights. Rather than the political dynamic in the 1930s, which led to the widespread protection of trade union rights and greater bargaining power for workers, the current financial crisis seems to have strengthened, not weakened, liberal market approaches. Despite initial optimism, it appears that the financial crisis did not delegitimize the neoliberal financial system, but rather resulted in a "patch up" of the existing system.[20]

As labor unions continue to lack strong bargaining power and political legitimacy, the legal and rights strategy remains an option. There has emerged a significant literature from labor studies that debates the usefulness of using human rights frames as a means to pursue workers' and unions' interests. A significant group of scholars and activists, such as Lance Compa and Roy Adams in Canada, have written about the utility of promoting workers' rights as human rights.[21] These authors argue that workers' use of the international human rights framework has provided a means to protect their interest against encroaching neoliberal conditions. However, dissenters such as Joseph McCartin and Nelson Lichtenstein argue that rights have superseded the past union strategies that focused on industrial democracy and building organizational power as a means for protecting workers' interests.[22]

Lichtenstein has gone so far as to say that "rights conscious liberalism . . . has also undermined the legal basis of union power."[23] Just as the Conservative government used the language of rights to give individual workers recourse against possibly repressive trade unions, these scholars argue that the language of rights has been used to undermine union solidarity by trade unions' foes. When this strategy is adopted by trade union leaders, it results in focusing members away from rank and file activism and toward judicial means of pursuing protections, shifting trade union laws from the legislatures to the courts.[24]

Although it is true that many of the narrow and often neoliberal interpretations of human rights seem congruent with neoliberal goals, the international human rights regime, both in its origins and current form, is very different than this narrow interpretation.[25] The international human rights regime, based on the United Nations documents and the Universal Declaration, include a wide variety of rights, including socioeconomic rights and rights for groups and collectivities. As this book has argued, certain political and economic conditions favor a narrow interpretation of human rights generally and labor rights specifically, but it is short-sighted to allow the neoliberal interpretation to remain authoritative. The "thicker" and more robust understanding of trade union rights, which include protections for unions and collective activity, is a long-standing one protected by several international institutions who seek to protect these rights despite dominant political and economic interests. The fact that an institution such as the ILO's Committee on Freedom of Association exists to act as an arbiter between workers, states, and employers provides a forum for workers to challenge this neoliberal interpretation of rights. As Lance Compa has argued, "without grounding in basic rights, workers' organizing and bargaining [are] vulnerable to shifts in the economy and in economic policy."[26] Making trade union rights a fundamental part of national or global citizenship is not a panacea, but rather an important starting point for effective union politics.

The dissenters are correct, though, to point out that the union strategy of using institutions such as the International Labour Organization as a means to challenge the neoliberal turn is not always effective. These case studies showed that while the presence of institutions' criticism of state practices was not a sufficient condition for changes in state behavior, it did strengthen the unions' bargaining power with the state. However, without the role played by international criticism of state behavior in each of the three case studies, it seems unlikely that the unions in question would have won the concessions they were granted. This book has argued that both ideational and material interests matter in understanding how international norms influence domestic politics. While the initial normative condemnations of a state's failure to protect trade union rights can be inconsequential, they can also be the start of a political process that changes how actors evaluate the appropriateness of certain laws and state activities. Being able to claim that a given behavior constitutes a rights violation remains a useful strategy for organized labor. The statutory protection of basic trade union rights, however, do not have a taken for granted quality even in these richer, democratic countries. In this book's case studies, states did not engage in "social learning" and internalization of strong trade union rights, but rather the confluence between a state's political economic interests and the normative negotiation process positively influenced legal outcomes for workers.

APPENDIX I

Kucera's Measure of Freedom of Association and Collective Bargaining

Civil liberties

Murder or disappearance of union members or organizers

Other violence against union members or organizers

Arrest, detention, imprisonment, or forced exile for union members or activities

Interference with union rights of assembly, demonstration, free opinion, free expression

Seizure or destruction of union premises or property

Right to establish and join union and workers' organizations

General prohibitions

General absence resulting from socioeconomic breakdown

Previous authorization requirements

Employment conditions on nonmembers in union

Dismissal or suspension for union membership or activities

Interference of employers (attempt to dominate unions)

Dissolution or suspension of union by administrative authority

Only workers' committees and labour councils permitted

Only state-sponsored or other single union permitted

Exclusion of tradeable industrial sectors from union membership

Exclusion of other sectors or workers from union membership

Other specific de facto problems or acts of prohibition

Right to establish and join federations or confederations of unions, without previous authorization

Other union activities

Right to elect representation in full freedom
Right to establish constitutions and rules
General prohibition of union/federation participation in political activities
Union control of finances

Right to bargain collectively

General prohibitions
Prior approval by authorities of collective agreements
Compulsory binding arbitration
Intervention of authorities
Scope of collective bargaining restricted by nonstate employees
Exclusion of tradeable industrial sectors from right to bargain collectively
Exclusion of other sectors of workers from right to bargain collectively
Other specific de facto problems or acts of prohibition

Right to strike

General prohibitions
Previous authorization required by authorities
Exclusion of tradeable industrial sectors from right to strike
Exclusion of other sectors or workers from right to strike
Other specific de facto problems or acts of prohibition

Export processing zones

Restricted rights in EPZs

Source: David Kucera, "Core Labour Standards and Foreign Direct Investment," *International Labour Review* 141 (2002): 42–43.

APPENDIX II

Number of Unions/Unionization Rate in Korea: 1987–2003

	Trade Unions	*Union Members (thousands)*	*Unionization Rate*
1987	4,086	1,267	18.5
1989	7,861	1,983	19.8
1991	7,656	1,803	17.2
1994	7,025	1,659	14.5
1995	6,606	1,615	13.8
1996	6,424	1,599	13.3
1997	5,733	1,484	12.2
1998	5,560	1,401	12.6
1999	5,637	1,480	11.9
2000	5,698	1,526	12.0
2001	6,150	1,568	12.0
2002	6,506	1,606	11.6
2003	6,257	1,550	11.0

Source: Republic of Korea: Ministry of Labor, *Labor Administration 2006*, 83.

Percentage of GPD Growth in Korea, 1961–2006

Year	*GDP Growth (Annual %)*	*Year*	*GDP Growth (Annual %)*
1961	4.936	1984	8.103
1962	2.458	1985	6.802
1963	9.532	1986	10.619
1964	7.561	1987	11.104
1965	5.19	1988	10.641
1966	12.7	1989	6.744
1967	6.1	1990	9.155
1968	11.7	1991	9.393
1969	14.1	1992	5.876
1970	8.345	1993	6.134
1971	8.244	1994	8.537
1972	4.467	1995	9.169
1973	12.035	1996	6.999
1974	7.182	1997	4.651
1975	5.948	1998	-6.854
1976	10.572	1999	9.486
1977	9.995	2000	8.486
1978	9.295	2001	3.837
1979	6.783	2002	6.970
1980	-1.488	2003	4.730
1981	6.163	2004	4.198
1982	7.325	2005	4.198
1983	10.775	2006	4.993

Source: World Bank, and World Bank. International Economics Dept. Development Data Group. *World Development Indicators*, 2008.

APPENDIX III

Case Disputes and U.S. Law

Comparison to Case Country Disputes

Korea

The United States, unlike in Korea in the 1990s, does not have any laws outlawing the expression of solidarity, advice, or support by third parties in industrial disputes. While the United States regulates "secondary" actions, this is very distinct from the ban on solidarity activity that the Korean government enforced. The Korean government limited free speech as well as advisement of outside parties to striking workers. On the contrary, the United States does not regulate the activities of unions' allies in the context of strikes, although sympathy and solidarity strike actions are strictly regulated under the secondary action ban. (Other industrialized countries, such as Japan, and most EU countries except the United Kingdom, allow for secondary strike activity.[1]) The Supreme Court, however, has ruled that private-sector workers' freedom of expression is defined not by constitutional guarantees, but rather Section 7 of the NLRA, which is a less powerful protection.[2]

With regard to trade union pluralism, the United States, according to its follow-up report to the ILO's Declaration on Fundamental Principles and Rights at Work, does not maintain any requirements in terms of affiliation for trade union registration. While workers' organizations need to go through either that National Labor Relations Board or the appropriate state or federal authorized election to get recognized status, this procedure is meant to ensure majority support. While only one union is recognized for collective bargaining purposes in a workplace, multiple trade unions are allowed at the national and industrial level. In addition, workers may form multiple organizations in a workplace.

There are no federal restrictions or protections for teachers' basic trade union rights, including the rights to collective action, or civil servants' basic trade union rights. Teachers' trade union rights are determined at the state level, and most states protect legally recognized rights for teachers. Even those states that do not legally recognize rights for teachers allow teachers' unions to engage in informal, voluntary collective bargaining. In fact, a 1995 study of teachers' unions in eleven states that lack legal protection of teachers' bargaining rights showed that unions significantly influenced teacher's salaries and other work conditions, especially in larger districts.[3]

As for civil servants, the law varies based on state regulations. Federal-level civil servants have had trade union rights since the 1960s, although federal employees do not have the right to strike. State-level civil servants have varying degrees of trade union rights protections. The AFL-CIO has reported that about half of all states do not protect or sufficiently protect state-level civil servants rights, but there are no federal prohibitions on state and local civil servants' trade union rights. Strike rights for state and local public-sector workers vary from state to state.[4]

United Kingdom

The practices in the United Kingdom case are illegal in the United States. The NLRA forbids blacklists, as employers may not discriminate or retaliate against employers because of union activity, past or present. In cases of discriminatory dismissals, the NLRB can issue a cease and desist, and order the employer to provide backpay. However, as the NLRA has problems with enforcement, these provisions may not be sufficient to protect workers, because discriminatory motives can be difficult to prove.[5]

In the United States, the employer cannot offer individual contracts to preclude collective bargaining. This was determined in the Supreme Court case *J.I. Case Co. v. NLRB*, 321 U.S. 332 (1944). The Supreme Court argued that employees could not give up their collective bargaining rights with an employer, although unions may negotiate contracts that create a minimum floor, and allow individuals to bargain contracts in addition to the collective agreement. Likewise, in *NLRB v. Exchange Parts Inc.* 375 U.S. 405 (1964), the Court ruled that it is illegal for an employer to use threats of reduced benefits or promises of additional benefits to undermine collective bargaining.[6]

The compulsory recognition that established the U.K. Employment Relations Act 1999 also differs from the U.S. system. While the bill continues to prioritize the established voluntary recognition mechanism, it also provides a compulsory recognition procedure as a last resort. On the contrary, the NLRA only allows voluntary recognition if majority support has been demonstrated. If workers and the employer cannot reach a voluntary recognition agreement, the Central Arbitration Committee will step in. The Central Arbitration Committee may either order the employer to recognize the union (if the union can demonstrate majority support), or may authorize a secret ballot. If a majority of workers participating in the ballot support the union, and this majority equals at least 40 percent of all eligible members in a bargaining unit, then the union will gain statutory recognition. Only workplaces with at least twenty-one employees may seek compulsory recognition, which grants such rights to 31 percent of the total workforce. The vast majority of employers, however, still choose voluntary recognition.[7] Once recognized, the union has the right to collective bargaining over pay, working hours, and holidays. This is slightly more difficult than in the United States, where only a simple majority of eligible *ballots cast* is necessary to demonstrate majority support. In the United States very few unions are certified through voluntary recognition. Most go through NLRB or similar elections.

Canada

In the United States, legislating over existing collective agreements in the public sector has not been a noticeable problem, according to AFSCME. State and federal governments have intervened in public-sector collective bargaining. Federal employees are forbidden from striking, according the 1978 Federal Labor Relations Act. Should a dispute arise within the bargaining process, the Federal Conciliation and Mediation Services helps to mediate conflicts with federal employees. If voluntary measures do not work, either side in a federal employment dispute may request the services of the Federal Service Impasse Panel.[8]

The United States maintains many restrictions of state-level public-sector trade union rights. For example, a key principle in public-sector bargaining is the "sovereignty doctrine," which states that public-sector collective bargaining is determined by democratic processes. As a result of the sovereignty principle, certain public-sector working conditions may not be available for collective bargaining. Of the states that allow public-sector workers trade union rights, most provide strong protections for the provisions of services and therefore provide a high level of autonomy to public authorities.[9] Unilateral imposition of a public employer's terms for a collective agreement is possible, as in Canada. However, like the Supreme Court's decision, most state courts have recognized that this is only legal at an impasse, after employers have fulfilled their duty to good faith consultation and bargaining procedures. Some state courts have also argued that employers must use appropriate arbitration measures prior to unilateral implementation.[10] In most states, the public-sector labor relations code include provisions for conciliation, fact-finding, and interest arbitration procedures should bargaining agents be unable to reach a mutually satisfactory agreement.[11] Unions may file an unfair labor practice complaint, as per the statutes of their state public employment laws, should unilateral imposition violate principles of good faith bargaining. For example, in a 1986 dispute involving public employees in Wayne County, Michigan, a court found the employer's unilateral imposition of a final agreement during fact-finding request constituted an unfair labor practice.[12]

In recent years, various state governments have resorted to legislation to limit the bargaining abilities of public-sector unions. Since public-sector laws are determined by states, with few federal restrictions, this has largely gone unchallenged legally. Prior to the rash of 2011 bills, governors in Indiana, Kentucky, and Missouri unilaterally ended public-sector collective bargaining agreements and provisions.[13] This did not lead to any successful legal challenges. A lower state court in Wisconsin blocked the anti-collective bargaining rights bill in Wisconsin, which severely limited the scope of bargaining for most public employees, mostly because of the irregular procedure by which the bill was passed. However, by June 2011, the state supreme court overturned this decision, allowing the controversial bill to become law, despite sustained popular action against the bill.[14]

NOTES

Chapter 1. The Precarious Position of Trade Union Rights in the Global Political Economy

Note to epigraph: International Trade Union Confederation, "ITUC Annual Survey: 101 Trade Unionists Murdered in 2009; Pressure on Workers' Rights Grows as Crisis Hits Jobs," International Trade Union Confederation, accessed December 2010, http://www.ituc-csi.org/ituc-annual-survey.html.

1. David Kucera, "Core Labour Standards and Foreign Direct Investment," *International Labour Review* 141 (2002): 31.

2. United Nations, World Summit for Social Development, *Report of the World Summit for Social Development*, Copenhagen, Denmark, March 6–12, 1995, A/CONF.1666//0, April 19, 1995.

3. Andreas F. Lowenfeld, "Congress and Cuba: The Helms-Burton Act," *American Journal of International Law* 90, no. 3 (July 1996): 424.

4. European Parliament, *The Charter of Fundamental Rights of the European Union*, accessed March 14, 2009, http://www.europarl.europa.eu/charter/default_en.htm.

5. The International Labour Organization is a specialized United Nations agency with representatives from almost every state in the world; it creates and monitors international labor standards. It has a unique tripartite structure that allows participation from governments, employers, and workers' organizations.

6. International Labour Organization, *Your Voice at Work. Global Report Under the Follow-up to the ILO Declaration on Fundamental Principles and Rights at Work. Report of the Director-General,* 2000, http://www.ilo.org/global/What_we_do/Publications/ILOBookstore/Orderonline/Books/lang—en/docName—WCMS_PUBL_9221115046_EN/index.htm.

7. Robert O'Brien, "Continuing Incivility: Labor Rights in a Global Economy," *Journal of Human Rights* 3, no. 2 (2004): 212.

8. Mark Anner and Teri Caraway, "International Institutions and Workers' Rights: Between Labor Standards and Market Flexibility," *Studies in Comparative International Development* 45, no. 2 (May 2010): 158, 160.

9. Edward Weisband and Christopher J. Colvin, "Empirical Analysis of International

Confederation of Free Trade Unions (ICFTU) Annual Surveys," *Human Rights Quarterly* 22, no. 1 (2000): 170.

10. International Labour Organization, "Freedom of Association and Effective Recognition of the Right to Collective Bargaining," *ILO Declaration on Fundamental Principles and Rights at Work* (2003), accessed April 24, 2008, http://www.ilo.org/dyn/declaris/declarationweb.static_jump?var_language=EN&var_pagename=issuesfreedom.

11. The ICFTU is now called the International Trade Union Confederation (ITUC) and represents 168 million workers from 155 countries and territories and has 311 national affiliates. International Trade Union Confederation, ITUC CSI IGB, "Who Are We?" *International Trade Union Confederation Homepage: General Information*, 2008, accessed April 21, 2008, http://www.ituc-csi.org/spip.php?rubrique57.

12. International Confederation of Free Trade Unions, *Annual Survey of Violations of Trade Union Rights 2001* (Brussels, Belgium: ICFTU Press, 2001).

13. Edward Weisband, "Discursive Multilateralism: Global Benchmarks, Shame, and Learning in the ILO Labor Standards Monitoring Regime," *International Studies Quarterly* 44, no. 4 (2000): 643.

14. This book uses the term "trade union rights" because the International Trade Union Confederation, formerly the International Confederation of Free Trade Unions, uses this term in their Annual Survey of Trade Union Rights Violations. The ILO uses "Freedom of Association" to refer to this set of rights, and other scholars, such as Moseley and Uno, refer to these rights as "collective labor rights." See Layna Mosley and Saika Uno, "Racing to the Bottom or Climbing to the Top? Economic Globalization and Collective Labor Rights," *Comparative Political Studies* 40, no. 8 (2007): 924.

15. This term comes from Irish economist John Kells Ingram, who rejected the idea that the market alone should determine the "price" of labor, and argued instead that higher moral principles should also influence labor outcomes. See Paul O'Higgins, "'Labour Is Not a Commodity'—an Irish Contribution to International Labour Law," *Industrial Law Journal* 26, no. 3 (1997): 287.

16. Philip Alston, "Core Labor Standards' and the Transformation of the International Labor Rights Regime," *European Journal of Industrial Relations* 15, no. 3 (2004): 458.

17. Trade union rights are separate from individual-level worker rights, such as the rights to safe conditions, sick leave, holidays, etc. See María Victoria Murillo, "Partisanship Amidst Convergence: The Politics of Labor Reform in Latin America," *Comparative Politics* 37, no. 4 (July 2005): 442.

18. Mita Aggarwal, "International Trade, Labor Standards, and Labor Market Conditions: An Evaluation of the Linkages," *USITC, Office of Economics Working Paper No. 95-06- C* (June), 1995.

19. Teri L. Caraway, "Labor Rights in East Asia: Progress or Regress?" *Journal of East Asian Studies* 9, no. 2 (May 26, 2009): 156.

20. Kenneth W. Abbott and Duncan Snidal, "Hard and Soft Law in International Governance," *International Organization* 54, no. 3 (Summer 2000): 421–456.

21. This claim is contentious, however. See Virginia Leary, "The Paradox of Workers'

Rights as Human Rights," in *Human Rights, Labor Rights, and International Trade*, ed. Lance A. Compa and Stephen F. Diamond (Philadelphia: University of Pennsylvania Press, 1996), 31.

22. Martha Finnemore and Kathryn Sikkink, "International Norm Dynamics and Political Change," *International Organization* 52, no. 4 (1998): 887–917.

23. Wayne Sandholtz, "Dynamics of International Norm Change: Rules Against Wartime Plunder," *European Journal of International Relations* 14, no. 1 (2008): 102.

24. Mark Anner, "Two Logics of Labor Organizing in the Global Apparel Industry," *International Studies Quarterly* 53, no. 3 (2009): 546.

25. Many other human rights activists, such as the case of the Mothers of the Plaza de Mayo, presented their concerns to a global audience. See Margaret E. Keck and Kathryn Sikkink, *Activists Beyond Borders: Advocacy Networks in International Politics* (Ithaca, N.Y.: Cornell University Press, 1998), 95.

26. Leary, "The Paradox of Workers' Rights as Human Rights," 44.

27. Darren Hawkins, "Explaining Costly International Institutions: Persuasion and Enforceable Human Rights Norms," *International Studies Quarterly* 48, no. 4 (December 1, 2004): 785.

28. T. Risse, "'Let's Argue!': Communicative Action in World Politics," *International Organization* 54, no. 1 (2000): 1–40.

29. Abbott and Snidal, "Hard and Soft Law in International Governance," 427.

30. Salient norms are those that "give rise to feelings of obligation by social actors and, when violated, engender regret or a feeling that the deviation or violations require justification." See Andrew P. Cortell and James W. Davis, "Understanding the Domestic Impact of International Norms: A Research Agenda," *International Studies Review* 2, no. 1 (2000): 69.

31. Tonia Novitz, *International and European Protection of the Right to Strike: A Comparative Study of Standards Set by the International Labour Organization, the Council of Europe and the European Union*, Oxford Monographs on Labour Law (Oxford: Oxford University Press, 2003), 182.

32. See Barbara Geddes, "How the Cases You Choose Affect the Answers You Get: Selection Bias in Comparative Politics," *Political Analysis* 2, no. 1 (January 1, 1990): 131–150; Gary King, Robert Owen Keohane, and Sidney Verba, *Designing Social Inquiry: Scientific Inference in Qualitative Research* (Princeton, N.J.: Princeton University Press, 1994), 129.

33. Alexander L. George and Andrew Bennett, *Case Studies and Theory Development in the Social Sciences* (Cambridge, Mass.: MIT Press, 2005), 23.

34. Douglas Dion, "Evidence and Inference in the Comparative Case Study," *Comparative Politics* 30, no. 2 (January 1998): 128; John Gerring, *Case Study Research: Principles and Practices* (Cambridge: Cambridge University Press, 2007), 27; 1. See also Bernhard Ebbinghaus, "When Less Is More," *International Sociology* 20, no. 2 (June 1, 2005): 144.

35. Charles C. Ragin, *The Comparative Method: Moving Beyond Qualitative and Quantitative Strategies* (Berkeley: University of California Press, 1989), 36.

36. While the Canadian case focuses exclusively on British Columbia, a subnational political unit, comparing this to national units is appropriate because the vast majority of labor relations law is determined at the provincial level. See H. W. Arthurs, "National Traditions in Labor Law Scholarship: The Canadian Case," *Comparative Labor Law and Policy Journal* 23, no. 2 (2002): 649.

37. Maria L. Cook, "International Labor Standards and Domestic Labor Advocates: Unions, Labor Reform, and Workers' Rights in Latin America," paper presented at the Annual Meeting of the International Studies Association, San Diego, 2006.

38. In 1999, South Korea had a trade union density of 11 percent, while Canada and the United Kingdom had 28.1 percent and 30.1 percent. See Organization for Economic Cooperation and Development, *Stat Extracts: Trade Union Density*, accessed June 1, 2009, http://stats.oecd.org/Index.aspx?DataSetCode=UN_DEN.

39. Anne-Marie Slaughter, "International Law in a World of Liberal States," *European Journal of International Law* 6, no. 4 (1995): 503–538.

40. Abram Chayes and Antonia Handler Chayes, "On Compliance," *International Organization* 47, no. 2 (1993): 188.

41. Jose Alvarez, "Do Liberal States Behave Better? A Critique of Slaughter's Liberal Theory," *European Journal of International Law* 12, no. 2 (2001): 186; Slaughter, "International Law in a World of Liberal States," 514; Jeffrey T. Checkel, "International Norms and Domestic Politics: Bridging the Rationalist—Constructivist Divide," *European Journal of International Relations* 3, no. 4 (1997): 478.

42. Benjamin Radcliff and Patricia Davis, "Labor Organization and Electoral Participation in Industrial Democracies," *American Journal of Political Science* 44, no. 1 (January 2000): 132–141.

43. Abbott and Snidal, "Hard and Soft Law in International Governance."

44. Eyāl Benveniśtî and Moshe Hirsch, *The Impact of International Law on International Cooperation: Theoretical Perspectives* (Cambridge: Cambridge University Press, 2004), 118.

45. World Bank, "High Income Countries," *Country and Lending Groups Data,* accessed September 2010, http://data.worldbank.org/about/country-classifications/country-and-lending-groups#High_income.

46. George and Bennett, *Case Studies and Theory Development in the Social Sciences,* 206.

47. Gerring, *Case Study Research: Principles and Practices,* 155.

48. This is now called the "Directorate for Employment, Labour and Social Affairs." See Organisation of Economic Cooperation and Development, "About," *Directorate for Employment, Labour and Social Affairs*, accessed October 17, 2011, http://www.oecd.org/about/0,3347,en_2649_33729_1_1_1_1_1,00.html.

49. The international normative obligations were created at the federal level. However, the provincial government did respond to the ILO Committee on Freedom of Association's requests for additional information.

Chapter 2. Negotiations and Norms

1. These rights are distinct from the individual-level worker protections that states can provide, though they often have the same outcome as collective bargaining agreements. Although states may provide many of the benefits of collective bargaining through statutory protection, trade union rights are valued because they promote existing rights within the workplace, whether these rights are determined through collective bargaining or statutory provision. In addition, institutions such as the ILO privilege trade union rights because they provide representational rights for workers.

2. This has varied based on context. Adams argues that in Canada and the United States, trade union rights were seen only as economic rights (valuable in their instrumental ability to bring about economic outcomes for workers), which is different than the international/continental European approach that values trade union rights as civil and economic rights. Roy J. Adams, "From Statutory Right to Human Right: The Evolution and Current Status of Collective Bargaining," *Just Labour* 12 (2008): 51.

3. International Labour Organization Freedom of Association Committee, *Freedom of Association: Digest of Decisions and Principles of the Freedom of Association Committee of the Governing Body of the ILO* (Geneva: International Labour Organization, 2006), 1.

4. Jack Donnelly, *Universal Human Rights in Theory and Practice* (Ithaca, N.Y.: Cornell University Press, 2003).

5. Richard P. McIntyre, *Are Workers Rights Human Rights?* (Ann Arbor: University of Michigan Press, 2008), 2.

6. Abbott and Snidal, "Hard and Soft Law in International Governance," 423.

7. See Dietrich Rueschemeyer, Evelyne Huber, and John D. Stephens, *Capitalist Development and Democracy* (Chicago: University of Chicago Press, 1992); August H. Nimtz, *Marx and Engels: Their Contribution to the Democratic Breakthrough* (Buffalo: SUNY Press, 2000); A. Belden Fields, *Rethinking Human Rights for the New Millennium* (New York: Palgrave Macmillan, 2003).

8. Harold Dunning, "The Origins of Convention No. 87 on Freedom of Association and the Right to Organize," *International Labour Review* 137, no. 2 (March 1998): 150.

9. Charles Tilly, "Globalization Threatens Labor's Rights," *International Labor and Working-Class History* 47 (1995): 5.

10. Tilly, "Globalization Threatens Labor's Rights," 8.

11. Dunning, "The Origins of Convention No. 87 on Freedom of Association and the Right to Organize," 151.

12. Tilly, "Globalization Threatens Labor's Rights," 8.

13. See Nimtz, *Marx and Engels,* and J. van Daele, "'Engineering Social Peace': Networks, Ideas, and the Establishment of the International Labour Organization," *International Review of Social History* 50 (2005): 435–466.

14. Tilly, "Globalization Threatens Labor's Rights," 8; Dunning, "The Origins of Convention No. 87 on Freedom of Association and the Right to Organize," 151.

15. Sumner M. Rosen, "Protecting Labor Rights in Market Economies," *Human Rights Quarterly* 14, no. 3 (1992): 372.

16. Dunning, "The Origins of Convention No. 87 on Freedom of Association and the Right to Organize," 152.

17. International Trade Secretariats are loose transnational federations of trade unions typically organized along sectors. They often facilitate meetings and other communications between affiliated organizations, and are now called "Global Union Federations"; the International Metalworkers' Federation is an example. See Terry Boswell and Dimitris Stevis, "Globalization and International Labor Organizing: A World-System Perspective," *Work and Occupations* 24, no. 3 (1997): 289.

18. Ishay, *History of Human Rights,* 149. While Ishay recognizes that Marx rejected the "rights of man" discourses as obscuring fundamental problems within bourgeois society, she maintains that the First International was the world's first federative human rights organization.

19. For a fuller account on the First and Second International, see Nimtz, *Marx and Engels.*

20. Van Daele, "'Engineering Social Peace,'" 440.

21. Dunning, "The Origins of Convention No. 87 on Freedom of Association and the Right to Organize," 153–154.

22. Van Daele, "'Engineering Social Peace,'" 448.

23. See A. J. R. Groom and Paul Taylor, "Functionalism and International Relations," in *Functionalism: Theory and Practice in International Relations*, ed. A. J. R. Groom and Paul Taylor (New York: Crane, Russak, 1975), 3–4; Victor-Yves Ghebali, "The League of Nations and Functionalism," in *Functionalism: Theory and Practice in International Relations*, ed. A. J. R. Groom and Paul Taylor (New York: Crane, Russak, 1975), 141–161.

24. International Labour Organization, "ILO Constitution," International Labour Organization home page, accessed June 5, 2009, http://www.ilo.org/public/english/about/iloconst.htm#annex.

25. Patrick Macklem, "The Right to Bargain Collectively in International Law: Workers' Right, Human Right, International Right?" in *Labour Rights as Human Rights*, ed. Phillip Alston (Oxford: Oxford University Press, 2005), 64.

26. Van Daele, "Engineering Social Peace," 449.

27. Robert W. Cox, "Labor and Hegemony," *International Organization* 31, no. 3 (1977): 388.

28. Christine Kaufmann, *Globalisation and Labour Rights: The Conflict Between Core Labour Rights and International Economic Law* (Oxford: Hart, 2007), 49.

29. Simon Deakin, "The Right to Bargain Collectively," in *Labor Rights as Human Rights*, ed. Phillip Alston (Oxford: Oxford University Press, 2005), 64.

30. Because of the politics in Switzerland, where the ILO is located, during this time the ILO temporarily moved to Montreal, Canada, in 1940. Christopher C. Joyner, *The United Nations and International Law* (Cambridge: Cambridge University Press, 1997), 211.

31. The declaration was later incorporated into the ILO's constitution. See Dun-

ning, "The Origins of Convention No. 87 on Freedom of Association and the Right to Organize," 157.

32. Swepston, "Human Rights Law and Freedom of Association," 170.

33. International Labour Organization, "ILO Constitution."

34. Macklem, "The Right to Bargain Collectively," 70.

35. John Ruggie, "International Regimes. Transactions, and Change: Embedded Liberalism in the Post War Economic order," *International Organization* 36, no. 2(1982): 387. Ruggie argued that the rejection of market rationality was evident in the interwar period as well. But the postwar period resulted in a "near universal" demand for social protection from the market. Ruggie, "International Regimes, Transactions, and Change," 388.

36. See Johannes Morsink, *The Universal Declaration of Human Rights* (Philadelphia: University of Pennsylvania Press, 2000), 169.

37. Roy Lewis, "Reforming Industrial Relations: Law, Politics, and Power," *Oxford Review of Economic Policy* 7, no. 1: 61. See also Tilly, "Globalization Threatens Labor's Rights," 10.

38. O'Brien, "Continuing Incivility," 205.

39. Since the OECD lacks a legal basis for promoting trade union rights, it is also not included in this discussion.

40. See Leary, "The Paradox of Workers' Rights as Human Rights," 116–118.

41. The ILO typically uses the term "freedom of association" to include the range of trade union rights.

42. Leary, "The Paradox of Workers' Rights as Human Rights," 110.

43. Eric Gravel, Isabelle Duplessis, and Bernard Gernigon, *The Committee on Freedom of Association: Its Impact Over 50 Years* (Geneva: International Labour Organization, 2001), 3.

44. Dunning, "The Origins of Convention No. 87 on Freedom of Association and the Right to Organize," 157.

45. The International Labor Conference is the ILO committee of the whole that meets once a year in Geneva. The structure is also tripartite, including two representatives of government, one business and one trade union representative from each member state, as well as their advisors. International Labour Organization, "About the ILC—International Labour Conference (ILC)," 2008, accessed September 13, 2009, http://www.ilo.org/global/What_we_do/Officialmeetings/ilc/AbouttheILC/lang--en/index.htm.

46. It should be noted that the freedom to not associate has been established in the ILO and other institutions' jurisprudence.

47. Novitz, *International and European Protection of the Right to Strike*, 116–117.

48. Swepston, "Human Rights Law and Freedom of Association," 171.

49. Morsink, *The Universal Declaration of Human Rights*, 168–173.

50. Ibid., 180.

51. Kaufmann, *Globalisation and Labour Rights*, 34.

52. Ibid., 35.

53. Lance A. Compa and Human Rights Watch, *Unfair Advantage: Workers' Freedom of Association in the United States Under International Human Rights Standards* (New York: Human Rights Watch, 2000), 41.

54. Kaufmann, *Globalisation and Labour Rights*, 44.

55. Office of the United Nations High Commissioner for Human Rights, "International Covenant on Economic, Social and Cultural Rights New York, 16 December 1966," *Office of the United Nations High Commissioner for Human Rights*, 2007, http://www2.ohchr.org/english/bodies/ratification/3.htm.

56. Novitz, *International and European Protection of the Right to Strike*, 117.

57. Office of the United Nations High Commissioner for Human Rights, "International Covenant on Economic, Social and Cultural Rights New York, 16 December 1966."

58. The Council of Europe is a distinct organization from the European Union. The European Union is an evolving organization that originated from the efforts of six countries—Germany, Italy, France, Luxembourg, the Netherlands, and Belgium—to deepen economic ties and cooperation, in an effort to prevent the enmities of World War II from reemerging. The first treaty from which current institutions evolved was the European Coal and Steel Community treaty, which later became the basis of the European Economic Community, and later the Common Market. Desmond Dinan, *Ever Closer Union: An Introduction to European Integration*, 3rd ed. (Boulder, Colo.: Palgrave Macmillan, 2005), 2–5.

59. The European Committee of Social Rights replaced the Committee of Independent Experts in 1996, although this did not come into practice immediately. The scope of the United Kingdom case involved the Committee of Independent Experts. Council of Europe, "The European Social Charter at a Glance," *Human Rights: European Social Charter*, accessed May 2, 2008, http://www.coe.int/t/e/human_rights/esc/1_general_presentation/CharterGlance_en.asp#TopOfPage.

60. D. J. (David John) Harris and John Darcy, *The European Social Charter* (Ardsley, N.Y.: Transnational Publishers, 2001), 3.

61. Council of Europe, "Convention for the Protection of Human Rights and Fundamental Freedoms as amended by Protocol no. 11" (Council of Europe, 2003), http://www.echr.coe.int/NR/rdonlyres/D5CC24A7-DC13-4318-B457-5C9014916D7A/0/englishAnglais.pdf.

62. Council of Europe, "European Social Charter, Turin 18.X.1961," Council of Europe - ETS no. 035, 2008, http://conventions.coe.int/treaty/en/treaties/html/035.htm.

63. These articles include the right to work, the right to organize; the right to bargain collectively; the right to social security; the right to social and medical assistance; the right to social, legal, and economic protection of the family; and the right to protection and assistance for migrant workers and their families.

64. The U.K. is also bound to Articles 1, 13, 16, and 19 of the hard-core articles. Additional commitments include: Paragraphs 2, 3, 4, and 5 of Article 2; Article 3; Paragraphs 1, 2, 4, and 5 of Article 4; Paragraphs 2, 3, 5, 6, 9, and 10 of Article 7; Paragraph 1 of Article 8; Articles 9, 10, and 11; Paragraph 1 of Article 12; Articles 14, 15, 17, and 18.

Council of Europe, "List of Declarations Made with Respect to Treaty No. 035," *Council of Europe Treaties*, 2008, accessed March 13, 2008, http://conventions.coe.int/Treaty/Commun/ListeDeclarations.asp?NT=035&CM=8&DF=07/11/2005&CL=ENG&VL=1.

65. See Ishay, *History of Human Rights*, 262.

66. See David Harvey, *A Brief History of Neoliberalism* (Oxford: Oxford University Press, 2005).

67. Nick Couldry, *Why Voice Matters: Culture and Politics After Neoliberalism* (New York: Sage Publications, 2010), 4.

68. Matthias Kipping, "American Management Consulting Companies in Western Europe, 1920 to 1990: Products, Reputation, and Relationships," *Business History Review* 73, no. 2 (1999): 191. Like other aspects of economic liberalization, government deregulation of labor markets and subsequent dismantling of trade union rights protections have spread through policy diffusion channels.

69. Harvey, *A Brief History of Neoliberalism*, 2–3.

70. See Neil Brenner and Nik Theodore, "Cities and the Geographies of 'Actually Existing Neoliberalism,'" *Antipode* 34, no. 3 (2002): 350.

71. Ulirch Brand and Nicola Sekler, "Postneoliberalism: Catch-all Word or Valuable Analytical and Political Concept?—Aims of a Beginning Debate," *Development Dialogue* 51, no. 1 (2009): 6.

72. Beth A. Simmons and Zachary Elkins, "The Globalization of Liberalization: Policy Diffusion in the International Political Economy," *American Political Science Review* 98, no. 1 (2004): 171–189.

73. See Helga Leitner, Jamie Peck, and Eric S. Sheppard, *Contesting Neoliberalism: Urban Frontiers* (New York: Guilford Press, 2007).

74. Rowan M. Abouharb and David L. Cingranelli, "The Effects of Structural Adjustment Agreements on Government Respect for Workers' Rights," presented at the University of North Carolina Workshop on Labor Rights and Multinational Production, Chapel Hill, 2006, 6.

75. Timothy Besley and Robin Burgess, "Can Labour Regulation Hinder Economic Performance?: Evidence from India," *Quarterly Journal of Economics* 19, no. 1 (2002): 91.

76. Juan Botero et al., *The Regulation of Labor*, NBER Working Paper no. 9756 (Cambridge, Mass.: National Bureau of Economic Research, 2003).

77. Alvaro Forteza and Martin Rama, *Labor Market Rigidity and the Success of Economic Reforms Across More Than One Hundred Countries*, Policy Research Working Paper 2521 (Washington, D.C.: World Bank Development Research Group, 2001).

78. For information about firms' pursuit of "employment flexibility," see Guy Standing, *Global Labour Flexibility: Seeking Distributive Justice* (New York: Palgrave Macmillan, 1999), 103.

79. The *Doing Business* indicators themselves give low labor flexibility rates to a number of countries that are quite rich, such as France, Germany, and Japan. Singapore was ranked the highest in 2007, meaning they had the fewest restrictions for businesses hiring and firing workers. See World Bank Group, "Employing Workers."

80. Blanpain et al., *The Global Workplace*, 9.

81. Keith Maskus, *Should Core Labor Standards Be Imposed Through International Trade Policy?* Policy Research Working Paper Series (World Bank, 1997).

82. Organisation for Economic Co-operation and Development, *Trade, Employment and Labor Standards: A Study of Core Workers' Rights and International Trade* (Paris: OECD, 1996).

83. Roger Blanpain, et al., *The Global Workplace: International and Comparative Employment Law—Cases and Materials* (Cambridge: Cambridge University Press), 10.

84. Hugh Collins, K. D. Ewing, and Aileen McColgan, *Labour Law: Text and Materials* (Oxford: Hart, 2001), 33.

85. Linda Cook, "More Rights, Less Power: Labor Standards and Labor Markets in East European Post-communist States," *Studies in Comparative International Development (SCID)* 45, no. 2 (June 1, 2010): 171.

86. Jim Stanford, "Testing the Flexibility Regime: Canadian Labour Market Performance in Internaional Context," in *Fighting Unemployment,: The Limits of a Free Market Orthodoxy,* ed. David R, Howell (Oxford: Oxford University Press, 2005), 119.

87. Anner and Caraway, "International Institutions and Workers' Rights," 158.

88. Couldry, *Why Voice Matters*, 5.

89. Anner and Caraway, "International Institutions and Workers' Rights," 163–165. The authors claim that the World Bank has given more attention to the labor standards than the IMF, but it still gives greater priority to labor market flexibility policies.

90. Fields, *Rethinking Human Rights for the New Millennium*, 139.

91. Chantelle Taylor, "NAFTA, GATT and the Current Free Trade System: A Dangerous Double Standard for Workers' Rights," *Denver Journal of International Law and Policy* 28, no. 4 (2000): 419.

92. Stanford, "Testing the Flexibility Paradigm," 119.

93. Stephen McBride and Russell A. Williams, "Globalization, the Restructuring of Labour Markets and Policy Convergence: The OECD 'Jobs Strategy,'" *Global Social Policy* 1, no. 3 (December 1, 2001): 292.

94. Caraway and Anner, "International Institutions and Workers' Rights"; Guy Standing, *Global Labour Flexibility: Seeking Distributive Justice* (New York: St. Martin's Press, 1999), 141.

95. David Craig and Doug Porter, "Poverty Reduction Strategy Papers: A New Convergence," *World Development* 31, no. 1 (January 2003): 53.

96. *Doing Business* is a project that "provides object measures of business regulations and their enforcement across 178 countries and selected cities." Its "Ease of Doing Business" index ranks 178 countries, based on whether the country's legal institutions promote a business-friendly environment. World Bank Group, "Employing Workers," *Doing Business*, 2008, accessed March 2, 2009, http://www.doingbusiness.org/ExploreTopics/EmployingWorkers/.

97. See Sangheon Lee, Deirdre McCann, and Nina Torm, "The World Bank's 'Employ-

ing Workers' Index: Findings and Critiques—A Review of Recent Evidence," *International Labour Review* 147, no. 4 (2008): 416–432.

98. Peter Bakvis, "How the World Bank and IMF Use the Doing Business Report to Promote Labour Market Deregulation in Developing Countries," International Confederation of Trade Unions, accessed June 21, 2008, http://www.icftu.org/www/PDF/doingbusinessicftuanalysis0606.pdf.

99. World Bank, "Revisions to EWI Indicators," Doing Business, April 29, 2009, http://www.doingbusiness.org/documents/EWI_revisions.pdf.

100. See International Trade Union Council, "ITUC Welcomes World Bank's Suspension of 'Doing Business' Labour Indicator," International Confederation of Trade Union Home Page: Economic and Social Policy, April 28, 2009, http://www.ituc-csi.org/spip.php?article3505&var_recherche=World%20Bank.

101. Sandrine Cazes and Alena Nešporová, "Introduction," in *Flexicurity: A Relevant Approach in Central and Eastern Europe*, ed. Sandrine Cazes and Alena Nešporová (Geneva: International Labour Organization, 2007), 2.

102. See Robert O'Brien, "Workers and World Order: The Tentative Transformation of the International Union Movement," *Review of International Studies* 26, no. 4 (October 2000): 535–555; Horst Siebert, "Labor Market Rigidities: At the Root of Unemployment in Europe," *Journal of Economic Perspectives* 11, no. 3 (1997): 37–54. This remains a controversial proposition in Western Europe, as critics of the neoliberal position argue that attributing the comparatively better performance of the U.K. and U.S. in the early 2000s purely to their labor flexibility is unfair and incomplete. See Robert A. Levine, "Anglo-Saxons vs. EMU: Labor 'Flexibility' Isn't a Cure-all," *International Herald Tribune*, March 6, 2002, Opinion section, http://iht.com/articles/2002/03/06/edlevine_ed3_.php.

103. Quoted in Blanpain et al., *The Global Workplace*, 9.

104. As Senator Wagner, namesake of the U.S.'s Wagner Act (National Labor Relations Act), stated in 1935, "Industrial tyranny is incompatible with a Republic Form of government." Nelson Lichtenstein, "The Rights Revolution," *New Labor Forum* 12, no. 1 (March 2003): 66.

105. O'Brien, "Continuing Incivility," 203.

Chapter 3. International Institutions and Their Protections of Trade Union Rights

1. Abbott and Snidal, "Hard and Soft Law in International Governance," 423.

2. Rodolfo Stavenhagen, "Indigenous Rights: Some Conceptual Problems," in *Constructing Democracy: Human Rights, Citizenship, and Society in Latin America*, ed. Elizabeth Jelin and Eric Hershberg (Boulder, Colo.: Westview Press, 1996), 141–159.

3. See Appendix I for the full range of behaviors.

4. K. D. Ewing, "The Human Rights Act and Labour Law," *Industrial Law Journal* 27, no. 4 (1998): 279.

5. International Labour Organization Freedom of Association Committee, *Freedom of Association: Digest of Decisions and Principles of the Freedom of Association Committee*

of the Governing Body of the ILO, paragraph 20. Here after paragraph references to this work will be cited parenthetically in the text.

6. The ILO has specifically included the following categories of workers as having the right to organize and join unions: civilians working in the armed services, firefighters, prison staff, customs officials, teachers, agricultural workers, plantation workers, airline workers, port workers, hospital personnel, temporary workers, workers in probationary periods, workers in export processing zones, domestic workers, and private security agents.

7. The ILO Committee on Freedom of Association has noted that workers in the following public industries are not engaged in the administration of the state: postal service, national radio and television, state-owned commercial enterprises, government agencies, education, air flight control personnel, public hospitals, and civil aviation as well as temporary workers in the public services.

8. The committee has identified these services as possibly constituting essential services: the hospital sector, electricity services, water supply services, telephone services, police and armed forces, firefighting services, public or private prison services, food provision and cleaners at schools, and air traffic controls. These industries are not essential services in the strict sense of the term: radio and television; petroleum sector; ports; banking; computer services related to taxation; department stores; metal and mining; general transport; airline pilots; fuel production, transportation, and distribution; railway services; metropolitan transportation; postal services; garbage collection; refrigeration; hotel services; construction; car manufacturing; agricultural activities; minting services; the education sector; government printing services; and mineral water bottling companies. Some nonessential services can become essential services over the duration, such as refuse collection. Ibid., 120–122.

9. Dunning, "The Origins of Convention No. 87 on Freedom of Association and the Right to Organize," 157.

10. International Labour Organization, "About the GB—Governing Body—Official meetings—What we do," *International Labour Organization*, 2008, accessed June 1, 2008, http://www.ilo.org/global/What_we_do/Officialmeetings/gb/AboutGB/lang--en/index.htm.

11. Lee Swepston, "Human Rights Law and Freedom of Association,: Development Through ILO Supervision," *International Labour Review*. 137, no, 2(1998), 175.

12. Gravel et al., *The Committee on Freedom of Association*, 10.

13. International Labour Organization, "Report of the Committee on Freedom of Association (15th Report)," *ILO Official Bulletin*, 38, no. 1 (1955).

14. Gravel et al., *The Committee on Freedom of Association*, 12–14.

15. Ibid., 13.

16. International Labour Organization, *Convention 87: Freedom of Association and Protection of the Right to Organise Convention, 1948*, accessed January 10, 2009, http://www.ilo.org/ilolex/cgi-lex/convde.pl?C087.

17. Novitz, *International and European Protection of the Right to Strike*, 201.

18. International Labour Organization, "About the ILO, Who we are: ILO Constitution."

19. Novitz, *International and European Protection of the Right to Strike*, 207.

20. Geraldo von Potobsky, "Freedom of Association: The Impact of Convention No. 87 and ILO Action," *International Labour Review* 137, no. 2 (March 1998): 205.

21. Abbott and Snidal, "Hard and Soft Law in International Governance," 410.

22. Ibid., 416.

23. Office of the United Nations High Commissioner for Human Rights, "International Covenant on Economic, Social and Cultural Rights New York, 16 December 1966."

24. Office of the United Nations High Commissioner for Human Rights, "Committee on Economic, Social and Cultural Rights," *Office of the United Nations High Commissioner for Human Rights- Treaty Bodies*, accessed November 12, 2007, http://www2.ohchr.org/english/bodies/cescr/index.htm.

25. Office of the United Nations High Commissioner for Human Rights, "Human Rights Committee: Monitoring Civil and Political Rights," *Office of the United Nations High Commissioner for Human Rights- Treaty Bodies*, accessed January 21, 2008, http://www2.ohchr.org/english/bodies/hrc/index.htm.

26. For example, the Human Rights Committee did not initially interpret the right to strike in its convention, arguing in the 1986 case *JB v. Canada* that legal prohibitions on public servants' strike rights were not violations of Article 22. But in 1999, the Human Rights Committee's Concluding Comments on Chile report found problems with Chile's legal restrictions on civil servants' rights to strike. See Macklem, "The Right to Bargain Collectively," 73.

27. Kaufmann, *Globalisation and Labour Rights*, 44.

28. United Nations High Commission on Human Rights, *Report on the Seventh Session of the Committee on Economic Social and Cultural Rights,* ESCR, 1993, Supp. No. 2 (UN Doc. E/1993/22), 1993, para. 245.

29. Abbott and Snidal, "Hard and Soft Law in International Governance," 405.

30. Office of the United Nations High Commissioner for Human Rights, "International Covenant on Economic, Social and Cultural Rights, New York, 16 December 1966."

31. Kaufmann, *Globalisation and Labour Rights*, 40.

32. Abbott and Snidal, "Hard and Soft Law in International Governance," 410.

33. The court was mostly a provisional body, and states need to submit themselves to the jurisdiction of the court under Article 46 for cases to be heard. See Council of Europe, *Information Document on the Court* (European Court of Human Rights), 1762893 (Strasbourg, September 2006), http://www.echr.coe.int/NR/rdonlyres/981B9082-45A4-44C6-829A-202A51B94A85/0/Informationdocumenton-theCourt_September2006_.pdf.

34. Council of Europe, "Historical Background (European Court of Human Rights),"

European Court of Human Rights: The Courts, accessed April 12, 2009, http://www.echr.coe.int/ECHR/EN/Header/The+Court/The+Court/History+of+the+Court.

35. Novitz, *International and European Protection of the Right to Strike*, 215, and European Court of Human Rights, *Rules of the Court* (Strasbourg: Council of Europe; Registry of the Court, 2006), 24.

36. S. K. Martens, "Commentary," in *Compliance with Judgments of International Courts*, ed. M. K. Bulterman and Martin Kuijer (The Hague: M. Nijhoff, 1996), 68.

37. For example, in *Schmidt and Dahlstrom v. Sweden* (1975) and *Swedish Engine Driver's Union v. Sweden* (1975), the court dismissed claims by unions for protections of their collective bargaining rights. See Macklem, "The Right to Bargain Collectively," 74.

38. K. D. Ewing, "The Human Rights Act and Labour Law," *Industrial Law Journal* 27, no. 4 (1998): 280.

39. Council of Europe, "The European Social Charter at a Glance."

40. Harris and Darcy, *The European Social Charter*, 298–304.

41. Ibid., 30.

42. Niamh Ann Casey and Council of Europe, *The Right to Organise and to Bargain Collectively: Protection Within the European Social Charter* (Strasbourg: Council of Europe, 1996), 12.

43. Ibid., 59–73.

44. Organisation for Economic Co-operation and Development, "Convention on the Organisation for Economic Co-operation and Development," Home: Legal Affairs, accessed April 4, 2008, http://www.oecd.org/document/7/0,3343,en_2649_34483_1915847_1_1_1_1,00.html.

45. Ibid.

46. Organisation for Economic Co-operation and Development, "About OECD," OECD: For a Better World Web site, accessed August 21, 2009, http://www.oecd.org/pages/0,3417,en_36734052_36734103_1_1_1_1_1,00.html.

47. Organisation for Economic Co-operation and Development, "OECD Codes of Liberalisation of Capital Movements and of Current Invisible Operations," *Home: Legal Affairs*, accessed August 22, 2009, http://www.oecd.org/document/63/0,3343,en_2649_34483_1826559_1_1_1_1,00.html.

48. James Salzman, "Labor Rights, Globalization and Institutions: The Role and Influence of the Organization for Economic Cooperation and Development," *Michigan Journal of International Law* 21 (2000): 780.

49. Ibid., 772.

50. These guidelines also established rules for environmental activities, consumer protections, science and technology, taxation, and competition rules for multinational enterprises. See Organisation for Economic Co-operation and Development, "Guidelines for Multinational Enterprises," *Directorate for Financial and Enterprise Affairs*, accessed April 1, 2008, http://www.oecd.org/department/0,3355,en_2649_34889_1_1_1_1_1,00.html.

51. Trade Union Advisory Committee, "About TUAC - TUAC - Trade Union Advisory Committee to the OECD," *Trade Union Advisory Committee to the OECD*, accessed March 14, 2008, http://www.tuac.org/en/public/tuac/index.phtml.

52. Salzman, "Labor Rights, Globalization and Institutions," 796–800.

53. Organisation for Economic Co-operation and Development, "On-Line Guide to OECD Intergovernmental Activity," *Organisation for Economic Co-operation and Development*, accessed February 25, 2008, http://webnet3.oecd.org/OECDgroups/.

Chapter 4. South Korea

1. Larry Jay Diamond and Pyong-guk Kim, "Introduction: Consolidating Democracy in South Korea," in *Consolidating Democracy in South Korea*, ed. Larry Jay Diamond and Pyong-guk Kim (Boulder, Colo.: L. Rienner, 2000), 6.

2. Yoonkyung Lee, "Divergent Outcomes of Labor Reform Politics in Democratized Korea and Taiwan," *Studies in Comparative International Development* 44, no. 1 (2009): 48. See also Maria Lorena Cook, *The Politics of Labor Reform in Latin America: Between Flexibility and Rights* (University Park: Pennsylvania State University Press, 2007).

3. This meant that only the certified trade union, the employer, and workers could be "involved" in any industrial dispute. This was leftover from the authoritarian period and was often used as the legal basis for many arrests of trade unionists.

4. Trade unionists and other actors emphasized nonlegislative issues in international forums as well, but this case focuses on the law, because legal changes provide a clear way to demarcate reforms.

5. Jeffrey T. Checkel, "International Institutions and Socialization in Europe: Introduction and Framework," *International Organization* 59, no. 4 (2005): 804.

6. Cold War politics dictated the refusal by key countries to recognize the separate statehood of North and South Korea until the 1990s. By 1990, the majority of countries were willing to separately recognize and grant membership to both Koreas. Ch'i-yŏng Pak, *Korea and the United Nations* (The Hague: Martinus Nijhoff Publishers, 2000), 66.

7. Korea took reservation to Article 22 in the International Covenant on Civil and Political Rights, although not to the corresponding clause in the Covenant on Economic Social and Cultural Rights. Office of the United Nations High Commissioner for Human Rights, "Declarations and Reservations: International Covenant on Civil and Political Rights," *Multilateral Treaties Deposited with the Secretary-General—TREATY I–IV—5.asp*, accessed September 21, 2008, http://www.unhchr.ch/html/menu3/b/treaty5_asp.htm.

8. While seven other states made a reservation on Article 22, only Korea's reservation resulted in objections. Korea's reservation reads, "The Government of the Republic of Korea [declares] that the provisions of paragraph 5 . . . of article 14, article 22 . . . of the Covenant shall be so applied as to be in conformity with the provisions of the local laws including the Constitution of the Republic of Korea." See United Nations Treaty Collection, "Chapter IV Human Rights: International Covenant on

Civil and Political Rights," accessed December 14, 2010, http://untreaty.un.org/unts/120001_144071/4/9/00003305.pdf.

9. Dong-One Kim, Jongsok Bae, and Changwon Lee, "Globalization and Labor Rights: The Case of Korea," in *Globalization and Labor in the Asia Pacific Region*, ed. Chris Rowley and John Benson, Studies in Asia Pacific Business (London: Frank Cass, 2000), 141.

10. Kwan Yeong Shin, "The Political Economy of Economic Growth in East Asia: South Korea and Taiwan," in *The Four Asian Tigers: Economic Development and the Global Political Economy*, ed. Eun Mee Kim (San Diego: Academic Press, 1998), 3–5.

11. Barry Wilkinson, "The Korea Labour Problem," *British Journal of Industrial Relations* 32, no. 3 (1994): 346.

12. Eun-Mee Kim, "Contradictions and Limits of a Developmental State: With Illustrations from the South Korean Case," *Social Problems* 40, no. 2 (1993): 235.

13. Yong Cheol Kim, "Industrial Reform and Labor Backlash in South Korea: Genesis, Escalation and Termination of the 1997 General Strike," *Asian Survey* 38, no. 12 (1998): 1145.

14. Kim Dong-One and Johngseok Bae, *Employment Relations and HRM in South Korea* (Aldershot: Ashgate, 2003), 144.

15. Koo, *Korean Workers*, 78.

16. Kim, "Contradictions and Limits of a Developmental State," 234.

17. Ibid., 234.

18. Bang-Soon Yoon, "Democratization and Gender Politics in South Korea," ed. Rita Mae Kelly, Mary E. Hawkesworth, and Briggitte Young (Lanham, Md.: Rowman & Littlefield, 2001), 181.

19. In the past, Korean presidents had been elected through indirect elections of an electoral college, with the presence of proto-opposition parties, although the leadership manipulated electoral rules to ensure success. See Sunhyuk Kim, "State and Civil Society in South Korea's Democratic Consolidation: Is the Battle Really Over," *Asian Survey* 37, no. 12 (1997): 1137.

20. The Great Workers' Struggle included estimated 4,000 strikes in 3,311 workplaces, involving 3.1 million workers. See Su-Hoon Lee, "Transitional Politics of Korea, 1987–1992: Activation of Civil Society," *Pacific Affairs* 66, no. 3 (1993): 354; Chong-sik Lee and Hyuk-Sang Sohn, "South Korea in 1993: The Year of Great Reform," *Asian Survey* 34, no. 1 (1994): 354. These limitations included the enterprise-level trade union monopoly, restrictions on trade union monopoly, and continued repression of trade union leaders. These grievances would form the basis of future internationally oriented complaints.

21. Koo, "Engendering Civil Society," 79.

22. See Appendix II.

23. Korean economists believed that this increase in wages was possible because of the ideal economic conditions of late 1980s, which were marked by "three lows": low interest rates, low oil prices, and low exchange rates of the yen to both the dollar and the

won. These conditions resulted in huge profits for Korean business. See Sunhyuk Kim, *The Politics of Democratization in Korea: The Role of Civil Society* (Pittsburgh: University of Pittsburgh Press, 2000); Bae and Lee, "Globalization and Labor Rights," 234.

24. The Federation of Korean Employers stated willingness to concede on economic issues, but not on freedom of association and other trade union autonomy issues. See Asia Monitor, *Min-Ju No-Jo South Korea's New Trade Unions*, 71.

25. Koo, *Korean Workers*, 170, 189. After issuing this decree, the state began to intervene again in industrial actions, such as the government crackdown at Poongsan Metal, Seoul Subway, and Hyundai Heavy Industry strikes.

26. John Synott, "Development, Education and the Teachers Union Movement in South Korea, 1989–1999," *Australian Journal of Politics and History* 47, no. 1 (2001): 142.

27. Asia Watch Committee (U.S.), *Retreat from Reform*, 30.

28. Korean Government Employees' Union, "Brief History of KGEU," *About KGEU: Korean Government Employees' Union*, accessed July 29, 2007, http://inter.kgeu.org/about/about.asp.

29. Synott, "Development, Education and the Teachers Union Movement in South Korea," 132.

30. This was found in section 3(5) of the Trade Union Act.

31. Kim Dae Jung ran under his opposition National Democratic Party. It is widely believed that President Park's victory was the result of massive vote fraud. See Aurel Croissant, "Strong Presidents, Weak Democracy? President, Parliaments and Political Parties in South Korea," *Korea Observer* 33, no. 1 (2002): 1–45.

32. International Labour Organization Freedom of Association Committee, *Freedom of Association: Digest of Decisions and Principles of the Freedom of Association Committee of the Governing Body of the ILO.*

33. Koo, *Korean Workers*, 194.

34. Kim, "Rethinking the New Beginning of the Democratic Union Movement in Korea," 493.

35. Kim, *The Politics of Democratization in Korea*, 80; Asia Watch Committee (U.S.), *Retreat from Reform: Labor Rights and Freedom of Expression in South Korea* (New York: Asia Watch Committee Human Rights Watch, 1990), 33.

36. International Labour Organization, "Report of the Committee on Freedom of Association (286th Report)," *ILO Official Bulletin* 76, ser. B, no. 1 (1993), 522.

37. Asia Watch Committee (U.S.), *Retreat from Reform*, 33.

38. Koo, *Korean Workers*, 190.

39. The Democratic Justice Party, the moderate party, merged with two more conservative parties to form the Democratic Liberal Party, which created a super majority coalition of 223 members. This new party excluded Kim Dae Jung's Party for Peace and Democracy. See Kim, "Rational Choice Theory and Third World Politics," 84. The name of this party self-consciously echoed Japan's long-ruling Liberal Democratic Party, as Korea has long sought to imitate Japan's economic and social practices. This party was an attempt to create the same sort of sustainable single-party dominance by uniting

elements of the prior regime and the centric opposition, as well as the regional appeal of Kim Young-Sam. See Bruce Cummings, "Civil Society in West and East," in *Korean Society: Civil Society, Democracy and the State,* ed. Charles K. Armstrong (London: Routledge, 2007), 27.

40. This court was established on September 1, 1988, as a European-style constitutional court with the mandate to protect and uphold the 1987 constitution. This is in contrast to the American system, which diffuses the power of constitutional review. A European system concentrates this power within one independent judicial body, which is meant to "emphasize the functionality and professionalism of constitutional adjudication." Republic of Korea, *The First Ten Years of the Korean Constitution Court* (Seoul: The Constitutional Court of Korea, 2001), 6.

41. Republic of Korea, "Constitutional Court," 28, and International Labour Organization, "Report of the Committee on Freedom of Association (286th Report)," 542.

42. Republic of Korea, "Constitutional Court," 251–252.

43. United States Department of State, *1996 Human Rights Report: Republic of Korea (South Korea)* (Bureau of Democracy, Human Rights and Labor, January 30, 1997), accessed June 20, 2009, http://www.state.gov/www/global/human_rights/1996_hrp_report/southkor.html.

44. Koo, *Korea Workers*, 197, and Kim, "Rethinking the New Beginning of the Democratic Union Movement in Korea," 494.

45. International Labour Organization, "Report of the Committee on Freedom of Association (286th Report)," 564.

46. Asia Watch, *Retreat from Reform*, 33.

47. International Labour Organization, "Report of the Committee on Freedom of Association (286th Report)," 566.

48. Ibid., 521, 523, 525.

49. Ibid., 521. It should be noted that protection of due process rights was not a concern in these complaints, as the trade unionists who were imprisoned were also charged and tried.

50. The government claimed that since its acceptance into the ILO, it had been committed to making trade unions more independent and democratic, although it did not provide any examples. The communication did cite the earlier legal changes that allowed for an easier union certification process. Ibid., 532.

51. Ibid., 543.

52. For example, the government report stated that a Mr. B. Y. Lee and Mr. S. H. Lee "were arrested for attacking the legitimate Government on issues irrelevant to the protection of workers' rights and interests, or for holding or participating in illegal meetings and riots which directly threatened the public order through threats, arson and the like." Other trade unionists had been arrested for threatening national security for passing out pamphlets promoting Korean unification "with the purpose of destabilizing Korea's democratic society," or for violating the solidarity ban law. Ibid., 554.

53. Ibid., 535.

54. The government reported the creation of the "Committee on Labor Laws" on April 24, 1992, which would explore possible amendments to key labor legislation, and possibly change laws in accordance with the committee's recommendations. In addition, the government had established a "Founders' Committee" in May 1992, composed of eight legal experts but no trade union representatives. This committee was charged with studying issues such as trade union pluralism and the solidarity activities ban. Ibid., 528, 532.

55. Ibid., 554.

56. Interestingly, this communication from the Roh Tae Woo administration came in late 1992, preceding the infamous "Asian values" argument expressed by Asian delegates at the World Conference on Human Rights in Vienna. See Amartya Kumar Sen and Carnegie Council on Ethics and International Relations, *Human Rights and Asian Values*, Morgenthau Memorial Lecture on Ethics & Foreign Policy, no. 16 (New York: Carnegie Council on Ethics and International Affairs, 1997), 9.

57. International Labour Organization, "Report of the Committee on Freedom of Association (286th Report)," 557.

58. Ibid., 560.

59. Ibid., 530.

60. Ibid., 529–531.

61. Citing the teachers unions' own written materials, which promoted broader economic and social changes, the government called the union an anti-democratic and anti-systemic organization that was negatively influencing students. Ibid., 545.

62. Ibid., 535.

63. Ibid., 553.

64. Ibid., 562.

65. Ibid., 563.

66. Ibid., 563.

67. Ibid., 564.

68. Ibid., 568.

69. Ibid., 568.

70. Ibid., 569.

71. Kim, "State and Civil Society in South Korea's Democratic Consolidation," 1141.

72. Hong-Young Lee, "South Korea in 1992: A Turning Point in Democratization," *Asian Survey* 33, no. 1 (1993): 33.

73. Lee and Sohn, "South Korea in 1993," 5. Existing investment rules did not encourage much foreign direct investment in South Korea as the other "Asian tigers." Instead, the government made arrangements for purchase of foreign technologies and relied on domestic production. See Robert Wade, "From 'Miracle' to 'Cronyism': Explaining the Great Asian Slump," *Cambridge Journal of Economics* 22, no. 6 (November 1, 1998): 693–706.

74. These reforms include the following: greater accountability of public officials, more transparent political contribution policies, and curbing both the National Security Police and the draconian National Security Law. See Sung Deuk Hahm and Kwang

Woong Kim, "Institutional Reforms and Democratization in Korea: The Case of the Kim Young Sam Administration, 1993–1998," *Governance* 12, no. 3 (1999): 479.

75. See Wilkinson, "The Korea Labour Problem," 341–343.

76. Chong-sik Lee and Hyuk-Sang Sohn, "South Korea in 1994: A Year of Trial," *Asian Survey* 35, no. 1 (1995): 30.

77. Kim and Bae, *Employment Relations and HRM in South Korea*, 97.

78. International Labour Organization, "Report of the Committee on Freedom of Association" (291st Report), *ILO Official Bulletin* 76, ser. B, no. 3 (1994), 409.

79. Ibid., 242.

80. Ibid., 406.

81. Ibid., 401.

82. Ibid., 403.

83. Ibid., 245.

84. Johnryn Mo, "Political Culture and Legislative Gridlock: Politics of Economic Reform in Precrisis Korea," *Comparative Political Studies* 34, no. 5 (June 2001): 480.

85. Jin Kyoon Kim, "Rethinking the Beginning of the Democratic Labour Movement in Korea from the 1987 Great Workers' Struggle to the Construction of the Korean Trade Union Council (Chunnohyup) and the Korean Confederation of Trade Union (KCTU)," *Inter-Asia Cultural Studies* 1, no. 3 (2000): 491–502.

86. Oona A. Hathaway, "Do Human Rights Treaties Make a Difference," *Yale Law Journal* 111 (2002): 2002–2004.

87. Won-Duk Lee and Byoung-Hoon Lee, "Korean Industrial Relations in the Era of Globalization," *Journal of Industrial Relations* 45, no. 4 (2003): 506.

88. Hahm and Kim, "Institutional Reforms and Democratization in Korea," 483–484.

89. Susan Noakes, "Building a New International Image: After Years of Isolation, Former Hermit Kingdom Seeks to Boost its Influence on World Stage. However, Korea's Biggest Test May be Whether Its Application to Join the OECD Is Accepted," *Financial Post* (Toronto, Canada), July 29, 1995, 28.

90. Michael Baker, "Invitation by Rich Nations 'Club' Puts S. Korea on Notice," *Christian Science Monitor,* October 15, 1996, 6.

91. Eduardo Lachica, "Korea Discovers Joining OECD Is Hard Work," *New York Times*, October 19, 1995, 1.

92. Steven Brull, "Two Steps Forward, How Many Back?" *Businessweek*, April 1, 1996, 18.

93. Mexico's ease of entry was largely a function of U.S. support. See Lachica, "Korea Discovers Joining OECD Is Hard Work," 1.

94. Organisation for Economic Co-operation and Development, "Becoming a Member of the OECD: the Accession Process," OECD country Web sites, accessed March 30, 2008, http://www.oecd.org/document/11/0,3343,en_33873108_33844430_1958091_1_1_1_1,00.html.

95. Korea only had to implement 65 percent of the OECD code on financial liberalization (while the average member's financial system complied with 89 percent of

the code). See John Burton and Robert Taylor, "South Korea Braces for Restructuring: OECD Membership Will Promote Shift Towards Market Economy, Writes John Burton," *Financial Times*, October 14, 1996. According to Chalmers Johnson, this was still a huge amount of rapid regulation, and OECD membership was the prize for Korea's "self-inflicted wounds." Chalmers Johnson, "Economic Crisis in East Asia: The Clash of Capitalisms," *Cambridge Journal of Economics* 22 (1998): 653–661.

96. Robert Wade and Frank Veneroso, "The Asian Crisis: The High Debt Model Versus the Wall Street-Treasury-IMF Complex," *New Left Review* I/228, no. 3-23 (April 1998): 9.

97. Prior to this, a company could request layoff permission, but this required court approval and supervision. Such a process intentionally created prohibitive opportunity costs and was largely was avoided. Kim, "Industrial Reform and Labor Backlash in South Korea," 1146–1147.

98. Richard Dicker and Human Rights Watch/Asia, *South Korea: Labor Rights Violations Under Democratic Rule* (New York: Human Rights Watch/Asia, 1995).

99. "South Korea to Join OECD," *Kyodo News Service: Japanese Economic Newswire*, October 11, 1996.

100. United Nations High Commission on Human Rights, *Concluding Observations/ Comments of Committee on Economic, Social and Cultural Rights: Republic of Korea* (UN Doc E/C.1/1995/3, 1995), 3017.

101. It held its inaugural congress on November 11, 1995, representing 862 enterprise-level unions, with 418,000 members. Kim, "Rethinking the Beginning of the Democratic Labour Movement in Korea," 493–495.

102. The government refused to grant them legal recognition, as the KCTU's objectives overlapped with the objectives of the FKTU, and also because of the status of some of its officers. The KCTU's president was arrested for an outstanding arrest warrant for violation of "third party intervention" under LDAA (section 13(2) and 45(2)) for making statements about the railway and subway workers' strike in June 1994, and had been in hiding for eighteen months. The government warned the KCTU to stop using the title "trade union" in their name. International Labour Organization, "Report of the Committee on Freedom of Association (304th Report)," *ILO Official Bulletin* 79, ser. B, no. 2 (1996), 225–227.

103. Ibid., 231.

104. Ibid., 240.

105. Ibid., 252.

106. Insoo Jeong, "OECD Recommendations on Labor Issues and Korean Compliance with Evaluations: Labor Law, Relations, Market and Social Security," presented at the Korea–OECD Conference; Korea in the OECD Perspective: Shaping up for Globalization, Seoul, South Korea, 2000, 5.

107. John Burton, "Seoul to Reform Trade Union Laws," *Financial Times*, April 25, 1996, News: Asia-Pacific section, 4.

108. Salzman, "Labor Rights, Globalization and Institutions," 802. Evidence of its

basis on the ILO's understanding of "internationally accepted labor standards" can be found in the 1996 communication from John Evans, the TUAC general secretary, in response to the initial labor law legislation changes, which refer to basic labor rights in the language of the ILO's conventions. The communication from TUAC read, "Ahead of Korea becoming a member of the OECD this month, your government made a solemn commitment to the OECD to reform its existing laws and regulations on industrial relations to bring them in line with internationally accepted standards, including those covering basic human rights such as freedom of association and collective bargaining. Instead of honouring this commitment, the current legislation represents a giant step backwards." John Burton, "Seoul Labour Law Attacked at OECD," *Financial Times*, January 2, 1997, 3.

109. Koo, "Dilemma of Empowered Labor in Korea," 237.

110. "South Korea's Kim Vows Labor Reform," *United Press International*, April 24, 1996, Financial section.

111. "Kim: Militant Moderate or Civilian Dictator?" *Financial Times*, September 2, 1996, News: Asia-Pacific section, 3.

112. "South Korea's Judgment," *International Herald Tribune*, August 28, 1996, online edition, Opinion section.

113. Burton and Montagnon, "Labour Law Pledge Backfires on Kim," 6.

114. "South Korea Formally Becomes 29th Member of OECD," *Xinhua News Agency*, December 12, 1996.

115. "OECD Unions Urge Korea to Veto Labour Law," *Agence France Presse*, December 31, 1996, International News section.

116. John Burton, "Seoul Threat to International Union Team," *Financial Times*, January 14, 1997, News: Asia-Pacific section. However, a minority of the presidential commission and the Kim Young Sam administration were truly sympathetic to improving labor rights. See Koo, "The Dilemma of Empowered Labour in Korea," 238.

117. Kim and Bae, *Employment Relations and HRM in South Korea*, 100.

118. "Political Conflicts on the Horizon Over Government Revision Bill on Labor," *Korea Herald*, December 3, 1996.

119. The "three pillars" of Korean industrial relations had been: seniority-based (as opposed to performance-based) wages, lifetime employment, and enterprise unions. See Kim et al., "Globalization and Labor Rights," 141.

120. The new bill allowed layoffs for a wider range of justifiable conditions, such as changing economic conditions, productivity concerns, and technology needs. International Labour Organization, "Report of the Committee on Freedom of Association (306th Report)," *ILO Official Bulletin* 80, ser. B, no. 1 (1997), 199–200.

121. The new law also ended the practice of paying full-time union officials. While this law provoked anger because of its practical effects on day-to-day union operations, it remains outside of the scope of this study. See Kim, "Industrial Reform and Labor Backlash in South Korea," 1149.

122. B. C. Koh, "South Korea in 1996: Internal Strains and External Challenges." *Asian Survey* 37, no. 1 (1997): 3.

123. Reid G. Miller, "New South Korean Labor Law Pleases No One," *Associated Press*, December 13, 1996, Business News section.

124. Ibid. The ruling party had only a very small majority. In addition, during the same predawn session, a new law that re-authorized the activities of the notorious Agency of National Security Planning was passed, allowing the agency to once again spy on Korean citizens.

125. Koo, "The Dilemma of Empowered Labour in Korea," 239.

126. "Tigers and Pussy Cats: South Korea Learns Democracy the Hard Way," *Guardian* (London), January 14, 1997, 12.

127. Koo, *Korean Workers,* 1.

128. Koo, "Engendering Civil Society," 84.

129. "ILO Calls on S. Korea to Respect Unions' Rights," *Kyodo News Service: Japanese Economic Newswire,* January 15, 1997.

130. Ju-Yeon Kim, "South Korean Striking Workers Clash with Riot Police," *Associated Press,* December 28, 1996, International News section.

131. John Burton, "Seoul to Reform Trade Union Laws," *Financial Times,* April 25, 1996, News: Asia-Pacific section, 3.

132. Larry Elliot, "Workface: Echoes of UK in Streets of Seoul," *Guardian* (London), January 8, 1997, City Page section, 19.

133. Burton and Montagnon, "Labour Law Pledge Backfires on Kim," 6.

134. Afterward, the Economic, Labour and Social Affairs Committee began to go regularly visit Korea to monitor its labor laws. See Kim and Bae, *Employment Relations and HRM in South Korea,* 99.

135. Burton and Montangon, "Labour Law Pledge Backfires on Kim," 6.

136. See Burton, "Seoul Threat to International Union Team," 6.

137. Barry James, "OECD Panel Faults Seoul on Labor Law Provisions," *International Herald Tribune,* January 24, 1997, online edition, 4.

138. Kevin Sullivan, South Korean Leader Retreats On Controversial Labor Laws," *Washington Post,* January 22, 1997, A14.

139. John Burton, "Kim Agrees to Review Korea Labour Law," *Financial Times*, January 22, 1997, London edition, News: Asia-Pacific section, 6.

140. John Burton, "Seoul Rebuked Over Labour Reform," *Financial Times*, January 24, 1997, 10; "Seoul Vows to Ease Labour Law," *Independent* (London), January 24, 1997, 13.

141. "OECD Censures South Korea Over Labour Law," *Weekend Australian*, January 25, 1997.

142. "South Korea Says New Labour Law a 'Domestic Issue,'" *Agence France-Presse,* January 24, 1997, International News section.

143. Kim and Bae, *Industrial Relations and HRM in South Korea,* 100.

144. Korean Confederation of Trade Unions Former International Representative, personal interview with author, Seoul, South Korea, June 14, 2006.

145. International Labour Organization, "Report of the Committee on Freedom of Association (306th Report)," 318.

146. Ibid., 319.

147. Ibid., 329.

148. Ibid., 330.

149. Ibid., 333–345.

150. Ibid., 309.

151. John Burton, "Seoul Police Set to Seize Union Leaders," *Financial Times,* January 10, 1997, 5.

152. International Labour Organization, "Report of the Committee on Freedom of Association (306th Report)," 203.

153. Korean Confederation of Trade Unions former international representative, personal interview with author, Seoul, South Korea, June 14, 2006.

154. The government admitted to having only $30.5 billion in foreign reserves, far less than the IMF's requirement of at least three months' worth of import bills. See Wade and Veneroso, "The Asian Crisis: The High Debt Model Versus the Wall Street-Treasury-IMF Complex," and David Kang, *Crony Capitalism: Corruption and Development in South Korea and the Philippines* (Cambridge: Cambridge University Press, 2002).

155. John Burton, "Seoul Under Pressure on 'Shameful' IMF Deal," *Financial Times,* November 24, 1997, 2. There was strong contention between the Korean representative and the IMF over the details of the package, such as the schedule for closing nonperforming banks; growth targets; and controls on foreign capital, banking, and corporate sectors. See Republic of Korea, "Korea Letter of Intent, December 3, 1997," International Monetary Fund, December 3, 1997, accessed December 10, 2007, http://www.imf.org/external/np/loi/120397.htm.

156. John Burton, "S. Korean Markets Soar After $57 Billion IMF-led Deal," *Financial Times,* December 5, 1997, News: Asia-Pacific section.

157. Peter Montagnon, "This Is an Unusual Situation," *Financial Times*, December 12, 1997, Comment and Analysis section, 19.

158. The IMF sought to make the financial sector "more transparent, market-oriented, better supervised, and free from political interference in business decisions." Republic of Korea, "Korea Letter of Intent, December 3, 1997."

159. A chaebol is a large, often family-owned private corporation/conglomerate that typically enjoys close ties to the government. For example, the SK corporation engaged in telecommunications, energy, trade/services, petrochemicals, real estate, banking, etc. See Kang, *Crony Capitalism,* 53.

160. Republic of Korea, "Korea Letter of Intent, December 3, 1997."

161. Clay Chandler, "S. Korea's Kim Proves Mettle in Financial Crisis; President-Elect Gains Support for Savvy Economic Strategy," *Washington Post*, September 29, 1997, A1.

162. It should be noted that business elites' fears of Kim Dae Jung having communist

sympathies were not reflected in his own political statements. His commitment to free markets was well documented in his 1985 campaign book *Mass Participation Economy* in which he laid out his extensive plans for "democratizing" and liberalizing Korea's statist economy. See Dae Jung Kim, *Mass-Participatory Economy: A Democratic Alternative for Korea* (Cambridge, Mass.: Center for International Affairs, Harvard University; University Press of America, 1985).

163. Mary Jordan, "A Dubious Victory Awaits in S. Korea: Presidential Winner Faces Crisis of Faith, Economy," *Washington Post*, December 14, 1997, A1; Steven Mufson and Washington Post Foreign Service, "Seoul's Financial Markets Plunge in Crisis of Confidence; Kim Assures Nation Economic Reform Is on Track," *Washington Post*, December 20, 1997, A1; Nicholas D. Kristof, "South Korean President Fails to Placate Foes," *New York Times*, January 23, 1997.

164. Chandler, "S. Korea's Kim Proves Mettle in Financial Crisis," A01.

165. Ibid., A01.

166. Republic of Korea, Korean Tripartite Commission, *Major Agreements of the Korean Tripartite Commission (1998–2006)* (Seoul: Korean Tripartite Commission, 2006), http://www.lmg.go.kr/bbs/down.asp?code=e_bbs52&number=26&seq=1&mime=doc.

167. Republic of Korea, Korean Tripartite Commission, *Major Agreements of the Korean Tripartite Commission.*

168. Ibid., 12–13.

169. Dong-Eun Lee, personal interview with author, Seoul, South Korea, June 16, 2006.

170. Kiu-Sik Bae (Korea Labor Institute), personal interview with author, Seoul, South Korea, June 5, 2006.

171. Dae-uop Chang and Jun-ho Chae, "The Transformation of Korean Labour Relations Since 1997," *Journal of Contemporary Asia* 34, no. 4 (2004): 433.

172. The ILO committee had urged Korea to accept this mission several times, arguing that a mission's input might be necessary "so that the government can take its views into account with a view to fully implementing freedom of association principles." International Labour Organization, "Report of the Committee on Freedom of Association (306th Report)," 347.

173. In report issued by the high-level commission, the Korean government justifies why basic rights for groups of workers such as teachers and public servants have not been passed. For example, the Grand National Party members, who walked out of the Tripartite Commission before negotiations finished, argued that the public did not support teachers' unionization rights. The Korean Teachers' Union, on the other hand, argued that in fact according to their polls, they had the support of 70 percent of the public and 90 percent of all teachers. International Labour Organization, "Report of the Committee on Freedom of Association (309th Report)," *ILO Official Bulletin* 81 ser. B, no. 1 (1998), annex.

174. Ho-Geun Lee (Korean Tripartite Commission), personal interview with author, Seoul, South Korea. June 12, 2006.

175. Mi-young Ahn, "Seoul Pushes for Labour Reform," *Deutsche Presse-Agentur*, October 25, 1996; Nicholas D. Kristof, "South Korean Unions Agree to Negotiate on Job Layoffs," *New York Times*, January 15, 1998, 12.

176. John Burton, "Seoul to Make It Easier to Sack Finance Workers; First Relaxation of Nation's Rigid Labour Laws," *Financial Times*, January 14, 1998.

177. International Labour Organization, "Report of the Committee on Freedom of Association (309th Report)," 154.

178. During the financial crisis, trade unions were threatening a general strike as a response to talk of labor flexibility reform, and therefore the state needed their approval to prevent a strike that could worsen Korea's chances for economic recovery. See Kristof, "South Korean Unions Agree to Negotiate on Job Layoffs," 12.

179. Young-Lee Goh, interview with author, Seoul, South Korea, July 6, 2006.

180. Republic of Korea, Ministry of Labour, *Labor Administration 2006* (Seoul: Ministry of Labor, 2006), 83.

181. Ibid., 84.

182. Ibid., 84.

183. These laws allowed the KCTU to gain legal status after the Teachers' Union was registered. International Labour Organization, "Report of the Committee of Freedom of Association (311th Report)," *ILO Official Bulletin* 81, ser. B, no. 3 (1998), 319, 467.

184. Robert Putnam argues that domestic actors sometimes use international pressures, such as IMF agreements, to bring about politically difficult changes that the governments themselves support. See Robert Putnam, "Diplomacy and Domestic Politics: The Logic of Two Level Games," *International Organization* 42, no. 3 (Summer 1998): 427–460.

185. Kim, *Mass-Participatory Economy*, 20.

186. International Labour Organization, "Report of the Committee of Freedom of Association (311th Report)," 314.

187. Kim Dong-il and Lee Seung-chan were dismissed in summer 1998 for their involvement in the Public Servants' Works Council Preparation Committee, which was loosely affiliated with the KCTU. While the local courts ruled for their reinstatement, this retaliation demonstrated the government's continued insistence on limiting civil servant trade union rights. See International Labour Organization, "Report of the Committee of Freedom of Association (324th Report)," *ILO Official Bulletin* 84, ser. B, no. 1 (2001), 394.

188. The committee responded that the fact that "companies are facing 'economic difficulty' [was] not a free pass to ignore the existence of unions and erode workers' basic rights." In addition, Kim Dae Jung's government justified the continued trade union monopoly on the enterprise level as necessary in order to avoid excessive competition between unions. International Labour Organization, "Report of the Committee of Freedom of Association (320th Report)," 494.

189. Amnesty International, *South Korea: Briefing for the ASEM Foreign Ministers'*

Meeting. Amnesty International Index 10R 30/07/1999, Distr: SC/CC/CO, International Secretariat, London, March 1999.

190. For example, during a peaceful sit-down strike by Hyundai Motor Workers' Union, riot police broke up the strike with tear gas, tanks, forklifts, cranes, fire engines, water cannons, and steel pipes. They also arrested over 2,000 unionists. While recognizing that the clash between riot police and strikers may not have been entirely peaceful, the committee did condemn Korea's reliance on police in breaking up strikes on workplace premises. International Labour Organization, "Report of the Committee of Freedom of Association (320th Report)," 523.

191. Amnesty International, "Republic of Korea (South Korea): Summary of Concerns and Recommendations to Candidates for the Presidential Elections in December 2002," ASA 25/007/2002, November 6, 2002, http://www.amnesty.org/en/library/info/ASA25/007/2002.

192. Stig Jutterström, "Interview with Dan Byun-Ho," *International Metalworkers' Federation*, July 31, 2000, accessed July 7, 2007, http://www.imfmetal.org/main/index.cfm?id=103&lid=2&cid=3285&title=Number:%202-2000.

193. The 2000 ILO committee report referred to the Mando Machinery Workers' Union strike. Though the strike was illegal, it was the result of an employer violation of an existing collective agreement and illegal layoffs. The government complained that the strikers' actions, which included a sit-down occupation and the erection of a barricade at the front gate to stop the flow of people and products, resulted in the "disabling of normal operation of the company." As a result of the police response, 2,458 strikers were arrested, although no workers were detained. As a point of comparison, compare these tactics to the 1930s sit-down strikes in the United States. Under current U.S. law, this would be considered an "unfair labor practices" strike, and therefore would receive stronger protections. International Labour Organization, "Report of the Committee of Freedom of Association (311th Report)," 319, 467.

194. International Labour Organization, "Report of the Committee of Freedom of Association (320th Report)," *ILO Official Bulletin* 83, ser. B, no. 1 (2000), 524.

195. Ibid., 524.

196. Organisation for Economic Co-operation and Development, *Pushing Ahead with Reform in Korea Labour Market and Social Safety-Net Policies*, complete ed. (Paris: OECD, 2000), 13.

197. For example, Mr. Hwang argued that many strikes became violent, as unionists would occupy university buildings or damage property. However, as the ILO committee had claimed in earlier investigations, Mr. Hwang did not inform the committee that the state often reacted with strong law and order punitive measures to any "illegal" strikes, which often provoked violence. Rather, the government has characterized general labor militancy as violent and disruptive activity. United Nations High Commission on Human Rights, United Nations Human Rights Committee, *Summary Record of the 1792nd Meeting: Republic of Korea. 22/11/99* CCPR/C/SR.1792, Summary Record, 1999.

198. United Nations High Commission on Human Rights, United Nations Human Rights Committee, *Summary Record of the 1792nd Meeting: Republic of Korea.*

199. International Labour Organization, "Report of the Committee of Freedom of Association (320th Report)," 510.

200. United Nations High Commission on Human Rights, *Report of the Human Rights Committee, Vol. 1*, General Assembly, Official Records, Fifty-Fifth Session, Supplement No. 40 (A/55/40), (New York, 2000), p. 26.

201. International Labour Organization, "Report of the Committee of Freedom of Association (320th Report)," 464.

202. International Labour Organization, "Report of the Committee of Freedom of Association (310th Report)," *ILO Official Bulletin* 81, ser. B, no. 2 (1998), 210. The members of the second tripartite committee included: Ministry of Labor and Ministry of Finance and Economy (2), Korean Employers Federation and Korean Federation of Industries (2), FKTU, KCTU (2), political parties (National Congress for New Politics, United Liberal Democrats, GNP), and 5 academics.

203. United Nations High Commission on High Rights, *Summary Record of the 13th Meeting of the Committee on Economic Social and Cultural Rights (Republic of Korea),* E/C.12/2001/SR.13 (7/5/2001), 2001, 46.

204. "Choice Between Model of Establishment or Untried Independent Thinking," *Times* (London), December 18, 2002.

205. James Brooke, "New Leader in Korea Emphasizes Foreign Ties," *New York Times,* January 17, 2003, online edition, Business section.

206. Ibid.

207. Republic of Korea, Ministry of Labor, *Labor Administration 2006.*

208. Hyoung-Woo Chung and Hae Young Chung, personal interview with author, Seoul, South Korea, June 27, 2006.

209. Both the KCTU and the FKTU refused to participate in this regional meeting in protest to the persistent labor rights violations and repression.

210. Dae-Hwan Kim (former Minister of Labor), personal interview with author, Seoul, South Korea, July 22, 2006.

211. International Labour Organization, "Report of the Committee on Freedom of Association (331st Report)," *ILO Official Bulletin* 86, ser. B, no. 2 (2003), 328.

212. Ibid., 327.

213. Ibid., 334, 339.

214. The committee stated, "The Committee notes with interest the latest government communications which have indicated not only an overall desire and willingness to resolve most, if not all, of the outstanding issues in this case, but have also demonstrated concrete progress made in achieving a positive framework for the promotion of harmonious industrial relations through a certain number of special pardons granted to imprisoned trade unionists." Ibid., 341.

215. Ibid., 336–338.

216. The Public Officials Union Act only granted these rights to civil servants below

grade 5. Grades 5 and higher were excluded because they were considered "managerial." There are 9 grades within the Korean civil services, and this law excluded a high number of workers. International Labour Organization, "Report of the Committee on Freedom of Association (346th Report)," *ILO Official Bulletin* 90, ser. B, no. 2 (2007), 541.

217. This included arrests of KGEU members and leaders as well as direct repression from riot police that tried to stop the KGEU from holding a rally in October 2004. Police with search warrants entered 47 of the KGEU's 207 branch offices to take union computers and files related to a union election. See International Labour Organization, "Report of the Committee on Freedom of Association (340th Report)," *ILO Official Bulletin* 94, ser. B, no. 1 (2006), 710–716.

218. International Labour Organization, "Report of the Committee on Freedom of Association (340th Report)," 710.

219. Ibid., 737.

220. Ibid., 739.

221. Ibid., 739.

222. Ibid., 781.

223. United Nations High Commission on Human Rights, *Concluding Observations of the Human Rights Committee: Consideration of Reports Submitted by State Parties Under Article 40 of the Covenant (Republic of Korea)*, CCPR/C/KOR/CO/3, Concluding Observations/Comments, 2006, 19.

224. International Labour Organization, "Report of the Committee on Freedom of Association (346th Report)," 615.

225. Ibid., 692.

226. The report stated that government's regret that "many major misunderstandings on the Korean situation remain or continue to occur because of some trade unions' exaggerated or false arguments." Ibid., 615.

227. Ibid., 674.

228. Ibid., 688.

229. Ibid., 618

230. Ibid., 628.

231. Ibid., 705.

232. Ibid., 707.

233. Ibid., 625–637.

234. Korean Confederation of Trade Unions, *KCTU Counter-Report on the South Korean Government's Report to the UN Human Rights Committee* (Seoul: Korean Confederation of Trade Unions, October 10, 2006).

235. Republic of Korea, Ministry of Labour, *The Position of Korean Government on the ICFTU/TUAC/GUF Mission Report* (Seoul: Ministry of Labor, October 24, 2006).

236. The report also included pictures of these trade unionists acting violently and unreasonably in the appendix. Ibid.

237. Korean Labor News Network, "Korea Labor Ministry Issues Response to the

TUAC Report," October 25, 2006, accessed May 1, 2008, http://www.labordan.net/yubi/bbs/board.php?bo_table=m4_04&wr_id=246&page=14.

238. Republic of Korea, Korean Tripartite Commission, *Major Agreements of the Korean Tripartite Commission (1998–2006).*

239. International Labour Organization, "Report of the Committee on Freedom of Association (346th Report)," *ILO Official Bulletin* 90, ser. B, no. 2 (2007), 621, and Korea International Labour Foundation, "Tripartite Representatives Agreed on Road Map for Advancement of Industrial Relations Laws and Systems," *Labor Today* (Korean International Labour Foundation), September 11, 2006.

240. Organisation for Economic Co-operation and Development, *2007 Follow up to the Council Monitoring Mandate on Korean Labor Law and Industrial Relations Reform, Report by the Chair of the Employment, Labor and Social Affairs Committee* C(2007)9, 2007, 9.

241. Ibid., 9.

242. Korean Teachers' Union representative, personal interview with author, Seoul, South Korea, July 5, 2006.

243. Magda Kowalczuk, "S. Korea-Labor: Striking Workers Put Critical Spotlight on Seoul," *IPS-InterPress Service Tokyo,* January 7, 1997.

244. International Labour Organization, "Report of the Committee on Freedom of Association (346th Report)," 542.

245. International Labour Organization, "Report of the Committee on Freedom of Association (353rd Report)," *ILO Official Bulletin* 92, ser. B, no. 1 (2009), 667.

246. Korean Confederation of Trade Unions Policy Representative, personal interview with author, Seoul, South Korea, June 26, 2006.

247. Korean Metalworkers Federation Representative, personal interview with author, Seoul, South Korea, June 3, 2006.

248. Ho-Geun Lee (Korean Tripartite Commission), personal interview with author.

Chapter 5. United Kingdom

1. Tonia Novitz, "International Promises and Domestic Pragmatism: To What Extent Will the Employment Relations Act 1999 Implement International Labour Standards Relating to Freedom of Association," *Modern Law Review* 63, no. 3 (2000): 381.

2. Jonathan Hollowell, *Britain Since 1945* (Oxford: Blackwell Publishing, 2002), 435.

3. See John Hendy and Institute of Employment Rights, *A Law Unto Themselves: Conservative Employment Laws: A National and International Assessment* (London: Institute of Employment Rights, 1993).

4. Otto Kahn-Freund, "The Illegality of a Trade Union," *Modern Law Review* 7, no. 4 (1944): 192–205. This was largely established by court decisions and several laws.

5. Brian Towers, "Two Speed Ahead: Social Europe and the UK After Maastricht," *Industrial Relations* 23, no. 2 (1992): 86.

6. Anne C. L. Davies, *Perspectives on Labour Law* (Cambridge: Cambridge University Press, 2004), 4.

7. John Pencavel, "The Surprising Retreat of Union Britain," in *Seeking a Premier Economy: The Economic Effects of British Economic Reforms, 1980–2000,* ed. David E. Card, Richard Blundell, and Richard B. Freeman (Chicago: University of Chicago Press, 2004), 194.

8. These laws included the Trade Union Act of 1871, which excluded trade unions from "restraint of trade" provisions and the 1875 Conspiracy and Protection of Property Act, which gave trade unions' normal activity immunity from criminal prosecutions. The Trade Dispute Act of 1906 protected unions and striking organizers from tort liability. Hendy, "A Law Unto Themselves," 15.

9. Employers would also provide time off for trade union officials and other resources (such as a check-off procedure to facilitate union dues collection) for trade unions. See Rafael Gomez, Alexander Bryson, and Paul Willman, "The End of an Affair?The Decline in Employers' Propensity to Unionize," in *Union Organization and Activity in Britain 2,* ed. John E. Kelly and Paul Willman (London: Routledge, 2004), 138.

10. Kenneth William Wedderburn, "Freedom of Association and Philosophies of Labour Law," *Industrial Law Journal* 18, no. 1 (1989): 15.

11. Bob Simpson, "The Changing Face of British Collective Labour Law," *Oxford Journal of Legal Studies* 21, no. 4 (2001): 710.

12. Hendy, "A Law Unto Themselves," 1993.

13. David Marsh, *The New Politics of British Trade Unionism: Union Power and the Thatcher Legacy* (Ithaca, N.Y.: Cornell University Press, 1992), 41–50.

14. Pencavel, "The Surprising Retreat of Union Britain," 188.

15. Ibid., 196.

16. Donley T. Studlar, *Great Britain: Decline or Renewal* (Boulder, Colo.: Westview Press, 1996), 84.

17. Hollowell, *Britain Since 1945,* 431.

18. Earl A. Reitan, *The Thatcher Revolution: Margaret Thatcher, John Major, Tony Blair, and the Transformation of Modern Britain* (Boulder, Colo.: Rowman & Littlefield, 2003), 24.

19. Towers, "Two Speed Ahead: Social Europe After Maastricht," 86.

20. Trevor Colling, "What Space for Unions on the Floor of Rights?Trade Unions and the Enforcement of Statutory Individual Employment Rights," *Industrial Law Journal* 35, no. 2 (2006): 142.

21. This quote is attributed to Norman Lamont, the former Chancellor of the Exchequer. At the time, unemployment stood at four million, and Lamont considered this positive because it would help lower wages and production costs. Hendy, *A Law Unto Themselves,* 28.

22. Pencavel, *The Surprising Retreat of Union Britain,* 197.

23. The ILO stated that "whilst it is true that most of the legislative measures under consideration are not incompatible with the requirements of the Convention, there is a point at which the cumulative effect of legislative changes which are in themselves consistent with the principles of freedom of association may nevertheless, by virtue of

their complexity and extent, constitute an incursion upon the rights guaranteed by the Convention." International Labour Organization, "Summary of Reports on Ratified Conventions (Articles 22 and 35 of the Constitution)," *Comments of the Committee of Experts on the Application of Conventions and Recommendations, International Labour Conference,* 76th session, 1989, 241.

24. Hendy, *A Law Unto Themselves,* 46.

25. Pencavel, *The Surprising Retreat of Union Britain,* 202.

26. Whether or not British unions deserved such blame is unclear. By the mid-1990s, there was a near academic consensus that unionized British firms were less profitable than nonunionized ones. There was also a simultaneous increase in firm productivity and trade union density starting from the early 1980s (although this could also be attributed to elimination of exchange controls). See John T. Addison and W. Stanley Siebert, "Union Security in Britain," *Journal of Labor Research* 19, no. 3 (6, 1998): 509.

27. Hendy, *A Law Unto Themselves,* 56.

28. Hollowell, *Britain Since 1945*, 431.

29. K. D. Ewing, *Britain and the ILO* (London: Institute of Employment Rights, 1994), 38.

30. International Labour Organization, *United Kingdom: Committee of Experts on the Application of Conventions and Recommendations: Individual Observation Concerning Convention No. 151, Labour Relations (Public Service),* ILOLEX Document No. 061994GBR151, 1994.

31. International Labour Organization, "Report of the Committee on Freedom of Association (211th Report)," *ILO Official Bulletin* 64, ser. B, no. 3 (1981), 63.

32. Ewing, *Britain and the ILO,* 23.

33. International Labour Organization, "Report of the Committee on Freedom of Association (275th Report)," 68.

34. Ibid.

35. Hendy, *A Law Unto Themselves,* 61.

36. Ibid., 81.

37. A White Paper is a publication by the government that sets out the agenda and details for future policy on a subject matter. It is typically the basis of a future bill, but it is released publicly prior to introduction in Parliament to allow for public feedback. See United Kingdom Parliament, "Glossary: White Paper," accessed November 10, 2010, http://www.parliament.uk/site-information/glossary/white-paper;John Gennard and Graham Judge, *Employee Relations,* 4th ed. (London: CIPD Publishing, 2005).

38. Ibid., 56.

39. Great Britain, Employment Dept. Group, *Industrial Relations in the 1990s: Proposals for Further Reform of Industrial Relations and Trade Union Law,* Cm, 1602 (London: HMSO, 1991), 1.

40. Ibid., 1.

41. Ibid., 2–3.

42. Ibid., 7.
43. Ibid., 7.
44. Ibid., 4–5.
45. Ibid., 10.
46. Ibid., 7.
47. Ibid., 7.
48. *Wilson and the National Union of Journalists; Palmer, Wyeth and National Union of Rail, Maritime and Transport Workers; Doolan and others v. United Kingdom* [2002] IRLR 128. Hereafter referred to in notes as *Wilson et al. v. UK.*
49. Stephen Cavalier, personal interview with author, London, January 10, 2007.
50. *David William Wilson v. Associated Newspapers Ltd. [1990]* ITR 10516/90/LS.
51. National Union of Journalists (former secretary general), Interview with author, London, United Kingdom, November 29, 2006.
52. *Wilson et al. v. UK.*
53. The employers were engaged in a deliberative attempt to reshape labor relations within the Associated Newspapers group. This group included the *Evening Standard, Mail on Sunday,* and *Daily Mail.* The editors decided to end the collective relationship between the newspapers and journalists by March 31, 1990, and replace them with individual-level contracts. The editors perceived a need for this shift because of new "commercial needs, modernisation, and political change." The editors told the union representatives that they were reorganizing to directly interact with staff, and therefore no longer needed a "third force." The employers claimed that they were not violating the existing legal provisions protecting trade union membership because they did not threaten the rights of employees to join and become trade union members. The employers admitted offering a 4.5 percent pay increase only to those who signed individual contracts but argued that this was not intended as a penalty. According to the court report, the employers claimed that "withdrawal of collective bargaining rights . . . could not constitute the penalizing of individual employees [and] a trade union member has no right in law to be individually and collectively represented by his/her trade union." *David William Wilson v. Associated Newspapers Ltd.* [1990] ITR 10516/90/LS., 22.
54. National Union of Journalists, phone interview with author.
55. This section of the act stated: "every employee shall have the right not to have action (short of dismissal) taken against him as an individual by his employer for the purpose of (a) preventing or deterring him from being or seeking to become a member of an independent trade union, or penalising him for doing so; or (b) preventing or deterring him from taking part in the activities of an independent trade union at any appropriate time, or penalising him for doing so." United Kingdom, *Employment Protection (Consolidation) Act 1978,* accessed June 17, 2008, http://www.legislation.gov.uk/ukpga/1978/44/section/23/enacted.
56. The tribunal ruled against other claims of Wilson that he had been prevented from being a trade union member. [1990] ITR 10516/90/LS.
57. John Hendy, QC, personal interview with author, London, January 10, 2007.

58. The employers justified this switch to individual contracts as a system for which "individual merit and contribution for an employee may be recognised and rewarded." At the tribunal, the employers admitted that they did engage in action short of dismissal against the workers who refused to sign individual contracts, but not with the *purpose* of preventing membership of a trade union. Instead the employers claimed to have engaged in omission, having failed to pay the same increase to those workers who did not sign the individual-level contract. They reiterated that the purpose was not penalty, but instead incentive and benefits for those employees who did accept the individual contracts. Replacing the collective agreement with individual contracts would lead to greater managerial efficiency. *Mr. T. A. E. Palmer, Mr. B. Stedman, and Mr. A.E. Wyeth v. Associated British Ports* [1991] ITR. 3367, 3367, 3367, 17/24.

59. [1991] ITR. 3367, 3367, 3367.

60. The amounts were £2,850 for Mr. Palmer, £2,020 for Mr. Wyeth, and £1,560 for Mr. Stedman. [1991] ITR. 3367, 3367, 3367, 18/25.

61. *Associated British Ports v. Palmer & Ors* [1993] IRLR 63.

62. The *Daily Mail*'s initial offer to its employees stated that the union could continue to represent members for grievance and disciplinary procedures. See *Associated Newspapers Ltd v. Wilson* [1992] ICR 681.

63. The Employment Appeals Tribunal claimed that 138 members of the NUJ having signed the individual contracts suggested that membership was not threatened nor were the new conditions substantively different. [1992] ICR 681, 13-15.

64. *Associated British Ports v. Palmer & Ors* [1993] IRLR 63.

65. *Associated British Ports v. Palmer & Ors*, 11-15.

66. *Associated British Ports v. Palmer; Associated Newspapers v. Wilson* [1994] ICR 97 (CA), 98.

67. Novitz, "International Pressures and Domestic Pragmatism," 390.

68. National Union of Journalists, personal interview with author.

69. The decision referred to a prior case, the 1990 *Discount Tobacco and Confectionery Ltd. v. Armitage,* in which the Employment Appeal Tribunal argued that their trade union membership included use of trade union services and activity. The *Discount Tobacco* decision stated, "the activities of a trade union officer in negotiating and elucidating terms of employment is . . . the outward and visible manifestation of trade union membership . . . we see no genuine distinction between membership of a union, on the one hand, and making use of the essential services of a union, on the other."[1994] ICR, 102.

70. The Court of Appeals also referred to the prior decision in the case of *National Coal v. Ridgeway*. According to the *National Coal* decision, granting a pay raise only to employees who signed individual contracts constituted action taken against the individual. The court also upheld the prior decision of the Industrial Tribunal, which argued that Associated Newspapers consciously deprived the union of all functional ability (except for health and safety), "effectively rendering the union powerless and thus membership pointless." [1994] ICR, 107.

71. Quoted in [1994] ICR, 109.

72. The act was introduced by Mrs. Shepard, the Employment Secretary, who called it "a tidying up exercise . . . [no] part of a war against unions. There was a war in the 1980s but that is now over." It should also be noted that the 1993 act also ended the Wages Councils, which had effectively helped to maintain "social wages" for the lowest-paid workers, with attention to regional economic conditions. See David Goodhart, "War with Trade Unions is Over Says Shephard," *Financial Times* (London), July 16, 1992.

73. International Labour Organization, "Report of the Committee on Freedom of Association (302nd Report)," *ILO Official Bulletin* 79, ser. B, no. 1 (1996).

74. Novitz, "International Promises and Domestic Pragmatism," 390.

75. National Union of Journalists, "The Wilson Case: Who Said What," National Union of Journalists Web site, 2002, accessed September 17, 2008, http://212.67.198.213/nuj/inner.php?docid=277.

76. The Trades Union Congress is similar in function to the United States' American Federation of Labor/ Congress of Industrial Organizations, as it serves as national level umbrella organization, uniting 58 affiliated unions and over 6 million members in 2011. It helps advise on both national and European level policy, and has historically maintained strong ties to the Labour Party. See Trades Union Congress, "About the TUC," *Trades Union Congress*, accessed October 18, 2011, http://www.tuc.org.uk/the_tuc/index.cfm?mins=2&minors=2&majorsubjectID=19.

77. International Labour Organization, "Report of the Committee on Freedom of Association (294nd Report)," *ILO Official Bulletin* 78, ser. B, no. 2 (1994), 166.

78. Hendy, personal interview with author, London.

79. *Wilson and the National Union of Journalists; Palmer, Wyeth and National Union of Rail, Maritime and Transport Workers; Doolan and Others v. United Kingdom* [2002] IRLR 128.

80. International Labour Organization, "Report of the Committee on Freedom of Association (294th Report)," 201.

81. This was now encapsulated within section 146 of the Trade Union and Labour Relations Consolidation Act of 1992.

82. Novitz, "International Promises and Domestic Pragmatism," 390.

83. *Associated Newspapers Ltd. v. Wilson and Association British Ports PLC v. Palmer* [1995] 2 AC 454.

84. Ibid., 172.

85. Ibid.

86. Hendy, *A Law Unto Themselves*, 56.

87. International Labour Organization, "Report of the Committee on Freedom of Association (302nd Report)," 40.

88. International Labour Organization, "Report of the Committee on Freedom of Association (294th Report)," 166.

89. Ibid., 193.

90. Ibid., 199.

91. Ibid., 202.

92. Workers at the Sheerness Steel company were offered a new contract without collective bargaining with the established union, the Iron and Steel Trades Confederation. The new contracts required that workers give up union membership, even though an overwhelming majority of workers wanted to continue collective bargaining. Management threatened to fire any workers who refused to so. It also would not allow unions representatives onto the worksite. International Labour Organization, "Report of the Committee on Freedom of Association (304th Report)," 477–482.

93. Ibid., 486.

94. International Labour Organization, "Report of the Committee on Freedom of Association (302nd Report)." The ILO echoed these decisions in its reports on case no. 1852, which also involved Section 13 of the Trade Union Reform and Employment Rights Act.

95. International Labour Organization, "Report of the Committee on Freedom of Association (304th Report)," 494.

96. Ibid., 495.

97. United Nations High Commission on Human Rights, *Summary Record of the 37th Meeting: United Kingdom of Great Britain and Northern Ireland,* E/C.12/1997/SR.37, 1998, 28-38.

98. United Nations High Commission on Human Rights, *Concluding Observations of the Committee on Economic, Social and Cultural Right* E/C.12/1/Add.19, 1997, 11, 23.

99. Wilson and the National Union of Journalists, Palmer, Wyeth and the National Union of Rail, Maritime and Transport Workers, Doolan and others, *Applicant's Response to Observations of the Government of the United Kingdom* (Strasbourg: European Court of Human Rights, March 13, 2000), 9–10.

100. Council of Europe, Committee of Independent Experts on the European Social Charter, *European Social Charter: Conclusions/Committee of Independent Experts of the European Social Charter XIII-3* (Strasbourg: Council of Europe, 1996), 108.

101. Great Britain, Department of Trade and Industry, *Review of the Employment Relations Act 1999: Government Response* (London: Department of Trade and Industry, 2003), 11.

102. Creighton Breen, "ILO and Freedom of Association in the UK," in *Human Rights and Labour Law: Essays for Paul O'Higgins*, ed. Paul O'Higgins et al., Studies in Labour and Social Law (New York: Mansell, 1994), 23.

103. Trades Union Congress (employment rights officer), personal interview with author, London, November 23, 2006.

104. Hendy, personal interview with author.

105. Novitz, "International Promises and Domestic Pragmatism," 383.

106. The Labour Party had won 43.2 percent of the vote (compared to 30.7 percent for the Conservatives) and 418 parliamentary seats (compared to the Conservatives' 165) in a parliament of 659. Matthew Leeke, *UK Election Statistics 1945–2003* (London:

House of Commons Library, 2003), accessed June 17, 2008, http://www.parliament.uk/commons/lib/research/rp2003/rp03-059.pdf.

107. This was unlike in South Korea, where the ruling party did not always enjoy a majority of parliamentary seats and thus had to compromise with opposition party members.

108. The shadow cabinet is the leadership of the official opposition party, which criticizes the party in power and offers policy alternatives. Shadow cabinets include officers that mirror the positions held by the actual Parliament. See Iain Mclean and Alistair McMillan, "Shadow Cabinet," *The Concise Oxford Dictionary of Politics* (Oxford: Oxford University Press, 2009), 482.

109. Philip Bassett, "Fear of a Return to the Seventies Haunt Talk of Union Recognition," *The Times* (London), March 28, 1997, sec. Business.

110. Philip Bassett, "GCHQ Move Signals Mild Change in Climate for Unions," *The Times* (London), May 16, 1997.

111. Ewen Macaskill, "The Election: The Unions: Ties that Bind Ever Less Closely: Blair Vowed to Sever Old Link," *Guardian*, April 4, 1997, 13.

112. Despite Labour's caution regarding trade unions, the Conservative government won the 1992 election. It should also be noted that the degree of party loyalty among trade union members also decreased. Only 33 percent of trade union members voted Labour in 1983, 42 percent in 1987. David Goodhart, "Election 92; Labour Keeps Its Distance but Is Tied to Dependence," *Financial Times* (London), March 13, 1992, 6; and David Goodhart, "Election 1992: Unions Review Party Funding," *Financial Times* (London), April 9, 1992.

113. Tony Blair, *Tony Blair in His Own Words*, ed. Paul Richards (London: Politico's, 2004), 90.

114. M. Hall, "Government Unveils Proposals for a Fairer Workplace," *European Industrial Relations Observatory Online*, June 28, 1998, accessed July 10, 2007, http://www.eurofound.europa.eu/eiro/1998/06/feature/uk9806129f.htm.

115. Robert Taylor, "Backtracking Embitters Trade Union Old Guard," *Financial Times*, April 7, 1997, News section.

116. Ibid., 20.

117. The Conservatives, as well conservative newspapers such as the *Daily Mail*, also criticized Labour for taking funds from unions. See Macaskill, "The Election: The Unions," 13.

118. After the Tories reported that the Labour manifesto would include a proposal for a statutory provision for union recognition, Tory leaders stated that such restoration of trade union rights would "send a chill down the spine" of British industry, calling the proposal "industrial blackmail." Gordon Brown, the shadow chancellor, mistakenly stated that judges would determine disputes over which workers qualified within a bargaining unit, and this caused confusion and controversy. As a result, shadow foreign secretary Robin Cook quickly corrected him, saying that disputes would be referred to a Central Arbitration Committee to mediate such disputes. Rebecca Smithers and

Michael White, "Tories Start Scare on Unions," *Guardian,* March 26, 1997, Home Page section. See also Ean Higgins, "Tories Exploit Bad Old Days of Unionism," *The Australian,* March 26, 1997, World section, 10.

119. Ean Higgins, "Labour's Tremors Before the Landslide," *The Australian,* April 30, 1997, Local section, 1.

120. Robert Taylor, "Backtracking Embitters Trade Union Old Guard," 11.

121. National Union of Journalists (former secretary general), phone interview with author

122. Ibid.

123. Stephen Cavalier, personal interview with author, London, January 10, 2007.

124. The Labour government would still refuse to allow compensation for workers fired during legal strike activity and would not obligate employers to rehire those workers who successfully filed an unfair dismissal claim. The government also wanted to maintain the ban on secondary pickets and closed shops. Robert Taylor, "Government Heads for Clash on Labour Laws, Ministers Under Pressure to Scrap Tory Employment Legislation after ILO Upholds Complaints Against Britain," *Financial Times*, June 6, 1997, News section.

125. Great Britain, Department for Education and Employment, *UK Argues for Jobs and Supports Employments at IL* (London: Department for Education and Employment, June 10, 1997).

126. Ibid.

127. The issue of blacklisting was immediately addressed in the first round of trade union reforms in 1999 and the changes to data privacy acts in 1998. The Data Privacy Act 1998 prohibited the processing of "sensitive" personal information, including trade union membership. The Employment Relations Act 1999 illegalized the "compilation, dissemination and use of lists" regarding trade union membership or activities for use by employers. The committee noted these changes in 2000 and this recommendation and communication process with the United Kingdom was considered successful. See International Labour Organization, "Report of the Committee of Freedom of Association (323rd Report)," *ILO Official Bulletin* 83, ser. B, no. 3 (2000), 72–80.

128. The New Labour government's communications repeatedly categorized the Co-Steel issue as a union recognition problem, not a trade union discrimination issue. In its response to the ILO committee, the government claimed that this problem could be readily addressed within the employment tribunals because of the provisions of the 1999 Employment Relations Act, which included a provision for statutory union recognition. International Labour Organization, "Report of the Committee of Freedom of Association (318th Report)," *ILO Official Bulletin* 82, ser. B, no. 3 (1999), 82.

129. Blair, *Tony Blair in His Own Words,* 1.

130. Great Britain, *Fairness at Work,* 2.13.

131. Novitz, "International Promises and Domestic Pragmatism," 380.

132. Great Britain, *Fairness at Work,* 4.24, 4.25.

133. Stephen Wood and John Goddard, "The Statutory Union Recognition Pro-

cedure in the Employment Relations Bill: A Comparative Analysis," *British Journal of Industrial Relations* 37, no. 2 (1999): 204–208.

134. Blanpain et al., *The Global Workplace*, 361.

135. *Employment Relations Act 1999* (U.K.), Chapter 26, accessed May 23, 2008, www.opsi.gov.uk/acts/acts1999/pdf/ukpga_19990026_en.pdf.

136. Great Britain, Department of Trade and Industry, *Review of the Employment Relations Act 1999: Government Response.*

137. The blacklist situation was a pernicious issue that remains a difficulty for British trade unionists. In the 1980s, an organization called the Economic League held and circulated data on an estimated 22,000 individuals allegedly considered "trade union militants," mostly in the construction industry, which allowed employers to discriminate against these individuals. In many cases, the information was proved to be inaccurate. Some of the individuals on the list had merely been shop stewards and had recruited other workers to become trade union members. Prior to 1999, British law did not make such practices illegal, nor did it allow for strong redress for discrimination by employers. See International Labour Organization, "Report of the Committee on Freedom of Association (283rd Report)," *ILO Official Bulletin* 75, ser. B, no. 2 (1992), 424–426. Recent information has demonstrated that additional changes in the law have failed to adequately protect British construction workers from such practices as recently as 2010. See Keith Ewing, "Labour Leaves Blacklisted High and Dry," *Guardian,* March 10, 2010, accessed October 21, 2010, http://www.guardian.co.uk/commentisfree/2010/mar/10/labour-leaves-blacklisted-high-dry.

138. Fredman and Morris wrote in their analysis that the different opinions between the European Commission on Human Rights and the ILO "highlights the inconsistencies between the various international instruments which protect the freedom of association." Sandra Fredman and Gillian Morris, "Recent Cases: Freedom of Association," *Industrial Law Journal* 17, no. 1 (1988): 105–108.

139. International Labour Organization, "Report of the Committee on Freedom of Association (275th Report)."

140. This had been mentioned in the white paper and also in campaign literature. See Novitz, "International Promises and Domestic Pragmatism," 391; Ewing, "Freedom of Association and Employment Relations Act 1999," 287.

141. Such an individual contract would not count as a "detriment."

142. *Employment Relations Act 1999* (U.K.) 1999, Sections 17(1), 17(2), 17(4).

143. Trades Union Congress, *The Employment Relations Act: A TUC Guide* (London: Anderson Lambert, 1999), 41.

144. Ewing, "Freedom of Association and the Employment Relations Act 1999," 288.

145. Novitz, "International Promises and Domestic Pragmatism," 391.

146. Trades Union Congress, *General Council Report 2002: Chapter 1,* accessed June 12, 2008, http://www.tuc.org.uk/congress/tuc-6423-f0.cfm.

147. Simpson, "The Changing Face of British Collective Labour Law," 713. See also Collins, Ewing, and McColgan, *Labour Law Text and Materials,*737.

148. The TUC and Liberty, a British human rights organization focused on domestic issues, were not parties to the ECtHR case, but later entered supporting submissions.

149. Wilson and the National Union of Journalists, Palmer, Wyeth and the National Union of Rail, Maritime and Transport Workers, Doolan and others, *Applicant's Response to Observations of the Government of the United Kingdom*, 7.

150. Ibid.

151. Trades Union Congress, and Liberty, *Joint Submission by Liberty and the Trade Unions Congress: Third Party Intervention to the Court*, Applications 30668/96, 30671/96, 30678/96 (Strasbourg: European Court of Human Rights, 2000).

152. United Kingdom, *Observations of the Government*, Application No. 30668/96; 30671/96; 30678/96 (European Court of Human Rights, 1999), 5.

153. Ibid., 13.

154. Prior decisions had established a "right to be heard" for trade unions under Article 11, but the U.K. government argued that this does not imply a right to recognition or collective bargaining.

155. Ibid., 26.

156. Ibid., 30.

157. National Union of Journalists, "NUJ Hero's Great Euro Victory on Union Rights," National Union of Journalists Web site, 2002, accessed April 21, 2008, http://www.nuj.org.uk/inner.php?docid=276.

158. [2002] IRLR 128, para. 15–20.

159. [2002] IRLR 128, para. 19.

160. Section 17 granted the Secretary of State the right to regulate when employers provided independent contracts different than a collective agreement through coercion, but not because of higher pay or other forms of monetary benefits. See earlier section.

161. Keith Ewing, John Hendy, Bob Simpson, and Stephen Cavalier, *Wilson and Palmer Briefing* (London: Institute for Employment Rights, 2002).

162. *Employment Relations Act 2004* (U.K.), accessed June 1, 2008, http://www.opsi.gov.uk/acts/acts2004/ukpga_20040024_en_1.htm.

163. To determine the *sole or main* purpose to such an offer would be determined by evidence of whether the employers had recently tried to change or did not want to use agreed-upon arrangements for collective bargaining. A tribunal could look to see if the employer at the time of the contracts had not wanted to enter into arrangements with the union for collective bargaining. *Employment Relations Act 2004* (U.K.).

164. Alan L. Bogg, "Employment Relations Act 2004: Another False Dawn for Collectivism?" *Industrial Law Journal* 34, no. 1 (2005): 73.

165. *Employment Relations Act 2004* (U.K.).

166. Great Britain Parliament, Joint Committee on Human Rights, *Legislative Scrutiny: Sixth Progress Report: Thirteenth Report of Session 2004–04* (London: Stationery Office, 2004), 104.

167. U.K. based law professor, personal interview with author, London, December 5, 2006.

168. Abbott and Snidal, "Hard and Soft Law in International Governance."

169. The Committee of Ministers is the executive arm of the Council of Europe and is composed of the foreign affairs ministers of member states.

170. Council of Europe, "How the Execution of Judgments Works (European Court of Human Rights)," *European Court of Human Rights—The Court*, accessed April 1, 2008, http://www.echr.coe.int/ECHR/EN/Header/The+Court/Execution/How+the+execution+of+judgments+works.

171. K. D. Ewing, *Human Rights at Work* (London: Institute of Employment Rights, 2000), 4.

172. Aileen McCabe, "Blair Is Making a Difference Already: Sweeping Changes Felt in Monetary Policy, Relations with Europe, Hospital Closings, etc.," May 14, 1997, *Gazette*, News section.

173. Colin Hay, "That Was Then, This Is Now: The Revision of Policy in the 'Modernisation' of the British Labour Party, 1992–97," *New Political Science* 20, no. 1 (1998): 7–25.

174. M. Wickham-Jones, "New Labour in the Global Economy: Partisan Politics and the Social Democratic Model," *British Journal of Politics and International Relations* 2, no. 1 (2000): 2.

175. Robert Peston, "Blair Sets Out 10-point 'Covenant'; Brown Admits a $1.5bn Revenue Shortfall as Labour Manifesto is Launched," *Financial Times*, April 4, 1997, 1.

176. Labour Party (of Great Britain), "New Labour Because Britain Deserves Better: Britain Will Be Better with New Labour," 1997 Labour Party Manifesto, accessed March 19, 2009, http://www.labour-party.org.uk/manifestos/1997/1997-labour-manifesto.shtml.

177. Glenda Korporaal, "Blair Has Every Opportunity to Reshape Britain," *Sydney Morning Herald* (Australia), May 5, 1997, International News section, 38.

178. The Social Chapter, a document of social regulations for the European Community, is different from the similarly named European Social Charter, the much older social and economic human rights code for the Council of Europe. David Wighton, "Blair Fudges EU Differences Between Parties: Labour Leader Launches Personal Attack on a Prime Minister 'Without Authority to Negotiate,'" *Financial Times*, April 22, 1997, News section, 10.

179. The Social Chapter was a major initial victory for the emergent transnational workers' rights movement that would also play a role in linking labor rights with South Korea's OECD membership and labor rights to NAFTA.

180. John Palmer, "Poll Shows British Majority Backs Controversial EEC Social Charter," *Guardian*, May 19, 1989.

181. The 1988 *Employment in the 1990s* White Paper stated, in relation to the EEC, that the United Kingdom would oppose any "unnecessary regulation which raise[s] the cost of employment, which make the labour market less flexible or which erect new barriers to jobs." The Department of Education, *Fact Pack, People, Jobs and Progress*

claimed, "government economists have estimated that the direct cost of [the EEC] proposal to UK employers alone would be at least £30 billion." John Palmer, "EEC Faces Opposition Over 'Workers Rights' Proposals," *Guardian*, May 19, 1988, News section.

182. John Palmer, "Poll Shows British Majority Backs Controversial EEC Social Charter."

183. Labour Party (of Great Britain), "It's Time to Get Working Again: British Labour Party Election Manifesto: 1992," *Political Science Resources*, Keele University (UK), 1992, http://www.psr.keele.ac.uk/area/uk/man/lab92.htm.

184. Shada Islam, "Britain's European Partners Hope for Constructive Partnership," *Deutsche Presse-Agentur*, April 30, 1997.

185. For example, French Foreign Minister de Charette and German Chancellor Kohl interpreted the election as a move away from British Euro-skepticism. EU Commission President Santer stated at an Intergovernmental Conference that the need for British leadership was clear. German Foreign Minister Kinkel said that the Blair victory was evidence of the British commitment to Europe and the European process. See Sarah Helm, "The World Warms to Blair's Victor: Europe Hopes Poll Will Lance Euroskeptic Boil," *Independent* (London), May 3, 1997, International section, 12. In addition, Socialist members of the European Parliament in Strasbourg evidently cheered "wildly" at the news of Blair's election. See Gary Younge, "Europeans Think He's a New JFK. Really," *Observer*, May 11, 1997, News section.

186. Labour Party (of Great Britain), "New Labour Because Britain Deserves Better: Britain Will Be Better with New Labour," *1997 Labour Party Manifesto*, accessed March 12, 2009, http://www.labour-party.org.uk/manifestos/1997/1997-labour-manifesto.shtml.

187. Ewing, *Human Rights at Work*.

188. K. D. Ewing, "The Human Rights Act and Parliamentary Democracy," *Modern Law Review* 62, no. 1 (1999): 81.

189. Great Britain, Department of Health, "Questions and Answers on the Human Rights Act 1998: Department of Health—Managing Your Organisation," *Department of Health: Human Rights*, 2007, accessed February 12, 2009, http://www.dh.gov.uk/en/Managingyourorganisation/Equalityandhumanrights/Humanrights/DH_4136018.

190. *Human Rights Act 1998* (U.K.), accessed January 11, 2009, http://www.opsi.gov.uk/ACTS/acts1998/ukpga_19980042_en_1.

191. Trades Union Congress, personal interview with author.

192. Hendy, personal interview with author.

193. K. D. Ewing, "The Implications of Wilson and Palmer," *Industrial Law Journal* 32, no. 1 (March 1, 2003): 5.

194. Ewing, *Human Rights at Work*, 16.

195. Cavalier, personal interview with author.

196. Trades Union Congress, personal interview with author.

197. This is due to the bylaws of the European Court. In order to qualify for admissibility, a litigant must have exhausted all domestic legal venues and not have gone to another international legal institution, such as the European Court of Justice. Since the

ILO's Committee on Freedom of Association was not necessarily the same case, as a trade union made the representation, the *Wilson* case was not disqualified.

198. Collins et al., *Labour Law Text and Materials*, 739.

199. Hendy, personal interview with author.

200. U.K.-based law professor, personal interview with author.

201. Bogg, "Employment Relations Act 2004," 73.

202. National Union of Journalists, phone interview with author. The law states that only a worker or a former worker can make such a complaint to an industrial tribunal.

203. Ibid., 74.

204. Ibid., 74.

205. "According to the complainant KGEU, the proposed 'individual contacts,' 'home visits,' and 'telephone calls' to persuade the person in question and his/her family members are serious human rights violations. The establishment of 'persuasion teams' to conduct individual contacts to press for withdrawal of membership is an abuse of the state's power." International Labour Organization, "Report of the Committee on Freedom of Association (346th Report)."

206. Great Britain Parliament, Joint Committee on Human Rights, *Legislative Scrutiny: Sixth Progress Report: Thirteenth Report of Session 2004–04*), 39–41.

207. Ibid., 83.

208. *Mr. B. Davies and Others v. Asda stores* [2006] UKET 2501510/05, 2006.

Chapter 6. Canada

1. Canadian Broadcast Corporation, "Health Care Workers Hurt by Bill 29 to Receive Compensation by Christmas," CBC News, November 10, 2008, accessed August 12, 2009, http://www.cbc.ca/canada/british-columbia/story/2008/11/10/bc-compensation-payout-arrangement.html.

2. International Labour Organization, "Report of the Committee on Freedom of Association (357th Report)," *ILO Official Bulletin* 92, ser. B, no. 2 (2010): 30–34.

3. See Roy J. Adams, *Labour Left Out: Canada's Failure to Protect and Promote Collective Bargaining as a Human Right* (Ottawa: Canadian Center for Policy Alternatives, 2006); H. D. Woods and Canada, *Canadian Industrial Relations: The Report of Task Force on Labour Relations* (Ottawa: Privy Council Office, 1968). This tradition is not without its contention, however.

4. Derek Fudge and John Brewin, *Collective Bargaining in Canada: Human Right or Canadian Illusion?* (Black Point, Nova Scotia: Fernwood, 2006).

5. The British Columbia Federation of Labour called it "uncharacteristically blunt language." See British Columbia Federation of Labour, *Workers Demand Repeal of Bills Violating International Rights: UN Body Condemns Campbell's Liberals for Legislation Trampling Workers Rights* (Vancouver: British Columbia Federation of Labour News Archives, March 26, 2003).

6. Fudge and Brewin, *Collective Bargaining in Canada.*

7. Canada, Human Resources and Social Development Canada, "Canadian Rati-

fication of ILO Conventions," *Labour: Building Fair and Productive Workplaces*, 2005, accessed May 14, 2008, http://www1.servicecanada.gc.ca/en/lp/ila/Representing_Canada/Canada_ratification_ILO.shtml.

8. Canada: Foreign Affairs and International Trade, "Six Principal Human Rights Treaties," *Canada's International Human Rights Policy*, 2007, accessed April 12, 2008, http://www.dfait-maeci.gc.ca/foreign_policy/human-rights/hr1-rights-en.asp#1.

9. Lawrence Helfer, *Understanding Change in International Organizations: Globalization and Innovation in the ILO*, Working Paper (Nashville, Tenn.: Vanderbilt University Law School Public Law and Legal Theory, 2005).

10. In contrast, the American and Mexican governments have largely ignored their obligations under this agreement.

11. Canada, Human Resources and Social Development Canada, "Canadian Ratification of ILO Conventions."

12. Fudge and Brewin, *Collective Bargaining in Canada*, 16.

13. Poisson and Torbin, quoted in Roy J. Adams, "Implications of the International Human Rights Consensus for Canadian Labour and Management," *Canadian Labour and Employment Law* 9 (2002): 125–145.

14. See Fudge, "Labour Is Not a Commodity." See also Panitch and Swartz, *From Consent to Coercion*; and Adams, *Labour Left Out*, for more documentation on Canada's failures.

15. Fudge and Brewin, *Collective Bargaining in Canada*, 65.

16. Leo Panitch and Donald Swartz, *From Consent to Coercion: The Assault on Trade Union Freedoms* (Aurora, Ont.: Garamond Press, 2003); Larry Savage, "Workers' Rights as Human Rights: Organized Labor and Rights Discourse in Canada," *Labor Studies Journal* 34, no. 1 (March 2009): 12.

17. The Privy Council was the highest national court prior to the establishment of the Canadian Supreme Court, based heavily on a British model.

18. Robert Burgess Stewart, "Canada and International Labor Conventions," *American Journal of International Law* 32 (1938): 47–48.

19. *Attorney-General for Canada v. Attorney-General for Ontario*, [1937] A.C. 326 (P.C.).

20. Ran Hirschl, "'Negative' Rights vs. 'Positive' Entitlements: A Comparative Study of Judicial Interpretations of Rights in an Emerging Neo-Liberal Economic Order," *Human Rights Quarterly* 22 (2000): 1060–1098.

21. Quoted in Gordon Digiacomo, *Federalism and Labour Policy in Canada*, Working Papers, (Kingston: Institute of Intergovernmental Relations, Queen's University, 2001).

22. Arthurs, "National Traditions in Labor Law Scholarship," 649.

23. Gene Swimmer, "Public Sector Labour Relations in an Era of Restraint and Restructuring: An Overview," in *Public-Sector Labour Relations in an Era of Restraint and Restructuring*, ed. Gene Swimmer (Oxford: Oxford University Press, 2001).

24. Gene Swimmer and Tim Bartkiw, "The Future of Public Sector Collective Bargaining in Canada," *Journal of Labor Research* 24 (2003): 586.

25. This means that government or public authorities may sidestep the usual collective bargaining process and legislate the new collective agreement, which does not consider the unions' interests. It is unilateral because the bargaining process has been removed.

26. Swimmer and Bartkiw, "The Future of Public Sector Collective Bargaining in Canada," 587.

27. Brad Underwood, personal interview with author, Victoria, Canada, October 17, 2006.

28. Michael Howlett and Keith Brownsey, "From Timber to Tourism: The Political Economy of British Columbia," in *Politics, Policy and Government in British Columbia,* ed. R. K. Carty (Vancouver: University of British Columbia Press, 1996), 18.

29. Donald E. Blake, "The Politics of Polarization: Parties and Election in British Columbia," in *Politics, Policy and Government in British Columbia*, ed. R. K. Carty (Vancouver: University of British Columbia Press, 1996), 72.

30. The Commonwealth Cooperative Federation was a Depression era social democratic third party created in Calgary in 1932, based on a "farmer-labor" alliance. It soon spread to other provinces. See David Laycock, "The Depression and Third Party Development," *Center for Canadian Studies at Mt. Allison University: The Prairie Roots of Canada's Political "Third Parties,* 2001, accessed November 15, 2010, http://www.mta.ca/faculty/arts/canadian_studies/english/about/study_guide/roots/depression.html.

31. British Columbia has a first-past-the-post unicameral legislature. Institutionally this results in overrepresentation of slightly dominant parties. The CCF won an electoral plurality in 1941, but the party was excluded from the governing coalition, formed by the splintered right parties. Blake, "The Politics of Polarization," 68.

32. "Provincialization" meant the transition of key industries from private to public ownership at the provincial level.

33. Howlett and Brownsey, "From Timber to Tourism."

34. The government led by W. A. C. Bennett's party was called Social Credit. The Social Credit Party had emerged from a right-wing populist provincial movement that started in neighboring Alberta.

35. The British Columbia Social Credit government of W. A. C. Bennett in 1950s consolidated the resource-based economy and greatly expanded public-sector employment. Both of these measures were seen as a necessary political response to the left's demands for greater public ownership in the province, yet ironically weakened the Social Credit's power base. Ibid., 28.

36. Blake, "The Politics of Polarization," 75.

37. Keith Brownsey and Michael Howlett, "British Columbia: Politics in a Post-Staples Economy," in *The Provincial State in Canada: Politics in the Provinces and Territories*, ed. Keith Brownsey and Michael Howlett (Peterborough, Ont., Canada: Broadview Press, 2001), 23.

38. The vast majority of the workers affected by the rights-violating Liberal govern-

ment's laws passed in 2001 and 2002 were in the Hospital Employees Union; 85 percent of these workers were female. See Barbara McClintock, "Female Trouble," in *Liberalized: The Tyee Report on British Columbia Under Gordon Campbell's Liberals*, ed. David Beers (Vancouver: New Star Books, 2005), 19.

39. Valerie Matthews Lemieux and Steven Barrett, "Charter Protection Extended to Collective Bargaining- How Far Does it Reach?" *CCPA Review Labour Notes* (Ontario, Canadian Centre for Policy Alternatives, December 2007).

40. British Columbia Government and Service Employees' Union, personal interview with author, Burnaby, Canada, October 5, 2006.

41. Howlett and Brownley, "British Columbia," 323.

42. Howlett and Brownley, "From Timber to Tourism," 29.

43. Mike Morton, Office of the Premier of British Columbia, personal interview with author, Victoria, British Columbia, October 19, 2006.

44. Over 30 percent of British Columbia's exports went to Japan and the other East Asian newly industrial countries in 1996. During this period, British Columbia's resource-based economy with strong ties to Asian markets suffered from a number of macroeconomic factors, including the East Asian Financial Crisis, low commodity prices for natural resources and high real estate interest rates. See David Fairey, *Behind the Numbers: BC's NDP Government: Spendthrift or Overly Restrained?* CCPA: Behind the Numbers. (Ontario: Canadian Center for Policy Alternatives, March 31, 2001).

45. The Liberal Party in 2001 was made up of the now defunct Social Credit Party, the British Columbia Reform party, and the remnants of the old Liberal Party, which had suffered from electoral marginality since the 1950s. Chuck Puchmayr, (MLA), personal interview with author, New Westminster, Canada, October 28, 2006.

46. Morton, personal interview with author.

47. British Columbia Liberal Party, *A New Era for British Columbia: A Vision for Hope and Prosperity for the New Decade and Beyond* (Vancouver: BC Liberal Party, 2001) (emphasis in the original).

48. Don Wright and British Columbia, *Towards a Better Teacher Bargaining Model in British Columbia: Report to Honourable Graham Bruce on the Teacher Collective Bargaining* (Victoria: British Columbia Ministry of Education/Ministry of Skills Development and Labour, 2003).

49. Jim Sinclair and Angela Schira, "Code Breaks: BC Federation of Labour," *Democrat*, September 9, 2001.

50. Diane McDonald and David Fairey, *Old Policies in Liberal "New Era" Labour Platform: A Backgrounder on the BC Liberals' Proposed Labour Policy Changes* (Ottawa: Canadian Center for Policy Alternatives, 2001).

51. British Columbia Liberal Party, *A New Era for British Columbia: A Vision for Hope and Prosperity for the New Decade and Beyond.*

52. National Union of Public and General Employees, *Unions Challenge Bill 29, B.C.'S Contract-Busting Law* (Ottawa: National Union of Public and General Employees,

May 29, 2002), accessed April 12, 2008, http://www.nupge.ca/news_2002/news_my02/n29my02b.htm.

53. British Columbia Legislative Assembly, "Official Report of Debates of the Legislative Assembly (HANSARD) Vol. 24, No. 7 (HTML)," *2004 Legislative Session: 5th Session, 37th Parliament Hansard*, accessed April 10, 2008, http://www.leg.bc.ca/Hansard/37th5th/h40428p.htm.

54. Legislative Library British Columbia, *Electoral History of British Columbia Supplement, 1987–2001* (Victoria: Legislative Library of British Columbia, 2002).

55. International Labour Organization, "Report of the Committee on Freedom of Association (330th Report)," *ILO Official Bulletin* 86, ser. B, no. 1 (2003), 269.

56. Jim Beatty and Craig McInnes, "Hospitals Will Close, Hansen Admits: Legislature Debates Controversial Labour Bills," *Vancouver Sun*, January 28, 2002.

57. Only Alberta had a lower debt-to-GDP ratio, largely due to the public royalties from its gas and oil industry. Furthermore, revised calculations demonstrated that instead of unsustainable deficits, the last two years of the NDP government had been characterized by budgetary restraints leading up to provincial budgetary surpluses of $617 million and $1.5 billion, respectively. The immediate tax cuts disproportionately benefited the highest income bracket, with the top 16 percent of income earners receiving over half the tax cut, and the top 50,000 earners in British Columbia receiving enough money to settle the labor disputes in question. See Seth Klein and Marc Lee, *BC's Fiscal Choices: Submission to the British Columbia Fiscal Review Panel* (Vancouver: Canadian Center for Policy Alternatives, July 2001).

58. Bill 27 (Education Services Collective Agreement Act) legislated a new collective agreement for the teachers. Bill 28 (Public Education Flexibility and Choice Act) and Bill 29 (Health and Social Services Delivery Improvement Act) override existing provisions in collective agreements in the name of public services flexibility. See International Labour Organization, "Report of the Committee on Freedom of Association (330th Report)"; British Columbia Legislative Assembly, "Official Report of Debates of the Legislative Assembly. 2003 Legislative Session: 4th Session, 37th Parliament, Vol. 14, No. 11 (HTML)," *Official Report of Debates of the Legislative Assembly (Hansard)*, April 29, 2004, accessed March 11, 2008, http://www.leg.bc.ca/hansard/37th4th/h30429p.htm; British Columbia Legislative Assembly, "Official Report of Debates of the Legislative Assembly (HANSARD) Vol. 24, No. 7 (HTML)"; British Columbia Legislative Assembly, "Official Report of Debates of the Legislative Assembly (Hansard) Monday, April 14, 2008, Vol 30, Number 7," *Legislative Assembly of British Columbia*, accessed April 14, 2008, http://www.leg.bc.ca/hansard/38th4th/h80414p.htm#11283.

59. Russ Francis, "Tearing Up Deals," *Monday Magazine*, February 21, 2003.

60. Ibid.

61. Canadian Press, "Legislation Draws Union Wrath," *Alberni Valley Times* (British Columbia), January 29, 2002, B.C. section, 2.

62. This led to unsympathetic ruling from the British Columbia Supreme Court in September 2003 and the Appeal Court of British Columbia in July 2004. The Supreme

Court of Canada agreed to accept the case on appeal in 2005. See British Columbia General and Service Employees Union, *Alert* (Vancouver: British Columbia General and Service Employees Union, April 21, 2005).

63. The Canadian Labour Congress is the national, pan-industrial labor union federation, similar to the U.S. AFL-CIO.

64. The NUPGE represents direct government employees; and the British Columbia Government and Service Employees Union (BCGEU) is the local union federation associated with the NUPGE. CUPE-BC, on the other hand, represents local and municipal government employees, including support staff at schools. The Hospital Employees' Union and the Health Sciences Association (HSA) are affiliated under CUPE-BC. The HEU represents hospital service workers, in such areas as maintenance and laundry, while the HSA represents technicians and specialists. The British Columbia Nurses' Association is a union federation for nurses, and the BC Teachers' Federation represents public school teachers. See International Labour Organization, "Report of the Committee on Freedom of Association (330th Report)," 245–259.

65. The Health Science Association included over 10,000 health care and social services professionals, which included paramedics and community health service and support workers. See Health Sciences Association of British Columbia, "About: Who we are," accessed January 21, 2009, http://www.hsabc.org/content.php?id=2&sid=4&pid=0.

66. International Labour Organization, "Report of the Committee on Freedom of Association (330th Report)," 249.

67. See Chapter 3 for more information on how the committee has interpreted essential services.

68. International Labour Organization, "Report of the Committee on Freedom of Association (330th Report)," 249, 294.

69. Ibid., 250–252.

70. International Labour Organization, "Report of the Committee on Freedom of Association (330th Report)," 249, 253–259.

71. The exact language of the committee's recommendation was: "Recalling that the right to strike is one of the essential means through which workers and their organizations may promote and defend their economic and social interest [see Digest, op. cit., para. 475], the Committee concludes that the provisions of Bill No. 18 which make education an essential service are in violation of freedom of association principles and should be repealed." Ibid., 297.

72. The committee stated, "there were no adequate consultations, and that Bill No. 27 unilaterally imposed a legislative settlement for a period of three years in the education sector, thereby not respecting the autonomy of the bargaining parties. The Committee reiterates here the comments made in Case No. 2166 concerning both the excessive length of this imposed agreement and the limited possibility of variation even if the parties would later agree upon modifications. The Committee firmly requests the Government to avoid in future having recourse to such legislated settlement, and strongly hopes that the next round of negotiations will be held in accordance with the principles mentioned above." Ibid., 298.

73. Ibid., 295–300.

74. This was the subject of case 2180, brought by the Canadian Labour Congress and the National Union of Public and General Employees (NUPGE), which is the national federation to which the British Columbia Government and Service Employees' Union and the Health Science Association belong.

75. The other bills in question, Bills 15 and 28, had legislated collective agreements that had already expired.

76. International Labour Organization, "Report of the Committee on Freedom of Association (330th Report)," 249, 302.

77. Ibid., 305.

78. The communications from the government were sent July 26, 2002, August 8, 2002, January 4, 2004, March 2, 2009, and March 8, 2010.

79. International Labour Organization, "Report of the Committee on Freedom of Association (330th Report)," 249, 267, 269, 276, 283.

80. Ibid., 286. The government listed as examples minimum wages, hours, work standards, and mandatory health and safety regulations.

81. Ibid., 286.

82. Ibid., 286.

83. Charles R. Epp, "Do Bills of Rights Matter? The Canadian Charter of Rights and Freedoms," *American Political Science Review* 90, no. 4 (1996): 769.

84. June M. Ross, "Limitations on Human Rights in International Law: Their Relevance to the Canadian Charter of Rights and Freedoms," *Human Rights Quarterly* 6, no. 2 (1984): 181.

85. Canada Department of Justice, "Canadian Charter of Rights and Freedoms," Justice Laws Website, accessed March 19, 2008, http://laws.justice.gc.ca/en/Charter/index.html#garantie.

86. These cases were officially known as *Reference Re Public Service Employee Relations Act (Alberta), PSAC v. Canada,* and *RWDSU v. Saskatchewan.*

87. These court cases include Reference re Public Services Employee Relations Act (Alberta), *PSAC v. Canada*, and *RWDSU v. Saskatchewan*. All three cases were decided in 1987. See Paul C. Weiler, "The Charter at Work: Reflections on the Constitutionalizing of Labour and Employment Law," *University of Toronto Law Journal* 40, no. 2 (1990): 124.

88. See International Labour Office and Freedom of Association Committee, *Freedom of Association: Digest of Decisions and Principles of the Freedom of Association Committee of the Governing Body of the ILO*. In addition, the 2002 ruling by the European Court of Human Rights case *Wilson et al. v. UK* also ruled that collective bargaining rights were necessary to protect workers' rights to form unions.

89. This is similar to the "race the bottom" concerns that led to the creation of an international labor protection regime.

90. Adams, "Implications of the International Human Rights Consensus for Canadian Labour and Management," and Fudge, *Collective Bargaining in Canada*.

91. *Health Services and Support-Facilities Subsector Bargaining Assn. v. British Columbia* [2003] BCJ No. 2107.

92. The Dunmore decision argued that freedom of association, as human rights obligations, included collective and individual-level protections. While collective bargaining itself was not protected by the Supreme Court's decision, the Court recognized the collective elements of these rights. See Fudge, *Collective Bargaining in Canada.*

93. These activities included making collective representations to an employer, adopting a majority political platform, and federating with other unions. The differences between "making collective representations" and collective bargaining are specified within the majority opinion. *Dunmore v. Ontario (Attorney General)* [2001] 3 SCR 1016, 207 D.LR (4th) 193, 2001 SCC 94.

94. Hirschl, "'Negative' Rights vs. 'Positive' Entitlements."

95. Ibid., 290.

96. International Labour Organization, "Report of the Committee on Freedom of Association (340th Report)," *ILO Official Bulletin* 94, ser. B, no. 1 (2006), 49. The next communication would occur in March 2009. International Labour Organization, "Report of the Committee on Freedom of Association (357th Report)," *ILO Official Bulletin* 92, ser. B, no. 2 (2010).

97. International Labour Organization, "Report of the Committee on Freedom of Association (340th Report)," 49.

98. British Columbia Teachers' Federation, personal interview with author.

99. Janet Steffenhagen, "Labour Lauds UN Slap at Liberals," *Vancouver Sun*, March 28, 2003.

100. Judith LaVoie, "UN Accuses Province of Labour Violations," *Times Colonist* (Victoria, British Columbia), March 20, 2003.

101. International Labour Organization, "Report of the Committee on Freedom of Association (340th Report)," 47.

102. Morton, personal interview with author.

103. This is similar to a tactic used in South Korea when the government wished to critique the legitimacy of the ILO's recommendations. British Columbia Legislative Assembly, "Official Report of the Debates of the Legislative Assembly [HANSARD], April 29, 2004, Vol. 14, No. 11 (HTML)," *2003 Legislative Session, 4th Session, 37th Parliament,* accessed March 18, 2009, http://www.leg.bc.ca/hansard/37th4th/h30429p.htm.

104. International Labour Organization, "Report of the Committee on Freedom of Association (354th Report)," *ILO Official Bulletin* 92, ser. B, no. 2 (2009), 40.

105. International Labour Organization, "Report of the Committee on Freedom of Association (340th Report)," 47.

106. Ibid., 27–29.

107. These included Bill 94, the Health Sector Partnerships Agreement Act, Bill 18, the Coastal Ferry Act, and the Railway and Ferries Bargaining Assistance Act (Bill 95). Bill 94 was a unilaterally imposed collective agreement that allowed for privatization of certain health services, and nullified existing collective agreement clauses and even sections of the

British Columbia Labour Relations Code. Bill 18 allowed for privatization of ferry services and severely restricted the scope of collective bargaining for BC ferry workers. Workers saw this as an attempt to de-unionize the ferry services. Bill 98 legislated the ferry workers back to work 48 hours after they called a legal strike and imposed a new 80-day "cooling off" period. International Labour Organization, "Report of the Committee on Freedom of Association (336th Report)," *ILO Official Bulletin* 83, ser. B, no. 1 (2005), 236–257.

108. Ibid., 269.

109. Ibid., 265.

110. *Health Services and Support - Facilities Subsector Bargaining Assn. v. British Columbia,* 2007 SCC 27, [2007] 2 S.C. R. 391, accessed June 10, 2009, http://scc.lexum.umontreal.ca/en/2007/2007scc27/2007scc27.html, herein referred to as *Health Services.*

111. Interestingly, the Supreme Court did not find Bill 29 to violate nondiscrimination protections— Section 15—of the Charter, even though the majority of workers within the health care union were women. *Health Services,* paragraph 165.

112. Kirk Markin, "Collective Bargaining Is a Right, Top Court Rules," *Globe and Mail,* June 9, 2007, online edition, Justice Report section.

113. Only one judge dissented in part. It should be noted that this judge did not dissent with the general principle that collective bargaining was protected by the charter. Instead, the dissenting opinion stated that in this particular instance in British Columbia, the curtailing of collective bargaining should have been permitted.

114. *Health Services,* 28.

115. *Health Services,* 41.

116. P.C. 1003, passed in 1939 as part of a federal order-in-council, set up a statutory system of trade union recognition and legal basis for collective bargaining, modeled after the 1935 National Labor Relations Act. See Donald M. Wells, "Origins of Canada's Wagner Model of Industrial Relations: The United Auto Workers in Canada and the Suppression of 'Rank and File' Unionism, 1936–1953," *Canadian Journal of Sociology/ Cahiers Canadiens de Sociologie* 20, no. 2 (1995): 193–225.

117. *Health Services,* 67.

118. Ibid., 81.

119. Ibid., 78. Emphasis in the original.

120. Ibid., 72.

121. Ibid., 74.

122. Ibid., 76–77.

123. The justices specified the scope of the right to collective bargaining, which was expressed as a limited right. This right entitled workers to a process, not an outcome. Workers and employers had to willingly and in good faith engage in consultation, but this did not necessarily have to result in a collective agreement. Ibid., 91.

124. This is a stark contrast between the 2004 Employment Relations Act in the United Kingdom, in which inducements to effect collective bargaining were prohibited *only* in those instances in which the employers' primary intent was to end collective bargaining, not as a means to reward workers or other prerogatives.

125. Ibid, 91.

126. Ibid, 93.

127. Ibid, 121.

128. Ibid, 129. The Court did not recognize other clauses that the union argued were in violation of Charter rights as constituting violations. This included the parts of Bill 29 that allowed employers to contract out certain health services without allowing these employees "successor rights," which mandates the same rights and protections as under *existing* collective agreements.

129. Ibid., 138.

130. Ibid., 141.

131. Ibid., 159–160.

132. Ibid.,167, 171.

133. Ian Baily, "Campbell in No Rush to Respond to Landmark Ruling on Bill 29," *Globe and Mail*, June 12, 2007, British Columbia News section.

134. Markin, "Collective Bargaining Is a Right," A4.

135. Brian Etherington, "The BC Health Services and Support Decision—The Constitutionalization of a Right to Bargain Collectively in Canada—Where Did It Come from and Where Will It Lead?" *Comparative Labor Law and Policy Journal* 30 (2009): 715.

136. *Health Services*, 113.

137. National Union of Public and General Employees, 2008, "Settlement Agreement Reached in British Columbia on Bill 29," NUPGE Web site, accessed January 19, 2008, http://www.nupge.ca/news_2008/n29ja08b.htm.

138. British Columbia Ministry of Health, "Bill 29 Negotations: Tentative Settlement Agreement," *Backgrounder*, January 28, 2008, http://www2.news.gov.bc.ca/news_releases_2005-2009/2008health0010-000112-Attachment1.htm.

139. "Deal Aims to Resolve Bill 29 Dispute," *Globe and Mail* (Canada), January 29, 2008, online edition, National: British Columbia News; Labour; Health Care sections.

140. British Columbia Legislative Assembly, "Official Report of Debates of the Legislative Assembly (Hansard) Monday, April 14, 2008, Vol. 30, Number 7," and British Columbia, "Progress of Bills," 2008 Legislative Session: 4th Session, 38th Parliament, accessed June 1, 2009, http://www.leg.bc.ca/38th4th/votes/progress-of-bills.htm.

141. International Labour Organization, "Report of the Committee on Freedom of Association (354th Report)," *ILO Official Bulletin* 92, ser. B, no. 2 (2009), 37.

142. Ibid., 40.

143. Ibid., 42.

144. Ibid., 44.

145. National Union of Public and General Employees, "Unions Challenge Bill 29, B.C.'s Contract-Busting Law," Ottawa, May 29, 2002, accessed April 21, 2009, http://www.nupge.ca/news_2002/news_my02/n29my02b.htm.

146. However, these recommendations were rumored to have created quite a reaction at the federal level. British Columbia Poverty and Human Rights Center, personal interview with author, Vancouver, November 7, 2006.

147. British Columbia Coalition of Women's Centres, "BC CEDAW: BC Singled Out for Criticism by UN Committee," March 8, 2003, accessed April 1, 2008, http://www3.telus.net/bcwomen/archives/BCCEDAW_UNsubmission_jan_03_pressrel.html.

148. British Columbia Poverty and Human Rights Center, personal interview with author.

149. Risse, "'Let's Argue!'" 8.

150. British Columbia Poverty and Human Rights Center, personal interview with author.

151. Chuck Puchmayr (MLA), personal interview with author.

152. Even children below the age of twelve with the permission of the director of Employment Standards Branch could work. See David Fairey, *Eroding Worker Protections.*

153. Ibid.

154. Ibid., 7.

155. International Labour Organization, "Report of the Committee on Freedom of Association (330th Report)," 267.

156. Robert Matas, "BC Income Tax Cuts Now in Place," *Globe and Mail*, December 31, 2001.

157. International Labour Organization, "Report of the Committee on Freedom of Association (330th Report)," 249.

158. Beatty and McInnes, "Hospitals Will Close, Hansen Admits."

159. British Columbia Federation of Labour, personal interview with author, Vancouver, October 25, 2006.

160. See Judy Fudge, "The Supreme Court of Canada and the Right to Bargain Collectively: The Implications of the Health Services and Support Case in Canada and Beyond," *Industrial Law Journal* 37, no. 1 (2008): 25–48; Etherington, "The BC Health Services and Support Decision," 723.

161. William A. Shabas, "International Human Rights Law and the Canadian Courts," in *Human Rights in the Twenty-first Century: Prospects, Institutions and Processes*, ed. Thomas A. Cromwell et al. (Montreal: Editions Themis, 1997), 21–48.

162. *Health Services,* 19.

163. Ibid., 91.

164. Ibid., 95.

165. Etherington, "The BC Health Services and Support Decision," 732.

166. Fudge, "The Supreme Court of Canada and the Right to Bargain Collectively."

Conclusion

1. T. Risse, "'Let's Argue!'" 17.

2. While the political reaction to unions in South Korea was less extreme, unions were still blamed for their inflationary effects because of their wage gains in the late 1980s.

3. David Beetham, "What Future for Economic and Social Rights?" *Political Studies* 43, no. 1 (1995): 41–60.

4. For an explanation of this view, which Harvey does not necessarily endorse, see David Harvey, *A Brief History of Neoliberalism*, 179.

5. International Trade Union Confederation, "Internationally Recognized Core Labour Standards in the Republic of Korea," Report for the WTO General Council Review of the Trade Policies of Korea, Geneva, October 8 and 10, 2008, http://www.ituc-csi.org/IMG/pdf/Korea-_final.pdf, 4.

6. Ibid., 4.

7. Great Britain Parliament, Joint Committee on Human Rights, *Legislative Scrutiny: Sixth Progress Report: Fourteenth Report of Session 2005–06* (London: Stationery Office, 2006), 39–41.

8. Ibid., 102.

9. Eric Tucker, "The Constitutional Right to Bargain Collectively: The Ironies of Labour History in the Supreme Court of Canada," *Labour/ Le Travail* 61, no. 1 (2008): 158.

10. *Health Sciences*, 19.

11. Ibid., 19.

12. Eric Tucker, "The Constitutional Right to Bargain Collectively," 158.

13. Lemieux and Barrett, "Charter Protection Extended to Collective Bargaining."

14. Ibid.

15. Larry Savage, "Workers' Rights as Human Rights," 16.

16. Ibid., 18.

17. Amnesty International, "South Korea: Journalists' Arrests Threaten Press Freedom," *Press Releases,* March 24, 2009, accessed September 1, 2009, http://www.amnesty.org/en/for-media/press-releases/south-korea-journalists%E2%80%99-arrests-threaten-press-freedom-20090324.

18. International Labour Organization, "Report of the Committee on Freedom of Association (353rd Report)," *Official Bulletin* 92, ser. B, no. 1 (2009), 589.

19. Robert Wade, "Financial Regime Change," *New Left Review* 53 (October 2008): 7; Edward R. T. Challies and Warwick E. Murray, "Towards Post-Neoliberalism? The Comparative Politico-economic Transition of New Zealand and Chile," *Asia Pacific Viewpoint* 49, no. 2 (2008): 229.

20. Lucio Baccaro, "Labour and the Global Financial Crisis," *Socio-Economic Review* 8, no. 2 (April 1, 2010): 342.

21. See Compa and Human Rights Watch (Organization), *Unfair Advantage: Workers' Freedom of Association in the United States Under International Human Rights Standards.* See also Adams, *Labour Left Out.*

22. Lichtenstein, "The Rights Revolution," *New Labor Forum* 12, no. 1 (March 2003): 60–73. See also J. McCartin, "Democratizing the Demand for Workers' Rights."

23. Lichtenstein, "The Rights Revolution," 70.

24. Savage, "Workers' Rights as Human Rights," 17.

25. Ishay, *The History of Human Rights*, 9.

26. Lance Compa, "Response," *Dissent,* Winter 2005, 67.

Appendix III. Case Disputes and U.S. Law

1. Compa, *Unfair Advantage*, 32.

2. David L. Gregory, "The Right to Unionize as a Fundamental Human and Civil Right," *Mississippi College Law Review* 9 (1988): 141.

3. Malcolm M. Duplantis, Timothy D. Chandler, and Terry G. Geske, "The Growth and Impact of Teachers' Unions in States Without Collective Bargaining Legislation," *Economics of Education Review* 14, no. 2 (June 1995): 175.

4. International Labor Organization, *Country Baselines Under the ILO Declaration Annual Review (2000–2010)*, 213.

5. Douglas L. Leslie, *Labor Law in a Nutshell*, 5th ed. (St. Paul, Minn.: Thomson West, 2008), 97.

6. Leslie, *Labor Law in a Nutshell*, 20, 104.

7. Novitz, "International Promises and Domestic Pragmatism: To What Extent will the Employment Relations Act 1999 Implement International Labour Standards in Relation to Freedom of Association?" 388. Stephen Wood and John Goddard, "The Statutory Union Recognition Procedure in the Employment Relations Bill: A Comparative Analysis," *British Journal of Industrial Relations* 37, no. 2 (1999): 204–208.

8. International Labor Organization, *Country Baselines Under the ILO Declaration Annual Review (2000–2010): Freedom of Association and the Effective Recognition of the Right to Collective Bargaining (FACB)*, 211.

9. David Twomey, *Labor and Employment Law: Text and Cases*, 13th ed. (Mason, Ohio: Thompson West, 2006), 251.

10. Isidore Silver, *Public Employee Discharge and Discipline* (New York: Aspen Publishers, 2001), 111–112.

11. See Thomas Kochan, David B. Lipinsky, Mary Newhart, and Alan Benson, "The Long Haul Effects of Interest Arbitration: The Case of New York State's Taylor Law," *Industrial and Labor Relations Review* 63 (2009): 565–584.

12. Silver, *Public Employee Discharge and Discipline,* 112.

13. Gerald Friedman, "Labor and the Bush Administration: 'Down So Long, Seem Like Up to Me'," *Revue LISA/LISA e-journal*, 1 (March 4, 2010): 69–85.

14. Monica Davey, "Wisconsin Court Reinstates Law on Union Rights," *New York Times*, June 14, 2011, U.S./Politics section, http://www.nytimes.com/2011/06/15/us/politics/15wisconsin.html.

BIBLIOGRAPHY

Abbott, Kenneth W., and Duncan Snidal. "Hard and Soft Law in International Governance." *International Organization* 54, no. 3 (Summer 2000): 421–456.

Abouharb, Rowan M., and David L. Cingranelli. "The Effects of Structural Adjustment Agreements on Government Respect for Workers' Rights." Presented at the University of North Carolina Workshop on Labor Rights and Multinational Production, Chapel Hill, 2006.

Adams, Roy J. "From Statutory Right to Human Right: The Evolution and Current Status of Collective Bargaining." *Just Labour* 12 (2008): 48–67.

———. "Implications of the International Human Rights Consensus for Canadian Labour and Management." *Canadian Labour and Employment Law* 9 (2002): 125–145.

———. *Labour Left Out: Canada's Failure to Protect and Promote Collective Bargaining as a Human Right.* Ottawa: Canadian Center for Policy Alternatives, 2006.

Addison, John T., and W. Stanley Siebert. "Union Security in Britain." *Journal of Labor Research* 19, no. 3 (1998): 495–517.

Aggarwal, Mita. "International Trade, Labor Standards, and Labor Market Conditions: An Evaluation of the Linkages." USITC, Office of Economics Working Paper No. 95-06-C (June), 1995.

Ahn, Mi-young. "Seoul Pushes for Labour Reform." *Deutsche Presse-Agentur*, October 25, 1996.

Alston, Philip. "'Core Labor Standards' and the Transformation of the International Labor Rights Regime." *European Journal of Industrial Relations* 15, no. 3 (2004): 457–521.

Alvarez, Jose. "Do Liberal States Behave Better? A Critique of Slaughter's Liberal Theory." *European Journal of International Law* 12, no. 2 (2001): 183–246.

Amnesty International. "Republic of Korea (South Korea): Summary of Concerns and Recommendations to Candidates for the Presidential Elections in December 2002." ASA 25/007/2002, November 6, 2002. http://www.amnesty.org/en/library/info/ASA25/007/2002.

———. *South Korea: Briefing for the ASEM Foreign Ministers' Meeting.* Amnesty International Index 10R 30/07/1999. Distr: SC/CC/CO. International Secretariat, London, March 1999.

———. "South Korea: Journalists' Arrests Threaten Press Freedom." Press release,

March 24, 2009, http://www.amnesty.org/en/for-media/press-releases/south-korea-journalists%E2%80%99-arrests-threaten-press-freedom-20090324.

Anner, Mark. "Two Logics of Labor Organizing in the Global Apparel Industry." *International Studies Quarterly* 53, no. 3 (2009): 545–570.

Anner, Mark, and Teri Caraway. "International Institutions and Workers' Rights: Between Labor Standards and Market Flexibility." *Studies in Comparative International Development* 45, no. 2 (2010): 151–169.

Applicant's Response to Observations of the Government of the United Kingdom. Strasbourg: European Court of Human Rights, March 13, 2000.

Arthurs, H. W. "National Traditions in Labor Law Scholarship: The Canadian Case." *Comparative Labor Law and Policy Journal* 23, no. 2 (2002): 645–678.

Asia Monitor. *Min-Ju No-Jo South Korea's New Trade Unions: The Struggle for Free Trade Unions.* Hong Kong: Asia Monitor Resource Center, 1988.

Asia Watch Committee (U.S.). *Retreat from Reform: Labor Rights and Freedom of Expression in South Korea.* New York: Asia Watch Committee Human Rights Watch, 1990.

Associated British Ports v. Palmer & Ors [1993] IRLR 63.

Associated British Ports v. Palmer.

Associated Newspapers Ltd v. Wilson [1992] ICR 681.

Associated Newspapers v. Wilson [1994] ICR 97 (CA).

Associated Newspapers Ltd. v. Wilson and Association British Ports PLC v. Palmer [1995] 2 AC 454.

Attorney-General For Canada v. Attorney-General For Ontario [1937] A.C. 326 (P.C.).

Baccaro, Lucio. "Labour and the Global Financial Crisis." *Socio-Economic Review* 8, no. 2 (2010): 341–348.

Bae, Kiu-Sik (Korea Labor Institute). Personal interview with author. Seoul, Korea. June 5, 2006.

Baily, Ian. "Campbell in No Rush to Respond to Landmark Ruling on Bill 29." *Globe and Mail*, June 12, 2007, British Columbia News section.

Baker, Michael. "Invitation by Rich Nations 'Club' Puts S. Korea on Notice." *Christian Science Monitor* (Boston, Mass.), October 15, 1996, 6.

Bakvis, Peter. "How the World Bank and IMF Use the Doing Business Report to Promote Labour Market Deregulation in Developing Countries." International Confederation of Trade Unions Web site, accessed June 21, 2008, http://www.icftu.org/www/PDF/doingbusinessicftuanalysis0606.pdf.

Bassett, Philip. "Fear of a Return to the Seventies Haunt Talk of Union Recognition." *The Times* (London), March 28, 1997, Business section.

———. "GCHQ Move Signals Mild Change in Climate for Unions." *The Times* (London), May 16, 1997.

Beatty, Jim, and Craig McInnes. "Hospitals Will Close, Hansen Admits: Legislature Debates Controversial Labour Bills." *Vancouver Sun*, January 28, 2002.

Beetham, David. "What Future for Economic and Social Rights?" *Political Studies* 43, no. 1 (1995): 41–60.

Benveniśtî, Eyāl, and Moshe Hirsch. *The Impact of International Law on International Cooperation: Theoretical Perspectives.* Cambridge: Cambridge University Press, 2004.

Besley, Timothy, and Robin Burgess. "Can Labour Regulation Hinder Economic Performance?: Evidence from India." *Quarterly Journal of Economics* 19, no. 1 (2002): 91–136.

Blair, Tony. *Tony Blair in His Own Words.* Edited by Paul Richards. London: Politico's, 2004.

Blake, Donald E. "The Politics of Polarization: Parties and Election in British Columbia." In *Politics, Policy and Government in British Columbia*, edited by R. K. Carty, 67–84. Vancouver: University of British Columbia Press, 1996.

Blanpain, Roger, Susan Bisom-Rapp, William R. Corbett, Hilary K. Josephs, and Michael J. Zimmer. *The Global Workplace: International and Comparative Employment Law—Cases and Materials.* 1st ed. Cambridge: Cambridge University Press, 2007.

Bogg, Alan L. "Employment Relations Act 2004: Another False Dawn for Collectivism?" *Industrial Law Journal* 34, no. 1 (2005): 72–82.

Boswell, Terry, and Dimitris Stevis. "Globalization and International Labor Organizing: a World-System Perspective." *Work and Occupations* 24, no. 3 (1997): 288–307.

Botero, Juan, Simeon Djankov, Rafael La Porta, Florencio Lopez-de-Silanes, and Andrei Shleifer. *The Regulation of Labor.* NBER working paper no. 9756. Cambridge, Mass.: National Bureau of Economic Research, 2003.

Brand, Ulirch, and Nicola Sekler. "Postneoliberalism: Catch-all Word or Valuable Analytical and Political Concept?—Aims of a Beginning Debate." *Development Dialogue* 51, no. 1 (2009): 5–14.

Breen, Creighton. "ILO and Freedom of Association in the UK." In *Human Rights and Labour Law: Essays for Paul O'Higgins*, edited by Paul O'Higgins, K. D. Ewing, C. A. Gearty, and B. A. Hepple, 1–27. Studies in labour and social law. New York: Mansell, 1994.

Brenner, Neil, and Nik Theodore. "Cities and the Geographies of 'Actually Existing Neoliberalism.'" *Antipode* 34, no. 3 (2002): 349–379.

British Columbia Coalition of Women's Centres. "BC CEDAW: BC Singled Out for Criticism by UN Committee." March 8, 2003. Accessed April 1, 2008, http://www3.telus.net/bcwomen/archives/BCCEDAW_UNsubmission_jan_03_pressrel.html.

British Columbia Federation of Labour. Personal interview with author, Vancouver, Canada, October 25, 2006.

———. *Workers Demand Repeal of Bills Violating International Rights: UN Body Condemns Campbell's Liberals for Legislation Trampling Workers Rights.* Vancouver: British Columbia Federation of Labour News Archives, March 26, 2003.

British Columbia General and Service Employees Union. *Alert.* Vancouver: British Columbia General and Service Employees Union, April 21, 2005.

British Columbia Government and Service Employees' Union. Personal interview with author. Burnaby, Canada. October 5, 2006.

British Columbia Legislative Assembly. "Official Report of Debates of the Legislative

Assembly (HANSARD) Vol. 24, No. 7 (HTML)." 2004 Legislative Session: 5th Session, 37th Parliament Hansard, accessed April 10, 2008, http://www.leg.bc.ca/Hansard/37th5th/h40428p.htm.

———. "Official Report of Debates of the Legislative Assembly." 2003 Legislative Session: 4th Session, 37th Parliament, Vol. 14, No. 11 (HTML).

———. *Official Report of Debates of the Legislative Assembly (Hansard)*, April 29, 2004. Accessed March 11, 2008, http://www.leg.bc.ca/hansard/37th4th/h30429p.htm.

———. "Official Report of Debates of the Legislative Assembly (HANSARD)." Vol. 24, No. 7 (HTML);

———. "Official Report of Debates of the Legislative Assembly (Hansard)." Monday, April 14, 2008, Vol. 30, Number 7. Legislative Assembly of British Columbia, April 14, 2008. http://www.leg.bc.ca/hansard/38th4th/h80414p.htm#11283.

———. "Official Report of the Debates of the Legislative Assembly [HANSARD]." April 29, 2004, Vol. 14, No. 11 (HTML). 2003 Legislative Session, 4th Session, 37th Parliament. Accessed March 18, 2009, http://www.leg.bc.ca/hansard/37th4th/h30429p.htm.

———. "Official Report of Debates of the Legislative Assembly (Hansard)." Monday, April 14, 2008, Vol. 30, Number 7.

British Columbia. "Progress of Bills." 2008 Legislative Session: 4th Session, 38th Parliament. Accessed June 1, 2009, http://www.leg.bc.ca/38th4th/votes/progress-of-bills.htm.

British Columbia Liberal Party. *A New Era for British Columbia: A Vision for Hope and Prosperity for the New Decade and Beyond.* Vancouver: British Columbia Liberal Party, 2001.

British Columbia Ministry of Health. "BILL 29 Negotations: Tentative Settlement Agreement." *Backgrounder*, January 28, 2008. Accessed May 21, 2009, http://www2.news.gov.bc.ca/news_releases_2005-2009/2008HEALTH0010-000112-Attachment1.htm.

British Columbia Poverty and Human Rights Center. Personal interview with author. Vancouver, Canada. November 7, 2006.

British Columbia Teachers' Federation. *A Note From Your Teachers: A Report from the BCTF to Members of the Legislative Assembly, British Columbia Should Abide by International Law.* Vancouver: British Columbia Teachers' Federation, September 28, 2005.

Brooke, James. "New Leader In Korea Emphasizes Foreign Ties." *New York Times*, January 17, 2003, online edition, Business section.

Brownsey, Keith, and Michael Howlett. "British Columbia: Politics in a Post-Staples Economy." In *The Provincial State in Canada: Politics in the Provinces and Territories*, edited by Keith Brownsey and Michael Howlett, 309–334. Peterborough: Broadview Press, 2001.

Brull, Steven. "Two Steps Forward, How Many Back?" *Businessweek*, April 1, 1996, 18.

Burton, John. "Kim Agrees to Review Korea Labour Law." *Financial Times*, January 22, 1997, London edition, News: Asia-Pacific section, 6.

———. "Maturing South Korea Suffers Labour Pains: A Job for Life with the Big Groups Could Be a Thing of the Past, Writes John Burton." *Financial Times*, October 2, 1996.

———. "S. Korean Markets Soar after $57 Billion IMF-Led Deal." *Financial Times*, December 5, 1997, News: Asia-Pacific section.

———. "Seoul to Make It Easier to Sack Finance Workers; First Relaxation of Nation's Rigid Labour Laws." *Financial Times*, January 14, 1998.

Burton, John, and Peter Montagnon. "Labour Law Pledge Backfires on Kim: Seoul Could Face the OECD's Unprecedented Censure." *Financial Times*, January 21, 1997, 6.

Burton, John, and Robert Taylor. "South Korea Braces for Restructuring: OECD Membership Will Promote Shift Towards Market Economy, Writes John Burton." *Financial Times*, October 14, 1996.

———. "Seoul Labour Law Attacked at OECD." *Financial Times*, January 2, 1997, 3.

———. "Seoul Police Set to Seize Union Leaders." *Financial Times*, January 10, 1997, 5.

———. "Seoul Rebuked Over Labour Reform." *Financial Times*, January 24, 1997, 10.

———. "Seoul to Reform Trade Union Laws." *Financial Times*, April 25, 1996, News: Asia-Pacific section, 4.

———. "Seoul Threat to International Union Team." *Financial Times*, January 14, 1997, News: Asia-Pacific section.

———. "Seoul Under Pressure on 'Shameful' IMF Deal." *Financial Times*, November 24, 1997, 2.

Canada Department of Justice. "Canadian Charter of Rights and Freedoms." Justice Laws Web site. Accessed March 19, 2008, http://laws.justice.gc.ca/en/Charter/index.html#garantie.

Canada Foreign Affairs and International Trade. "Six Principal Human Rights Treaties." *Canada's International Human Rights Policy*, 2007. Accessed April 12, 2008, http://www.dfait-maeci.gc.ca/foreign_policy/human-rights/hr1-rights-en.asp#1.

Canada Human Resources and Social Development. "Canadian Ratification of ILO Conventions." *Labour: Building Fair and Productive Workplaces*, 2005. http://www1.servicecanada.gc.ca/en/lp/ila/Representing_Canada/Canada_ratification_ILO.shtml.

Canadian Broadcast Corporation. "Health Care Workers Hurt by Bill 29 to Receive Compensation by Christmas." CBC News, November 10, 2008. http://www.cbc.ca/canada/british-columbia/story/2008/11/10/bc-compensation-payout-arrangement.html.

Canadian Press. "Legislation Draws Union Wrath." *Alberni Valley Times* (British Columbia), January 29, 2002, B.C. section, 2.

Caraway, Teri L. "Labor Rights in East Asia: Progress or Regress?" *Journal of East Asian Studies* 9, no. 2 (May 26, 2009): 153–186.

Casey, Niamh Ann, and Council of Europe. *The Right to Organise and to Bargain Collec-*

tively: Protection Within the European Social Charter. Strasbourg: Council of Europe Publishers, 1996.

Cavalier, Stephen. Personal interview with author. London, United Kingdom. January 10, 2007.

Cazes, Sandrine, and Alena Nešporová. "Introduction." In *Flexicurity: A Relevant Approach in Central and Eastern Europe*, edited by Sandrine Cazes and Alena Nešporová, 1–8. Geneva, Switzerland: International Labour Organization, 2007.

Chandler, Clay. "S. Korea's Kim Proves Mettle in Financial Crisis; President-Elect Gains Support for Savvy Economic Strategy." *Washington Post*, September 29, 1997.

Chang, Dae-uop, and Jun-ho Chae. "The Transformation of Korean Labour Relations Since 1997." *Journal of Contemporary Asia* 34, no. 4 (2004): 427–448.

Chayes, Abram, and Antonia Handler Chayes. "On Compliance." *International Organization* 47, no. 2 (1993): 175–205.

Checkel, Jeffrey T. "International Institutions and Socialization in Europe: Introduction and Framework." *International Organization* 59, no. 04 (2005): 801–826.

———. "International Norms and Domestic Politics." *European Journal of International Relations* 3, no. 4 (December 1, 1997): 473–495.

"Choice Between Model of Establishment or Untried Independent Thinking." *The Times* (London), December 18, 2002.

Chung, Hyoung-Woo, and Hae Young Chung. Personal interview with author. Seoul, South Korea, June 27, 2006.

Colling, Trevor. "What Space for Unions on the Floor of Rights? Trade Unions and the Enforcement of Statutory Individual Employment Rights." *Industrial Law Journal* 35, no. 2 (2006): 140–160.

Collins, Hugh, K. D. Ewing, and Aileen McColgan. *Labour Law: Text and Materials*. Oxford: Hart, 2001.

Compa, Lance. "Response." *Dissent*, Winter 2005, 66-68.

Compa, Lance A., and Human Rights Watch. *Unfair Advantage: Workers' Freedom of Association in the United States Under International Human Rights Standards*. New York: Human Rights Watch, 2000.

Cook, Linda. "More Rights, Less Power: Labor Standards and Labor Markets in East European Post-communist States." *Studies in Comparative International Development* 45, no. 2 (2010): 170–197.

Cook, Maria L. "International Labor Standards and Domestic Labor Advocates: Unions, Labor Reform, and Workers' Rights in Latin America." Paper presented at the Annual Meeting of the International Studies Association, San Diego, Calif., March 2006.

———. *The Politics of Labor Reform in Latin America: Between Flexibility and Rights*. University Park: Pennsylvania State University Press, 2007.

Cortell, Andrew P., and James W. Davis. "Understanding the Domestic Impact of International Norms: A Research Agenda." *International Studies Review* 2, no. 1 (2000): 65–87.

Couldry, Nick. *Why Voice Matters: Culture and Politics After Neoliberalism*. New York: Sage Publications, 2010.
Council of Europe. "Convention for the Protection of Human Rights and Fundamental Freedoms as amended by Protocol no. 11." Council of Europe, 2003, http://www.echr.coe.int/NR/rdonlyres/D5CC24A7-DC13-4318-B457-5C9014916D7A/0/englishAnglais.pdf.
———. "List of Declarations Made with Respect to Treaty No. 035." *Council of Europe Treaties*, 2008. Accessed March 13, 2008, http://conventions.coe.int/Treaty/Commun/ListeDeclarations.asp?NT=035&CM=8&DF=07/11/2005&CL=ENG&VL=1.
Council of Europe. "European Social Charter, Turin 18.X.1961." *Council of Europe - ETS no. 035*, 2008. Accessed July 19, 2009, http://conventions.coe.int/treaty/en/treaties/html/035.htm.
———. "How the Execution of Judgments Works (European Court of Human Rights)." *European Court of Human Rights—The Court*. Accessed April 1, 2008, http://www.echr.coe.int/ECHR/EN/Header/The+Court/Execution/How+the+execution+of+judgments+works.
———. *Information Document on the Court* (European Court of Human Rights). 1762893 (Strasbourg, September 2006). http://www.echr.coe.int/NR/rdonlyres/981B9082-45A4-44C6-829A-202A51B94A85/0/InformationdocumentontheCourt_September2006_.pdf.
———. "Historical Background (European Court of Human Rights)." *European Court of Human Rights: The Courts*. Accessed April 12, 2009, http://www.echr.coe.int/ECHR/EN/Header/The+Court/The+Court/History+of+the+Court.
———. "The European Social Charter at a Glance." *Human Rights: European Social Charter*. Accessed May 2, 2008, http://www.coe.int/t/e/human_rights/esc/1_general_presentation/CharterGlance_en.asp#TopOfPage.
———. Committee of Independent Experts on the European Social Charter. *European Social Charter. Conclusions/Committee of Independent Experts of the European Social Charter XIII-3*. Strasbourg: Council of Europe, 1996.
Cox, Robert W. "Labor and Hegemony." *International Organization* 31, no. 3 (1977): 385–424.
Craig, David, and Doug Porter. "Poverty Reduction Strategy Papers: A New Convergence." *World Development* 31, no. 1 (2003): 53–69.
Croissant, Aurel. "Strong Presidents, Weak Democracy? President, Parliaments and Political Parties in South Korea." *Korea Observer* 33, no. 1 (2002): 1–45.
Cummings, Bruce. "Civil Society in West and East." In *Korean Society: Civil Society, Democracy and the State,* edited by Charles K. Armstrong, 9–32. London: Routledge, 2007.
van Daele, Jasmine. "'Engineering Social Peace': Networks, Ideas, and the Establishment of the International Labour Organization." *International Review of Social History* 50 (2005): 435–466.
Davey, Monica. "Wisconsin Court Reinstates Law on Union Rights." *New York Times*,

June 14, 2011, U.S. / Politics section, http://www.nytimes.com/2011/06/15/us/politics/15wisconsin.html.

Davies, Anne C. L. *Perspectives on Labour Law.* Cambridge: Cambridge University Press, 2004.

Mr. B. Davies and Others v. Asda stores [2006] UKET 2501510/05, 2006.

Deakin, Simon. "Social Rights in a Globalized Economy." In *Labour Rights as Human Rights*, edited by Phillip Alston, 25–61. Oxford: Oxford University Press, 2005.

"Deal Aims to Resolve Bill 29 Dispute." *Globe And Mail* (Canada), January 29, 2008, online edition, National: British Columbia News; Labour; Health Care sections.

Diamond, Larry Jay, and Pyong-guk Kim. "Introduction: Consolidating Democracy in South Korea." In *Consolidating Democracy in South Korea*, edited by Larry Jay Diamond and Pyong-guk Kim, 1–20. Boulder, Colo.: L. Rienner, 2000.

Dicker, Richard, and Human Rights Watch/Asia. *South Korea: Labor Rights Violations Under Democratic Rule.* New York: Human Rights Watch/Asia, 1995.

Digiacomo, Gordon. *Federalism and Labour Policy in Canada.* Working Papers (Queen's University (Kingston, Ont.), Institute of Intergovernmental Relations). Kingston: Institute of Intergovernmental Relations, Queen's University, 2001.

Dinan, Desmond. *Ever Closer Union: An Introduction to European Integration.* 3rd ed. Boulder, Colo.: Palgrave Macmillan, 2005.

Dion, Douglas. "Evidence and Inference in the Comparative Case Study." *Comparative Politics* 30, no. 2 (1998): 127–145.

Donnelly, Jack. *Universal Human Rights in Theory and Practice.* Ithaca, N.Y.: Cornell University Press, 2003.

Dunmore v. Ontario (Attorney General) [2001] 3 S.C. R. 1016, 207 D.LR (4th) 193, 2001 SCC 94.

Dunning, Harold. "The Origins of Convention No. 87 on Freedom of Association and the Right to Organize." *International Labour Review* 137, no. 2 (1998): 149–168.

Duplantis, Malcolm M., Timothy D. Chandler, and Terry G. Geske. "The Growth and Impact of Teachers' Unions in States Without Collective Bargaining Legislation." *Economics of Education Review* 14, no. 2 (June 1995): 167–178.

Ebbinghaus, Bernhard. "When Less Is More." *International Sociology* 20, no. 2 (June 1, 2005): 133–152.

Elliot, Larry. "Workface: Echoes of UK in Streets of Seoul." *Guardian* (London), January 8, 1997, The Guardian City Page section, 19.

Employment Relations Act 1999 (U.K.). Chapter 26, accessed May 23, 2008, www.opsi.gov.uk/acts/acts1999/pdf/ukpga_19990026_en.pdf.

Employment Relations Act 2004 (U.K.). Accessed June 1, 2008, http://www.opsi.gov.uk/acts/acts2004/ukpga_20040024_en_1.htm.

Epp, Charles R. "Do Bills of Rights Matter? The Canadian Charter of Rights and Freedoms." *American Political Science Review* 90, no. 4 (1996): 765–779.

Etherington, Brian. "The B.C. Health Services and Support Decision—The Constitutionalization of a Right to Bargain Collectively in Canada: Where Did It Come

From and Where Will It Lead?" *Comparative Labor Law and Policy Journal* 30, no. 4 (2009): 715–749.

European Parliament. *The Charter of Fundamental Rights of the European Union*, 21/02/2001. Accessed March 14, 2009, http://www.europarl.europa.eu/charter/default_en.htm.

Ewing, K. D. *Britain and the ILO*. London: Institute of Employment Rights, 1994.

———. "The Human Rights Act and Labour Law." *Industrial Law Journal* 27, no. 4 (1998): 275–292.

———. "The Human Rights Act and Parliamentary Democracy." *Modern Law Review* 62, no. 1 (1999): 79–99.

———. "The Implications of Wilson and Palmer." *Industrial Law Journal* 32, no. 1 (March 1, 2003): 1–22.

Ewing, Keith. "Labour Leaves Blacklisted High and Dry." *Guardian* (London), March 10, 2010. Accessed October 21, 2010, http://www.guardian.co.uk/commentisfree/2010/mar/10/labour-leaves-blacklisted-high-dry.

Ewing, Keith, John Hendy, Bob Simpson, and Stephen Cavalier. *Wilson and Palmer Briefing*. London: Institute for Employment Rights, 2002.

European Court of Human Rights. *Rules of the Court*. Strasbourg: Council of Europe; Registry of the Court, 2006.

Fairey, David. *Behind the Numbers: BC's NDP Government: Spendthrift or Overly Restrained? CCPA: Behind the Numbers*. Vancouver: Canadian Center for Policy Alternatives, March 31, 2001.

———. *Eroding Worker Protections: British Columbia's New 'Flexible' Employment Standards*. Vancouver: Canadian Center for Policy Alternatives British Columbia Office, 2005.

Fields, A. Belden. *Rethinking Human Rights for the New Millennium*. New York: Palgrave Macmillan, 2003.

Finnemore, Martha, and Kathryn Sikkink. "International Norm Dynamics and Political Change." *International Organization* 52, no. 4 (1998): 887–917.

Forteza, Alvaro, and Martin Rama. *Labor Market Rigidity and the Success of Economic Reforms Across More Than One Hundred Countries*. Policy Research Working Paper 2521. Washington, D.C.: World Bank Development Research Group, 2001.

Francis, Russ. "Tearing Up Deals." *Monday Magazine*, February 21, 2003.

Fredman, Sandra, and Gillian Morris. "Recent Cases: Freedom of Association." *Industrial Law Journal* 17, no. 1 (1988): 105–108.

Friedman, Gerald. "Labor and the Bush Administration: 'Down So Long, Seem Like Up to Me.'" *Revue LISA/LISA e-journal*, no. 1. (March 4, 2010): 69–85.

Fudge, Derek, and John Brewin. *Collective Bargaining in Canada: Human Right or Canadian Illusion?* Black Point, Nova Scotia: Fernwood, 2006.

Fudge, Judy. "'Labour Is Not a Commodity': The Supreme Court of Canada and the Freedom of Association." *Saskatchewan Law Review* 67 (2004): 425–453.

———. "The Supreme Court of Canada and the Right to Bargain Collectively: The Implications of the Health Services and Support Case in Canada and Beyond." *Industrial Law Journal* 37, no. 1 (2008): 25–48.

Geddes, Barbara. "How the Cases You Choose Affect the Answers You Get: Selection Bias in Comparative Politics." *Political Analysis* 2, no. 1 (January 1, 1990): 131–150.

Gennard, John, and Graham Judge. *Employee Relations.* 4th ed. London: CIPD Publishing, 2005.

George, Alexander L., and Andrew Bennett. *Case Studies and Theory Development in the Social Sciences.* Cambridge, Mass.: MIT Press, 2005.

Gerring, John. *Case Study Research: Principles and Practices.* Cambridge: Cambridge University Press, 2007.

Ghebali, Victor-Yves. "The League of Nations and Functionalism." In *Functionalism: Theory and Practice in International Relations,* edited by A. J. R. Groom and Paul Graham Taylor, 141–161. New York: Crane, Russak, 1975.

Goh, Young-Lee. Personal interview with author. Seoul, South Korea, July 6, 2006.

Gomez, Rafael, Alexander Bryson, and Paul Willman. "The End of an Affair? The Decline in Employers' Propensity to Unionize." In *Union Organization and Activity in Britain,* edited by John E. Kelly and Paul Willman. London: Routledge, 2004.

Goodhart, David. "Election 92; Labour Keeps Its Distance but Is Tied to Dependence." *Financial Times* (London), March 13, 1992, 6.

———. "Election 1992: Unions Review Party Funding." *Financial Times* (London), April 9, 1992.

———. "War with Trade Unions Is over Says Shephard." *Financial Times* (London), July 16, 1992.

Gravel, Eric, Isabelle Duplessis, and Bernard Gernigon. *The Committee on Freedom of Association: Its Impact over 50 Years.* Geneva: International Labour Office, 2001.

Great Britain, Employment Dept. Group. *Industrial Relations in the 1990s: Proposals for Further Reform of Industrial Relations and Trade Union Law.* Cm, 1602. London: HMSO, 1991.

Great Britain, Department for Education and Employment. *UK Argues for Jobs and Supports Employments at ILO.* London: Department for Education and Employment, June 10, 1997.

Great Britain, Department of Health. "Questions and Answers on the Human Rights Act 1998: Department of Health- Managing Your Organisation." *Department of Health: Human Rights,* (2007). Accessed February 12, 2009, http://www.dh.gov.uk/en/Managingyourorganisation/Equalityandhumanrights/Humanrights/DH_4136018.

Great Britain, Department of Trade and Industry. *Fairness at Work.* London: Stationery Office, 1998.

Great Britain, Department of Trade and Industry. *Review of the Employment Relations Act 1999: Government Response.* London: Department of Trade and Industry, 2003.

Great Britain, Parliament. Joint Committee on Human Rights. *Legislative Scrutiny: Sixth Progress Report: Fourteenth Report of Session 2005–06.* London: Stationery Office, 2006.

Groom, A. J. R., and Paul Taylor. "Functionalism and International Relations." In *Functionalism: Theory and Practice in International Relations*, edited by A. J. R. Groom and Paul Graham Taylor, 1–6. New York: Crane, Russak, 1975.

Hahm, Sung Deuk, and Kwang Woong Kim. "Institutional Reforms and Democratization in Korea: The Case of the Kim Young Sam Administration, 1993–1998." *Governance* 12, no. 3 (1999): 479–499.

Hall, M. "Government Unveils Proposals for a Fairer Workplace." *European Industrial Relations Observatory Online*, June 28, 1998. Accessed July 10, 2007, http://www.eurofound.europa.eu/eiro/1998/06/feature/uk9806129f.htm.

Harris, D. J. (David John), and John Darcy. *The European Social Charter*. Ardsley, N.Y.: Transnational Publishers, 2001.

Harvey, David. *A Brief History of Neoliberalism.* Oxford: Oxford University Press, 2005.

Hathaway, Oona A. "Do Human Rights Treaties Make a Difference." *Yale Law Journal* 111 (2002): 1935–2042.

Hawkins, Darren. "Explaining Costly International Institutions: Persuasion and Enforceable Human Rights Norms." *International Studies Quarterly* 48, no. 4 (December 1, 2004): 785.

Hay, Colin. "That Was Then, This Is Now: The Revision of Policy in the 'Modernisation' of the British Labour Party, 1992–97." *New Political Science* 20, no. 1 (1998): 7–25.

Health Sciences Association of British Columbia. "About: Who we are." Accessed January 21, 2009, http://www.hsabc.org/content.php?id=2&sid=4&pid=0.

Health Services and Support-Facilities Subsector Bargaining Assn. v. British Columbia [2003] B.C.J. No. 2107.

Helfer, Lawrence. *Understanding Change in International Organizations: Globalization and Innovation in the ILO.* Working paper. Nashville, Tenn.: Vanderbilt University Law School Public Law and Legal Theory, 2005.

Helm, Sarah. "The World Warms to Blair's Victor: Europe Hopes Poll Will Lance Euroskeptic Boil." *Independent* (London), May 3, 1997, International section, 12.

Hendy, John QC. Personal interview with author. London, January 10, 2007.

Hendy, John, and Institute of Employment Rights. *A Law Unto Themselves: Conservative Employment Laws: A National and International Assessment.* London: Institute of Employment Rights, 1993.

Higgins, Ean. "Tories Exploit Bad Old Days of Unionism." *Australian,* March 26, 1997, World section, 10.

Hirschl, Ran. "'Negative' Rights vs. 'Positive' Entitlements: A Comparative Study of Judicial Interpretations of Rights in an Emerging Neo-Liberal Economic Order." *Human Rights Quarterly* 22, no. 4 (2000): 1060–1098.

Hollowell, Jonathan. *Britain Since 1945.* Oxford: Blackwell Publishing, 2002.

Howlett, Michael, and Keith Brownsey. "From Timber to Tourism: The Political Economy of British Columbia." In *Politics, Policy and Government in British Columbia*, edited by R. K. Carty, 18–31. Vancouver: University of British Columbia Press, 1996.

Human Rights Act 1998 (U.K.). Accessed January 11, 2009, http://www.opsi.gov.uk/ACTS/acts1998/ukpga_19980042_en_1.

"ILO Calls on S. Korea to Respect Unions' Rights." *Kyodo News Service: Japanese Economic Newswire*, January 15, 1997.

International Labour Organization. "About the GB—Governing Body—Official meetings—What we do." International Labor Organization Web site. Accessed June 1, 2008, http://www.ilo.org/global/What_we_do/Officialmeetings/gb/AboutGB/lang--en/index.htm.

———. "About the ILO, Who We Are: ILO Constitution." International Labor Organization Web site, accessed June 5, 2009, http://ilo.org/public/english/about/iloconst.htm#annex.

———. "About the ILC—International Labour Conference (ILC)." ILO Home: What We Do, accessed September 13, 2009, http://www.ilo.org/global/What_we_do/Officialmeetings/ilc/AbouttheILC/lang--en/index.htm.

———. *Convention 87: Freedom of Association and Protection of the Right to Organise Convention, 1948*. Accessed January 10, 2009, http://www.ilo.org/ilolex/cgi-lex/convde.pl?C087.

———. "Freedom of Association and Effective Recognition of the Right to Collective Bargaining." *ILO Declaration on Fundamental Principles and Rights at Work* (2003), accessed April 24, 2008, http://www.ilo.org/dyn/declaris/DECLARATIONWEB.static_jump?var_language=EN&var_pagename=ISSUESFREEDOM.

———. "Report of the Committee on Freedom of Association (15th Report)." *ILO Official Bulletin* 38, no. 1 (1955).

———. "Report of the Committee on Freedom of Association (211th Report)." *ILO Official Bulletin* 64, ser. B, no. 3 (1981).

———. "Report of the Committee on Freedom of Association (275th Report)." *ILO Official Bulletin* 73, ser. B, no. 3 (1990).

———. "Report of the Committee on Freedom of Association (278th Report)." *ILO Official Bulletin* 74, ser. B, no. 2 (1991), 89.

———. "Report of the Committee on Freedom of Association (283rd Report)." *ILO Official Bulletin* 75, ser. B, no. 2 (1992).

———. "Report of the Committee on Freedom of Association (291st Report)." *ILO Official Bulletin* 76, ser. B, no. 3 (1994).

———. "Report of the Committee on Freedom of Association (286th Report)." *ILO Official Bulletin* 76, ser. B, no. 1 (1993).

———. "Report of the Committee on Freedom of Association (294th Report)." *ILO Official Bulletin* 78, ser. B, no. 2 (1994).

———. "Report of the Committee on Freedom of Association (302nd Report)." *ILO Official Bulletin* 79, ser. B, no. 1 (1996).

———. "Report of the Committee on Freedom of Association (304th Report)." *ILO Official Bulletin* 79, ser. B, no. 2 (1996).

———. "Report of the Committee on Freedom of Association (306th Report)." *ILO Official Bulletin* 80, ser. B, no. 1 (1997).
———. "Report of the Committee on Freedom of Association (309th Report)." *ILO Official Bulletin* 81, ser. B, no. 1 (1998).
———. "Report of the Committee of Freedom of Association (310th Report)." *ILO Official Bulletin* 81, ser. B, no. 2 (1998).
———. "Report of the Committee of Freedom of Association (311th Report)." *ILO Official Bulletin* 81, ser. B, no. 3 (1998).
———. "Report of the Committee of Freedom of Association (318th Report)." *ILO Official Bulletin* 82, ser. B, no. 3 (1999): 82.
———. "Report of the Committee of Freedom of Association (320th Report)." *ILO Official Bulletin* 83, ser. B, no. 1 (2000).
———. "Report of the Committee of Freedom of Association (323rd Report)." *ILO Official Bulletin* 83, ser. B, no. 3 (2000).
———. "Report of the Committee of Freedom of Association (324th Report)." *ILO Official Bulletin* 84, ser. B, no. 1 (2001).
———. "Report of the Committee on Freedom of Association (330th Report)." *ILO Official Bulletin* 86, ser. B, no. 1 (2003).
———. "Report of the Committee on Freedom of Association (331st Report)." *ILO Official Bulletin* 86, ser. B, no. 2 (2003).
———. "Report of the Committee on Freedom of Association (336th Report)." *ILO Official Bulletin* 83, ser. B, no. 1 (2005).
———. "Report of the Committee on Freedom of Association (340th Report)." *ILO Official Bulletin* 94, ser. B, no. 1 (2006).
———. "Report of the Committee on Freedom of Association (346th Report)." *ILO Official* Bulletin 90, ser. B, no. 2 (2007).
———. "Report of the Committee on Freedom of Association (353rd Report)." *ILO Official Bulletin* 92, ser. B, no. 1 (2009).
———. "Report of the Committee on Freedom of Association (357th Report)." *ILO Official Bulletin* 92, ser. B, no. 2 (2010).
———. "Summary of Reports on Ratified Convention (Articles 22 and 35 of the Constitution)." *Comments of the Committee of Experts on the Application of Conventions and Recommendations, International Labour Conference,* 76th session, 1989.
———. *United Kingdom. Committee of Experts on the Application of Conventions and Recommendations: Individual Observation Concerning Convention No. 151, Labour Relations (Public Service).* ILOLEX Document No. 061994GBR151, 1994.
———. *Your Voice at Work. Global Report Under the Follow-up to the ILO Declaration on Fundamental Principles and Rights at Work. Report of the Director-General,* 2000. Accessed September 21, 2009, http://www.ilo.org/global/What_we_do/Publications/ILOBookstore/Orderonline/Books/lang—en/docName—WCMS_PUBL_9221115046_EN/index.htm.
International Labour Organization Committee on Freedom of Association. *Freedom of*

Association: Digest of Decisions and Principles of the Freedom of Association Committee of the Governing Body of the ILO. Geneva: International Labour Organization, 2006.

International Trade Union Confederation. "ITUC Annual Survey: 101 Trade Unionists Murdered in 2009; Pressure on Workers' Rights Grows as Crisis Hits Jobs." *International Trade Union Confederation*. Accessed November 13, 2010, http://www.ituc-csi.org/ituc-annual-survey.html.

———. ITUC CSI IGB, "Who Are We?" International Trade Union Confederation Homepage: General Information. Accessed April 21, 2008, http://www.ituc-csi.org/spip.php?rubrique57.

———. "Internationally Recognized Core Labour Standards in the Republic of Korea." Report for the WTO General Council Review of the Trade Policies of Korea, Geneva, October 8 and 10, 2008. http://www.ituc-csi.org/IMG/pdf/Korea-_FINAL.pdf, 4.

International Trade Union Council. "ITUC Welcomes World Bank's Suspension of 'Doing Business' Labour Indicator." International Confederation of Trade Union Home Page: Economic and Social Policy, accessed April 28, 2009, http://www.ituc-csi.org/spip.php?article3505&var_recherche=World%20Bank.

International Confederation of Free Trade Unions. *Annual Survey of Violations of Trade Union Rights 2001*. Brussels, Belgium: ICFTU Press, 2001.

Ishay, Micheline. *The History of Human Rights: From Ancient Times to the Globalization Era*. 2nd ed. Berkeley: University of California Press, 2008.

Islam, Shada. "Britain's European Partners Hope for Constructive Partnership." *Deutsche Presse-Agentur*, April 30, 1997.

James, Barry. "OECD Panel Faults Seoul on Labor Law Provisions." *International Herald Tribune*, January 24, 1997, online edition, 4.

Jeong, Insoo. "OECD Recommendations on Labor Issues and Korean Compliance with Evaluations: Labor Law, Relations, Market and Social Security." Paper presented at the Korea-OECD Conference; Korea in the OECD Perspective: Shaping up for Globalization, Seoul, Korea, 2000.

Johnson, Chalmers. "Economic Crisis in East Asia: The Clash of Capitalisms." *Cambridge Journal of Economics* 22 (1998): 653–661.

Jordan, Mary. "A Dubious Victory Awaits in S. Korea: Presidential Winner Faces Crisis of Faith, Economy." *Washington Post*, December 14, 1997, A1.

Joyner, Christopher C. *The United Nations and International Law*. Cambridge: Cambridge University Press, 1997.

Jutterström, Stig. "Interview with Dan Byun-Ho." *International Metalworkers' Federation*, July 31, 2000. Accessed July 7, 2007, http://www.imfmetal.org/main/index.cfm?id=103&lid=2&cid=3285&title=Number:%202-2000.

Kahn-Freund, Otto. "The Illegality of a Trade Union." *Modern Law Review* 7, no. 4 (November 1, 1944): 192–205.

Kang, David. *Crony Capitalism: Corruption and Development in South Korea and the Philippines*. Cambridge: Cambridge University Press, 2002.

Kaufmann, Christine. *Globalisation and Labour Rights: The Conflict Between Core Labour Rights and International Economic Law.* Oxford: Hart, 2007.

Keck, Margaret E., and Kathryn Sikkink. *Activists Beyond Borders: Advocacy Networks in International Politics.* Ithaca, N.Y.: Cornell University Press, 1998.

Keter, Bill. *Employment Relations Bill. Research Paper* 04/03. Business and Transport Section. House of Commons Library, January 7, 2004.

Kim, Dae Jung. *Mass-Participatory Economy: A Democratic Alternative for Korea.* Cambridge, Mass.: Center for International Affairs, Harvard University; University Press of America, 1985.

Kim, Dae-Hwan. Personal interview with author. Seoul, South Korea, July 22, 2006.

Kim, Dong-One, and Johngseok Bae. *Employment Relations and HRM in South Korea.* Aldershot: Ashgate, 2003.

Kim, Dong-One, Johngseok Bae, and Changwon Lee. "Globalization and Labor Rights: The Case of Korea." In *Globalization and Labor in the Asia Pacific Region*, edited by Chris Rowley and John Benson, 133–153. Studies in Asia Pacific Business. London: Frank Cass, 2000.

Kim, Eun-Mee. "Contradictions and Limits of a Developmental State: With Illustrations from the South Korean Case." *Social Problems* 40, no. 2 (1993): 228–249.

Kim, HeeMin. "Rational Choice Theory and Third World Politics: The 1990 Party Merger in Korea." *Comparative Politics* 30, no. 1 (1997): 83–100.

Kim, Hyun-Joon. "A Brief History of the Korean Teachers' Movement." Seoul, Korea, 1997.

Kim, Jin Kyoon. "Rethinking the Beginning of the Democratic Labour Movement in Korea: From the 1987 Great Workers' Struggle to the Construction of the Korean Trade Union Council (Chunnohyup) and the Korean Confederation of Trade Union (KCTU)." *Asia Cultural Studies* 1, no. 3 (2000): 421–502.

Kim, Ju-Yeon. "South Korean Striking Workers Clash with Riot Police." *Associated Press*, December 28, 1996, International News section.

"Kim: Militant Moderate or Civilian Dictator?" *Financial Times*, September 2, 1996, News: Asia-Pacific section, 3.

Kim, Sunhyuk. "State and Civil Society in South Korea's Democratic Consolidation: Is the Battle Really Over." *Asian Survey* 37, no. 12 (1997): 1135–1144.

———. *The Politics of Democratization in Korea: The Role of Civil Society.* Pittsburgh, Pa.: University of Pittsburgh Press, 2000.

Kim, Yong Cheol. "Industrial Reform and Labor Backlash in South Korea: Genesis, Escalation and Termination of the 1997 General Strike." *Asian Survey* 38, no. 12 (1998): 1142–1160.

King, Gary, Robert Owen Keohane, and Sidney Verba. *Designing Social Inquiry: Scientific Inference in Qualitative Research.* Princeton, N.J.: Princeton University Press, 1994.

Kipping, Matthias. "American Management Consulting Companies in Western Europe, 1920 to 1990: Products, Reputation, and Relationships." *Business History Review* 73, no. 2 (1999): 190–220.

Klein, Seth, and Marc Lee. *BC's Fiscal Choices: Submission to the British Columbia Fiscal Review Panel.* Vancouver: Canadian Center for Policy Alternatives, July 2001.

Kochan, Thomas, David B. Lipinsky, Mary Newhart, and Alan Benson. "The Long Haul Effects of Interest Arbitration: The Case of New York State's Taylor Law." *Industrial and Labor Relations Review* 63 (2009): 565–584.

Koh, B. C. "South Korea in 1996: Internal Strains and External Challenges." *Asian Survey* 37, no. 1 (1997): 1–9.

Kolben, Kevin. "Labor Rights as Human Rights." *Virginia Journal of International Law* 50, no. 2 (2010): 449–484.

Koo, Hagen. "The Dilemmas of Empowered Labor in Korea: Korean Workers in the Face of Global Capitalism." *Asian Survey* 40, no. 2 (April 2000): 227–250.

———. "Engendering Civil Society: The Role of the Labor Movement." In *Korean Society: Civil Society, Democracy and the State*, edited by Charles Armstrong, 73–94. 2nd ed. London: Routledge, 2007.

———. *Korean Workers: The Culture and Politics of Class Formation.* Ithaca, N.Y.: Cornell University Press, 2001.

Korean Confederation of Trade Unions. *KCTU Counter-Report on the South Korean Government's Report to the UN Human Rights Committee.* Seoul: Korean Confederation of Trade Unions, October 10, 2006.

Korean Confederation of Trade Unions (former international representative). Personal interview with author. Seoul, South Korea, June 14, 2006.

Korean Confederation of Trade Unions (policy representative). Personal interview with author, Seoul, South Korea, June 26, 2006.

Korean Government Employees' Union. "Brief History of KGEU." About KGEU: Korean Government Employees' Union Web site, accessed July 29, 2007, http://inter.kgeu.org/about/about.asp.

Korea International Labour Foundation. "Tripartite Representatives Agreed on Road Map for Advancement of Industrial Relations Laws and Systems." *Labor Today* (Korean International Labour Foundation), September 11, 2006.

Korean Labor News Network. "Korea Labor Ministry Issues Response to the TUAC Report." October 25, 2006. Accessed May 1, 2008, http://www.labordan.net/yubi/bbs/board.php?bo_table=m4_04&wr_id=246&page=14.

Korean Metalworkers Federation Representative. Personal interview with author, Seoul, South Korea, June 3, 2006.

Korean Teachers' Union representative. Personal interview with author. Seoul, South Korea, July 5, 2006.

Korporaal, Glenda. "Blair Has Every Opportunity to Reshape Britain." *Sydney Morning Herald* (Australia), May 5, 1997, International News section, 38.

Kōshiro, Kazutoshi. "Introduction." In *Employment Security and Labor Market Flexibility: An International Perspective*, edited by Kazuyoshi Kōshiro, 11–31. Detroit: Wayne State University Press, 1992.

Kowalczuk, Magda. "S. Korea-Labor: Striking Workers Put Critical Spotlight on Seoul." *IPS-InterPress Service,* Tokyo, January 7, 1997.

Kristof, Nicholas D. "South Korean President Fails to Placate Foes." *New York Times,* January 23, 1997.

———. "South Korean Unions Agree to Negotiate on Job Layoffs." *New York Times,* January 15, 1998, 12.

Kucera, David. "Core Labour Standards and Foreign Direct Investment." *International Labour Review* 141 (2002): 31–69.

Labour Party (of Great Britain). "New Labour Because Britain Deserves Better: Britain Will Be Better with New Labour." 1997 Labour Party Manifesto. Accessed March 19, 2009, http://www.labour-party.org.uk/manifestos/1997/1997-labour-manifesto.shtml.

———. "It's Time to Get Working Again: British Labour Party Election Manifesto: 1992." *Political Science Resources,* Keele University (UK), 1992.

Lachica, Eduardo. "Korea Discovers Joining OECD Is Hard Work." *New York Times,* October 19, 1995, 1.

LaVoie, Judith. "UN Accuses Province of Labour Violations." *Times Colonist* (Victoria, British Columbia), March 20, 2003.

Laycock, David. "The Depression and Third Party Development." *Center for Canadian Studies at Mt. Allison University: The Prairie Roots of Canada's Political "Third Parties,"* 2001. Accessed November 15, 2010, http://www.mta.ca/faculty/arts/canadian_studies/english/about/study_guide/roots/depression.html.

Leary, Virginia. "The Paradox of Workers' Rights as Human Rights." In *Human Rights, Labor Rights, and International Trade,* edited by Lance A. Compa and Stephen F. Diamond, 22–47. Philadelphia: University of Pennsylvania Press, 1996.

Lee, Chong-sik, and Hyuk-Sang Sohn. "South Korea in 1993: The Year of Great Reform." *Asian Survey* 34, no. 1 (1994): 1–9.

———. "South Korea in 1994: A Year of Trial." *Asian Survey* 35, no. 1 (1995): 28–36.

Lee, Dong-Eun. Personal interview with author. Seoul, South Korea, June 16, 2006.

Lee, Ho-Geun (Korean Tripartite Commission). Personal interview with author. Seoul, South Korea, June 12, 2006.

Lee, Hong-Young. "South Korea in 1992: A Turning Point in Democratization." *Asian Survey* 33, no. 1 (1993): 32–43.

Lee, Sangheon, Deirdre McCann, and Nina Torm. "The World Bank's 'Employing Workers' Index: Findings and Critiques—A Review of Recent Evidence." *International Labour Review* 147, no. 4 (2008): 416–432.

Lee, Su-Hoon. "Transitional Politics of Korea, 1987–1992: Activation of Civil Society." *Pacific Affairs* 66, no. 3 (1993): 351–367.

Lee, Won-Duk, and Byoung-Hoon Lee. "Korean Industrial Relations in the Era of Globalization." *Journal of Industrial Relations* 45, no. 4 (2003): 505–520.

Lee, Yoonkyung. "Varieties of Labor Politics in Northeast Asian Democracies: Political Institutions and Union Activism in Korea and Taiwan." *Asian Survey* 46, no. 5 (October 1, 2006): 721–740.

Leeke, Matthew. *UK Election Statistics 1945–2003*. London: House of Commons Library, 2003. Accessed June 17, 2008, http://www.parliament.uk/commons/lib/research/rp2003/rp03-059.pdf.

Legislative Library British Columbia. *Electoral History of British Columbia Supplement, 1987–2001*. Victoria: Legislative Library of British Columbia, 2002.

Leitner, Helga, Jamie Peck, and Eric S. Sheppard. *Contesting Neoliberalism: Urban Frontiers*. New York: Guilford Press, 2007.

Lemieux, Valerie Matthews, and Steven Barrett. "Charter Protection Extended to Collective Bargaining—How Far Does it Reach?" *CCPA Review Labour Notes*. Ontario, Canadian Centre for Policy Alternatives, December 2007.

Leslie, Douglas L. *Labor Law in a Nutshell*. 5th ed. St. Paul, Minn.: Thomson West, 2008.

Lewis, Roy. "Reforming Industrial Relations: Law, Politics, and Power." *Oxford Review of Economic Policy* 7, no. 1 (1991): 60–75.

Levine, Robert A. "Anglo-Saxons vs. EMU: Labor 'Flexibility' Isn't a Cure-all." *International Herald Tribune*, March 6, 2002, Opinion section, http://iht.com/articles/2002/03/06/edlevine_ed3_.php.

Lichtenstein, Nelson. "The Rights Revolution." *New Labor Forum* 12, no. 1 (March 2003): 60–73.

Lowenfeld, Andreas F. "Congress and Cuba: The Helms-Burton Act." *American Journal of International Law* 90, no. 3 (July 1996): 419–434.

Macaskill, Ewen. "The Election: The Unions: Ties that Bind Ever Less Closely: Blair Vowed to Sever Old Link." *Guardian*, April 4, 1997, 13.

Macklem, Patrick. "The Right to Bargain Collectively in International Law: Workers' Right, Human Right, International Right?" In *Labour Rights as Human Rights*, edited by Phillip Alston, 61–84. Oxford: Oxford University Press, 2005.

Markin, Kirk. "Collective Bargaining Is a Right, Top Court Rules." *Globe and Mail*, June 9, 2007, online edition, Justice Report section.

Marsh, David. *The New Politics of British Trade Unionism: Union Power and the Thatcher Legacy*. Ithaca, N.Y.: Cornell University Press, 1992.

Martens, S. K. "Commentary." In *Compliance with Judgments of International Courts*, edited by M. K Bulterman and Martin Kuijer, 172. The Hague: M. Nijhoff, 1996.

Maskus, Keith. *Should Core Labor Standards Be Imposed Through International Trade Policy?* Policy Research Working Paper Series. The World Bank, 1997.

Matas, Robert. "BC Income Tax Cuts Now in Place." *Globe and Mail*, December 31, 2001.

McBride, Stephen, and Russell A. Williams. "Globalization, the Restructuring of Labour Markets and Policy Convergence: The OECD 'Jobs Strategy." *Global Social Policy* 1, no. 3 (December 1, 2001): 281–309.

McCabe, Aileen. "Blair Is Making a Difference Already: Sweeping Changes Felt in Monetary Policy, Relations with Europe, Hospital Closings, etc." *Gazette*, May 14, 1997, News section.

McClintock, Barbara. "Female Trouble." In *Liberalized: The Tyee Report on British Columbia Under Gordon Campbell's Liberals*, edited by David Beers, 17–37. Vancouver: New Star Books, 2005.

McDonald, Diane, and David Fairey. *Old Policies in Liberal "New Era" Labour Platform: A Backgrounder on the BC Liberals' Proposed Labour Policy Changes.* Ottawa: Canadian Center for Policy Alternatives, 2001.

McIntyre, Richard P. *Are Worker Rights Human Rights?* Ann Arbor: University of Michigan Press, 2008.

McLean, Iain, and Alistair McMillan. *The Concise Oxford Dictionary of Politics.* Oxford: Oxford University Press, 2009.

Miller, Reid G. "New South Korean Labor Law Pleases No One." *Associated Press*, December 13, 1996, Business News section.

Mo, Johnryn. "Political Culture and Legislative Gridlock: Politics of Economic Reform in Precrisis Korea." *Comparative Political Studies* 34, no. 5 (June 2001): 467–492.

Montagnon, Peter. "This Is an Unusual Situation." *Financial Times*, December 12, 1997, Comment and Analysis section, 19.

Morsink, Johannes. *The Universal Declaration of Human Rights.* Philadelphia: University of Pennsylvania Press, 2000.

Morton, Mike, Office of the Premier of British Columbia. Personal interview with author, Victoria, British Columbia, October 19, 2006.

Mosley, Layna, and Saika Uno. "Racing to the Bottom or Climbing to the Top? Economic Globalization and Collective Labor Rights." *Comparative Political Studies* 40, no. 8 (2007): 923–948.

Mufson, Steven, and Washington Post Foreign Service. "Seoul's Financial Markets Plunge in Crisis of Confidence; Kim Assures Nation Economic Reform Is on Track." *Washington Post*, December 20, 1997, A1.

Murillo, María Victoria. "Partisanship Amidst Convergence: The Politics of Labor Reform in Latin America." *Comparative Politics* 37, no. 4 (July 2005): 441–458.

National Union of Journalists. "The Wilson Case: Who Said What." National Union of Journalists Web site, 2002, accessed September 17, 2008, http://212.67.198.213/nuj/inner.php?docid=277.

———. "NUJ Hero's Great Euro Victory on Union Rights." National Union of Journalists Web site, 2002, accessed April 21, 2008, http://www.nuj.org.uk/inner.php?docid=276.

National Union of Journalists (former secretary general), phone interview with author, London, United Kingdom, November 29, 2006.

National Union of Public and General Employees. "Unions Challenge Bill 29, B.C.'s Contract-Busting Law," Ottawa, May 29, 2002, accessed April 21, 2009, http://www.nupge.ca/news_2002/news_my02/n29my02b.htm.

———. 2008. "Settlement Agreement Reached in British Columbia on Bill 29." NUPGE Web site, accessed January 19, 2009, http://www.nupge.ca/news_2008/n29ja08b.htm.

Nimtz, August H. *Marx and Engels: Their Contribution to the Democratic Breakthrough.* Buffalo: SUNY Press, 2000.

Noakes, Susan. "Building a New International Image: After Years of Isolation, Former Hermit Kingdom Seeks to Boost its Influence on World Stage. However, Korea's Biggest Test May Be Whether Its Application to Join the OECD Is Accepted." *Financial Post* (Toronto, Canada), July 29, 1995.

Novitz, Tonia. *International and European Protection of the Right to Strike: A Comparative Study of Standards Set by the International Labour Organization, the Council of Europe and the European Union.* Oxford monographs on labour law. Oxford: Oxford University Press, 2003.

———. "International Promises and Domestic Pragmatism: To What Extent Will the Employment Relations Act 1999 Implement International Labour Standards Relating to Freedom of Association." *Modern Law Review* 63, no. 3 (2000): 379–393.

O'Brien, Robert. "Continuing Incivility: Labor Rights in a Global Economy." *Journal of Human Rights* 3, no. 2 (2004): 203–214.

———. "Workers and World Order: The Tentative Transformation of the International Union Movement." *Review of International Studies* 26, no. 4 (October 2000): 535–555.

"OECD Censures South Korea over Labour Law." *Weekend Australian*, January 25, 1997.

"OECD Unions Urge Korea to Veto Labour Law." *Agence France Presse*, December 31, 1996, International News section.

Office of the United Nations High Commissioner for Human Rights. "Committee on Economic, Social and Cultural Rights." *Office of the United Nations High Commissioner for Human Rights—Treaty Bodies*, accessed November 12, 2007, http://www2.ohchr.org/english/bodies/cescr/index.htm.

———. "Declarations and Reservations: International Covenant on Civil and Political Rights." *Multilateral Treaties Deposited with the Secretary-General—TREATY I-IV--5.asp*, accessed September 21, 2008, http://www.unhchr.ch/html/menu3/b/treaty5_asp.htm.

———. "Human Rights Committee: Monitoring Civil and Political Rights." *Office of the United Nations High Commissioner for Human Rights-Treaty Bodies.* Accessed January 21, 2008, http://www2.ohchr.org/english/bodies/hrc/index.htm.

———. "International Covenant on Economic, Social and Cultural Rights New York, 16 December 1966." *Office of the United Nations High Commissioner for Human Rights*, 2007. Accessed March 13, 2008, http://www2.ohchr.org/english/bodies/ratification/3.htm.

O'Higgins, Paul. "Labour Is Not a Commodity—An Irish Contribution to International Labour Law." *Industrial Law Journal* 26 (1997): 225–234.

Organisation for Economic Co-operation and Development. "About OECD." OECD: For a Better World Web site, accessed August 21, 2009, http://www.oecd.org/pages/0,3417,en_36734052_36734103_1_1_1_1_1,00.html.

———. "Becoming a Member of the OECD: The Accession Process." OECD country

Web site, accessed March 30, 2008, http://www.oecd.org/document/11/0,3343,en_33873108_33844430_1958091_1_1_1_1,00.html.
———. "Convention on the Organisation for Economic Co-operation and Development." Home: Legal Affairs, accessed April 4, 2009, http://www.oecd.org/document/7/0,3343,en_2649_34483_1915847_1_1_1_1,00.html.
———. "Guidelines for Multinational Enterprises," *Directorate for Financial and Enterprise Affairs*. Accessed April 1, 2009, http://www.oecd.org/department/0,3355,en_2649_34889_1_1_1_1_1,00.html.
———. "Labour and the OECD: The Role of the TUAC (Policy Brief)." Public Affairs Division, Public Affairs and Communications Directorate, December 2008, http://www.tuac.org/en/public/tuac/0812_TuacRole.pdf.
———. "OECD Codes of Liberalisation of Capital Movements and of Current Invisible Operations." *Home: Legal Affairs*. Accessed August 22, 2009, http://www.oecd.org/document/63/0,3343,en_2649_34483_1826559_1_1_1_1,00.html.
———. *The OECD Jobs Study: Facts, Analysis, Strategies*. Paris: OECD Publications and Information Centre, 1994.
———. "On-Line Guide to OECD Intergovernmental Activity." *Organisation for Economic Co-operation and Development*. Accessed February 25, 2008, http://webnet3.oecd.org/OECDgroups/.
———. *Pushing Ahead with Reform in Korea Labour Market and Social Safety-Net Policies*. Paris: OECD, 2000.
———. *Stat Extracts: Trade Union Density*. Accessed June 1, 2009, http://stats.oecd.org/Index.aspx?DataSetCode=UN_DEN.
———. *Trade, Employment and Labor Standards: A Study of Core Workers' Rights and International Trade*. Paris: OECD, 1996.
———. *2007 Follow up to the Council Monitoring Mandate on Korean Labor Law and Industrial Relations Reform, Report by the Chair of the Employment, Labor and Social Affairs Committee*. C(2007)9, 2007.
Pak, Ch'i-yŏng. *Korea and the United Nations*. The Hague: Martinus Nijhoff Publishers, 2000.
Palmer, John. "EEC Faces Opposition over 'Workers Rights' Proposals." *Guardian*, May 19, 1988, News section.
———. "Poll Shows British Majority Backs Controversial EEC Social Charter." *Guardian*, May 19, 1989.
Mr. T. A. E. Palmer, Mr. B. Stedman, and Mr. A.E. Wyeth v. Associated British Ports. [1991] ITR. 3367, 3367, 3367, 17/24.
Panitch, Leo, and Donald Swartz. *From Consent to Coercion: The Assault on Trade Union Freedoms*. Aurora, Ont.: Garamond Press, 2003.
Park, James. "World Bank Doing Business on the Backs of Workers." AFL-CIO Now Blog News, October 4, 2007, http://blog.aflcio.org/2007/10/04/world-bank-doing-business-on-backs-of-workers/.
Pencavel, John. "The Surprising Retreat of Union Britain." In *Seeking a Premier Economy: The Economic Effects of British Economic Reforms, 1980–2000*, edited by David

E. Card, Richard Blundell, and Richard B. Freeman, 191–232. Chicago: University of Chicago Press, 2004.

Peston, Robert. "Blair Sets Out 10-point 'Covenant'; Brown Admits a $1.5bn Revenue Shortfall as Labour Manifesto is Launched." *Financial Times*, April 4, 1997, 1.

"Political Conflicts on the Horizon over Government Revision Bill on Labor." *Korea Herald*, December 3, 1996.

von Potobsky, Geraldo. "Freedom of Association: The Impact of Convention No. 87 and ILO Action." *International Labour Review* 137, no. 2 (March 1998): 195–222.

Puchmayr, Chuck (MLA). Personal interview with author. New Westminster, Canada, October 28, 2006.

Putnam, Robert. "Diplomacy and Domestic Politics: The Logic of Two Level Games." *International Organization* 42, no. 3 (1998): 427–460.

Radcliff, Benjamin, and Patricia Davis. "Labor Organization and Electoral Participation in Industrial Democracies." *American Journal of Political Science* 44, no. 1 (January 2000): 132–141.

Ragin, Charles C. The *Comparative Method: Moving Beyond Qualitative and Quantitative Strategies*. Berkeley: University of California Press, 1989.

Republic of Korea. *The First Ten Years of the Korean Constitution Court*. Seoul: The Constitutional Court of Korea, 2001.

———. "Korea Letter of Intent, December 3, 1997." International Monetary Fund, December 3, 1997. http://www.imf.org/external/np/loi/120397.htm.

———. "Constitution of the Republic of Korea, 1948." UCLA Center for East Asian Studies: East Asian Studies Documents, 2007. http://www.international.ucla.edu/eas/documents/korea-constit.htm.

Republic of Korea, Korean Tripartite Commission. *Major Agreements of the Korean Tripartite Commission (1998–2006)*. Seoul: Korean Tripartite Commission, 2006. http://www.lmg.go.kr/bbs/down.asp?code=e_bbs52&number=26&seq=1&mime=doc

Republic of Korea, Ministry of Labor. *Labor Administration 2006*. Seoul: Ministry of Labor, 2006.

———. *The Position of Korean Government on the ICFTU/TUAC/GUF Mission Report*. Seoul: Ministry of Labor, October 24, 2006.

Reitan, Earl A. *The Thatcher Revolution: Margaret Thatcher, John Major, Tony Blair, and the Transformation of Modern Britain*. Boulder, Colo.: Rowman & Littlefield, 2003.

Risse, T. "'Let's Argue': Communicative Action in World Politics." *International Organization* 54, no. 1 (2000): 1–40.

Rosen, Sumner M. "Protecting Labor Rights in Market Economies." *Human Rights Quarterly* 14, no. 3 (1992): 371–382.

Ross, June M. "Limitations on Human Rights in International Law: Their Relevance to the Canadian Charter of Rights and Freedoms." *Human Rights Quarterly* 6, no. 2 (1984): 180–223.

Rueschemeyer, Dietrich, Evelyne Huber Stephens, and John D. Stephens. *Capitalist Development and Democracy*. 1st ed. Chicago: University of Chicago Press, 1992.

Ruggie, John Gerard. "International Regimes, Transactions, and Change: Embedded Liberalism in the Postwar Economic Order." *International Organization* 36, no. 2 (Spring 1982): 379–415.

Salzman, James. "Labor Rights, Globalization and Institutions: The Role and Influence of the Organization for Economic Cooperation and Development." *Michigan Journal of International Law* 21 (2000): 770–848.

Sandholtz, Wayne. "Dynamics of International Norm Change: Rules Against Wartime Plunder." *European Journal of International Relations* 14, no. 1 (March 1, 2008): 101–131.

Savage, Larry. "Workers' Rights as Human Rights: Organized Labor and Rights Discourse in Canada." *Labor Studies Journal* 34, no. 1 (March 2009): 8–20.

Seidman, Gay. *Beyond the Boycott: Labor Rights, Human Rights, and Transnational Activism*. New York: Russell Sage Foundation, 2007.

———. "Deflated Citizenship: Labor Rights in a Global Era." In *People Out of Place: Globalization, Human Rights, and the Citizenship Gap*, edited by Alison Brysk, 109–129. New York: Routledge, 2004.

"Seoul Vows to Ease Labour Law." *Independent* (London), January 24, 1997, 13.

Sen, Amartya Kumar, and Carnegie Council on Ethics and International Relations. *Human Rights and Asian Values*. Morgenthau Memorial Lecture on Ethics and Foreign Policy, no. 16. New York: Carnegie Council on Ethics and International Affairs, 1997.

Shabas, William A. "International Human Rights Law and the Canadian Courts." In *Human Rights in the 21st Century: Prospects, Institutions and Processes*, edited by Thomas A. Cromwell, Helene Dumont, Danielle Pinard, and Canadian Institute for the Administration of Justice, 21–48. Montreal: Editions Themis, 1997.

Shin, Kwan Yeong. "The Political Economy of Economic Growth in East Asia: South Korea and Taiwan." In *The Four Asian Tigers: Economic Development and the Global Political Economy*, edited by Eun Mee Kim, 3–32. San Diego, Calif.: Academic Press, 1998.

Siebert, Horst. "Labor Market Rigidities: At the Root of Unemployment in Europe." *Journal of Economic Perspectives* 11, no. 3 (1997): 37–54.

Silver, Isidore. *Public Employee Discharge and Discipline*. New York: Aspen Publishers, 2005.

Simmons, Beth A., and Zachary Elkins. "The Globalization of Liberalization: Policy Diffusion in the International Political Economy." *American Political Science Review* 98, no. 01 (2004): 171–189.

Simpson, Bob. "The Changing Face of British Collective Labour Law." *Oxford Journal of Legal Studies* 21, no. 4 (2001): 705–718.

Sinclair, Jim, and Angela Schira, "Code Breaks: BC Federation of Labour." *Democrat*, September 9, 2001.

Slaughter, Anne-Marie. "International Law in a World of Liberal States." *European Journal of International Law* 6, no. 4 (1995): 503–538.

Smithers, Rebecca, and Michael White. "Tories Start Scare on Unions." *Guardian*, March 26, 1997, Home Page section.

"South Korea Formally Becomes 29th Member of OECD." *Xinhua News Agency*, December 12, 1996.

"South Korea to Join OECD." *Kyodo News Service: Japanese Economic Newswire*, October 11, 1996.

"South Korea's Judgment." *International Herald Tribune*, August 28, 1996, online edition, Opinion section.

"South Korea's Kim Vows Labor Reform." *United Press International*, April 24, 1996, Financial section.

"South Korea Says New Labour Law a 'Domestic Issue.'" *Agence France-Presse*, January 24, 1997, International News section.

Standing, Guy. *Global Labour Flexibility: Seeking Distributive Justice*. New York: Macmillan, 1999.

Stanford, Jim. "Testing the Flexibility Paradigm: Canadian Labor Market Performance in International Context." In *Fighting Unemployment: The Limits of a Free Market Orthodoxy*, edited by David R. Howell, 119–155. Oxford: Oxford University Press, 2005.

Stavenhagen, Rodolfo. "Indigenous Rights: Some Conceptual Problems." In *Constructing Democracy: Human Rights, Citizenship, And Society In Latin America*, edited by Elizabeth Jelin and Eric Hershberg, 141–159. Boulder, Colo.: Westview Press, 1996.

Steffenhagen, Janet. "Labour Lauds UN Slap at Liberals." *Vancouver Sun*, March 28, 2003.

Stewart, Robert Burgess. "Canada and International Labor Conventions." *American Journal of International Law* 32 (1938): 36–62.

Studlar, Donley T. *Great Britain: Decline Or Renewal*. Boulder, Colo.: Westview Press, 1996.

Sullivan, Kevin. "South Korean Leader Retreats On Controversial Labor Laws." *Washington Post*, January 22, 1997, A14.

Swepston, Lee. "Human Rights Law and Freedom of Association: Development Through ILO Supervision." *International Labour Review* 137, no. 2 (March 1998): 169–194.

Swimmer, Gene. "Public Sector Labour Relations in an Era of Restraint and Restructuring: An Overview." In *Public-Sector Labour Relations in an Era of Restraint and Restructuring*, edited by Gene Swimmer, 1–35. Oxford: Oxford University Press, 2001.

Swimmer, Gene, and Tim Bartkiw. "The Future of Public Sector Collective Bargaining in Canada." *Journal of Labor Research* 24 (2003): 579–596.

Synott, John. "Development, Education and the Teachers Union Movement in South Korea, 1989–1999." *Australian Journal of Politics and History* 47, no. 1 (2001): 130–148.

Taylor, Chantelle. "NAFTA, GATT and the Current Free Trade System: A Dangerous Double Standard for Workers' Rights." *Denver Journal of International Law and Policy* 28, no. 4 (2000): 401–434.

Taylor, Robert. "Backtracking Embitters Trade Union Old Guard." *Financial Times*, April 7, 1997, News section.

———. "Government Heads for Clash on Labour Laws, Ministers Under Pressure to Scrap Tory Employment Legislation after ILO Upholds Complaints Against Britain." *Financial Times*, June 6, 1997, News section.

"Tigers and Pussy Cats: South Korea Learns Democracy the Hard Way." *Guardian* (London), January 14, 1997, 12.

Tilly, Charles. "Globalization Threatens Labor's Rights." *International Labor and Working-Class History* 47 (1995): 1–23.

Towers, Brian. "Two Speed Ahead: Social Europe and the UK After Maastricht." *Industrial Relations* 23, no. 2 (1992): 83–89.

Trade Union Advisory Committee. "About TUAC—TUAC—Trade Union Advisory Committee to the OECD." Trade Union Advisory Committee to the OECD Web site, accessed March 14, 2008, http://www.tuac.org/en/public/tuac/index.phtml.

Trades Union Congress (employment rights officer), personal interview with author, London, November 23, 2006.

Trades Union Congress. *General Council Report 2002: Chapter 1,* accessed June 12, 2008 http://www.tuc.org.uk/congress/tuc-6423-f0.cfm.

———. *The Employment Relations Act: A TUC Guide*. London: Anderson Lambert, 1999.

Trades Union Congress, and Liberty. *Joint Submission by Liberty and the Trade Unions Congress. Third Party Intervention to the Court.* Applications 30668/96, 30671/96, 30678/96. Strasbourg: European Court of Human Rights, 2000.

Tucker, Eric. "The Constitutional Right to Bargain Collectively: The Ironies of Labour History in the Supreme Court of Canada." *Labour / Le Travail* 61, no. 1 (2008): 151–180.

Twomey, David. *Labor & Employment Law: Text and Cases.* 13th ed. Mason, Oh.: Thompson West, 2006.

U.K. based law professor, personal interview with author, London, December 5, 2006.

Underwood, Brad. Personal interview with author. Victoria, Canada, October 17, 2006.

United Kingdom. *Employment Protection (Consolidation) Act 1978,* accessed June 17, 2008, http://www.legislation.gov.uk/ukpga/1978/44/section/23/enacted.

———. *Observations of the Government*. Application No. 30668/96; 30671/96; 30678/96. European Court of Human Rights, 1999.

United Kingdom Parliament. "Glossary: White Paper." Accessed November 10, 2010, http://www.parliament.uk/site-information/glossary/white-paper.

United Nations Treaty Collection. "Chapter IV Human Rights: International Covenant on Civil and Political Rights." Accessed December 14, 2010, http://untreaty.un.org/unts/120001_144071/4/9/00003305.pdf.

United Nations High Commission on Human Rights. *Concluding Observations/ Comments of Committee on Economic, Social and Cultural Rights: Republic of Korea.* UN Doc E/C.1/1995/3, 1995.

———. *Concluding Observations of the Human Rights Committee: Consideration of Reports Submitted by State Parties Under Article 40 of the Covenant (Republic of Korea)*. CCPR/C/KOR/CO/3, Concluding Observations/Comments, 2006.

———. *Concluding Observations of the Committee on Economic, Social and Cultural Right*. E/C.12/1/Add.19, 1997.

———. *Report of the Human Rights Committee, Vol. 1*, General Assembly, Official Records, Fifty-Fifth Session, Supplement No. 40 (A/55/40), New York, 2000.

———. *Report on the Seventh Session of the Committee on Economic Social and Cultural Rights*. ESCR, 1993, Supp. No. 2 (UN Doc. E/1993/22), 1993.

———. *Summary Record of the 13th Meeting of the Committee on Economic Social and Cultural Rights (Republic of Korea)*. E/C.12/2001/SR.13 (7/5/2001), 2001.

———. *Summary Record of the 37th Meeting: United Kingdom of Great Britain and Northern Ireland*. E/C.12/1997/SR.37, 1998.

United Nations High Commission on Human Rights, United Nations Human Rights Committee. *Summary Record of the 1792nd Meeting: Republic of Korea, 22/11/99*. CCPR/C/SR.1792, Summary Record, 1999.

United Nations, World Summit for Social Development. *Report of the World Summit for Social Development*. Copenhagen, Denmark, March 6–12, 1995, A/CONF.1666//0, April 19, 1995.

United States Department of State. *1996 Human Rights Report: Republic of Korea (South Korea)*. Bureau of Democracy, Human Rights and Labor, January 30, 1997, accessed June 20, 2009, http://www.state.gov/www/global/human_rights/1996_hrp_report/southkor.html.

Verite. *Emerging Markets Research Project: Year-End Report: Prepared for the California Public Employees Retirement System (CalPERS)*. Amherst, Mass.: Verite, December 2006. http://www.calpers.ca.gov/eip-docs/investments/assets/equities/international/permissible-2007/verite-report-2006.pdf.

Wade, Robert. "From 'Miracle' to 'Cronyism': Explaining the Great Asian Slump." *Cambridge Journal of Economics* 22, no. 6 (November 1, 1998): 693–706.

———. "Financial Regime Change." *New Left Review* 53 (October 2008): 5–21.

Wade, Robert, and Frank Veneroso. "The Asian Crisis: The High Debt Model Versus the Wall Street-Treasury-IMF Complex." *New Left Review* I/228, no. 3 (April 1998).

Weiler, Paul C. "The Charter at Work: Reflections on the Constitutionalizing of Labour and Employment Law." *University of Toronto Law Journal* 40, no. 2 (1990): 117–212.

Weisband, Edward. "Discursive Multilateralism: Global Benchmarks, Shame, and Learning in the ILO Labor Standards Monitoring Regime." *International Studies Quarterly* 44, no. 4 (2000): 643-666.

Weisband, Edward, and Christopher J. Colvin. "An Empirical Analysis of International Confederation of Free Trade Union (ICFTU) Annual Surveys." *Human Rights Quarterly* 22, no. 1 (2000): 167–186.

Wedderburn, Kenneth William. "Freedom of Association and Philosophies of Labour Law." *Industrial Law Journal* 18, no. 1 (1989): 1–38.

Wells, Donald M. "Origins of Canada's Wagner Model of Industrial Relations: The United Auto Workers in Canada and the Suppression of 'Rank and File' Unionism,

1936–1953." *Canadian Journal of Sociology/Cahiers Canadiens de Sociologie.* 20, no. 2 (1995): 193–225.

Wickham-Jones, M. "New Labour in the Global Economy: Partisan Politics and the Social Democratic Model." *British Journal of Politics and International Relations* 2, no. 1 (2000): 1–25.

Wighton, David. "Blair Fudges EU Differences Between Parties: Labour Leader Launches Personal Attack on a Prime Minister 'Without Authority to Negotiate.'" *Financial Times*, April 22, 1997, News section, 10.

Wilkinson, Barry. "The Korea Labour Problem." *British Journal of Industrial Relations* 32, no. 3 (1994): 339–358.

David William Wilson v. Associated Newspapers Ltd. [1990] ITR 10516/90/LS.

Wilson and the National Union of Journalists; Palmer, Wyeth and National Union of Rail, Maritime and Transport Workers; Doolan and Other v. United Kingdom [2002] IRLR 128.

Wilson and the National Union of Journalists, Palmer, Wyeth and the National Union of Rail, Maritime and Transport Workers, Doolan and others. *Applicant's Response to Observations of the Government of the United Kingdom.* Strasbourg: European Court of Human Rights, March 13, 2000.

Wood, Stephen, and John Goddard. "The Statutory Union Recognition Procedure in the Employment Relations Bill: A Comparative Analysis." *British Journal of Industrial Relations* 37, no. 2 (1999): 203–245.

Woods, H. D., and Canada. *Canadian Industrial Relations: The Report of Task Force on Labour Relations.* Ottawa: Privy Council Office, 1968.

World Bank. "High Income Countries." *Country and Lending Groups Data.* Accessed September 21, 2010, http://data.worldbank.org/about/country-classifications/country-and-lending-groups#High_income.

———. "Revisions to EWI Indicators." Doing Business. April 29, 2009. Accessed November 17, 2009, http://www.doingbusiness.org/documents/EWI_revisions.pdf.

———. International Economics Dept. Development Data Group. *World Development Indicators 2008.* Washington, D.C.: World Bank Publishers, 2008.

World Bank Group. "Employing Workers." *Doing Business*, 2008. Accessed March 2, 2009. http://www.doingbusiness.org/ExploreTopics/EmployingWorkers/.

Wright, Don, and British Columbia. *Towards a Better Teacher Bargaining Model in British Columbia: Report to Honourable Graham Bruce on the Teacher Collective Bargaining.* Victoria: British Columbia Ministry of Education/Ministry of Skills Development and Labour, 2003.

Yoon, Bang-Soon. "Democratization and Gender Politics in South Korea." In *Gender, Globalization, and Democratization,* edited by Rita Mae Kelly, Mary E. Hawkesworth, and Briggitte Young, 171–194. Lanham, Md.: Rowman & Littlefield Publishers, 2001.

Younge, Gary. "Europeans Think He's a New JFK. Really." *Observer*, May 11, 1997, News section.

INDEX

Abbott, George, 183
Abbott, Kenneth W., 3, 57, 61, 64
Act on Establishment and Operation of Teachers' Unions, 98, 201
Act on Establishment and Operation of Workplace Associations for Public Officials, 98
Adams, Roy, 207
affiliation rights, 49
Agency of National Security Planning, 240n.124
agricultural workers (Canada), 186
American Declaration of Human Rights, 115
American Federation of Labor (AFL), 23, 27–28
Amnesty International, 82, 99–100, 206
antiunion discrimination, 45–46; British Columbia, 188, 195; United Kingdom, 114, 119, 124–25, 127, 129, 130, 132, 133, 137, 138, 141
arrests of unionists (South Korea), 67, 75–76, 79, 80, 99–100, 236n.52, 244n.190, 245n.193, 246n.217
Arthurs, Harry, 40
Asda, 154
Asian financial crisis (1997), 6, 92–101, 163, 197
Asian Regional Meeting (ILO, 2006), 103
Asia-Pacific Economic Cooperation summit (1994), 81
assembly rights (South Korea), 67
Associated British Ports, 125
Associated British Ports v. Palmer and Others, 123. *See also Wilson/Palmer* cases
Associated Newspapers, 124, 126, 127, 251n.53
Associated Newspapers v. Wilson, 123. *See also Wilson/Palmer* cases
associations of workers, 20
Attorney General for Canada v. Attorney General for Ontario, 159
Australia, 108
Austria, 61, 82

Bae Kiu-Sik, 95
Bakvis, Peter, 38–39
Bartkiw, Tim, 160–61
Belgian Police case, 142–43
Belgium, 21, 30, 61
Besley, Timothy, 35
Bill of Rights (Canada), 172
blacklisting, 46, 119, 137, 139, 140, 256–67n.137, 256n.127
Blair, Tony, 113, 128, 134–37, 139, 147–50, 198–99, 203. *See also* New Labour government (UK)
Botero, Juan, 35
Bringing Rights Home (Labour Party, UK), 150
Britain, 24. *See also* United Kingdom
British Columbia, Canada: economic growth in, 192, 198; labor standards in, 186; partisan politics and labor rights in, 162–63; strikes in, 194; transition in economy of, 163; British Columbia Business Council, 185; British Columbia case study, 155–92; and Canada's commitments to international law,

British Columbia, Canada: (*cont'd*) 157–60; conclusions from, 194, 196–98, 200–202, 204–7; federal and provincial division of labor, 157; *Health Services* case, 11, 177–84; interviews in, 13; and lack of international institutional support, 187–89; legal changes, 12; mechanisms of change, 5–6; normative negotiations, 167–84; political history of trade union rights, 161–67; politics of trade union rights, 160–61; theoretical implications of, 184–89; U.S. law compared to, 217–18
British Columbia Court of Appeals, 177
British Columbia Federation of Labour, 164
British Columbia Government and Service Employees Union (BCGEU), 265n.64
British Columbia Liberal Party, 163–65, 264n.45
British Columbia Nurses' Association, 265–66n.64
British Columbia Poverty and Human Rights Center, 187
British Columbia Teachers' Federation (BCTF), 164, 266n.64
British North America Act (Canada), 159, 172
Brown, Gordon, 128, 148, 255n.118
Bruce, Graham, 166, 175–76, 186
Building Prosperity—Flexibility, Efficiency and Fairness at Work (Labour Party, UK), 135–36
Burgess, Robin, 35
Business and Industry Advisory Council (BIAC), 82, 104

Camdessus, Michael, 93
Campbell, Gordon, 164–65, 174, 182
Canada, 9, 157–58; and American Declaration of Human Rights, 115; cases brought before ILO Committee from, 159; collective agreements, 116, 161; commitments to human rights, 202; commitments to international law, 157–60; federalism in, 159–60; federal-provincial conflicts, 159–60; federal respect for/compliance with trade union rights, 158; as "high income country," 10; ILO leadership of, 158; industrial relations practices, 116; interactions with international institutions, 194; international promotion of trade union rights by, 158; lack of constitution and human rights guarantees, 172; local trade union rights, 158–59; in OECD, 61; provincial governments' collective agreements, 161; South Korea pressured by, 108. *See also* British Columbia case study
Canada-Brazil Memorandum of Understanding on Labour Cooperation, 158
Canada-Chile Agreement on Labour Cooperation, 158
Canada-Costa Rica Agreement on Labour Cooperation, 158
Canadian Charter of Rights and Freedoms, 155–56, 166, 172–74, 177–84, 187, 205
Canadian Labour Congress, 27, 166
Canadian Labour Law Casebook Group, 182
Canadian Supreme Court, 155–56, 172–74, 177–84
Canadian Teachers' Federation, 166
Canadian Union of Public Employees-British Columbia (CUPE-BC), 167, 265n.64
case selection, 8–11
case studies: normative negotiations in, 5; research design, 8–13
Cavalier, Stephen, 137, 143, 152
Central Arbitration Committee, 217
Central Arbitration Council, 138
Chae Jun-ho, 95
Chang Dae-uop, 95
Charter of Fundamental Rights (2000), 2
child labor laws (British Columbia), 186
Church of England, 21
church-related workers' organizations, 21, 22
civil rights, 31; in Canada, 159; individual-level, 45; legalization of, 29; in the United Kingdom, 128
civil servants' rights: South Korea, 66, 70–71, 75, 76, 86, 90, 95, 98, 99, 101–6, 109, 110; United Kingdom, 120, 137, 139, 140; United States, 216. *See also* public sector workers
closed shops. *See* security clauses
Coastal Ferry Act (Bill 98), 268n.107
Code of Liberalisation of Capital Movements, 62

Code of Liberalisation of Current Invisible Operations, 62
Cold War: and European Court of Human Rights, 152; and human rights covenants, 29; and international norms, 19, 26, 27, 33; and Korean teachers' organizations, 71; and neoliberalism, 34; and OECD establishment, 61
collective action rights, 18, 20; British Columbia, 173, 174; importance of, 196; South Korea, 67, 68, 69, 75, 88, 90, 99, 101, 104, 110; United Kingdom, 117–21. *See also* strike rights
collective agreements: British Columbia, 161, 165, 167–69, 176, 177, 181, 183, 186, 187; Canada, 116; government interference with, 49; OECD rule for, 63; South Korea, 116; United Kingdom, 116, 120, 123–25, 132, 143, 145
collective bargaining, 18, 46–48; British Columbia, 156, 158, 160–62, 165, 168, 171–74, 177–84, 187, 191; COIE on, 133; under different national industrial relations systems, 47–48; Human Rights Committee view of, 56; and ILO Convention 87, 56; Kucera's measure of, 211–12; in labor flexibility regime, 36; OECD rule for, 63; and public-sector labor costs, 161; South Korea, 68, 69, 104, 110; state obligation to protect, 49; and trade union membership, 130; United Kingdom, 114, 116, 118, 120–25, 129–33, 138–39, 141–43, 145–46, 151, 152; utility of, 35
collective laissez faire (UK), 115–16
collective rights of trade unions, 42, 43, 46–49
Combination Acts of 1799, 20
Commission of Inquiry (ILO), 180
Commission on Human Rights, 28, 29
Committee of Experts (European Social Charter); interpretation of trade union rights by, 60–61; and United Kingdom case study, 142
Committee of Experts on the Application of Conventions and Recommendations (CEACR), 48, 51, 60–61, 132; in British Columbia case study, 180; in United Kingdom case study, 121, 133, 139; and United Kingdom's strike restrictions, 120; Committee of Independent Experts (COIE, Council of Europe), 31; monitoring by, 60; as source of research information, 12; in United Kingdom case study, 121, 133, 144; Committee of Ministers (Council of Europe), 58–60, 133, 146
Committee on Economic, Social and Cultural Rights (CESCR); interpretation of legal commitments, 55–57; and right to strike, 30; as source of research information, 12; in South Korea case study, 83, 101; in United Kingdom case study, 132–33
Committee on Labor Laws, 236n.54
Committee on the Elimination of Discrimination Against Women (CEDAW), 185, 187, 188, 190
commodification of labor, 37
common law (UK), 115–16
Community Charter of the Fundamental Social Rights of Workers, 134
Compa, Lance, 207, 208
competitiveness, 77, 193, 197–98
compliance with trade union rights; analyzing depth of, 7–8; in case studies, 9, 10; depth of, 203–6; ILO promotion of, 54; and multiple recommendations from international institutions, 199–201; and states' human rights commitments, 202–3; and types of disputes, 201–2. *See also individual case studies*
Concluding Observations of the Human Rights Committee (1999), 179
Confederation of British Industries, 139
Congress of Industrial Organizations, 27
Conservative governments (UK), 11, 113, 115, 117–23, 128, 133–34, 198, 200
Conservative Party (UK), 118, 134, 136, 141, 147, 149
Conspiracy and Protection of Property Act of 1875, 248n.8
Constitutional Court (South Korea), 73
construction workers (Canada), 186
constructivist norm theory, 193
constructivist tradition, in international relations, 3, 196
control variables (in case studies), 9–11

Convention for the Protection of Human Rights and Fundamental Freedoms (1953), 31. *See also* European Convention on Human Rights
Convention on the OECD (1960), 61–62
Cook, Maria L., 9
Cook, Robin, 128, 255n.118
Cooperative Commonwealth Federation (CCF), 162, 263n.30
core labor standards, 2, 3
Council of Europe, 31–32, 226n.58; Committee of Ministers, 58, 60, 133, 146; European Convention on Human Rights, 31–32; European Court of Human Rights, 31, 32; European Social Charter, 32–33; expelling members from, 146; human rights categories in, 29; human rights documents of, 115; interpretation of legal commitments, 57–61, 65; protection of trade union rights by, 30–31; sources of information from, 12; United Kingdom in, 115. *See also specific bodies*
Council of Global Unions, 63
Council of Ministers (OECD), 59, 83, 85, 87, 107, 108
Court of Appeals (UK), 123, 127–29
Cox, Robert, 24
Creighton, Breen, 133
Cuba, 1
cultural rights, legalization of, 29
Czechoslovakia, 68
Czech Republic, 83

Daily Mail, 123–25, 127
Dan Byung Ho, 99–100
Data Protection Act of 1998, 139
Declaration of Educational Democratization, 71
Declaration of Fundamental Principles and Rights at Work (1998), 2, 158
Declaration of Philadelphia (1944), 24–27
decommodification of labor, 3, 34
democracy; linking trade union rights to, 28; and oppression of unions, 193; rights seen as "essential" for, 31; South Korean transition to, 70; in the United Kingdom, 119
Democratic Justice Party (South Korea), 235n.29
Democratic Liberal Party (South Korea), 235n.29
democratic pluralism, 82
democratic rights, in pre-industrial regimes, 20
demonstrations (South Korea), 99
Denmark, 21, 30, 61
Department of Trade and Industry (UK), 154
dependent variables (in cases), 8, 9, 11
Deschamps, Justice (Canada), 182
Digest of Cases (ILO Committee on Freedom of Association), 14, 45, 106
Discount Tobacco and Confectionary Ltd. v. Armitage, 252n.69
dismissals; South Korea, 69, 74, 78; United Kingdom, 114, 119, 120, 124, 126, 127, 132, 139, 140, 145
dispatch workers (South Korea), 94
dispute intervention (South Korea), 70
dispute resolution (UK), 117
Doing Business (World Bank), 38, 227n.79, 228n.96
domestic legal activism; British Columbia, 190; United Kingdom, 123–29
domestic norms and laws; British Columbia, 172–73; during industrialization period, 20
Dunmore v. Ontario (Attorney General) (2001), 174

Ebbinghaus, Bernhard, 21
economic conditions, 195; in British Columbia, 160–61, 163, 165, 171, 176, 187; and embedded liberalism, 25; and international labor rights regime, 24; as justification for curtailing trade union rights, 198; and South Korean labor law reforms, 77, 79–80, 99, 102; and states' approach to trade union rights, 4; and strikes, 194; in the United Kingdom, 117, 118, 121–22; economic growth/development; in British Columbia, 163, 198; as control factor in case studies, 10; as goal of case study states, 197–98; OECD standards for, 62; and regulation of labor markets, 35; in South Korea, 68–69, 198; and UK trade union rights, 121; and unemployment, 118

economic interests, effect of labor rights on, 37
Economic League, 139
economic protection regime, 25
economic recession, 197
economic rights, 29, 31, 196–97
economic standards labor rights perspective, 22
Economic Surveys of Korea (OECD), 12
education services (British Columbia), 164, 166, 171, 175–76, 183. *See also* teachers' rights
Education Services Collective Agreements Act (Bill 27), 165–66, 168–70, 187–89
election certification (UK), 120
elections, trade union, 48–49
Elections Law (South Korea), 95
embedded liberalism, 25, 33, 34
Employing Workers Index, 38–39
Employment, Labour and Social Affairs Committee (ELSA), 63–64, 82, 84, 85, 87–89, 104, 107–8
Employment Appeal Tribunals (UK), 123, 126–27, 140, 178
Employment Department (UK), 121
Employment Insurance system (South Korea), 92
employment practices, Anglo-American, 34
Employment Protection Act of 1975, 117
Employment Protection (Consolidation) Act of 1978, 124–26, 129
Employment Relations Act of 1999, 138–42, 201–3
Employment Relations Act of 2004, 144–46, 153–54, 174, 182, 203
employment relationship, 20–21. *See also* United Kingdom case study
Employment Standards Act, 186
Employment Standards Branch (Canada), 186
enforcement, 2; by European Court of Human Rights, 59, 146; by ILO bodies, 54–55; lack of strong mechanisms for, 193
Engels, Friedrich, 21
England, 20, 21
entitlements, 7
"essential services," 230nn.7–8
"essential services" strikes, 45–47, 50, 167–69, 184
Etherington, Brian, 182
Europe, 21–23, 148–50. *See also* European Union (EU)
European Central Bank, 149
European Coal and Steel Community treaty, 226n.58
European Commission of Human Rights, 59, 139, 141, 151, 200. *See also* European Court of Human Rights
European common market, 149
European Convention for the Protection of Human Rights and Fundamental Freedoms, 115, 141, 142
European Convention on Human Rights, 203; on compensation for violations, 146; legal obligations under, 42–44; obligations under, 59; protection of trade union rights by, 31–32; in United Kingdom case study, 114, 142–44, 150–53
European Court of Human Rights, 31, 143, 200, 203, 206, 260n.197; adjudication procedures, 58; cases brought before, 57–58; enforcement by, 59, 146; interpretation of legal commitments, 57–60, 65; legal rulings of, 10, 44; protection of trade union rights by, 32; as source of research information, 12; in United Kingdom case study, 114, 123, 141–53
European Social Charter, 31; Additional Protocol of 1989, 121; Committee of Independent Experts, 12, 31, 60–61; interpretation of legal commitments, 60–61, 65; legal obligations under, 42–44; protection of trade union rights by, 32–33; UK and expansion of, 134; and United Kingdom case study, 147, 153; United Kingdom's ratification of, 115; and United Kingdom's violation of rights, 121, 133
European Social Committee, 60, 226n.59
European Trade Union Council, 63
European Union (EU), 1–2, 108, 115, 149–50, 226n.58. *See also individual countries*
Ewing, Keith, 140

Fact-Finding and Conciliation Commission on Freedom of Association (ILO), 51–52
Fairness at Work (UK), 137–38

fairness principles (UK), 119, 133
Federal Conciliation and Mediation Services, 217
federalism (Canada), 159–60
Federal Labor Relations Act of 1978, 217
Federal Service Impasse Panel, 217
Federation of Korean Trade Unions (FKTU), 71, 73, 83, 86, 87, 93, 97
ferry workers (British Columbia), 164, 176
financial control, of trade unions, 48
financial crises; of 2008, 207; Asian, 6, 92–101, 163, 197
financial institutions, public support for trade union rights from, 2
Financial Times, 136
First International, 22, 224n.18
flexicurity, 39
Fordist production regime, 33, 34, 196
Forteza, Alvaro, 35
foundational conditions for trade union rights, 19
Founders Committee (South Korea), 79
France, 20, 24, 30, 61, 82
freedom not to associate, 60
freedom of association, 18, 27; British Columbia, 156, 162, 167, 172–74, 177–81, 187; Human Rights Committee view of, 56; Kucera's measure of, 211–12; OECD rule for, 63; South Korea, 76, 88, 90, 95, 101, 105, 107; United Kingdom, 122, 131, 133, 152; utility of, 35
free trade agreements (Canada), 158
Free Trade Area of the Americas, 158
Fudge, Derek, 157, 191
functionalism, 19, 23

Germany, 21, 61, 68, 82
global economy, 33–34, 193
global human rights regime, 20, 25
globalization; competitive pressures of, 34; and labor flexibility regime, 36; pressures of, 4; and security created by trade unions, 193; in South Korea case study, 80–91; trade union rights in context of, 2; "weakened state" thesis of, 160
global labor protection regime, 3, 20
Global North, 2, 62
Global South, 62
Global Union Federation, 106, 224n.17
Globe and Mail, 178, 182, 183
Gompers, Samuel, 23
Governing Body (ILO), 51, 52, 103
Governing Committee (European Social Charter), 60
Government Communications Headquarters (GCHQ), 120, 137, 139, 140, 200–202
governments; and autonomous running of trade unions, 48; Canadian federal-provincial conflict between, 159–60; dictation of working conditions by, 47; international focused political interest of, 5; labor market flexibility policies of, 35; legal changes correlating with changes in, 11–12 (*See also* United Kingdom case study); and prohibition of multiple federations, 49, 71. *See also* states; *specific governments, e.g.:* Liberal government (British Columbia)
Grand National Party (South Korea), 97, 98
"Great Compromise" (South Korea), 94
Great Depression, 196
Great Workers' Struggle (South Korea), 70, 194, 234n.20
Greece, 61
Guardian newspaper, 87
Gustafsson case, 142–43

Hansenne, Michael, 87
hard law, 3, 57
Harvey, David, 34
Hathaway, Oona A., 80
Health and Social Services Delivery Improvement Act (Bill 29), 128, 165–66, 169–70, 176–84, 187–89, 194, 204–5
health care services (British Columbia), 164–66, 169, 171, 176–84
Health Care Services Collective Agreements Act (Bill 15), 167, 168, 170, 188
Health Care Services Continuation Act (Bill 2), 167, 168, 170, 178, 188
health conventions, 22
Health Sciences Association (HSA), 167, 265n.64, 266n.65
Health Sector Partnerships Agreement Act (Bill 94), 268n.107
Health Services Support-Facilities Subsection Bargaining Association v. British Columbia, 11, 177–84, 189, 191, 204

Health Statutes Amendment Act (Bill 26), 183
Helms-Burton Act, 1
Hendy, John, 124–25, 128, 134, 151, 152
High-Level Tripartite Representative Meetings, 106
history of trade union rights, 18–26; changes in support for rights, 33–40; ILO, 23–25; during industrialization period, 19–20; international institutions' incorporation of trade union rights, 26–27; from national to international norms, 19–26; new normative global regime, 25–26; professional legal and reform organizations, 22–23; rights to organize and act collectively, 20; secular trade unions, 23; transnational promotion of rights, 22; workers' rights organizations, 20–22
Hospital Employees Union (British Columbia), 166, 263n.38, 265n.64
House of Lords (UK), 123, 129, 132, 140, 142
human rights; in British Columbia, 171, 185; in Canada, 186–88; Canadian Charter of Rights and Freedoms, 155–56, 166, 172–74, 177–84, 187, 205; classical view of, 42; current dominant interpretation of, 197; European Convention on Human Rights, 31; European Court of Human Rights, 31, 144; European Social Charter, 31; as individualistic vs. collective, 8; International Covenant on Civil and Political Rights, 29; International Covenant on Economic, Social and Cultural Rights, 29; international human rights regime, 25; within neoliberalism, 198–99; and OECD membership, 82–83; in pre-industrial regimes, 20; in South Korea, 66; trade union rights as, 3–5, 29–30, 40, 59–60, 206–9; union security clauses as violations of, 59; in the United Kingdom, 115, 148, 150–51; workers' rights as, 207–8
Human Rights Act of 1998 (UK), 150–51
Human Rights Act of 1999 (UK), 173, 203
Human Rights Commission (Canada), 185
Human Rights Watch, 82
Humphrey, John, 28
Hungary, 83
Hwang, Mr., 100
Iceland, 61
illegal strikes, 50; South Korea, 76, 100, 106, 245n.197; United Kingdom, 120
ILO Conventions; Canada's ratification of, 157–59, 172; Convention 87, 30, 56, 172, 177, 179; Convention 98, 30; legal obligations under, 42–44, 55; protection of trade union rights by, 27–29; United Kingdom's denouncement of, 134; United Kingdom's ratification of, 115; United Kingdom's violation of, 130–32
Implementing the OECD Jobs Strategy (OECD Economic and Development Review committee, 1997), 38
income levels, 10, 81
independent variables (in cases), 11
Indiana, 218
individual labor protections, 3, 8; British Columbia, 172, 177; Canada, 186; importance of, 196; provided by states, 18; rights of union members, 42, 43, 45–46; states' curtailment of, 36; trade union rights vs., 3, 220n.17, 223n.1. *See also* United Kingdom case study
Industrial Inquiry Commission (British Columbia), 183
industrialization period, 19–20
Industrial Relations Act of 1971, 117
Industrial Relations in the 1990s (UK Employment Department), 121–23
Industrial Relations Roadmap (South Korea), 103, 104, 107
industrial relations systems: and collective bargaining rights, 47–48; South Korea, 68–70, 75, 240n.119; United Kingdom, 114–16, 121–23, 138
Industrial Training Act of 1964, 117
Industrial Tribunals (UK), 117, 123–27, 129, 156
ING Barings Hong Kong, 92
Ingram, John Kells, 24, 220n.15
Institute of Employment Rights, 144–45
institutional "fatigue," 111
Inter-American Conference of Ministries of Labour, 158
International Association for Labor Legislation, 21–23

International Confederation of Free Trade Unions (ICFTU), 2, 74, 78, 79, 88, 106, 166, 220n.11
International Congress on Labor Legislation, 22
International Court of Justice, 139
International Covenant on Civil and Political Rights (ICCPR), 29, 30; Canada's ratification of, 158; Canadian Supreme Court on, 179; and individual complaints of rights violations, 57; legal obligations under, 43, 57; South Korea's ratification of, 68; state parties to, 55; United Kingdom's ratification of, 115
International Covenant on Economic, Social and Cultural Rights (ICESCR), 29–30; Canada's ratification of, 158; Canadian Supreme Court on, 179; legal obligations under, 43, 44, 57; and South Korean campaign to join OECD, 80; South Korea's obligations under, 110; South Korea's ratification of, 68; state parties to, 55; United Kingdom's ratification of, 115
International Federation of Building and Woodworkers, 74
International Federation of Journalists, 74
International Federation of Trade Unions, 23
International Herald Tribune, 85, 96
international human rights regime, 25, 42, 208
international institutions, 27–33; in British Columbia case study, 157, 184, 187–90; codified protections of trade union rights by, 26–33; enforcement mechanisms of, 2–3; incorporation of trade union rights by, 26–27; and influence on states, 9–10; interaction of case study states and, 195–96; interpretive authority of, 6–7; and labor flexibility policies, 36; length and frequency of interaction with, 111; multiple recommendations from, 199–201; in normative negotiation process, 4–5; as platforms to critique rights violations, 193; in South Korea case study, 73–81, 87, 95–98, 102; and trade unions' interpretation of human rights law, 6; in United Kingdom case study, 114, 133–34, 151–53; variation in interpretations of state obligations, 44; and *Wilson/Palmer* case, 53. *See also individual institutions*
International Labor Conference, 28, 48, 51, 103, 137, 172, 225n.45
international labor conventions, 22. *See also* ILO Conventions
International Labor Institute, 42
international labor rights regime, 24, 34
international labor standards, 22
International Labour Organization (ILO); Canada as founding member of, 158; and Canadian federal-provincial conflict, 159; collective bargaining convention, 28; commitment to trade union rights by, 2; Constitution of, 26, 27, 54; described, 219n.5; freedom of association convention, 28; on globalization and trade union rights, 2; Governing Body, 51, 52, 103; history of, 23–25; ICESCR on, 30; and protections of rights, 26; in South Korea case study, 74–81, 83, 89, 102; South Korea's leadership role in, 103; in United Kingdom case study, 147, 153; United Kingdom in, 114–15; on value of trade union rights, 18. *See also* ILO Conventions; *specific committees*
International Labour Organization Committee on Freedom of Association (ILO committee), 44–55, 206, 208; in British Columbia case study, 156, 159, 165–77, 179–80, 183–84, 187, 189–91; Canadian cases brought before, 159; collective rights of trade unions, 46–49; *Digest of Cases*, 14, 45; functions of, 52; individual rights of union members, 45–46; interpretation of legal commitments, 52–55, 65; and non-ratifying member states, 52; proceedings of, 12; recommendations made by, 199–200; in South Korea case study, 83, 84, 88–90, 100, 101, 103–6; states' obligations, 49–51; Tripartite Mission, 96; in United Kingdom case study, 121, 123, 130–32, 137, 139, 142, 144
International Labour Review, 180
international laws; influence of, in Canada, 159; liberal states' likelihood of following, 9; trade union sub-rights under, 41–44
International Metalworkers' Union, 88

International Monetary Fund (IMF); criticism of, 207; emergency loan to United Kingdom, 117; and labor flexibility policies, 38; labor-related conditions of, 34; neoliberalism of, 37; public support for trade union rights from, 2; and South Korean rescue package, 92–93
international norms; behavior of states shaped by, 3–4; in British Columbia case study, 155–56, 177; change from national to, 19–26; contesting of, 194–95; created by OECD, 62; early support for, 21; and hostility to trade union rights, 33; liberal states' likelihood of following, 9; political consensus surrounding, 19; recognition of trade union rights as, 19; in South Korea case study, 99, 102, 104–6; states' internalization of, 67, 209; states' interpretations of, 4, 196; states' specific obligations created by, 42, 44; sub-rights and principles, 41–44; trade union rights as, 3, 193; in United Kingdom case study, 137–38; United Kingdom commitments to, 115
international obligations; South Korea case study, 67–68, 73–74; United Kingdom case study, 128
international trade secretariats (ITS), 22, 224n.17
International Trade Union Confederation (ITUC), 39, 220n.11
international trade union rights, 23
International Workingmen's Association, 22
interviews, research, 12–13
Ireland, 21, 30, 61
Iron and Steel Trades Confederation, 253n.92
Italy, 30, 61

Japan, 38, 69, 215
JB v. Canada, 231n.26
J.I. Case Co. v. NLRB, 216
job security: and labor market flexibility, 197; OECD rule for, 63; security clauses (closed shops), 47, 119, 122, 138, 151–52; in South Korea, 69, 87
Jobs Study (OECD, 1994), 38
Johnson, Don, 85
Joint Committee on Human Rights (UK), 154, 204
judicial process, as mechanism for change, 5–6. *See also* British Columbia case study

Kahn-Freund, Otto, 116
Kentucky, 218
Kim Dae Hwan, 103
Kim Dae Jung, 12, 92–93, 96, 99, 135, 242n.162
Kim Dae Jung administration (South Korea), 93–101
Kim Young Sam, 108, 203
Kim Young Sam administration (South Korea), 77–92, 198
Koo, Hagen, 69
Korea Labor Institute, 77, 95
Korean Confederation of Trade Unions (KCTU), 80, 83, 84, 86, 87, 89, 90, 93, 95, 97, 106, 107
Korean Employers Federation, 95
Korean Federation of Industries, 97
Korean Government Employees Union (KGEU), 104–6, 201
Korean Teachers' Union, 74–77, 90, 201
Korean Trade Union Congress (KTUC), 72, 74–77, 80
Korean Tripartite Commission, 93–97
Kucera, Dave, 42, 211–12
Kunkook University (South Korea), 104

Labor Administration (South Korean Labor Ministry), 98
Labor Dispute Adjustment Act, 72
labor (labor market) flexibility regime, 35–39; British Columbia, 166, 171, 177, 183; South Korea, 69, 82, 86, 90, 94–98; United Kingdom, 122–23; and violations of trade union rights, 197
Labor Monitoring Process (OECD), 64
labor rights; and economic interests, 37; and labor flexibility regime, 35; states' changing views of, 42. *See also* workers' rights; *individual case studies*
labor standards; in British Columbia, 186; as ethical good, 24; evenness of, 19; international, 22–24; OECD rule for, 63; transnational institutionalization of, 23

Labour Conventions Case (Canada), 159
Labour governments (UK), 117, 134–38, 142, 147, 150, 153, 198–99
Labour Party (UK), 113, 118, 128, 134–36, 147–51
Labour Relations Board (British Columbia), 168
Labour Trilogy cases (Canada), 173–74, 177–78, 182, 191
Law Concerning Special Measures for Safeguarding National Security (South Korea), 71
law(s); domestic, 20; hard vs. soft, 3; human rights, 29; international, 9, 41–44; for negotiations over workplace issues, 47; trade union rights in, 36; workers' rights, 21
layoffs, 90, 92–96, 107, 181
Le Chapelier law of 1791 (France), 20
LeDain, Gerald Eric, 173
Lee Dong-Eung, 95
Leeds conference (1916), 23
Lee Ho-Guen, 96
legal changes, changes in government correlated with, 11–12
legalization of obligations; and European Court of Human Rights, 58–59; and European Social Charter, 61; human rights, 20; and ILO Committee on Freedom of Association, 55; and OECD, 62, 64; political and civil rights, 29; social, economic, and cultural rights, 29; trade union rights, 10, 26
legal organizations, professional, 22–23
Leo XIII, pope, 21–22
Liberal government (British Columbia), 156–57, 160–61, 165–66, 171, 172, 175, 176, 183–90, 196, 198
liberalism, embedded, 25, 33, 34
Lichtenstein, Nelson, 207–8
lifetime employment (South Korea), 69
logic of appropriateness (legitimacy), 3, 4
logic of consequences (self-interest), 3–4
Luxembourg, 30, 61

Maastricht Treaty, Social Chapter of, 134, 149, 150, 259n.178
MacPhail, Joy, 18–189
Major, John, 118. *See also* Conservative governments (UK)
Mando Machinery Workers' Union strike, 245n.193
Mareska, Daniel, 20
market functioning, neoliberalism and, 34
Marx, Karl, 20
McCartin, Joseph, 207
McIntosh, Lord, 141
mechanisms for change, 5–8
Methodist churches, 21
Method of Agreement, 9
methodology, research, 11–13
Mexico, 82, 83
Michigan, 218
middle class (South Korea), 87
Mill, John Stuart, 9
"minimum floor" of standards (Canada), 186
minimum wage (British Columbia), 186
Ministry of Government Administration and Home Affairs (South Korea), 99
Ministry of Labor (South Korea), 86, 103
Ministry of Labour (Canada), 175
Missouri, 218
modernization (UK New Labour), 148
monitoring; of European Social Charter, 60; by Human Rights Committee and CESCR, 56–57; by OECD, 62, 64; of South Korean unions and workers, 69, 80–108, 200. *See also individual monitoring organizations*
monopoly union system (South Korea), 66, 71–72, 75, 76, 104, 107, 108, 110
multinational corporations, 2, 63
Murdoch, Rupert, 136–37
Myanmar, 54

National Coal v. Ridgeway, 252n.70
National Congress for New Politics (South Korea), 86
National Labor Relations Act (NLRA), 215–17
National Labor Relations Board (NLRB), 215, 216
National Security Law (South Korea), 85
National Union of Journalists (NUJ), 124, 126, 136–37, 141
National Union of Public and General Employees (NUPGE), 157, 166, 265n.64
National Union of Rail, Maritime and Transport Workers, 125 (UK), 141

Necker, Jacques, 20
negative rights (UK), 116
neoclassical economics, 35
neoliberalism, 34, 205–7; in British Columbia, 156; challenging, 208–9; and economic regime, 39–40; and financial crisis of 2008, 207; human rights in context of, 198–99; and interpretations of human rights, 208; and labor (labor market) flexibility regime, 35–39; political criticism of, 39; in the United Kingdom, 147
Nepal, 39
Netherlands, 21, 30, 38, 61, 68
"New Britain," 148
Newcastle Employment Tribunal (UK), 154
New Democratic Party (NDP), 162, 163, 166
New Democratic Party government (British Columbia), 163–65, 265n.57
New Korea Party (South Korea), 86
New Labour (UK), 6, 12, 113, 135–36, 147–50
New Labour government (UK), 134–36, 147, 151, 198, 201–2
New Social Contract (UK), 117
New Zealand, 38
NLRB v. Exchange Parts Inc., 216
noncompliance, 9, 10
nondiscrimination, 45–46, 63
nongovernmental organizations (NGOs); in British Columbia, 183, 187–88; public support for trade union rights from, 1; repression of rights claimed by, 40; and South Korea's OECD membership, 82; submissions to UN Human Rights Committee and CESCR, 56
nonstate actors, 1, 2, 40
normative global regime, 25, 183
normative negotiation process, 196, 209; British Columbia, 156, 157, 167–84; defined, 4; evaluating, 12; as mechanism for change, 6–7, 196; political conditions leading to success of, 8–9; as political process, 196; South Korea, 67, 73–91, 96, 108; United Kingdom, 130–41, 147
norms; and Canadian federal-provincial conflicts, 160; contested, 36; domestic, 20, 21; influence of, 193; recognition of trade union rights as, 19; in trade union rights, 18. *See also* international norms
North American Agreement on Labour Cooperation, 158
North American Free Trade Agreement (NAFTA), 1, 158
Norway, 21, 30, 61
no-work/no-pay strike procedure (South Korea), 86
nurses' rights (British Columbia), 168, 182–83

Oakes test (Canada), 181
obligations; of case study states, 195–96; legalization of, 10; positive obligations of states, 42, 44, 49–51; in trade union rights, 7
obstruction of business laws (South Korea), 100–101, 106, 110, 201
Official Bulletin (ILO), 12
Ontario, Canada, 159
open market economy, 82
Organization for Economic Cooperation and Development (OECD), 6; commitments required by, 82; countries' positions on legal instruments of, 82; Directorate of Employment Labour and Social Affairs, 63–64; Economic Surveys of Korea, 12; interpretation of legal commitments, 61–65; and labor (labor market) flexibility, 35, 38; Labor Monitoring Process, 64; legal authority of, 10; membership in, 62–63; purpose of, 61; in South Korea case study, 80–91, 101–8, 200, 203; Special Monitoring Process, 64; and Trade Union Advisory Committee/Council, 63. *See also specific committees and topics*
Owen, Robert, 20

Palmer, Terrence, 125, 141, 142
Palmer v. Associated British Ports, 129. *See also Wilson/Palmer* cases (UK)
Paris Peace Conference (1919), 23
Park Chung-hee, 71
peace, industrial and international, 24
People, Jobs and Opportunity (UK), 121
Phillips, Lord, 144
picketing (UK), 121, 122, 138
Poland, 83

political conditions; in British Columbia, 156, 162–63, 183, 185; as foundation for trade union rights, 19; and hostility to trade union rights, 33; and ILO establishment, 24; and international labor rights regime, 24; as mechanism for change, 5, 6; and states' approach to trade union rights, 4; for successful normative negotiation process, 8–9. *See also* South Korea case study
political consensus, surrounding norms, 19
Political Funds Act, 95
political rights, 31; individual-level, 45; legalization of, 29
Portugal, 61
post-neoliberalism, 207
power of unions, limiting; British Columbia, 187; United Kingdom, 119, 122
Presidential Commission on Industrial Relations Reform (South Korea), 85, 86
prior notification of solidarity actions, 107, 120, 122, 165
private sector workers; in British Columbia, 162; pay increases in exchange for relinquishment of rights by (*see* United Kingdom case study); right to collective bargaining, 46–47; right to form and join workers' rights organizations, 45
privatization, 34
Privy Council (Canada), 159
process tracing, 11–12
Professional Institute of Public Service of Canada v. Northwest Territories (Commissioner) [1990] (PIPSC), 173–74
professional legal and reform organizations, 22–23
property rights (Canada), 159
protection of trade union rights, 41–65; in Cold War period, 26; Council of Europe, 30–31, 57–61, 65; difficulties of, 196–97; European Convention, 31–32; European Court of Human Rights, 32, 57–60, 65; European Social Charter, 32–33, 60–61, 65; and globalization, 193; ILO Committee on Freedom of Association, 44–51, 52–55, 65; ILO Conventions and Universal Declaration of Human Rights, 27–29; ILO Fact-Finding and Conciliation Commission on Freedom of Association, 51–52; individual labor protections vs., 3; in industrialization period, 20; international institutions' codified protections, 26–33; legal protection, 9; national, 20; Organization for Economic Cooperation and Development, 61–65; political goals/interests vs., 193; preference for and resistance to, 19; states' obligations for, 36, 42, 44, 46, 49–51; sub-rights and principles, 41–44; UN Committee on Economic, Social and Cultural Rights, 55–57, 65; UN Human Rights Committee, 55–57, 65; UN Human Rights Covenants, 29–30
protection of workers; from discrimination, 45–46; as underlying assumption of trade union rights, 42
protests (South Korea), 100
Protocol 14 of the European Community Treaty on Social Policy, 149. *See also* Social Chapter, Maastricht Treaty
provincialization, 162
Public Education Flexibility and Choice Act (Bill 28), 165–66, 168–70, 187–89
Public Education Servants Act, 71
Public Officials Act, 71
Public Officials Trade Union Act, 104, 105, 246n.216
public opinion toward unions, 117–19, 194
Public School Act, 71
public sector workers, 8; British Columbia, 155–57, 160, 162–71, 173, 176, 177, 182–84, 187; curbing rights of, 194; cutting costs of, 161; right of affiliation for, 49; right to collective bargaining by, 46–47; right to form and join workers' rights organizations, 45; South Korea, 66, 70–71, 90; United Kingdom, 117, 120; United States, 217–18. *See also* civil servants' rights
Public Services International, 166
public support for trade union rights, 1–2
Puchmayr, Chuck, 185–86

Railway and Ferries Bargaining Assistance Act (Bill 95), 268n.107
Rama, Martin, 35
rationalist perspective, 10
reasonable limits standards, 181

recession, 197
Reed, Hannah, 151
reform organizations, professional, 22–23
regulation of labor markets, 35, 138
repression of trade unions (South Korea), 69, 72, 74–78, 80, 97, 99, 104
Rerum Novarum, 21–22
research design, 8–13; case selection, 8–11; methodology, 11–13
retraining, 96, 103, 183
rights; to collective action, 18, 20; to collective bargaining, 46–48; to freedom of association, 18, 27; of individual workers, 42, 43, 45–46; to organize, 68, 133; to strike, 18, 26–30; sub-rights of, 41–44. *See also* trade union rights; *specific types of rights, e.g.*: political rights
Roh Moo Hyun, 109
Roh Moo Hyun administration (South Korea), 102–8, 200
Roh Tae Woo, 69–70, 72
Roh Tae Woo administration (South Korea), 74–77
Ruggie, John, 25
Russian Revolution, 24, 196
Ryder, Guy, 1

safety conventions, 22
safety regulations (British Columbia), 186
Savage, Larry, 206
Scandinavian countries, 82. *See also individual countries*
Schabas, William, 191
Schricke, Christian, 84
Scott, F. R., 159–60
"Scrutiny of Bills" (Joint Committee on Human Rights), 204
Seattle Ministerial Meetings (1999), 37
secondary collective actions; United Kingdom, 122, 138; United States, 215
Second International, 22
secular trade unions, 23
security clauses (closed shops), 47, 119, 122, 138, 151–52
shadow cabinet, 134, 254n.108
Sherness Steel, 253n.92
Skills Development and Labour Statutes Amendment Act (Bill 18), 168–70, 268n.107
Smith, Andrew, 137
Smith, John, 150
Snidal, Duncan, 3, 57, 61, 64
Social Agreement to Overcome the Economic Crisis (South Korea), 94
Social Chapter, Maastricht Treaty, 134, 149, 150, 259n.178
social clause (Canadian trade treaties), 158
Social Contributions and Labor Taxes index (World Bank), 39
social dumping, 24
socialism (British Columbia), 162
Socialist Bloc countries, 28, 30
Socialist states, 26
social learning, 196, 209
social movements, public support for trade union rights from, 2
social partner bargaining, 94
social rights, 29, 31–33, 196–97
social safety net (South Korea), 96, 103
soft law, 3, 22, 55
solidarity activities; importance of, 196; South Korea, 66, 72, 73, 75, 76, 86, 90, 104, 107–9; United Kingdom, 122, 138; United States, 215
South African strike law, 52
South American countries, 30
South Korea; characteristics of, 9; collective agreements, 116; commitments to human rights, 202; compliance, 10; economic growth, 198, 213; election of presidents, 234n.19; as "high income country," 10; and ILO convention ratification, 158; ILO leadership role of, 103; industrial relations practices, 116; interactions with international institutions, 194; legal changes correlating with changes in government, 12; OECD monitoring of, 64; political learning in, 67; recent transition in, 66; restructured government, 81; strikes, 194; unions and unionization, 213
South Korea case study, 66–112; Asian financial crisis and aftermath, 92–101; campaign to join OECD, 80–91; conclusions from, 194, 197–203, 206; end of OECD monitoring process, 103–8; forms of international engagement, 102–8; globalization, 80, 81;

South Korea case study,
industrial relations, 68–70; influence of international institutions, 95–98; initial interactions with international organizations, 73–81; interviews in, 13; key years divisions in, 10–11; Kim Dae Jung administration, 92–101; Kim Young Sam administration, 77–92; mechanism of change in, 5, 6; Roh Moo Hyun administration, 102–8; Roh Tae Woo administration, 74–77; trade union rights disputes, 70–73; trade union rights obligations, 67; Tripartite Commission, 93–97; U.S. law compared to, 215–16
South Korean Central Intelligence Agency, 69
South Korean Foreign Ministry, 88, 89
sovereignty doctrine (US), 217
Spain, 61
"Special Announcement on Maintaining Civic Security and Law and Order" (South Korea), 70
Special Monitoring Process (OECD), 64, 87–88
states; and allowance of vs. responsibility for rights, 26–27; behavior shaped by international norms, 3–4; in case studies, 195–96 (*See also individual case studies*); and codified protections, 19; compliance with trade union rights, 7–8; construction of trade union rights, 193; curtailment of individual labor protections, 36; declared commitment to trade union rights, 40; and early workers' organizations, 20; human rights commitments, 202–3; interpretations of international norms, 4, 196; in the normative negotiation process, 4, 5; and obligations to protect trade union rights, 36; positive obligations of, 42, 44, 46, 49–51; public support for trade union rights, 1; responsibilities to international laws, 33; scope of responsibilities to trade union rights, 18–19; softening of stances on trade union rights disputes, 206–7; tangible benefits provided to workers, 18; variation in interpretations of obligations, 44
Statute of the Council of Europe, 59
Stedman, Brian, 125
strike ballot initiatives (UK), 119, 120, 138
strike breaking, by states, 50–51
strike rights, 18; British Columbia, 164, 171, 174, 176, 184, 191; during Cold War era, 26; Committee of Experts on, 61; explicit inclusion of, 27; Human Rights Committee view of, 56; in ICESCR, 30; as individual vs. collective right, 30; limitations of, 50; South Korea, 67, 76, 100, 104–6, 110; state obligation to protect, 49–50; United Kingdom, 116, 119–21, 136, 139, 152; and Universal Declaration of Human Rights, 28–29; for workers in "essential services," 45–47, 50
strikes; British Columbia, 164, 167, 194; as cost-cutting measure, 161; South Korea, 81, 87, 97, 99–101, 108, 194, 244n.190, 245n.193, 245n.197; United Kingdom, 117, 118, 122, 139, 194
sub-rights, 41–44
substantial interference standard, 180, 191
successor rights, 168
Suddaby, Clay, 166
Supreme Court (Canada), 174, 175, 177, 189–91, 200, 204–7
Supreme Court (US), 215, 216
Sweden, 21, 30, 61
Swedish Engine Drivers case, 142–43
Swimmer, Gene, 160–61
Switzerland, 21, 61
sympathy strikes (UK), 121

Taiwan, 77
Teachers' Pay and Conditions Act of 1987, 120
teachers' rights; British Columbia, 156, 162, 164, 166, 168, 176, 177, 184; South Korea, 66, 70–71, 73–77, 76, 86, 90, 94, 95, 97, 98, 101, 110; United Kingdom, 120; United States, 216
Thatcher, Margaret, 115, 118, 149, 165. *See also* Conservative governments (UK)
third-party intervention (South Korea), 72
Trade, Employment, and Labour Standards (ELSA), 63–64
trade agreements, clauses reaffirming importance of trade union rights in, 1
Trade Dispute Act of 1906 (UK), 248n.8

trade guilds, 20
Trades Union Congress (TUC), 128, 130–32, 134, 139, 141, 152, 253n.76
Trades Union Council (UK), 135, 140
Trade Union Act (South Korea), 71, 84
Trade Union Act of 1871 (UK), 248n.8
Trade Union Advisory Committee/Council (TUAC), 63, 80, 82, 84, 87, 104, 106, 108
Trade Union and Labour Relations Adjustment Act (TULRAA), 85–90, 128
Trade Union and Labour Relations Adjustment Act (TULRAA, revised), 91–92
Trade Union and Labour Relations Consolidation Act of 1992 (UK), 119, 127, 128, 138, 140, 142, 145
trade union-led workers' organizations, 22
Trade Union Reform and Employment Rights Act of 1993 (UK), 128, 130, 131, 133, 139
trade union representation, trade union membership vs., 114. *See also* United Kingdom case study
trade union rights, 1–8; affiliation rights, 49; assumption underlying, 42; collective, 46–49; depth of state compliance with, 7–8; economic foundational basis of, 37; enforcement of, 2; foundational conditions for, 19, 24; historical changes in support for, 33–40; history of, 18–26; as human rights, 3–5, 29–30, 40, 59–60, 206–9; individual rights vs., 3, 220n.17, 223n.1; international, 23; intrinsic value of, 18; and labor flexibility regime, 35; mechanisms for changing, 5–8; and normative negotiation process, 6–7; and political goals/interests, 193; public support for, 1–2; related norms in, 18; research design, 8–13; utility of, 35–36; violations of, 2–3. *See also individual case studies; specific topics, e.g.:* protection of trade union rights
trade unions; autonomous running of, 48; and codified protections, 18–19; collective rights of, 42, 43, 46–49; defensiveness of, 193; diversity of complaints of, 7; in England, 21; legal personality of, 46; in national Fordist production regime, 33; in normative negotiation process, 4, 13; in post-World War II era, 25–26; repression of rights claimed by, 40; right to form and join, 45; secular, 23; violations reported by, 2. *See also* workers' rights organizations; *individual case studies; specific unions*
transit workers (British Columbia), 164
transnational management consultant industry, 34
transnational normative negotiations. *See* normative negotiation process
transnational organizations, 22
Tripartite Commission (South Korea), 93–97, 101, 106, 107
Tripartite Mission (ILO), 96, 97
Turkey, 61

UK Employment Department, 117
Ullswater Amendment (UK), 128–29, 131–33, 141, 143, 145, 194
unemployed workers, union membership of (South Korea), 95
unemployment; in British Columbia, 163; and economic growth, 118
unemployment benefits (South Korea), 94, 96, 103
UN Global Compact (2000), 2
union membership, right to trade union representation vs., 114. *See also* United Kingdom case study
UNISOM v. United Kingdom, 152
United Kingdom; characteristics of, 9; collective agreements in, 116; commitments to human rights, 202; in Council of Europe, 30; Golden Age of, 115; as "high income country," 10; interactions with international institutions, 194; legal changes correlating with changes in government, 12; in OECD, 61; as outsider in European Community, 148–49; protection of trade union rights in, 21; ratification of Social Charter by, 33; reduction of structural unemployment rate, 38; strikes in, 194. *See also individual countries*
United Kingdom case study, 113–54; Blair's New Labour government, 134–38; British industrial relations system, 114–16; commitments to international norms, 115; conclusions from, 194, 197–204;

United Kingdom case study, (*cont'd.*)
Conservative positions on labor unions, 121–23; domestic legal activism, 123–29; Employment Relations Act of 1999, 138–41; Employment Relations Act of 2004, 144–46; European Court of Human Rights, 141–46; history of commitments to trade union rights, 114–23; human rights as election issue, 150–51; implementation of European Court's rulings, 146–53; individual rights protections, 113, 114, 116–18; international institutions' recommendations, 151–53; interviews in, 13; mechanisms of change in, 6; New Labour and Conservative governments, 11; normative negotiation process, 130–41; Thatcher/Major government's approach to trade unions, 118–21; U.S. law compared to, 216–17; *Wilson/Palmer* case, 123–29
United Nations, 1, 67, 208. *See also specific bodies*
United Nations Covenants on Human Rights, 29–30, 42–44, 55–57
United Nations Economic and Social Council, 27, 28, 55
United Nations High Commission on Human Rights, 55
United Nations Human Rights Committee; in British Columbia case study, 187, 188; on freedom of association, 173; interpretation of legal commitments, 54–57; as source of research information, 12; in South Korea case study, 100–102, 105–7, 111–12; in United Kingdom case study, 123
United States; flexible labor markets of, 38; and ICESCR right to strike, 30; International Association for Labor Legislation, 21; labor rights-related reservations about South Korea, 82; in OECD, 61; public support for trade union rights, 1; and social provisions in post-WWI peace treaties, 24
United States law; comparison with British Columbia case study, 217–18; comparison with South Korea case study, 215–16; comparison with United Kingdom case study, 216–17
Universal Declaration of Human Rights, 18, 27–29, 208
University Teachers' Union (British Columbia), 168

Verité, 42
Versailles, Treaty of, 24, 159
Versailles Peace Conference (1919), 23
violations of trade union rights, 2–3; antiunion discrimination, 45–46; in case studies, 194–95; international institutions as platforms to critique, 193; investigations by Committee on Freedom of Association, 52–54; list of possible violations, 42; and neoliberalism, 36–37; public support vs., 2; reporting of, 52; states' reforms of, 8; unclear identification of, 32; and unpopular strikes, 194. *See also individual case studies*

wages; in British Columbia, 186; financial incentives in exchange for giving up union rights (*See* United Kingdom case study); in South Korea, 69, 70, 77
Washington Consensus, 34, 37
"weakened state" thesis of globalization, 160
Wedderburn, Professor Lord, 146, 204
welfare benefits; British Columbia, 190; South Korea case study, 96; United Kingdom, 117
Western states, 26, 30
West Germany, 61
wildcat strikes (UK), 119
Wilson, David, 123–25, 132, 137, 141, 142
Wilson/Palmer cases (UK), 114, 123–30, 132–33, 138, 140–47, 151–53, 202
Wilson v. Associated Newspapers Ltd., 129. *See also Wilson/Palmer* cases (UK)
Winter of Discontent (UK), 117, 118, 165, 194
Wisconsin, 218
Wolfensohn, James, 36–37
women's rights, 185, 188
workers' rights, 20–22, 229–30n.6; as human rights, 207–8; in industrialization period, 19–20; international liberal regime of, 24; protection from discrimination, 45–46;

transnational institutionalization of, 23; union security clauses as violations of, 59. *See also* trade union rights
workers' rights organizations; advocacy for freedom of association convention, 27; collective rights for, 46–49; freedom to join and establish, 45; history of, 20–22; legal personality of, 46. *See also* trade unions; *specific organizations*
workplace councils (South Korea), 106
World Bank; core labor standard-compliant loans by, 2; criticism of, 207; Employing Workers Index, 38–39; and labor flexibility policies, 38; labor-related conditions of, 34; neoliberalism of, 36–37; Social Contributions and Labor Taxes index, 39
World Confederation of Organizations of the Teaching Profession, 74
World Federation of Trade Unions, 27, 28
World Summit on Social Development (1995), 1
World Trade Organization (WTO), 37, 81
World War I, 23, 24, 196
World War II, 24, 25, 196
Wyeth, Arthur, 125, 141

Young, James and Webster v. United Kingdom, 151–52
Young Lee Goh, 97

ACKNOWLEDGMENTS

This book's examination of the role of human rights laws and frameworks was the result of much discussion, active collaboration, and collective learning. I owe much of my scholarly development and focus to the efforts of my dedicated advisor, Kathryn Sikkink, who presented a wonderful model of scholar/activist through her excellent work and mentorship during my time at the University of Minnesota. Professor Sikkink remains an amazing exemplar not only for her scholarly contributions, but also because of her continued engagement with political questions. Her critical support, advice, and encouragement have been indispensible to me as I have continued my scholarly career. In addition, Teri Caraway has also served above and beyond as a mentor, a reader, and a friend, and I remain grateful for her generosity and involvement in this project. The University of Minnesota was a wonderful place where young scholars of political science could remain actively engaged in political questions, despite the apolitical dominant stance of the discipline. Peter Agree at the University of Pennsylvania Press has been a patient, helpful, and generous editor, and I remain indebted for his willingness to work with such a green first-time author. Sandy Thatcher was also encouraging and instrumental in helping this book project come to fruition. I also would like to thank the two anonymous editors, whose useful comments and careful reading were instrumental in helping to transform the manuscript into a book.

As solidarity plays an important part in trade union struggles, it was through the solidarity of Minnesota colleagues that I have been able to grow as a scholar and a teacher. The contributions of Jonathan Havercroft, Isaac Kamola, Jonneke Koomen, Meghana Nayak, Jennifer Rutledge, Carrie Booth Walling, and the rest of the Minnesota Expat Writing Collective included comments on early drafts, assistance in developing ideas, general encouragement, and scholarly solidarity. Perhaps the cooperative spirit of the Upper Midwest taught us early on that scholarly pursuits are best done collectively, and I remain awed and humbled by our friendships and collaborations. I would also like to thank Kate Harshman for her advice on understanding the legal framework of U.S. labor rights.

I had the fortune of joining a community of supportive and encouraging colleagues at the John Jay College of Criminal Justice, City University of New York. Through the leadership of Harold Sullivan, I have been mentored and supported through my early years. A special thanks to Desmond Arias and Peter Romaniuk for encouragement and help in demystifying the publishing process. I would also like to thank my many bright and enthusiastic students, particularly in my research seminars, in helping me think about how one should present their research questions and findings. My dedicated research assistant and student Rizwan Ali Raja has also been helpful with the final manuscript preparation.

I would also like to thank the following funding sources that made field research and the revision process possible. The Association for Canadian Studies in the United States and the Canadian Studies Association's Graduate Student Fellowship, the Graduate School at the University of Minnesota, and the department of Political Science for financially supporting my field research. I owe many thanks to the cooperation of many busy leaders and activists of trade unions studied in this book. The Korean Confederation of Trade Unions, the British Trades Union Congress, and various trade unions in British Columbia were wonderful in their willingness to be interviewed and to share information. John Hendy QC was very helpful in generously providing comments on the United Kingdom chapter. And many thanks to my own union, the Professional Staff Congress at CUNY, for supporting the revision process.

A final thanks goes to my family. Steven Koskela is my partner and my greatest intellectual and emotional supporter; this book would not be possible without him. I dedicate this book to my parents, Keesun and Young Chan Kang, first-generation immigrants from South Korea who fostered intellectual curiosity, a commitment to social justice, and political interest in East Asia.

www.ingramcontent.com/pod-product-compliance
Ingram Content Group UK Ltd.
Pitfield, Milton Keynes, MK11 3LW, UK
UKHW041832031026
15587UKWH00002B/716

9 780812 244106